ADVANCED MATHEMATICS

BOOK 3

[METRIC]

THE
SCHOOL
MATHEMATICS
PROJECT

MATHEMATICS DEPARTMENT.

ADVANCED
MATHEMATICS
BOOK 3

[METRIC]

CAMBRIDGE
AT THE UNIVERSITY PRESS
1970

Published by the Syndics of the Cambridge University Press
Bentley House, 200 Euston Road, London N.W. 1
American Branch: 32 East 57th Street, New York, N.Y. 10022

© Cambridge University Press 1970

Library of Congress Catalogue Card Number: 67–28685

ISBN: 0 521 08107 6

First published 1968
Metric reprint 1970

Printed in Great Britain
at the University Printing House, Cambridge
(Brooke Crutchley, University Printer)

THE
SCHOOL MATHEMATICS
PROJECT

This project was founded on the belief, held by a group of practising school teachers, that there are serious shortcomings in traditional school mathematics syllabuses, and that there is a need for experiment in schools with the aim of bringing these syllabuses into line with modern ideas and applications. To this end, they have co-operated in devising a radically new syllabus which would more adequately reflect the nature and usages of mathematics and which, by spanning the whole secondary school course, would lead to new G.C.E. examinations at both O and A level.

This is not the place to describe the complex arrangements which this simple objective has required; the printed annual reports of the Project deal with such matters and are available on request to the Director at Westfield College, University of London. But perhaps acknowledgement could gratefully be expressed here of the financial support which has enabled the work to be done.

As for this series of publications, it is not claimed for one moment that the texts represent the best possible development of the subject—there is altogether too much of mathematics for that to be true of any course; but the material published in the series has been forged in the furnace of the classroom, and it is offered with a confidence all the greater for that.

It is naturally the hope of all those associated with the Project that these texts will encourage many other teachers of mathematics to strike out into new ways. Such teachers may be further encouraged by the knowledge that all the examining Boards—the Oxford and Cambridge, the Cambridge, the London, the Northern Joint, the Oxford, the Southern Universities Joint, the Welsh, and the Associated Examining Board—set joint G.C.E. examinations on syllabuses which, in general outline, follow the contents of these texts.

Finally, it may as well be admitted that this first English experiment in co-operative mathematical teaching has not been as radical, so far, as some of the much larger experiments in the U.S.A. and in Europe. But so long as we can avoid developing merely a new dogma, this does not matter, for above all we look forward to the possibility of a more or less continual process of change. It is to the beginnings of such a process that this series will, we hope, make a useful contribution.

The S.M.P. advanced texts are based on the original contributions of

P. G. Bowie	*G. S. Howlett	T. D. Morris
*H. M. Cundy	T. A. Jones	*D. A. Quadling
*J. H. Durran	M. J. Leach	G. D. Stagg
*L. E. Ellis	P. G. T. Lewis	B. Thwaites
*C. C. Goldsmith	*G. Merlane	*J. S. T. Woolmer

and are edited by Dr H. Martyn Cundy assisted by Miss E. Evans.

 * Those primarily concerned with this book are indicated by the asterisk.

Many other schoolteachers have been directly involved in the further development and revision of the material and the Project gratefully acknowledges the contributions which they and their schools have made.

CONTENTS

CONTENTS

PREFACE

In this, the third book of the S.M.P. Advanced level course, the various approaches of the previous books begin to merge, and the insights gained enable different branches of the subject to throw light upon one another. Thus, algebra is needed for the development of probability, and is illuminated by it; matrices find a new application in electrical networks; they in their turn illustrate the meaning of a differential equation, which is seen to be an all-pervasive contribution of analysis to the applications of mathematics.

The book opens with two linked chapters on probability, in which theoretical models are discussed for statistical behaviour. The earlier somewhat abstract treatment of polynomial forms now leads easily to the idea of a probability generator, and to the binomial model for the statistics of repeated dichotomous trials. The binomial theorem thus finds its natural place in a context of counting choices. Discussion of parameters to be selected for the model—sometimes called expected values—paves the way for an introduction to the idea of significance which is to come later.

Four Chapters—27, 29, 30 and 31—carry the analysis forward to the point where its applications become diverse and interesting. The guiding thread here is the differential equation, introduced first numerically and graphically, and then leading to new functions which are seen to be necessary for the analytical solution of simple types. These are, however, old functions in a new guise: logarithms met previously in an algebraic context, and exponential functions known from simple laws of growth. They find immediate application in electric phenomena, chemical reactions, and motion under resistance, all of which involve the linear differential equation.

Chapter 28 on programming is in effect a complete introduction to numerical mathematics, and can be used in many ways. It revises many techniques in the main course; it can be used with desk calculators to give practice in organizing a calculation and carrying out the computational work; and it can be a first step towards the mastery of a computer language such as Algol or Fortran. Brief outlines of these two languages are given in appendices.

Chapters 32 and 33 carry the development of mechanics a stage further; together they culminate in providing a mathematical model of the motion of a rocket, as one of the most important applications of the momentum principle. Energy and power are met in the chapter on Current Electricity, where it is assumed that they will be familiar from the physics course;

their mathematical treatment in the context of mechanics is left to the final book.

The final two chapters are devoted to algebra. That on complex numbers gives a systematic treatment of the complex field, first as an extension of the real field, and then as a field of ordered pairs. Isomorphisms with points, vectors, matrices, and the geometric transformations of translation and spiral similarity are brought out, and the chapter culminates in simple mappings of the complex number plane—the starting-point for much advanced work. The final chapter summarizes what we have learnt about polynomials, and discusses their zeros in the light of what we know about the complex number field. It has been felt advisable to include here a sketch of the way in which the fundamental theorem—that every polynomial over the complex field has a zero—can be proved, both because of the intrinsic interest of the topological approach, and because of the sense of finality which it confers on the long development of number systems.

It is probably necessary to repeat the warning that the examples are far more numerous than any single student's needs; many are suitable for discussion and for sharing round a class. Certain important examples are again printed in bold type. International standard units and symbols have been used in the electricity section, as well as in the mechanics.

The answers to exercises in this book will be published in the second volume of Hints and Answers to the advanced books. An overall *Companion to Advanced Mathematics* is also being prepared.

ACKNOWLEDGEMENTS

We are grateful to Broughton and Co. (Bristol) Ltd., for supplying the photograph of the *NIPPON Master* desk calculator reproduced in Chapter 28. We are again indebted to Mrs Elisabeth Muir for her careful typing of the MS of this book, and to Miss Elisabeth Evans for her assistance, especially with the diagrams. We record our gratitude to Dr D. G. Burnett-Hall for advice about the technicalities of Programming; to I.B.M. Research Laboratories at Hursley for the Fortran print-out on p. 1084; to the Oxford and Cambridge Schools Examination Board for permission to reproduce questions set in the S.M.P. A level examinations; and to the staff of the Cambridge University Press, who with patience and cheerfulness have converted the efforts of a wide variety of authors into a coherent and attractive text.

A NOTE ON METRICATION

(i) All quantities of money have been expressed in pounds (£) and new pence (p).

(ii) All measures have been expressed in metric units. The fundamental units of the Système International (that is the metric system to be used in Great Britain) are the metre, the kilogram and the second. These units have been used in the book except where practical class-room considerations or an estimation of everyday practice in the years to come have suggested otherwise.

(iii) The notation used for the abbreviations of units and on some other occasions conforms to that suggested in the British Standard publications PD 5686: 1967 and BS 1991: Part 1: 1967.

GLOSSARY OF SYMBOLS

Additional to those in earlier books

ALGEBRA

$_nC_i$ Number of selections of i things out of n

$$= \frac{n!}{i!\,(n-i)!}$$

$\binom{n}{i}$ Coefficient of t^i in the expansion of $(1+t)^n$
$= {}_nC_i$ when n is a positive integer and $0 \leqslant i \leqslant n$

C Field of complex numbers

z Complex number $x+jy$

$\bar{z}$ Conjugate of z; $x-jy$

$|z|$ Modulus of z; $+\sqrt{(x^2+y^2)}$

$\arg z$ Argument of z; θ, for which $\cos\theta:\sin\theta:1 = x:y:|z|$, and $-\pi < \theta \leqslant \pi$

$[r, \theta]$ Complex number with modulus r and argument θ; $r(\cos\theta+j\sin\theta)$

I, J The matrices $\begin{pmatrix} 1 & 0 \\ 0 & 1 \end{pmatrix}$, $\begin{pmatrix} 0 & -1 \\ 1 & 0 \end{pmatrix}$

CALCULUS

$\log a, \ln a$ Natural logarithm of a; $\displaystyle\int_1^a \frac{1}{x}\,dx$

e Base of natural logarithms; $1 = \displaystyle\int_1^e \frac{1}{x}\,dx$

$\exp$ Inverse of log; $y = \log x \Leftrightarrow x = \exp y$;
$\exp y = e^y$ for rational y

$\cosh x$ $\frac{1}{2}(e^x + e^{-x})$

$\sinh x$ $\frac{1}{2}(e^x - e^{-x})$

$T(x)$ Linear differential operator acting on x

CF Complementary function; general solution of $T(x) = 0$

PI Particular integral; any solution of $T(x) = f(x)$

xii

PROBABILITY

$E[x]$	Expected value of x
$G(t)$	Probability generator
μ	Theoretical mean; mean for probability model
σ^2	Theoretical variance; variance for probability model
$V[x]$	Expected variance of x

COMPUTING

READ A	Put next item on data tape into store A
$A := B$	Replace contents of store A by contents of store B
$A(I)$	Store whose address is given by the contents of store I
$A(I, J)$	Store located in an array by the contents of stores I and J
MOD (X)	Absolute value of contents of store X
SQRT (X)	Square root of contents of store X
INT (X)	Largest integer not greater than contents of store X
PRINT A	Output contents of store A

MECHANICS

qp	Displacement of P relative to Q
$\mathbf{r}_{12}$	$\mathbf{r}_2 - \mathbf{r}_1$; position vector of P_2 relative to P_1
$\longrightarrow$	Force
$\longrightarrow$	Velocity
$\overset{\longrightarrow}{I}$	Impulse, momentum
$\bar{\mathbf{r}}$	Position vector of centre of mass
$\bar{\mathbf{v}}$	Velocity of centre of mass
e	Coefficient of restitution

ELECTRICITY

D.C.	Direct current
A.C.	Alternating current
p.d.	Potential difference
e.m.f.	Electromotive force

Battery, positive terminal to left, with e.m.f. E and internal resistance r

Resistor with resistance R

Capacitor with capacitance C

Inductor with inductance L

Transformer

A.C. generator

Switch

UNITS (S.I.)

Quantity	Symbol for quantity	Name of unit	Symbol for unit
Charge	Q	coulomb	C
Current	i, I	ampere = coulomb/second	A
p.d., e.m.f.	V, E	volt = joule/coulomb	V
Resistance	R, r	ohm = volt/ampere	Ω
Energy	W	joule = newton-metre	J
Power	P	watt = joule/second	W
Capacitance	C	farad = coulomb/volt	F
Inductance	L	henry = ohm-second	H

25

BINOMIAL PROBABILITY FUNCTIONS AND THE BINOMIAL THEOREM

1. ATTRIBUTES AND THEIR REPRESENTATION

1.1   Statistical data can be of one of two kinds: quantitative or qualitative. For example, on a fishing expedition we might record the lengths of the fish caught—say 20 cm, 18 cm, 20 cm, 22 cm; we are then dealing with quantities. On the other hand, we might record types of fish—say brown trout, silver trout, grayling, rainbow trout; these are qualities.

Sometimes a list of quantities is converted into a list of qualities. Thus we might decide to throw back all fish less than 20 cm long and to accept the others. Instead of the lengths we would then record 'accept, reject, accept, accept' for the four fish in the catch.

Qualities of the kind described above are often called *attributes*. We can make frequency tables for the attributes in these examples:

Attribute	Frequency	Attribute	Frequency
Brown trout	2	Accepted	3
Grayling	1	Rejected	1
Rainbow trout	1		
Pike	0		

But we cannot handle the attributes as numbers. For example, in no sense can we talk about the 'mean attribute' in either table.

In this chapter we propose to consider especially trials whose outcomes can be specified in terms of one or other of just two attributes—the key either does or does not fit the lock, the answer to the problem is either right or wrong, the witness will either tell the truth or lie. Such a trial is called a *dichotomy*.

From the mathematical point of view the nature of the application is clearly unimportant. We shall therefore represent the two possible outcomes by abstract symbols A and B, so that the set of possibilities for any one trial is $\{A, B\}$. Sometimes A is described as 'success' and B as 'failure', but this should not be taken to imply that we are making any value judgements about the situation. We are merely setting up a mathematical model which will describe any dichotomy.

1.2   Let us suppose that two such trials are carried out, each having either A or B as a possible outcome. If we record the results of the two trials (so that BA, for example, denotes an outcome B from the first trial followed by an outcome A from the second) the possibility space has four elements

$$\{AA, AB, BA, BB\}.$$

Similarly for three successive trials we have a possibility space

$$\{AAA, AAB, ABA, ABB, BAA, BAB, BBA, BBB\}$$

with eight elements; and so on.

1.3   It is obviously unimportant what symbols are used to denote the two possible outcomes of a trial. As an alternative to that used above we might depict the situation by drawing a row of cells, one for each trial:

First trial	Second trial	Third trial

Fig. 1

A possibility for the sequence of three trials could then be indicated by inserting a tick for each success and a cross for each failure:

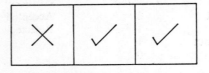

Fig. 2

Another interesting method is to use a code in which 1 represents success and 0 represents failure. For five trials in a row the symbol 11010 would then represent a record of two successes, one failure, another success and finally another failure. It will be noticed that these symbols may be read as numbers in the binary scale; and there is a one-one correspondence between possible outcomes of the sequence of five trials and the five-digit binary numbers from 00000 to 11111 (that is, from 0 to 2^5-1), giving thirty-two possibilities in all. This correspondence suggests a simple way of listing all the possibilities which ensures that each appears once and only once.

   As an example, we list the possible outcomes of a sequence of five trials, classifying them according to the number of successes in each. The binary numbers are put down in ascending order of magnitude, and we obtain the following table of results:

Outcome	Number of successes	Outcome	Number of successes	Outcome	Number of successes
00000	0	01011	3	10110	3
00001	1	01100	2	10111	4
00010	1	01101	3	11000	2
00011	2	01110	3	11001	3
00100	1	01111	4	11010	3
00101	2	10000	1	11011	4
00110	2	10001	2	11100	3
00111	3	10010	2	11101	4
01000	1	10011	3	11110	4
01001	2	10100	2	11111	5
01010	2	10101	3		

Now this is one method of classification. But it is often more relevant to record from the sequence of trials not the detail of each outcome but the total number of successes. If we do this the possibility space has just six elements {0, 1, 2, 3, 4, 5}, but some of these can arise in several different ways. The situation can then be analysed as follows:

Number of successes	Number of ways	Corresponding outcomes				
0	1	00000				
1	5	00001	00010	00100	01000	10000
2	10	$\begin{cases} 00011 \\ 01100 \end{cases}$	00101 10001	00110 10010	01001 10100	01010 11000
3	10	$\begin{cases} 00111 \\ 10101 \end{cases}$	01011 10110	01101 11001	01110 11010	10011 11100
4	5	01111	10111	11011	11101	11110
5	1	11111				

Notice that the numerical significance of the symbols for the different possibilities disappears when they are sorted according to numbers of successes.

Exercise A

1. You are going to make a statistical survey of the composition of your school. Suggest: (*a*) four sets of attributes, (*b*) four sets of quantities, that might be relevant.

2. A piece of wood 60 cm long is needed for a bookshelf. You are not prepared to waste more than 6 cm in cutting a plank down to size. The pieces available have lengths (in cm): 63·4, 68·4, 59·6, 55·2, 60·4, 65·2, 57·8, 70·0, 53·4, 67·4. Make a frequency table for the attributes 'too short', 'too long', 'acceptable'.

3. Suggest a situation in which the score on the face of a die is regarded as an attribute, and one in which it is regarded as a quantity.

4. On a ballot paper the names of five candidates P, Q, R, S, T are listed, with an empty box beside each. The voter has to place crosses in two of the boxes, leaving the other three blank. Make a list of all the different ways in which he can do this.

5. Analyse, as in Section 1.3, the possible outcomes for: (a) 4 repetitions, (b) 6 repetitions of a dichotomy.

6. If the possibility space for a single trial is a set of four attributes, how many possibilities are there for a sequence of three such trials? Generalize your answer.

7. In an examination a candidate may be awarded grade A, B or C in each subject. He sits four subjects in all. Describe a systematic way of writing down all the possible results he might achieve; and set down in a table the numbers of different ways in which he can obtain various results expressed in terms of totals of each grade. (For example, he can obtain three A's and one C in four ways.)

2. PROBABILITIES

2.1 We know from Chapter 20 (Book 2) that with each outcome of a trial may be associated a number called its probability. For a dichotomy, with outcomes symbolized by A and B, let us write

$$p \text{ (outcome is A)} = a, \quad p \text{ (outcome is B)} = b.$$

Since these two events are exclusive and exhaustive, it follows that

$$a+b = 1.$$

Suppose, for example, that a card is drawn from a pack, and that A and B refer to the drawing of a picture card and a number card respectively. Then $a = \frac{3}{13}$, $b = \frac{10}{13}$, and the sum of these is $\frac{13}{13}$, or 1.

2.2 Consider now a sequence of two trials, each with possibility space $\{A, B\}$. The probabilities of these outcomes in the two trials may, or may not, be the same. In the general case let the probabilities for the first trial be a_1, b_1, and those for the second trial a_2, b_2. The possibility space for the two trials together is $\{AA, AB, BA, BB\}$, and the problem arises of assigning probabilities to these possibilities.

Before this can be done it is necessary to specify more clearly the conditions under which the trials are conducted. In the work which follows we shall make two assumptions about these:

(i) We suppose that the probabilities a_2, b_2 are not affected by the result of the first trial. Thus in the card-drawing example cited above it would not be satisfactory to draw a second card from the 51 cards which remain after the first draw. For if the first card had been a picture card, the remaining pack would contain 11 picture cards and 40 number cards, giving probabilities $a_2 = \frac{11}{51}$ and $b_2 = \frac{40}{51}$; but if it had been a number card there would be 12 picture and 39 number cards left, and the probabilities would be $a_2 = \frac{12}{51}$ and $b_2 = \frac{39}{51}$. To satisfy the conditions laid down it must be

740

possible to give values to a_2, b_2 without ambiguity. Thus we might return the first-drawn card to the pack before making the second draw, in which case $a_2 = \frac{3}{13}$, $b_2 = \frac{10}{13}$, the same as a_1 and b_1. Or we might remove from the pack after the first draw a second card of the opposite kind to the card drawn, so as to leave for the second draw 11 picture cards and 39 number cards; then $a_2 = \frac{11}{50}$, $b_2 = \frac{39}{50}$.

(ii) Furthermore, we suppose that the results of the two trials are independent of each other. This would not happen, for example, if the draws were made from two packs which had the cards in an identical order before the trials and the top card were taken in each trial. This is an assumption whose validity is often doubted; the belief that 'since it came down heads last time it is more likely to be tails now' is one which dies hard.

Under these conditions the product rule for combining probabilities holds (see Chapter 20, Section 6.4) and we deduce at once for the two trials:

Possibility	Probability
AA	$a_1 a_2$
AB	$a_1 b_2$
BA	$b_1 a_2$
BB	$b_1 b_2$

2.3 Suppose now that the information about the sequence of two trials is re-organized in the manner suggested in Section 1.3, according to the number of successes. Counting A as 'success', the possibilities AB and BA will both come into the category of 'one success', and since these are exclusive we deduce:

Number of successes	Probability
0	$b_1 b_2$
1	$a_1 b_2 + b_1 a_2$
2	$a_1 a_2$

The form of the entries in the 'probability' column of this table should be carefully noticed. They are expressions which also appear in a quite different context. If we consider the polynomial G whose factorized form is

$$G = (b_1 + a_1 t) . (b_2 + a_2 t),$$

we find that $\qquad G = b_1 b_2 + (a_1 b_2 + b_1 a_2) t + a_1 a_2 t^2.$

Thus the coefficient of any power of t in G is equal to the probability of the corresponding number of successes in the sequence of trials. This link between probabilities and coefficients in a polynomial is central to the theme of this chapter.

Exercise B

1. By factorizing and simplifying, verify that the sum of the probabilities in the table at the end of Section 2.2 is 1.

2. What do the probabilities in Section 2.3 become when both trials have the same probabilities a, b of success and failure? What form does the polynomial G take in this case?

3. A boy reckons that there is a 60 % probability that he will pass in physics and a 70 % probability that he will pass in chemistry. Find the probabilities that he will pass in 0, 1, 2 subjects. Write down, in both factorized and expanded form, a polynomial whose coefficients are equal to the respective probabilities.

4. Driving through a town in light traffic the probability that the first traffic light is green is 0·25, and the probability that the second traffic light is green is 0·4. Find a polynomial whose coefficients give the probabilities of two hold-ups, one hold-up and a clear run. Evaluate these probabilities.

What difference might it make if the traffic were too heavy?

5. On my way to work I have to catch a bus which makes a somewhat un-reliable connection with a train. There is a probability of $\frac{3}{4}$ that I will catch the bus, and a probability of $\frac{2}{3}$ that the bus will make the connection with the train. Explain why the analysis of Section 2.2 does not apply to this situation.

6. Extend the results of Sections 2.2 and 2.3 to a sequence of three trials, giving the probabilities of 0, 1, 2, 3 successes and the corresponding polynomial G in both factorized and expanded form. Write down also the forms to which these simplify if the probabilities are the same for each trial.

7. A card is drawn from a pack and we record whether it is a picture or a number card. A second card of the opposite kind is then taken from the pack and the trial is repeated; and we proceed in this manner for up to twelve trials. If we start with a full pack, what is the probability of drawing a number card at the rth trial? Find the probability that the first three draws give one number and two picture cards (in any order).

2.4 Extension to a longer sequence. Having looked at sequences of two trials (Section 2.2) and three trials (Exercise B, Question 6), let us now consider in detail a sequence of five trials under similar conditions. We shall concentrate on the particular case in which the probabilities a, b of success and failure are the same for each trial, and shall calculate the probabilities of various numbers of successes. For this purpose the classification worked out in Section 1.3 will be found useful.

No successes. This can happen in only one way, indicated by the symbol 00000. The probability of this outcome is $b.b.b.b.b$, or b^5.

One success. There are five ways in which this can happen, coded as 00001, 00010, 00100, 01000, 10000. The probability of the outcome 00001

742

is $b.b.b.b.a$, or b^4a; that of the outcome 00010 is $b.b.b.a.b$, or b^4a again; and so on. We deduce that the probability of just one success is $5b^4a$.

Similar calculation over the rest of the possibility space leads to the following table of results:

Number of successes	Probability
0	b^5
1	$5b^4a$
2	$10b^3a^2$
3	$10b^2a^3$
4	$5ba^4$
5	a^5

The coefficients 1, 5, 10, 10, 5, 1 which appear in these expressions are numbers we have met before. They are, of course, just the numbers of different outcomes which give the corresponding numbers of successes, as set out in the table at the end of Section 1.3.

2.5 For the sequence of two trials we saw that the probabilities could also be found as the coefficients of powers of t in the polynomial

$$(b_1 + a_1 t).(b_2 + a_2 t).$$

With five trials and constant probabilities a, b the appropriate polynomial is

$$G = (b+at).(b+at).(b+at).(b+at).(b+at),$$

which can be expanded into the form

$$G = b^5 + 5b^4at + 10b^3a^2t^2 + 10b^2a^3t^3 + 5ba^4t^4 + a^5t^5.$$

The reason is not difficult to find. The terms of the polynomial are obtained by taking just one term (either b or at) from each factor and multiplying them together. For example, the terms involving t^1 arise as

$$b.b.b.b.at, \quad b.b.b.at.b, \quad b.b.at.b.b, \quad b.at.b.b.b, \quad at.b.b.b.b.$$

It is clear how these are related to the five elements

$$00001, \quad 00010, \quad 00100, \quad 01000, \quad 10000$$

in the classification of outcomes: we merely apply the rule that 'noughts' in the code indicate brackets from which the term b is taken, and 'ones' those from which at is taken. To get the power t^1 we must take at from just one of the five factors.

Similar reasoning can be used to establish the general result:

If each separate trial has probabilities a, b of resulting in success or failure, then the probability of i successes in a sequence of n trials is the same as the coefficient of t^i in the expanded form of $(b+at)^n$.

Example 1. What is the probability of throwing exactly three sixes in five throws of a fair die?

Notice that a score of six here is regarded as an attribute; the six has no numerical significance, but is simply a mark on one face of the die. If we count throwing a six as 'success', then $a = \frac{1}{6}$, $b = \frac{5}{6}$. The probability is therefore

$$10(\tfrac{5}{6})^2(\tfrac{1}{6})^3,$$

or about 0·03.

This number would appear as the coefficient of t^3 in the expansion of $(\frac{5}{6} + \frac{1}{6}t)^5$.

Exercise C

1. If each trial of a sequence has probabilities a, b of success and failure respectively, make out a table giving probabilities of various numbers of successes with: (*a*) 4 trials, (*b*) 6 trials. In each case give the associated polynomial G in both factorized and expanded form.

2. Four people each cut a pack of cards. What is the probability that three of them will get picture cards?

3. One-tenth of the peaches in a large consignment are bruised. What is the probability of getting just one bruised peach in a box of ten?

4. A marksman hits the bull with a probability of 0·8. What is the probability of scoring three or more bulls with five rounds?

5. Thirty per cent of candidates offered places on a certain course are expected to fail to reach the required entrance qualifications. In a batch of five selected candidates what is the most probable number of drop-outs on these grounds?

6. Express the following probabilities as the coefficients of certain powers of t in a certain expression:
 (*a*) the probability of 45 heads when a coin is spun 100 times;
 (*b*) the probability of 3 'twos' in 10 throws of a die;
 (*c*) the probability that 4 children in a class of 30 have names beginning with A, given that the proportion of such names in the population is 0·006.

7. For the polynomial G described in Section 2.5, give two reasons why $G(1) = 1$, one based on the expanded form of G and one on the factorized form.

3. PROBABILITY GENERATORS

The polynomials G described in Sections 2.3 and 2.5 will be called *probability generators,*† since in their expanded form they generate as coefficients the probabilities for the corresponding numbers of successes in the sequence of trials. In general, if the probabilities of obtaining

† The term in more common use is *probability generating function*. The authors have preferred 'probability generator' because the emphasis in this application is on polynomials as algebraic forms rather than on polynomial functions.

$0, 1, 2, \ldots$ successes as the result of some experiment are denoted by $p_0, p_1, p_2, \ldots,$† then the expression

$$G = p_0 + p_1 t + p_2 t^2 + \ldots$$

is the probability generator for that experiment.

We saw in Chapter 3 that a polynomial is in essence an assemblage of coefficients; and in defining a probability generator we assign no special significance to the 'indeterminate' t, which acts as a place-holder. It is called a 'dummy variable' or 'apparent variable', and it could be replaced by any other symbol without affecting the generator.

For a single trial with probabilities a, b of success and failure respectively, the probability generator is simply

$$b + at;$$

for the number of successes arising from this trial can only be 0 or 1, and their probabilities are $p_0 = b$ and $p_1 = a$.

For a sequence of two independent trials we found the probability generator

$$(b_1 + a_1 t) . (b_2 + a_2 t),$$

which is the product of the probability generators for the two trials separately. This 'product rule' for combining the probability generators for two independent trials can be shown to be true in general; and by applying it repeatedly we can obtain the probability generator

$$(b + at)^n$$

for a sequence of n trials each having probabilities a, b of success and failure.

A system of trials with probability generator $(b+at)^n$ is called a *binomial system*, because it is based on a power of the two-term, or 'binomial', expression $b+at$. It is also sometimes called *Bernoullian* after its first investigator Jacob Bernoulli (1654–1705), whose *Ars Conjectandi* was published posthumously in 1713. The function

$$n \to p_n,$$

where the probabilities p_n pertain to a binomial system of trials, is called a *binomial probability function*.

4. BINOMIAL COEFFICIENTS

Although the applications so far discussed have been to the theory of probability, an expansion such as

$$(b + at)^5 = b^5 + 5b^4 at + 10b^3 a^2 t^2 + 10b^2 a^3 t^3 + 5ba^4 t^4 + a^5 t^5$$

---

† Note that the suffixes here refer to the number of successes. They should not be confused with the suffixes in the notation $a_1 a_2, a_3, \ldots$ and $b_1, b_2, b_3, \ldots$ which indicated particular trials in the sequence (see Sections 2.2 and 2.3).

is of course a purely algebraic result. As such it is not restricted to situations in which a and b represent probabilities of success and failure in repeated trials; and it is valid whether or not $a+b = 1$. In fact, if we wish to study the expansion in its algebraic aspect it is more convenient to cast it in a simpler form, either writing $t = 1$, viz.

$$(b+a)^5 = b^5+5b^4a+10b^3a^2+10b^2a^3+5ba^4+a^5;$$

or writing $a = b = 1$, which gives

$$(1+t)^5 = 1+5t+10t^2+10t^3+5t^4+t^5.$$

The coefficients 1, 5, 10, 10, 5, 1 which appear in these expansions are called *binomial coefficients*. It is useful to have a general notation for these, and they are usually written

$$\binom{5}{0}, \quad \binom{5}{1}, \quad \binom{5}{2}, \quad \binom{5}{3}, \quad \binom{5}{4}, \quad \binom{5}{5}.$$

Thus $\binom{5}{3}$ stands for the coefficient of t^3 in the expansion of $(1+t)^5$. More generally, $\binom{n}{i}$ is the coefficient of t^i in the expansion of $(1+t)^n$. We can therefore write

$$(1+t)^n = \sum_{i=0}^{n} \binom{n}{i} t^i.$$

Notice also the forms:

$$(b+a)^n = \sum_{i=0}^{n} \binom{n}{i} b^{n-i}a^i;$$

and, in the application to probability,

$$(b+at)^n = \sum_{i=0}^{n} \binom{n}{i} b^{n-i}a^i t^i.$$

Exercise D

1. Give the values of

$$\binom{2}{1}, \quad \binom{3}{2}, \quad \binom{6}{6}, \quad \binom{4}{2}, \quad \binom{9}{0}, \quad \binom{7}{1}, \quad \binom{6}{2}.$$

2. Give the values of

$$\binom{n}{0}, \quad \binom{n}{1}, \quad \binom{n}{n-1}, \quad \binom{n}{n}$$

for any natural number n.

3. Write down, using the notation of binomial coefficients, a formula for the probability of i successes in a sequence of n trials, each of which has probabilities a, b of success and failure.

4. Give answers to Exercise C, Question 6 in the notation of binomial coefficients.

746

5. By writing down the actual values of the binomial coefficients for a few small values of n, guess a formula for the sum

$$\binom{n}{0}+\binom{n}{1}+\binom{n}{2}+\ldots+\binom{n}{n}.$$

Then give a proof of your result by giving a special value to t in the formula for the expansion of $(1+t)^n$.

6. Write down, for a few small values of n, the sums of alternate terms of the series in Question 5; that is,

$$\binom{n}{0}+\binom{n}{2}+\ldots \quad \text{and} \quad \binom{n}{1}+\binom{n}{3}+\ldots.$$

Guess a general result, and prove it by giving another special value to t in $(1+t)^n$.

7. Write out in expanded form:

(a) $(1-t)^5$;   (b) $(1+2t)^4$;   (c) $(2+a)^5$.

8. Give the value of

$$\binom{6}{0}+2\binom{6}{1}+4\binom{6}{2}+8\binom{6}{3}+\ldots+64\binom{6}{6}.$$

9. Prove that, if G is a probability generator, then $G(1) = 1$.

10. Which of the following are probability generators (not necessarily binomial)?

(a) $\frac{1}{25}+\frac{8}{25}t+\frac{16}{25}t^2$;

(b) $\binom{3}{0}+\binom{3}{1}t+\binom{3}{2}t^2+\binom{3}{3}t^3$;

(c) $\frac{1}{2}+\frac{1}{2}t-\frac{1}{2}t^2+\frac{1}{2}t^3$;

(d) $\frac{1}{2}(1+t^2)$;

(e) $\dfrac{1}{8}+\dfrac{1}{8}\left(\dfrac{8-t^3}{2-t}\right).$

5. PASCAL'S TRIANGLE

A method of obtaining successive sets of binomial coefficients, once one set is known, was developed by Pascal (1623–62) in a work published posthumously in 1664. We will illustrate it by deriving the expansion of $(1+t)^5$ from that of $(1+t)^4$, as follows:

$$(1+t)^4 = 1+4t+6t^2+4t^3+t^4$$
$$\Rightarrow (1+t)^5 = (1+t)^4.(1+t)$$
$$= (1+4t+6t^2+4t^3+t^4).(1+t)$$
$$= 1+(1+4)t+(4+6)t^2+(6+4)t^3+(4+1)t^4+t^5$$
$$= 1+5t+10t^2+10t^3+5t^4+t^5.$$

747

Thus the line of coefficients   1 4 6 4 1

gives rise to the next line   1 5 10 10 5 1

according to the scheme:

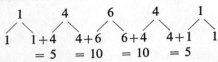

Starting in this way from $(1+t)^1$ we obtain the array of coefficients known as *Pascal's triangle*:

$$
\begin{array}{ccccccccc}
 & & & & 1 & & 1 & & \\
 & & & 1 & & 2 & & 1 & \\
 & & 1 & & 3 & & 3 & & 1 \\
 & 1 & & 4 & & 6 & & 4 & & 1 \\
1 & & 5 & & 10 & & 10 & & 5 & & 1 \\
1 & & 6 & & 15 & & 20 & & 15 & & 6 & & 1
\end{array}
$$

... .

... .

The general relation on which this is based is easily seen if the array is written in the notation of binomial coefficients:

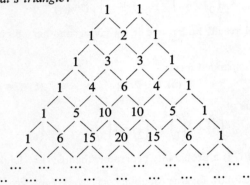

Thus

$$
\binom{4}{1} = \binom{3}{0} + \binom{3}{1}, \quad \binom{4}{2} = \binom{3}{1} + \binom{3}{2}, \quad \binom{4}{3} = \binom{3}{2} + \binom{3}{3};
$$

and clearly the array is built up by repeated application of the rule

$$
\binom{k+1}{i} = \binom{k}{i-1} + \binom{k}{i}.
$$

This is not quite sufficient by itself, since it is meaningless if we write $i = 0$ or $i = k+1$; at each stage in the construction of Pascal's triangle it is necessary to adjoin the number 1 at either end of the row. A complete inductive definition for the binomial coefficients is therefore:

(i) $\quad \dbinom{1}{0} = \dbinom{1}{1} = 1;$

(ii) $\quad \forall \, k \in N,$

$$\begin{cases} \dbinom{k+1}{0} = 1, \\[2mm] \dbinom{k+1}{i} = \dbinom{k}{i-1} + \dbinom{k}{i} \quad \text{for} \quad 1 \leqslant i \leqslant k, \\[2mm] \dbinom{k+1}{k+1} = 1. \end{cases}$$

Exercise E

1. (a) Extend Pascal's triangle as far as the tenth row.
   (b) Underline the binomial coefficients

$$\binom{8}{3}, \quad \binom{9}{7}, \quad \binom{10}{5}.$$

   (c) Continue the table further so as to calculate the binomial coefficients

$$\binom{11}{5}, \quad \binom{12}{8}, \quad \binom{13}{2}.$$

2. Use suitable expansions of $(1+t)^n$ to evalute exactly

$$(a) \ 1 \cdot 1^6; \qquad (b) \ 1 \cdot 2^4.$$

3. Using a table of binomial coefficients, evaluate correct to four places of decimals $1 \cdot 1^{20}$ and $0 \cdot 9^{20}$. As a check, repeat these calculations using logarithms. If there is any discrepancy between the two answers, account for it and say which is likely to be the more accurate.

4. A coin is tossed ten times. What is the probability that it will fall five heads and five tails?

5. The probability that a student will do a certain kind of calculation correctly is 40 %. What is the probability that he will get more than half the calculations right on a test of eight questions?

6. (a) Using the expanded forms for $(b+a)^n$ with suitable numbers substituted for a and b, make a table of powers of 11 up to the fifth power.
   (b) Make a table of powers of twelve in the scale of eleven up to the fifth power.
   (c) Make a table of powers of eleven in the scale of twelve up to the fifth power, and compare the results with the powers of 9 in the decimal scale.

7. Use the induction principle to prove that every row in Pascal's triangle is symmetrical about the middle.

8. Prove that
$$\binom{2n}{n} = 2\binom{2n-1}{n-1}.$$

9. Use the induction principle to prove that, if n is any natural number,

$$(a)\ \binom{n}{1} = n; \qquad (b)\ \binom{n}{2} = \tfrac{1}{2}n(n-1).$$

10. Write out in full the expansions of $(1+t)^3$ and $(1+t)^5$. Multiply them together and verify that the coefficients in the product are the same as those in the expansion of $(1+t)^8$. By writing all three expansions in the notation of binomial coefficients, prove that

$$\binom{3}{0}\binom{5}{4}+\binom{3}{1}\binom{5}{3}+\binom{3}{2}\binom{5}{2}+\binom{3}{3}\binom{5}{1} = \binom{8}{4}$$

and obtain a number of relations of a similar kind. Express all of these in the form of a general law.

By taking general powers in place of 3, 5 and 8, extend your result still further.

11. Write out the expansions of $(1+t)^6$, $(1-t)^6$ and $(1-t^2)^6$ in terms of binomial coefficients. By equating the product of the first two to the third, prove that

$$\binom{6}{0}\binom{6}{4}-\binom{6}{1}\binom{6}{3}+\binom{6}{2}\binom{6}{2}-\binom{6}{3}\binom{6}{1}+\binom{6}{4}\binom{6}{0} = \binom{6}{2}$$

and obtain some similar relations.

Extend these by using powers other than 6. Express all your results in the form of a general law.

6. COMBINATORIAL METHOD

6.1 Pascal's triangle affords a convenient method of calculating $\binom{n}{i}$ when n is a small number; but to use it to find, say, $\binom{30}{10}$ would involve a great deal of labour. It would be an advantage to have a formula which would enable us to calculate a coefficient such as this directly.

To obtain such a formula it is helpful to approach the problem from a different point of view; and we shall first recapitulate some of the earlier argument. We have observed that $\binom{5}{3}$, the coefficient of t^3 in the expansion of $(1+t)^5$, is equal to the number of five-digit binary code-numbers in which three of the digits are 1 and two are 0. In fact we have shown how to set up a one-one correspondence between such code-numbers and terms in the expansion of $(1+t)^5$; for example, the number 11010 is made to correspond to the term $t.t.1.t.1$ obtained by selecting the terms in bold type from the individual factors of

$$(1+t).(1+t).(1+t).(1+t).(1+t).$$

Now the binary code-numbers were previously used for indicating the incidence of success or failure in a sequence of trials, as an alternative to the notation

$$AABAB$$

or the display

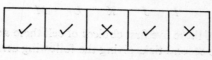

Fig. 3

The number $\binom{5}{3}$ could therefore be calculated as the number of different ways of placing three ticks in a line of five cells. (Notice that, once the ticks are placed, the crosses go willy-nilly into the empty spaces.)

Imagine therefore that we are presented with a line of five empty cells:

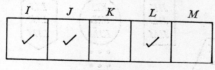

Fig. 4

We wish to find the number of ways in which three ticks can be placed in these cells. When considering the problem from this point of view it is usual to describe the number by the notation $_5C_3$. The letter C stands for 'combinations', another word for 'selections'; and the notation is read as 'the number of selections of 3 things (the cells with ticks in) out of 5'. Thus $\binom{5}{3}$ and $_5C_3$ are different symbols for the same number, the first being used when we are interested in the coefficients of a binomial expansion and the second when we concern ourselves with the combinatorial problem.

Any one of the selections can be described by naming the three cells in which ticks are placed. Thus the selection could be denoted by the symbol

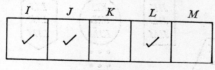

Fig. 5

IJL. Notice that the same selection could also be denoted by the symbols ILJ, or JIL, or JLI, or LIJ, or LJI; the order is immaterial. This selection therefore corresponds to a subset $\{I, J, L\}$ of three elements taken from the universal set $\{I, J, K, L, M\}$, and $_5C_3$ is the total number of subsets of three elements.

6.2 Calculation of $_5C_3$. We carry out the calculation by placing each of the three ticks in turn in empty cells:

(i) The first tick can be placed in any of the five cells

$$I \quad J \quad K \quad L \quad M$$

(ii) With each of these five first choices of cell there are four choices for the position of the second tick, giving the following arrangements:

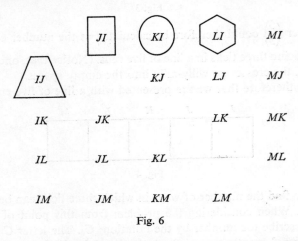

Fig. 6

Notice that arrangements such as KK are impossible. Once the first tick has been placed in cell K, this cell is not available for the second tick. This array contains 5.4, or 20 entries. It will be observed that it contains repetitions, such as JK and KJ; but it is simplest to defer discussion of these until later.

(iii) With each of these 20 choices there are three ways of placing the third tick. We give only a part of the complete array, but the method of extension should be obvious:

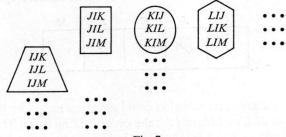

Fig. 7

This makes an array with 5.4.3, or 60 entries in all.

752

(iv) Finally, we must consider the question of repetition. It has already been remarked that a selection such as $\{I, J, L\}$ gives rise to six separate entries in the array: IJL, ILJ, JIL, JLI, LIJ and LJI. Thus the entries can be grouped into blocks of six, each block corresponding to just one selection. It follows that the number of distinct selections is $60 \div 6$, or 10. That is,

$$_5C_3 = \frac{5.4.3}{6} = 10.$$

6.3   The general result. The derivation of a general formula for $_nC_i$ proceeds along similar lines. We begin with n empty cells into which we wish to place i ticks. The first tick can be placed in any of n cells, the next in any of the remaining $(n-1)$ cells, and so on. When the final tick is about to be placed, $i-1$ cells have already been filled, so that there are still $n-(i-1)$, or $n-i+1$ cells available. We therefore obtain an array of

$$n.(n-1).(n-2).....(n-i+1)$$

entries.

It remains to find how many of these entries are equivalent, on the grounds that they are derived from the same selection. To do this, we take any selection of i cells and consider the number of different orders in which ticks might be placed in these; for example, in the special case discussed in Section 6.2 attention was concentrated on the cells I, J, L:

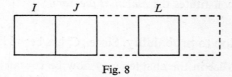

Fig. 8

The argument is similar to that already used. The first tick can be placed in any of i cells, the second in any of the remaining $(i-1)$ cells, and so on. Thus to each selection there correspond

$$i.(i-1).(i-2).....1$$

different entries in the array.

The number of distinct selections is therefore given by the formula

$$_nC_i = \frac{n(n-1)(n-2)....(n-i+1)}{i(i-1)(i-2)....1}.$$

6.4   Factorial formula for $_nC_i$. The formula just derived can be re-cast in terms of the factorial function. We note first that the denominator can be abbreviated to $i!$, the product of the first i natural numbers. The numerator

$$n(n-1)(n-2)....(n-i+1)$$

can be converted into the form

$$\frac{n(n-1)(n-2)....(n-i+1).(n-i)(n-i-1)....1}{(n-i)(n-i-1)....1},$$

which is

$$\frac{n!}{(n-i)!}.$$

It follows that

$$_nC_i = \frac{n!}{i!(n-i)!}.$$

This form is especially suitable in general theoretical work.

With this expression it is easy to calculate approximate values of the binomial coefficients for large n, using tables of $\log_{10} x!$. (See, for example, S.M.P. *Advanced Tables*, p. 70, where the function is tabulated up to $x = 100$. A formula due to Stirling is also given, which makes it possible to deal with even larger values of x.)

Substituting for $_nC_i$, or $\binom{n}{i}$, in the expansions set out in Section 4, we obtain the results

$$(1+t)^n = \sum_{i=0}^{n} \frac{n!}{i!(n-i)!} t^i$$

and

$$(b+a)^n = \sum_{i=0}^{n} \frac{n!}{i!(n-i)!} b^{n-i}a^i.$$

This last form constitutes the *binomial theorem*.

6.5 Application to probability.

Since $_nC_i$ has been identified with $\binom{n}{i}$, results given earlier in the chapter may now be re-stated in terms of the formula for $_nC_i$. In particular, in a sequence of n trials such that the probabilities of success and failure in each are a, b respectively, the probability of i successes is

$$p_i = \frac{n!}{i!(n-i)!} b^{n-i}a^i,$$

and the probability generator for this situation is

$$G = (b+at)^n = \sum_{i=0}^{n} \frac{n!}{i!(n-i)!} b^{n-i}a^i t^i.$$

*7. PROOF OF THE FORMULA FROM THE INDUCTIVE DEFINITION

A direct proof of the formula

$$\binom{n}{i} = \frac{n!}{i!(n-i)!}$$

754

may be given using the inductive definition for $\binom{n}{i}$ set out at the end of Section 5:

(i) $\binom{1}{0} = \binom{1}{1} = 1$;

(ii) $\forall\, k \in N$,

$$\begin{cases} \binom{k+1}{0} = 1, \\ \binom{k+1}{i} = \binom{k}{i-1} + \binom{k}{i} & \text{for } 1 \leqslant i \leqslant k, \\ \binom{k+1}{k+1} = 1. \end{cases}$$

The details are not entirely straightforward, since the statement to be proved involves two variables n, i. It is therefore necessary to use care in stating the proposition on which the induction argument is to be based. We take this as follows:

Proposition.

$$\binom{n}{i} = \frac{n!}{i!(n-1)!}, \quad \text{for all integers } i \text{ such that } 0 \leqslant i \leqslant n.$$

Thus if T denotes the truth set for this proposition, the statement $3 \in T$ involves *all* the following assertions:

$$\binom{3}{0} = \frac{3!}{0!3!}, \quad \binom{3}{1} = \frac{3!}{1!2!}, \quad \binom{3}{2} = \frac{3!}{2!1!}, \quad \binom{3}{3} = \frac{3!}{3!0!}.$$

In the course of the proof we shall need to use a definition for $n!$. One way of defining this inductively is:

(i) $0! = 1$;

(ii) for all integers $k \geqslant 0$, $(k+1)! = (k+1).k!$.

We now proceed as follows:

(i) Prove that $1 \in T$. For this we have to establish that

$$\binom{1}{0} = \frac{1!}{0!1!} \quad \text{and} \quad \binom{1}{1} = \frac{1!}{1!0!}.$$

This is immediate, since by the definition of $\binom{n}{i}$,

$$\binom{1}{0} = \binom{1}{1} = 1$$

and we know that $0! = 1$, $1! = 1$.

(ii) Prove that $k \in T \Rightarrow k+1 \in T$. That is, we take as known that

$$\binom{k}{i} = \frac{k!}{i!(k-i)!} \quad \text{for } 0 \leqslant i \leqslant k$$

and deduce that

$$\binom{k+1}{i} = \frac{(k+1)!}{i!(k+1-i)!} \quad \text{for} \quad 0 \leqslant i \leqslant k+1.$$

It is necessary to consider three separate cases:

(a) $i = 0$. Then

$$\binom{k+1}{i} = \binom{k+1}{0} = 1 \quad \text{(by definition),}$$

and $\qquad \dfrac{(k+1)!}{i!(k+1-i)!} = \dfrac{(k+1)!}{0!(k+1)!} = 1 \quad \text{(since } 0! = 1\text{)}.$

(b) $1 \leqslant i \leqslant k$. Then

$$\binom{k+1}{i} = \binom{k}{i-1} + \binom{k}{i} \quad \left(\text{by the inductive definition of } \binom{n}{i}\right)$$

$$= \frac{k!}{(i-1)!(k-i+1)!} + \frac{k!}{i!(k-i)!} \quad \text{(since } k \in T\text{)}.$$

Now the definition of $n!$ gives

$$\frac{1}{(i-1)!} = \frac{i}{i!} \quad \text{and} \quad \frac{1}{(k-i)!} = \frac{k-i+1}{(k-i+1)!}.$$

Making these substitutions in the preceding line,

$$\binom{k+1}{i} = \frac{k!i}{i!(k-i+1)!} + \frac{k!(k-i+1)}{i!(k-i+1)!}$$

$$= \frac{k!}{i!(k-i+1)!}\{i+(k-i+1)\}$$

$$= \frac{k!(k+1)}{i!(k-i+1)!}$$

$$= \frac{(k+1)!}{i!(k+1-i)!}, \quad \text{as required.}$$

(c) $i = k+1$. Then

$$\binom{k+1}{i} = \binom{k+1}{k+1} = 1 \quad \text{(by definition)}$$

and $\qquad \dfrac{(k+1)!}{i!(k+1-i)!} = \dfrac{(k+1)!}{(k+1)!0!} = 1 \quad \text{(since } 0! = 1\text{)}.$

This completes the proof of (ii); and (i) and (ii) together give all the requirements of the principle of mathematical induction. We have therefore proved the proposition stated.

Exercise F

1. Calculate $_{12}C_7$, $_{30}C_6$, $_{50}C_{47}$.

2. How could you tell, without knowing the formula, that

$$_nC_{n-i} = {_nC_i}?$$

3. A history paper contains 25 questions, of which candidates have to answer four. In how many different ways can the selection be made?

4. The judges at a local baby show have to choose five babies out of a field of 80 to go on to the county finals. How many different selections could they make?

If 50 boys and 30 girls are entered for the contest, what are the probabilities that they choose: (*a*) five boys, (*b*) two boys and three girls, if the sex of the babies does not influence their choice?

5. A football pools coupon lists 48 matches, and contestants are expected to name four which they think will result in draws. How many different selections are possible?

If when the results are published it turns out that there were eleven draws altogether, what is the probability of winning if the selection was made at random?

6. Use tables to find approximately the values of $_{80}C_{25}$, $_{200}C_{40}$.

7. Calculate the probabilities of an exact half-and-half split between heads and tails if a coin is tossed: (*a*) 10 times, (*b*) 100 times, (*c*) 1000 times.

Write a short paragraph in non-technical terms to account for the trend of your answers.

8. One-quarter of the population is thought to have watched the Cup Final on television. On this assumption, calculate the probability that a random sample of 100 people will contain: (*a*) 25, (*b*) 20, (*c*) 30 people who watched the programme.

9. Calculate the probability of being dealt a hand of 13 spades at bridge from a well-shuffled pack.

10. A bookshelf holds a family bible and k volumes of the *Encyclopedia Britannica*. A small child takes down i books from the shelf at random. Use this illustration to justify in terms of selections the relation

$$_{k+1}C_i = {_kC_{i-1}} + {_kC_i}.$$

11. Prove that, if p is a prime number, then $_pC_i$ is a multiple of p for $1 \leqslant i \leqslant p-1$. Is the converse true? Justify your answer.

12. Prove that the number of solutions of the equation

$$x_1 + x_2 + \ldots + x_m = n$$

in non-negative integers is

$$_{m+n-1}C_{m-1}.$$

8. RELATION BETWEEN SUCCESSIVE
BINOMIAL COEFFICIENTS

Let us now reverse the order of the factors in the denominator of the expression

$$\frac{n(n-1)(n-2)\ldots.(n-i+1)}{i(i-1)(i-2)\ldots.1}$$

(see Section 6.3), and write the binomial coefficient as the product of i fractions:

$$\binom{n}{i} = \frac{n}{1} \cdot \frac{n-1}{2} \cdot \frac{n-2}{3} \ldots. \frac{n-i+1}{i}.$$

(The notation $\binom{n}{i}$ is used in preference to ${}_n C_i$ because this form is of particular importance for binomial expansions.) Putting $i = 1, 2, 3, \ldots$ in turn, we find

$$\binom{n}{1} = \frac{n}{1},$$

$$\binom{n}{2} = \frac{n}{1} \cdot \frac{n-1}{2},$$

$$\binom{n}{3} = \frac{n}{1} \cdot \frac{n-1}{2} \cdot \frac{n-2}{3}, \quad \text{etc.}$$

This gives a very convenient way of calculating successive binomial coefficients, each being derived from its predecessor by multiplying by the next fraction in the sequence. For example, the coefficients in the expansion of $(1+t)^8$ are found as

$$1, \quad \tfrac{8}{1} = 8, \quad 8 \times \tfrac{7}{2} = 28, \quad 28 \times \tfrac{6}{3} = 56, \quad 56 \times \tfrac{5}{4} = 70, \quad 70 \times \tfrac{4}{5} = 56,$$

and so on.

In general,

$$\binom{n}{i+1} = \frac{n}{1} \cdot \frac{n-1}{2} \cdot \frac{n-2}{3} \ldots. \frac{n-i+1}{i} \cdot \frac{n-i}{i+1}$$

$$= \frac{n-i}{i+1} \binom{n}{i}.$$

Notice that this relation still holds when $i = 0$, since then

$$\binom{n}{i+1} = \binom{n}{1} = n$$

and

$$\frac{n-i}{i+1} \binom{n}{i} = \frac{n}{1} \binom{n}{0} = n.$$

We therefore have the basis of an inductive procedure for developing the binomial coefficients:

(i) $\binom{n}{0} = 1$;

(ii) for $0 \leqslant i \leqslant n-1$, $\binom{n}{i+1} = \dfrac{n-i}{i+1}\binom{n}{i}$.

Exercise G

1. Use the method described in Section 8 to develop the sequence of coefficients in the expansion of $(1+t)^{12}$. Show that it gives the coefficient of t^{12} as 1, and that if the rule is applied for integral values of i greater than 11 it gives all subsequent coefficients as 0.

2. Given that $\binom{22}{9} = 497\,420$, find $\binom{22}{10}$, $\binom{22}{11}$, $\binom{23}{13}$.

3. Given that $_{100}C_{20} \approx 5\cdot36 \times 10^{20}$, find $_{100}C_{21}$ and $_{100}C_{19}$.

4. Use the inductive relation devised in Section 8 to devise a flow diagram for the calculation of $\binom{n}{i}$.

5. A die is rolled 100 times. Write down a formula for p_i, the probability of getting i sixes, and prove that the ratio of p_{i+1} to p_i is

$$\frac{100-i}{5(i+1)}.$$

Given that p_{10} is approximately $0\cdot0213$, calculate (with the help of a slide rule) the probabilities of various numbers of sixes from 10 to 25, and show your results graphically.

6. A pack of cards is shuffled and cut 50 times. About how many times would you expect to show a spade? Write down a formula for the probability of obtaining i spades, and find the ratio of the probabilities of $i+1$ spades and i spades. Use this to find the number with the highest probability.

7. A gambler has a 20 % chance of winning a certain game. One evening he plays 100 games. If x denotes the probability that he will win exactly 20 of these, find in terms of x (to slide rule accuracy) the probabilities of winning 21, 22, ... times, and 19, 18, ... times; continue with these calculations each way until the probabilities are less than $0\cdot01x$. Draw a diagram showing the relative probabilities of different numbers of wins.

Use the fact that the total probability of 0, 1, ..., 100 wins is 1 to estimate the value of x.

8. In a sequence of n trials, each having probabilities a, b of success and failure, let p_i denote the probability of obtaining i successes. Prove that

$$p_{i+1} > p_i \Leftrightarrow i < na-b,$$

and deduce that the most probable number of successes lies within a distance 1 of na. What is the significance of the number na in this context?

9. BINOMIAL EXPANSIONS AND TAYLOR APPROXIMATIONS

9.1 We saw in Chapter 16 that the expansions for $(p+\alpha)^2$, $(p+\alpha)^3$, $(p+\alpha)^4$ consist of the same terms as the local Taylor approximations

$$f(p+\alpha) \simeq f(p)+f'(p)\alpha+\frac{f''(p)}{2!}\alpha^2+\ldots+\frac{f^{(m)}(p)}{m!}\alpha^m$$

for the square, cube and fourth power functions. We are now in a position to generalize this result.

Consider the function defined by

$$f(x) = x^n$$

and its Taylor approximations in a neighbourhood of $x = 1$, written in the form

$$f(1+t) \simeq f(1)+f'(1)t+\frac{f''(1)}{2!}t^2+\ldots+\frac{f^{(m)}(1)}{m!}t^m.$$

It is easily calculated that

$$\left.\begin{array}{l} f'(x) = nx^{n-1}, \\ f''(x) = n(n-1)x^{n-2}, \\ f'''(x) = n(n-1)(n-2)x^{n-3}, \\ \text{etc.} \end{array}\right\} \quad \text{so that} \quad \left\{\begin{array}{l} f'(1) = n, \\ f''(1) = n(n-1), \\ f'''(1) = n(n-1)(n-2), \\ \text{etc.} \end{array}\right.$$

Substituting the values of these derivatives in the Taylor approximation, we obtain the form

$$(1+t)^n \simeq 1+nt+\frac{n(n-1)}{2!}t^2+\frac{n(n-1)(n-2)}{3!}t^3+\ldots$$

continued to the appropriate number of terms; and we recognize this as the beginning of the binomial expansion.

If only a few terms of the Taylor approximation are taken, then the result is useful only over an interval of small values of t. The terms of the binomial expansion involving t^{m+1}, t^{m+2}, ..., t^n are then comparatively small. It is interesting to notice, however, that if the Taylor approximation is taken as far as the power t^n or higher, then the complete expansion is obtained; for the terms agree up to t^n, and when $m > n$

$$f^{(m)}(x) = 0.$$

In this case, therefore, the two expressions are exactly equal for all values of t.

9.2 The general binomial theorem. What is especially interesting about this approach to the binomial expansion is that, in developing the Taylor approximation, it is not necessary to restrict n to be a natural number. Thus polynomials of the form

$$1 + nt + \frac{n(n-1)}{2!} t^2 + \frac{n(n-1)(n-2)}{3!} t^3 + \dots,$$

taken as far as some power t^m, afford approximations to $(1+t)^n$ for small values of t, even if n is a negative integer or a general rational number.

Important special cases include:

$$\frac{1}{1+t} = (1+t)^{-1} = 1 - t + t^2 - t^3 + \dots;$$

$$\frac{1}{(1+t)^2} = (1+t)^{-2} = 1 - 2t + 3t^2 - 4t^3 + \dots;$$

$$\sqrt{(1+t)} = (1+t)^{\frac{1}{2}} = 1 + \tfrac{1}{2}t - \tfrac{1}{8}t^2 + \tfrac{1}{16}t^3 - \dots.$$

The interval of values of t over which these approximations are reliable depends, of course, on the number of terms used. It can in fact be proved that, if $-1 < t < 1$, the sum of the series converges to $(1+t)^n$ when the number of terms is increased indefinitely. This result was stated by Newton; it is known as the *general binomial theorem*, and may be written

$$(1+t)^n = \sum_{i=0}^{\infty} \frac{n(n-1)\dots(n-i+1)}{i!} t^i \quad \text{if} \quad -1 < t < 1.$$

Notice that when n is not a natural number the coefficients in the series never become zero. For practical purposes, therefore, it is always necessary to cut the series off at some power of t and to use a polynomial approximation; there is no possibility of achieving exact equality.

9.3 A similar approximation can be made to the more general binomial expression $(b+a)^n$, applying Taylor's formula to the function defined by $f(x) = x^n$ in a neighbourhood of $x = b$. But since each term then involves a factor such as b^n, b^{n-1}, ..., which is clumsy to handle when n is not a natural number, it is more convenient to write

$$(b+a)^n = b^n \left(1 + \frac{a}{b}\right)^n$$

and to use the form given in Section 9.2 with a/b written for t.

Example 2. Evaluate $\sqrt{10}$ to three places of decimals.

A convenient exact square near to 10 is 9, so we write

$$\sqrt{10} = (9+1)^{\frac{1}{2}}$$
$$= 9^{\frac{1}{2}}(1 + \tfrac{1}{9})^{\frac{1}{2}}$$
$$\simeq 3\left\{1 + \frac{1}{2} \cdot \frac{1}{9} - \frac{1}{8} \cdot \frac{1}{9^2} + \frac{1}{16} \cdot \frac{1}{9^3}\right\}$$
$$\simeq 3 + 0\cdot1667 - 0\cdot0046 + 0\cdot0003$$
$$\simeq 3\cdot162.$$

Example 3. A die is rolled repeatedly until a six appears. Find a generator for the probability that *r* non-sixes are thrown before the first six.

The probability of *r* non-sixes followed by a six is

$$(\tfrac{5}{6})^r \cdot \tfrac{1}{6}$$

The probability generator is therefore

$$\begin{aligned} G &= \tfrac{1}{6} + \tfrac{5}{6} \cdot \tfrac{1}{6}t + (\tfrac{5}{6})^2 \cdot \tfrac{1}{6}t^2 + (\tfrac{5}{6})^3 \cdot \tfrac{1}{6}t^3 + \ldots \\ &= \tfrac{1}{6}\{1 + \tfrac{5}{6}t + (\tfrac{5}{6}t)^2 + (\tfrac{5}{6}t)^3 + \ldots\} \\ &= 6^{-1}(1 - \tfrac{5}{6}t)^{-1} \\ &= (6 - 5t)^{-1} \\ &= \frac{1}{6 - 5t}. \end{aligned}$$

Notice that in this example the probability generator is not a polynomial, since there is no limit to the possible length of a run of bad luck.

Exercise H

1. Find approximations in the form of cubic polynomials to the following functions for small values of *t*:

(a) $\dfrac{1}{\sqrt{(1+t)}}$;

(b) $\dfrac{1}{(1+t)^3}$;

(c) $\sqrt[3]{(1+t)}$;

(d) $\sqrt{(4-t)}$;

(e) $\dfrac{1}{2+t}$;

(f) $\dfrac{3}{(3-t)^2}$.

2. Evaluate $\sqrt[3]{10}$ to three places of decimals.

3. Evaluate $1/\sqrt{50}$ and deduce the value of $\sqrt{2}$ to four places of decimals.

4. A gambler goes on playing until he loses a game, and then stops. If his probability of winning a game is 0·4, find a probability generator for the number of games he will play in all.

5. A die is rolled repeatedly until two sixes have appeared. Find the probability that there will be *r* non-sixes before the second six shows up, and find a generator for the probability function.
   Could your answer have been forecast from the result of Example 3?

6. Prove that the coefficient of t^i in the general binomial expansion of $(1-t)^{-n}$ is

$$\binom{n+i-1}{i}.$$

7. Use the fact that

$$(1+t)^n(1+t)^{-1} = (1+t)^{n-1}$$

to show that, if $0 \leqslant i \leqslant n-1$,

$$\binom{n}{i} - \binom{n}{i-1} + \binom{n}{i-2} - \ldots + (-1)^i\binom{n}{0} = \binom{n-1}{i}.$$

What is the value of the expression on the left if $i \geqslant n$?

Miscellaneous Exercise

1. An American city is designed on a square grid of streets, the intersections being labelled by integral Cartesian coordinates. The number of routes from $(0, 0)$ to (r, s) with the shortest possible distance of $r+s$ 'blocks' is denoted by $u(r, s)$. Prove that

$$u(r, s) = u(r-1, s) + u(r, s-1) \quad (r > 0, s > 0)$$

and give the values of $u(r, 0)$ and $u(0, s)$.

Draw a diagram of the lattice of street intersections, and mark against each the number of possible routes of this kind from $(0, 0)$. Guess a formula for $u(r, s)$, and then prove it either by induction or by some other argument.

2. If 20 pennies are tossed together, find the probabilities of getting 0, 1, 2, ..., 20 heads. (Use a table of binomial coefficients, and note that $2^{20} \simeq 1 \cdot 05 \times 10^6$.)

(*a*) If you want to assert that there is about a 95 % probability that the number of heads will lie between $10 \pm d$, what value would you give for d?

(*b*) If you want to assert that there is only about one chance in a thousand that there will be fewer than n heads, what value would you give for n?

With these values for d and n, give rather more precise values for the respective probabilities.

3. (*a*) Four dice are rolled and the number of sixes recorded. If the experiment is repeated 25 times, on how many occasions would you think it likely that you would get 0, 1, 2, 3, 4 sixes?

(*b*) If four dice are rolled 25 times, on how many occasions would you expect to get a triple or better (not necessarily of sixes)?

Carry out the experiments and compare the frequencies with the estimates you have made from the theory of probability.

4. In 1964 an assessment was being made by the Department of Education and Science (using a large sample of schools) of the proportion of leavers who were going on to a university. One school had seven leavers of whom two were going to a university; but in giving this information the school remarked that their figures were misleading, as their usual proportion was something like $\frac{3}{4}$. What is the probability that a sample as unrepresentative as this would occur in a randomly chosen year, and what action would you take if you were conducting the survey?

5. In a certain type of habitat the proportion of butterflies with wing spots is $\frac{3}{8}$. A sample of twelve butterflies collected in one location was found to contain only two with wing spots. Calculate the probability that such a sample (that is, one with two or fewer spotted butterflies out of twelve) could have been drawn by chance from the given type of habitat. Would this lead you to the conclusion that the sample collected must have come from some other habitat?

6. On a certain south-facing hillside the proportion of metre-squares which, when examined, are found to contain a plant of tormentil is $0 \cdot 4$. A botanist suspects that the north-facing hillside is less densely populated with the plant; he therefore carries out a survey and in twenty metre-squares he observes four with tormentil. On the hypothesis that the south-facing type of vegetation does in fact exist on the north-facing hillside and that the discrepancy is merely due to chance variation, what is the probability of a deficiency as large or larger than that observed? Discuss the botanist's suspicion in the light of his survey.

7. The first fifty digits of the decimal form for π are

3·141 592 653 589 793 238 462 643 383 279 502 884 197 169 399 375 1;

make a table showing the frequency of occurrence of the various digits.

In a random sequence of fifty digits what is the probability of getting: (a) one or fewer zeros, (b) nine or more threes? Do your answers support the theory that there is some significance in the irregular distribution in the first fifty digits of π?

Try to find out the value of π to a larger number of decimal places, and investigate whether this irregularity persists.

8. A certain commercial firm has ten agents looking for clients, and each agent sends an average of three clients a week in a 6-day week (but never two on the same day). What are the probabilities that on any day there will be: (a) 10, (b) 9 or more, (c) 8 or more, (d) 7 or more clients visiting the firm?

The firm arranges for a separate officer to look after each client during his whole-day visit. It is prepared to ask a client, or clients, to rearrange the day of visit if there will not be an officer available to accompany the visitor; but for administrative convenience it tries to avoid disrupting the original schedule in this way more than about once a week. How many officers should it keep available to look after clients?

9. Show that if n is a large number and r is comparatively small, then the first few terms of the binomial expansion of

$$\left(1 + \frac{r}{n}\right)^n$$

are approximately 1, r, $r^2/2!$, $r^3/3!$, etc.

Working to three places of decimals, find the difference between

$$(1\cdot002)^{1000} \quad \text{and} \quad \sum_{i=1}^{10} \frac{2^i}{i!}.$$

(Take $\log_{10} 1\cdot002 = 0\cdot0008677$.)

10. A factory is lit by 1000 fluorescent tubes, and on average three of these need replacing every week. Write down the probability generator giving the probabilities that in a particular week the number of tubes needing replacement is 0, 1, 2, 3, ...

Prove that the probability that none will need to be replaced is about 0·050. (Use $\log_{10} 0\cdot997 = \bar{1}\cdot9986952$.)

Let this probability be denoted by P. By considering the ratios of successive coefficients of the probability generator, prove that the successive probabilities are approximately P, $3P$, $3^2P/2!$, $3^3P/3!$, etc. Hence calculate these probabilities (working to three places of decimals) and display your results in a diagram. (The succession of probabilities in this question is called a *Poisson sequence*.)

SUMMARY

In a sequence of n trials, each having probabilities a, b of success and failure respectively, the probability of i successes is the coefficient of t^i in the expansion of

$$(b+at)^n.$$

This coefficient is

$$\binom{n}{i} b^{n-i}a^i,$$

where

$$\binom{n}{i} \text{ (or } _nC_i) = \frac{n!}{i!(n-i)!}$$

$$= \frac{n(n-1)(n-2)...(n-i+1)}{i(i-1)(i-2)...1}.$$

$_nC_i$ is the number of subsets of size i contained in a set of n elements.

The binomial theorem:

$$(b+a)^n = \sum_{i=0}^{n} \binom{n}{i} b^{n-i}a^i,$$

or

$$(1+t)^n = \sum_{i=0}^{n} \binom{n}{i} t^i, \quad \text{where} \quad n \in N.$$

Important relations:

$$\binom{k+1}{i} = \binom{k}{i-1} + \binom{k}{i};$$

$$\binom{n}{i+1} = \frac{n-i}{i+1} \binom{n}{i}.$$

The general binomial theorem:

For any rational number n,

$$(1+t)^n = \sum_{i=0}^{\infty} \frac{n(n-1)...(n-i+1)}{i!} t^i \quad \text{if} \quad -1 < t < 1.$$

26

PROBABILITY PARAMETERS

1. STATISTICS AND PROBABILITY

1.1 Statistical populations: a summary. Statistics is an experimental science. From a statistical experiment we derive a population (or maybe several populations) of either measurements or attributes. Each member of this population is an element of the set of possible outcomes of the experiment, known as the possibility space.

In this chapter we shall be concerned only with populations of measurements drawn from a possibility space of discrete elements

$$\{x_1, x_2, ..., x_n\},$$

such as sizes of families or cricket scores or prices of articles. Discussion of populations drawn from a continuum is deferred until a later chapter.

When we have obtained such a population we proceed to summarize the information in various ways—graphically perhaps, or by calculating various statistics such as the mean and standard deviation. We have seen that it is convenient for this purpose to use the frequency function f, which associates with each element x_i of the possibility space the number, $f(x_i)$, of occurrences in the population. We then define, for example, the mean m (or $\bar{x}$) by the equation

$$m = \frac{1}{N} \sum_{i=1}^{n} x_i f(x_i),$$

where N, the size of the population, is given by

$$N = \sum_{i=1}^{n} f(x_i).$$

For the purposes of this chapter we prefer to re-write this formula in terms of relative frequencies rather than actual frequencies. It will be recalled that these are the proportions of occurrences in the population of the various elements x_i (see Chapter 20, Section 2.3). Denoting the relative frequency of x_i by $q(x_i)$, we write

$$q(x_i) = \frac{f(x_i)}{N},$$

so that

$$m = \frac{1}{N} \Sigma x_i f(x_i)$$

$$= \Sigma x_i \cdot \frac{f(x_i)}{N}$$

$$= \Sigma x_i q(x_i).$$

It is of course obvious that the sum of the relative frequencies corresponding to all the elements of the possibility space is 1. Algebraically,

$$\Sigma q(x_i) = \Sigma \frac{f(x_i)}{N} = \frac{1}{N}\Sigma f(x_i) = \frac{1}{N}N = 1.$$

Example 1. A pair of dice is rolled 100 times, and the numbers of sixes recorded. There are two double-sixes, 25 single sixes and 73 throws with no sixes. Calculate the relative frequencies and deduce the mean number of sixes.

The possibility space is the set {0, 1, 2}, and the relative frequencies are as follows:

Number of sixes x_i	Relative frequency $q(x_i)$	$x_i q(x_i)$
0	0·73	0
1	0·25	0·25
2	0·02	0·04
	1·00	0·29

The third column of the table is used for the calculation of the mean. We deduce that the mean number of sixes is $m = 0.29$.

1.2 Probability models.

A scientist will not rest content with assembling and summarizing numerical data from experiments. He will hope to find recognizable patterns in his results, and to describe them in terms of some theory of more general application. For this purpose he creates a theoretical system, operating according to well-defined laws, which he hopes will mirror closely his experimental observations. Such a system is often described as a 'mathematical model'.

Any model for a particular situation will be set in the framework of some general theory. For an engineer this may be defined by the laws of Newtonian mechanics; for a geneticist it may be the Mendelian theory of inheritance. Similarly, the statistician constructs his models within the general framework of probability theory. He carries out calculations on probabilities according to laws such as those laid down in Chapter 20. If his model is a good one he will usually get close agreement between the probabilities he has calculated and the relative frequencies found from statistical experiment. Often it will be necessary to consider several alternative models (for example, using different initial probabilities or different probability functions) and to select for further study the one which agrees best with the results of experiment.

Imagine, for example, that we are interested in the flow of traffic along a certain stretch of road. Observation may suggest that about 30 % of the vehicles travel at speeds around 110 km/h, 58 % around 80 km/h,

10 % around 55 km/h, and 2 % around 15 km/h. We might then set up a model in which the idealized probability function for vehicle speeds is:

Speed	Probability
15	0·02
55	0·10
80	0·58
110	0·30

It will also be necessary to consider how the vehicles are spaced out on the road; how important, for example, is the effect of the traffic light in the town five miles back? To investigate this we might examine two alternative models: one based on the assumption that the spacing of vehicles is random, and one in which we suppose the traffic to emerge from the town in one-minute bursts followed by one-minute gaps. Proceeding in this way, we aim to set up a model of the situation which predicts a traffic flow in good agreement with experimental observations. When we are satisfied with our model, we may use it to examine theoretically the effect of changing certain factors: to estimate, for example, how much improvement could be expected from the construction of a mile of dual carriageway at a certain place.

The important point is that results in the theory of probability are established by mathematical reasoning and not by experiment. All that a statistical experiment and an associated probability model have in common is the possibility space. The applicability of the model rests on the belief that, in a large number of repetitions of a trial, the relative frequencies of the various elements of the possibility space will be approximately equal to the probabilities calculated theoretically.

2. EXPECTED VALUE

2.1 The situation in Example 1, in which a pair of dice is rolled and the number of sixes recorded, can be described by a probability model built around the concept of a perfectly fair die inserted randomly in the shaker. On this basis we assign *a priori* probabilities, taking all possible pairs of scores to be equally likely. Of the 36 possible pairs, one is a double-six and ten others contain one six. We therefore take the probabilities as follows:

Number of sixes	Probability
0	$\frac{25}{36}$
1	$\frac{10}{36}$
2	$\frac{1}{36}$

Now the validity of the model rests on the assumption that, in a long series of throws, the relative frequencies will approximate to these probabilities. If they did so exactly, then the mean would be

$$0 \times \tfrac{25}{36} + 1 \times \tfrac{10}{36} + 2 \times \tfrac{1}{36}$$
$$= \tfrac{1}{3}.$$

We notice that, in the actual experiment described in Example 1, the mean was approximately but not exactly equal to this value.

The quantity which we have calculated was obtained by replacing, in the formula for m, the relative frequency $q(x_i)$ of the element x_i by the probability $p(x_i)$ assigned to it in the model. It is therefore a kind of theoretical mean for the situation, given by the expression

$$\mu = \sum_{i=1}^{n} x_i p(x_i).$$

A measure of this kind, calculated from a probability function in the same way as a statistic is calculated from a frequency function, is called a *parameter*. It represents the value which the corresponding statistic would have if the relative frequencies in an experiment were exactly equal to the probabilities in the model.

The parameter μ is often called the *expected value of x*, or the *expectation*, and denoted by the symbol $E[x]$. It is a precisely defined quantity calculated from a probability function specified on a possibility space whose elements are quantities. $E[x]$ is not, of course, a function of x; it is rather a function of the whole set of elements of the possibility space together with their probabilities.

It is important to realize that expected value is defined only if the elements of the possibility space are quantities rather than attributes. For example, if a coin is tossed and

$$p \text{ (coin is a head)} = \tfrac{1}{2},$$
$$p \text{ (coin is a tail)} = \tfrac{1}{2},$$

then we do not define the 'expected value of the face'. We can, however, state that the expected value of the number of heads is $0.\tfrac{1}{2} + 1.\tfrac{1}{2} = \tfrac{1}{2}$. This is because in the first case the possibilities are the attributes $\{H, T\}$, whereas in the second case they are the numbers $\{0, 1\}$.

Example 2. In the game of crown-and-anchor the possible winnings for a unit stake are -1, 1, 2 and 3 units, and the probabilities of these are respectively $\tfrac{125}{216}$, $\tfrac{75}{216}$, $\tfrac{15}{216}$ and $\tfrac{1}{216}$.

Find the expected value of the winnings, and interpret the result.

The formula gives

$$E \text{ [winnings]} = (-1) \times \tfrac{125}{216} + 1 \times \tfrac{75}{216} + 2 \times \tfrac{15}{216} + 3 \times \tfrac{1}{216}$$
$$= -\tfrac{17}{216}$$
$$\simeq -0 \cdot 08.$$

3   SAM 3

This means that on average the player will lose 0·08 units for every unit staked, and will therefore probably lose about 8 % of his total stake in the long run.

This kind of analysis can obviously be applied to other situations, and in particular to other games. If the expected value of the gain is zero, the game is said to be 'fair'. If the expected value of the gain is W units, then the game can be made fair by charging the player an entry fee of W units each time he plays.

2.2 Interpretation of expected value. In probability theory we use the word 'expected' in a technical sense which does not carry all its everyday associations. First, it is important to notice that $E[x]$ corresponds to the mean and not to the mode. For example, if in the dice-rolling experiment of Example 1 a person were asked to state in advance how many sixes he would expect to get, he might well answer 'none': for 0 is the 'most probable' value in the possibility space. The expected value $E[x] = \frac{1}{3}$ as we have defined it is not even a value which can be attained in a single throw. The meaning of the statement 'the expected value is $\frac{1}{3}$' is that, over a large number of throws of the dice, we expect to get about one-third as many sixes as throws.

Moreover, even the modal value might not be 'expected' in the ordinary sense of the word. For example, it is easy to show that, in tossing a coin 10000 times the expected value of the number of heads (speaking technically) is 5000; and this time 5000 is also the most probable value. But we know from the theory of binomial probability that the probability of an experiment giving exactly 5000 heads and 5000 tails is

$$\binom{10000}{5000} (\tfrac{1}{2})^{5000} (\tfrac{1}{2})^{5000},$$

or about 0·008. This is small enough to occasion some surprise if such a conveniently symmetrical result turned up by chance.

Exercise A

1. Calculate the parameter μ for the vehicle speeds in the probability model described in Section 1.2.

2. A manufacturer makes shoes in sizes from 7 to 11, and markets them at a standard price of £2.50. The costs to him of making the five sizes are £1.65, £1.70, £1.80, £1.90, £1.95 and he estimates the demand at 12%, 35%, 28%, 14 %, 11 % respectively of his total order. Calculate the expected value of his profit per pair.

3. Take a block of 100 digits from a table of random numbers and calculate the relative frequencies of the ten digits. Hence find the mean value of the population of single-digit numbers.

Compare your answers with the theoretical probabilities for the occurrences of single-digit numbers selected at random, and the theoretical mean value.

4. A player rolls two dice and receives from the bank a prize of as many pence as the difference between his score and 7. Make a table of the probabilities of each size of prize and find his expected winning. Would 2 pence be a fair entry fee, and if not whom would it favour, and at what rate in the long run?

Carry out three runs, each of ten plays of the game, and find the mean profit per game for each of your runs, assuming an entry fee of 2 pence per game.

5. A game consists of three successive tosses of a coin. A player receives a penny for the first head, 2 pence for the second and finally 3 pence for the third (so that if he tosses two heads he gets $(1+2)$ pence). What would be a fair forfeit for 'no heads' if the game is to be fair without an entrance fee?

Carry out three runs, each of ten plays of the game, and find the mean receipts per game in each of your runs. (If you prefer it, simulate the game with a table of random numbers.)

6. Select 50 blocks of five digits from a table of random numbers, and record the number of multiples of 3 (including zero) that each contains. Calculate the relative frequencies of different scores in your population, and the mean value.

Compare your answers with the probabilities of the various scores and the expected value.

7. Calculate the probabilities of various numbers of sixes when three dice are rolled simultaneously, and the expected value of the number of sixes.

Repeat your calculations with four and five dice. Could the expected values have been guessed without finding the probabilities?

8. In a game of bridge I know that my two opponents hold six trumps between them. What is the expected value of the number of rounds of trumps I shall have to lead in order to clear both their hands of this suit?

3. VARIANCE

3.1 The analogy we have developed between the mean of a statistical population and the theoretical mean value for a corresponding probability model can be extended to other statistics, such as measures of spread, skewness, and so on.

After the mean m, the next statistic in order of importance is the standard deviation s, or its square which we call the variance. It will be recalled that the variance is the mean square deviation from the mean, given by the formula

$$s^2 = \frac{1}{N} \sum_{i=1}^{n} (x_i - m)^2 f(x_i).$$

This expression can be written as

$$\sum_{i=1}^{n} (x_i - m)^2 \frac{f(x_i)}{N},$$

so that the variance is given in terms of relative frequencies by the formula

$$s^2 = \sum_{i=1}^{n} (x_i - m)^2 q(x_i).$$

In defining a corresponding parameter for a probability model we replace the mean of the population by the theoretical mean for the model, and relative frequencies by probabilities. Thus the spread of elements of the possibility space in the probability model can be described by the parameter σ such that

$$\sigma^2 = \sum_{i=1}^{n} (x_i - \mu)^2 p(x_i).$$

As in the statistical situation we use the words *standard deviation* and *variance* to describe the parameters σ and σ^2 respectively. Notice the convention whereby a parameter for the probability model is denoted by the Greek letter corresponding to the Roman letter used for the analogous statistic.

Example 3. Compare the standard deviation for the population of numbers of sixes described in Example 1 with the standard deviation for the probability model.

For the statistical population,

$$s^2 = \Sigma(x_i - m)^2 q(x_i)$$
$$= (0 - 0.29)^2 \times 0.73 + (1 - 0.29)^2 \times 0.25 + (2 - 0.29)^2 \times 0.02$$
$$= 0.2459.$$

For the theoretical model the mean is $\frac{1}{3}$ and the probabilities are respectively $\frac{25}{36}$, $\frac{10}{36}$ and $\frac{1}{36}$ (see Section 2.1). Therefore

$$\sigma^2 = \Sigma(x_i - \mu)^2 p(x_i)$$
$$= (0 - \tfrac{1}{3})^2 \times \tfrac{25}{36} + (1 - \tfrac{1}{3})^2 \times \tfrac{10}{36} + (2 - \tfrac{1}{3})^2 \times \tfrac{1}{36}$$
$$= \tfrac{5}{18}$$
$$\simeq 0.2778.$$

The standard deviations for the experimental population and the theoretical model are therefore 0.496 and 0.527.

3.2 The calculations carried out in Example 3 are very unwieldy even for such a simple example, but fortunately it is possible to obtain the answers far more simply by adapting the formulae. We found in Chapter 12 that in calculating the variance we could make use of the relation

$$s^2 = \frac{1}{N}\Sigma(x_i - m)^2 f(x_i) = \frac{1}{N}\Sigma x_i^2 f(x_i) - m^2.$$

In terms of relative frequency this gives the two alternative forms

$$s^2 = \Sigma(x_i - m)^2 q(x_i) = \Sigma x_i^2 q(x_i) - m^2.$$

Similarly, for the theoretical probability model,

$$\sigma^2 = \Sigma(x_i - \mu)^2 p(x_i) = \Sigma x_i^2 p(x_i) - \mu^2.$$

We shall illustrate the use of these alternatives by working again the calculations of Example 3:

Experimental population

x_i	$q(x_i)$	$x_i q(x_i)$	$x_i^2 q(x_i)$
0	0·73	0	0
1	0·25	0·25	0·25
2	0·02	0·04	0·08
	1·00	$m = 0·29$	0·33

$$s^2 = 0·33 - (0·29)^2 = 0·2459.$$

Theoretical model

x_i	$p(x_i)$	$x_i p(x_i)$	$x_i^2 p(x_i)$
0	$\frac{25}{36}$	0	0
1	$\frac{10}{36}$	$\frac{10}{36}$	$\frac{10}{36}$
2	$\frac{1}{36}$	$\frac{2}{36}$	$\frac{4}{36}$
	1	$\mu = \frac{12}{36} = \frac{1}{3}$	$\frac{14}{36}$

$$\sigma^2 = \tfrac{14}{36} - (\tfrac{1}{3})^2 = \tfrac{5}{18} \simeq 0·2778.$$

There is clearly a considerable reduction in the labour of calculation using this method.

The equivalence of the two expressions for σ^2 can be established as follows:

$$\begin{aligned}
\Sigma(x_i - \mu)^2 p(x_i) &= \Sigma x_i^2 p(x_i) - \Sigma 2\mu x_i p(x_i) + \Sigma \mu^2 p(x_i) \\
&= \Sigma x_i^2 p(x_i) - 2\mu \Sigma x_i p(x_i) + \mu^2 \Sigma p(x_i) \\
&= \Sigma x_i^2 p(x_i) - 2\mu . \mu + \mu^2 . 1 \\
&= \Sigma x_i^2 p(x_i) - \mu^2,
\end{aligned}$$

since $\Sigma x_i p(x_i) = \mu$ and $\Sigma p(x_i) = 1$.

4. EXPECTED VALUE OF A FUNCTION

Just as $\mu = \Sigma x_i p(x_i)$ is the mean, or expected, value of x, so we may regard $\sigma^2 = \Sigma(x_i - \mu)^2 p(x_i)$ as the mean square deviation from the mean, or the 'expected' value of $(x - \mu)^2$. These two parameters are, in fact, special examples of a more general quantity, the *expected value of a function* $g(x)$, which we denote by $E[g(x)]$ and define by the formula

$$E[g(x)] = \sum_{i=1}^{n} g(x_i) p(x_i).$$

Clearly the formulae for μ and σ^2 are derived from this general expression by making the substitutions $g(x) = x$ and $g(x) = (x - \mu)^2$ respectively. Thus the equality

$$\mu = E[x]$$

is in line with this notation, and similarly we write

$$\sigma^2 = E[(x-\mu)^2].$$

Notice also that the equivalence of the two expressions for σ^2 established in Section 3.2 can be stated in the form

$$\sigma^2 = E[x^2] - \mu^2.$$

Other important examples of the concept of expected value of a function include the mean absolute deviation from a value k, defined as

$$E[|x-k|];$$

and skewness, usually defined as μ_3/σ^3, where

$$\mu_3 = E[(x-\mu)^3].$$

Example 4. A gambler rolls two dice and stands to lose £1 if he fails to throw a six, to win £2 if he throws one six, and to win £5 if he throws two sixes. Is the game fair?

We have two functions: a probability function p and a winnings function g (see Figure 1). Both have for domain the possibility space $\{0, 1, 2\}$ of numbers of sixes thrown.

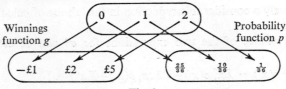

Fig. 1

We wish to find the expected value of the winnings function g with the probability function p. This is

$$E[g(x)] = (-£1) \times \tfrac{25}{36} + £2 \times \tfrac{10}{36} + £5 \times \tfrac{1}{36}$$
$$= 0,$$

so that the game is fair.

Exercise B

1. Calculate the standard deviation for the vehicle speeds in the probability model described in Section 1.2.

2. A probability model of a queueing situation gives the probabilities of finding 0, 1, 2, ..., 6 people in front of one on arrival as 0·14, 0·27, 0·27, 0·18, 0·09, 0·04, 0·01. Find the expected value of the length of the queue on arrival, and the variance.

3. With the data of Question 4 of Exercise A:

    (*a*) find the variance of the player's winnings ignoring the entrance fee;

    (*b*) if the entrance fee is twopence, find the variance of his profits;

    (*c*) if the entrance fee is such as makes the game fair, find the variance of his profits.

4. Blocks of five digits are selected from a table of random numbers, and the number of even digits in each block recorded. Calculate the probabilities of obtaining the various possible scores, and hence find the mean and variance.

Repeat this calculation if the digits counted are: (a) fives, (b) multiples of three (including zero), (c) those greater than two. Can you recognize any general pattern in your answers? If so, express it algebraically.

5. A casino offers its patrons a choice between three games, for each of which there is an entry fee of 1 franc. The possible winnings are:

Game 1. A 2 % probability of winning 20 francs.

Game 2. An 8 % probability of winning 5 francs.

Game 3. A 1 % probability of winning 20 francs and a 4 % probability of winning 5 francs (but you cannot win both).

In each game a winner also has his entry fee returned. For each game calculate the mean gain to the casino and the variance.

How should a casino proprietor adjust the mean and variance if (a) he wishes to ensure a steady income for himself, (b) he is interested in making a long-term profit whilst making the game superficially attractive to the player?

6. For the probability model of the dice-rolling experiment described in Section 2.1, find (i) the mean absolute deviation from 0, $\frac{1}{3}$ and 1; (ii) the skewness.

7. If the possibility space is the set $\{-2, -1, 0, 1, 2\}$ and $\mu = 0$, assign probabilities to the elements so as to make (a) the variance, (b) the skewness as large as you can.

8. If g and h are two functions whose domain is a possibility space for a given probability function, and if c and k are constants, prove that:

(a) $E[k] = k$;

(b) $E[g(x)+h(x)] = E[g(x)]+E[h(x)]$;

(c) $E[c.g(x)] = c.E[g(x)]$.

Prove directly from these rules that

$$E[(x-\mu)^2] = E[x^2]-\mu^2.$$

9. The variance $V[g(x)]$ of a function g is defined as $E[(g(x)-\gamma)^2]$, where $\gamma = E[g(x)]$. Using this definition and the results of Question 8, simplify $V[k]$, $V[x+k]$, $V[kx]$, where k is constant, and interpret your results.

10. Prove that

$$E[x(x-1)] = \sigma^2+\mu(\mu-1).$$

5. USE OF PROBABILITY GENERATORS

5.1 Generators as functions. For a probability function whose domain is the possibility space† $\{0, 1, 2, ...\}$, the probability generator has been defined as

$$G = \Sigma p_r t^r = p_0+p_1 t+p_2 t^2+...,$$

where the notation p_r is used for the probability of obtaining a 'score' of r (see Chapter 25, Section 3).

† The restriction of the possibility space to positive integers is not essential. A sum of the form $\Sigma p_r t^r$, where the variable r runs through any possibility space of discrete elements, can also be a probability generator. See, for example, Exercise C, Questions 2–4.

775

Now G has so far been regarded merely as an algebraic form which generates the sequence of probabilities; but such a form also defines a function
$$t \to G(t)$$
with domain a set of real numbers. We shall find that useful results about the probabilities can be obtained by carrying out analytical operations on this function.

We notice in passing that, for any probability generator,
$$G(1) = \Sigma p_r$$
$$= 1,$$
since this is the sum of the probabilities of all the elements of the possibility space.

5.2 Calculation of the mean. The mean 'score' is
$$\mu = E[r] = \Sigma r p_r.$$
Now the form of this sum suggests a connection with the derived function G'. In fact,
$$G(t) = \Sigma p_r t^r$$
$$\Rightarrow G'(t) = \Sigma r p_r t^{r-1}$$
$$\Rightarrow G'(1) = \Sigma r p_r,$$
so that
$$\mu = G'(1).$$

This result furnishes us with a very simple method of finding the mean if the probability generator is known.

5.3 Calculation of the variance. Further differentiation leads to a formula on similar lines for the variance. We have
$$G''(t) = \Sigma r(r-1) p_r t^{r-2},$$
so that
$$G''(1) = \Sigma r(r-1) p_r$$
$$= E[r(r-1)].$$

To connect this with the variance, we recall that
$$E[r^2] = \Sigma r^2 p_r = \sigma^2 + \mu^2 \quad \text{(see Sections 3.2 and 4)}$$
and
$$E[r] = \Sigma r p_r = \mu \quad \text{(see Section 2.1)}.$$
Subtracting,
$$E[r(r-1)] = \Sigma r(r-1) p_r = \sigma^2 + \mu^2 - \mu;$$
and since $\mu = G'(1)$,
$$G''(1) = \sigma^2 + \{G'(1)\}^2 - G'(1),$$
so that
$$\sigma^2 = G''(1) + G'(1) - \{G'(1)\}^2.$$

776

Example 5. Use the probability generator to find the mean and variance for the probability model of the dice-rolling situation described in Section 2.1.

The generator is
$$G(t) = \tfrac{25}{36} + \tfrac{10}{36}t + \tfrac{1}{36}t^2$$
$$= \tfrac{1}{36}(5+t)^2,$$

so that
$$G'(t) = \tfrac{1}{18}(5+t)$$

and
$$G''(t) = \tfrac{1}{18}.$$

From this we find $G'(1) = \tfrac{1}{3}$ and $G''(1) = \tfrac{1}{18}$, and the formulae derived above give
$$\mu = \tfrac{1}{3},$$
$$\sigma^2 = \tfrac{1}{18} + \tfrac{1}{3} - (\tfrac{1}{3})^2 = \tfrac{5}{18}.$$

5.4   Parameters for the binomial probability function.

An important application of the foregoing theory is to the binomial probability function. We have seen that for a sequence of n trials, each having probabilities a, b of success and failure (where $a+b = 1$), the probability generator for the various numbers of successes is
$$G(t) = (b+at)^n.$$

For this function,
$$G'(t) = na(b+at)^{n-1}$$

and
$$G''(t) = n(n-1)a^2(b+at)^{n-2};$$

so that
$$G'(1) = na(b+a)^{n-1} = na,$$

and
$$G''(1) = n(n-1)a^2(b+a)^{n-2} = n(n-1)a^2.$$

It follows that the expected value of the number of successes is
$$\mu = na$$

(as might be guessed, since the proportion of successes to be 'expected' is a); and that the variance is
$$\sigma^2 = n(n-1)a^2 + na - (na)^2$$
$$= na(1-a);$$

that is,
$$\sigma^2 = nab.$$

These two formulae are of great importance in probability theory and in applications in the field of statistical inference.

Exercise C

1. Write down the probability generator for single-digit numbers selected from a table of random numbers, and deduce the mean and standard deviation. Display your results on a histogram of probabilities, marking in the lines $x = \mu$ and $x = \mu \pm \sigma$.

2. With the data of Exercise A, Question 4, write down a probability generator for the player's winnings, and deduce the expected value of the winnings and the standard deviation. Display your results on a histogram of probabilities.

If the player has to pay an entry fee of twopence per game, write down a probability generator for his profits, and deduce from this the expected value of the profits and the standard deviation. Comment on your answers. (See also Exercise B, Question 3.)

3. For the game described in Exercise A, Question 5, assume that there is a forfeit of 18 pence if no heads show up. Write down a probability generator for the player's receipts and losses, and deduce the variance.

4. For a certain game the probabilities of winning various sums are specified by the probability generator $G(t)$, the expected value of the winnings is μ and the variance σ^2. Explain why the imposition of an entry fee of r units changes the probability generator for the player's profits to $t^{-r}G(t)$; and deduce values for the expected profits and the variance in terms of μ and σ.

5. A coin is tossed: (*a*) 10 times, (*b*) 100 times, (*c*) 1000 times. Calculate in each case the expected number of heads, and the standard deviation.

Which would surprise you more—3 heads and 7 tails in 10 tosses, or 300 heads and 700 tails in 1000 tosses? Justify your answer mathematically.

6. A die is rolled 100 times. It is estimated that there is about 95 % probability that the number of sixes lies between $\mu - 2\sigma$ and $\mu + 2\sigma$. What possible numbers of sixes lie within this interval?

7. A fully trained card-punch operator makes on average ten mistakes a day. If she punches N symbols per day in all, what is the probability that she makes a mistake in punching any single symbol? Prove that the standard deviation of the numbers of mistakes per day is very nearly $\sqrt{10}$.

8. A die is rolled repeatedly until a six appears. Use the probability generator to find the expected number of non-sixes that must be thrown before the first six, and the standard deviation of this number. (See Chapter 25, Section 9.3, Example 3.)

If rolling continues until a second six appears, find also a probability generator for the total number of non-sixes before the second six. Deduce the expected value of this number, and the standard deviation.

9. Thirty sets of four random digits were examined, and a success was recorded if a digit i satisfied $0 \leqslant i \leqslant k$, where k is some integer. The results were:

Number of successes in a set of 4 digits	Frequency
0	5
1	14
2	10
3	0
4	1

Calculate the mean number of successes in a set of four digits.

778

Explain why you would expect the relative frequency function to approximate to a binomial probability function, and find the expected number of successes in a set of four digits in terms of k. What value of k fits the data best? With this value of k calculate the probabilities and compare them with the observed relative frequencies.

Calculate also the variance of the observed population and the corresponding parameter for your probability model.

10. Forty sets of n random digits were examined and the number of zeros recorded:

Number of zeros	Frequency
0	26
1	12
2	2

What do you think was the value of n? With this value of n, calculate the probabilities of different numbers of zeros, and compare them with the relative frequencies. Compare also the variances for the experimental observations and the probability model.

11. In a certain experiment the mean and variance of the number of successes are m and s^2. On the assumption that the frequencies arise from a binomial process, what estimate would you make of b, and hence of a and n?

Carry out an experiment with a table of random numbers as follows. Select integers n and k (where $k < 10$); examine fifty sets of n random digits and record a success if a digit i satisfies $0 \leqslant i \leqslant k$. Make a frequency table of the various numbers of successes, and hence calculate the mean and variance. Substitute these statistics in the formulae you have found for the estimates of a and n; and compare your answers with the actual values of a and n on which your experiment was based.

12. A sequence of n binomial trials is carried out, with probability of success a. It is found that the number of successes is r. What was the probability of this result?

Regarding this probability as a function of a (n and r being determined by the experiment), find the value of a which maximizes it. What is the interpretation of your result?

Miscellaneous Exercise

1. The rules of a gambling game once played at St Petersburg were as follows. A player tosses a coin repeatedly until a head appears; if the head first appears on the nth toss, he receives 2^{n-1} units of prize money from the bank.

(a) In one version of the game there is a limit of ten tosses. If the player never throws a head then he wins no prize. What would be a suitable entry fee?

(b) What would be a suitable entry fee if the coin may be tossed an unlimited number of times?

(c) Find the probability generator for the total number of tosses in the unlimited game, and deduce the mean and variance of the length of run.

(d) If the bank will only pay 10000 units to any one player because of a shortage of funds, what is the probability that a player will 'break the bank'?

779

(e) If the game is played 256 times a night, what is the probability that the bank will not be broken during the course of the night? (Use the binomial theorem to get an approximate answer.)

(f) What is the probability that the bank will be broken in a season of 64 nights?

2. For a given possibility space and probability function, $E[x] = \mu$ and $E[(x-\mu)^2] = \sigma^2$. Prove that

(a) $E[x-k] = \mu - k$;

(b) $E[(x-k)^2] = \sigma^2 + (\mu-k)^2$.

Sketch the graphs of the functions $k \to E[x-k]$ and $k \to E[(x-k)^2]$ and hence give descriptions of μ and σ^2 in terms of properties of these functions.

Sketch also the graph of $E[|x-k|]$ and suggest definitions of parameters corresponding to the median and mean absolute deviation.

3. A particle may occupy any one of a number of points of space with position vectors $r_1, r_2, ..., r_n$. A probability function associates with each point the probability that the particle is located there. Suggest a definition of a 'mean position' for the particle which is independent of the origin from which the vectors are measured; and prove this property of independence from your definition.

4. In a pack of n cards, each of the scores $1, 2, ..., n$ appears on just one card. A card is drawn from the pack at random. Find formulae for the expected value of the score on the card, and the variance.

5. An underground railway system has n stations, each a mile from its neighbours, strung out on a single route through a city. Assuming that passengers are equally likely to travel between any pair of stations, find a formula for the expected value of the length of a journey.

If there are 14 stations and it costs £1 000 000 to operate the system for a year, and if it is estimated that 20 million journeys will be made during the year, how much per mile should the passengers be charged?

6. The probability generators for the numbers of successes in two independent experiments are

$$G = p_0 + p_1 t + p_2 t^2 + ...$$

and

$$H = q_0 + q_1 t + q_2 t^2 + ...$$

Interpret the expression

$$p_0 q_3 + p_1 q_2 + p_2 q_1 + p_3 q_0$$

(i) as a probability, (ii) as a coefficient in the expression $G.H$. Hence interpret $K = G.H$ as a probability generator.

Prove the following results directly from the definition of K, and interpret them:

(a) all the coefficients of K are non-negative;

(b) $K(1) = 1$;

(c) $K'(1) = G'(1) + H'(1)$;

(d) $K''(1) + K'(1) - \{K'(1)\}^2 = G''(1) + G'(1) - \{G'(1)\}^2 + H''(1) + H'(1) - \{H'(1)\}^2$.

Pairs of digits are taken from a table of random numbers, and their sum recorded. Write down the probability generator for this situation, and use the results just proved to find the mean and variance.

Generalize your results to sets of n digits.

7. Two *independent* experiments are performed. The possibility space for the first is $\{x_1, x_2\}$, and the probabilities assigned to these elements are u_1, u_2; the possibility space for the second is $\{y_1, y_2, y_3\}$ with probabilities v_1, v_2, v_3. From the results x, y of the two experiments the sum $x+y$ is formed. Write down the possibility space for this sum, and express the associated probabilities in terms of those specified above. Hence prove that

$$E[x+y] = E[x]+E[y].$$

Prove similarly that $\qquad E[xy] = E[x].E[y].$

Do these results hold good for possibility spaces with any number of elements? If so, write out your proofs for the more general case.

Take $E[x]$, $E[y]$ as new origins of measurement for the two possibility spaces, and define measures $X_i = x_i - E[x]$, $Y_j = y_j - E[y]$. Prove that $E[X+Y]$ and $E[XY]$ are both zero; and deduce, with the notation of Exercise B, Question 9, that

$$V[X+Y] = V[X]+V[Y].$$

Hence prove that $\qquad V[x+y] = V[x]+V[y].$

Find a similar expression for $V[x-y]$.

A machine makes cylindrical pegs of mean radius 9·00 mm. with standard deviation 0·03 mm, and another machine drills cylindrical holes of mean radius 9·05 mm with standard deviation 0·04 mm. If pegs and holes are paired randomly, and the maximum acceptable clearance is 0·05 mm, about what proportion of the pairs will make an acceptable fit? (Assume that about two-thirds of a population of this kind lie within one standard deviation of the mean.)

8. A bowler can bowl either off-breaks or googlies; the batsman has two shots, an off-drive or a hook. If the batsman off-drives an off-break, he will score 4, but if he off-drives a googly he will score only 1. If he hooks an off-break he will not score, but if he hooks a googly he will score 2. Prove that, if the batsman off-drives with probability p, and the bowler bowls off-breaks with probability q, then the expected value of the runs scored per ball is $5pq-p-2q+2$.

Prove that if $q > 0·2$ then it is best for the batsman always to off-drive, and that if $q < 0·2$ then he should always hook. Prove also that, if the batsman realizes this, then the bowler will keep runs down most effectively by choosing to bowl off-breaks with probability 0·2.

Find by a similar argument what is the batsman's best strategy if he is to make as many runs as possible. What will the scoring rate be if both batsman and bowler play their best strategy?

9. Carry through the argument of Question 8 in general terms when two players P, Q each have two plays available, and if the gain to A in the various cases is as follows:

		Q's play	
		1	2
P's play $\{$	1	a	b
	2	c	d

Discuss the situation first in which a and d are both greater than b and c. Then consider the case when d is greater than both b and c, a is greater than b, but a is less than c.

SUMMARY

Statistical population	Probability model
Possibility space $\{x_1, x_2, ..., x_n\}$	
Relative frequency $q(x_i)$ $\Sigma q(x_i) = 1$	Probability $p(x_i)$ $\Sigma p(x_i) = 1$
Mean: $m = \bar{x} = \Sigma x_i q(x_i)$	Mean (expected value): $\mu = E[x] = \Sigma x_i p(x_i)$
Variance: $s^2 = \overline{(x-m)^2}$ $\quad = \Sigma(x_i - m)^2 q(x_i)$	Variance: $\sigma^2 = E[(x-\mu)^2]$ $\quad = \Sigma(x_i - \mu)^2 p(x_i)$
Mean value of a function: $\overline{g(x)} = \Sigma g(x_i) q(x_i)$	Expected value of a function: $E[g(x)] = \Sigma g(x_i) p(x_i)$

In terms of probability generators
$$\mu = G'(1),$$
$$\sigma^2 = G''(1) + G'(1) - G'(1)^2.$$
For the binomial probability function
$$\mu = na,$$
$$\sigma^2 = nab.$$

27

INTRODUCTION TO DIFFERENTIAL EQUATIONS

1. THE IDEA OF A DIFFERENTIAL EQUATION

Consider the following statements:

(i) The tangent to a certain graph at every point P is at right-angles to the line OP.

(ii) The rate at which a rumour is spreading through the school depends on the number of people who have heard it already.

These statements are clearly capable of translation into mathematical language, and they imply the existence of a mathematical relationship. In (i) this will be a relationship between the coordinates (x, y) of points on the graph (see Figure 1). The gradient of a tangent is given by the derivative

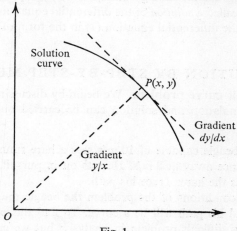

Fig. 1

dy/dx, and the gradient of OP is y/x. The fact that the tangent at P is at right-angles to OP is expressed by the rule for the gradients of perpendicular lines (see Chapter 13, Section 6.1):

$$\frac{dy}{dx} \cdot \frac{y}{x} = -1,$$

or

$$\frac{dy}{dx} = -\frac{x}{y}. \qquad (1)$$

783

In (ii) the relationship is between the number of people (z, say) who have heard the rumour and the time (t hours) which has elapsed since it was first introduced into the school. The rate at which the rumour is spreading is then measured by the derivative dz/dt. Our statement does not specify the exact law, but merely that there is a functional relationship connecting this rate with z. Let this function be denoted by the symbol f; then the statement is condensed into the equation

$$\frac{dz}{dt} = f(z). \tag{2}$$

It will be noticed that although each statement implies a mathematical relationship, this does not appear as an algebraic equation expressing y directly in terms of x, or z in terms of t; instead, it appears as an equation involving a derivative. For this reason an equation such as (1) or (2) is called a *differential equation*. We shall find that many scientific laws when translated into mathematical language take the form of differential equations.

Ultimately, however, we should like to be able to display the connection between x and y, or t and z, explicitly: either by an algebraic formula, or by a table showing corresponding values, or by a graph. Such an explicit formulation is called a *solution* of the differential equation. Figure 1 shows a solution for the differential equation (1) in the form of a graph.

2. SOLUTION BY STEP-BY-STEP METHODS

2.1 A pursuit curve problem. We begin by discussing an example in which the formulation and solution can be carried out in purely geometrical terms.

Example 1. A beagle capable of 10 m/s sees a hare running in a straight line some distance away at 8 m/s. He sets off in pursuit, heading always directly towards the hare. Trace his path.

To fulfil the conditions of the problem the beagle must change course continually, and his path will be a curve. To find the exact form of this curve is quite a difficult problem in analysis; but we can easily find an approximation to this curve in the form of a path made up of line-segments.

To do this, suppose that the beagle is rather slow-witted, and that he sights on the hare only once a second; then during the intervals between re-sighting he will run 10 m in a straight line towards the point where he last saw the hare. The paths of the hare and the beagle are illustrated in Figure 2. Initially they are H_0 and B_0 respectively. During the first second the hare runs from H_0 to H_1, and the beagle runs from B_0 to B_1 in the direction of H_0. He then adjusts his course, and whilst the hare runs from H_1 to H_2 the beagle runs from B_1 to B_2 in the direction of H_1; and so on.

The polygon $B_0B_1B_2\ldots$ is an approximation to the solution of the original problem. Clearly, a better approximation could be made by correcting course more frequently; thus by re-sighting ten times a second the beagle would steer a truer path. With a little anticipation of the hare's movements he could do better still.

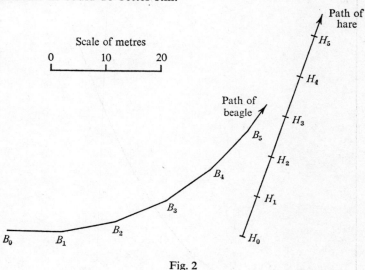

Fig. 2

2.2 A differential equation from dynamics.

A method similar to that used in the last example will now be applied to find, in the form of a table of values, a solution to a differential equation in which the data are given numerically.

Example 2. The acceleration of a space-rocket at various times after blast-off is given in the following table:

Time (seconds)	0	2	4	6	8	10
Acceleration (m/s²)	10	20	40	90	170	260

Investigate how the speed of the rocket varies with time.

We must first be clear how the speed is related to the acceleration. It was shown in Chapter 19 that acceleration is the instantaneous rate of change of velocity. In this example the rocket is moving in a straight line, the velocity and acceleration both being directed vertically upwards. The speed, v m/s, is therefore related to the acceleration, a m/s², by the simple equation

$$\frac{dv}{dt} = a.$$

4   SAM 3

Now our aim is to discover how v varies with t: this could be shown by a graph having the general form of Figure 3. What information have we which will help us to draw this graph? The answer is twofold:

(i) We know that the rocket is initially at rest on the launching pad. This is expressed mathematically by saying that $v = 0$ when $t = 0$.

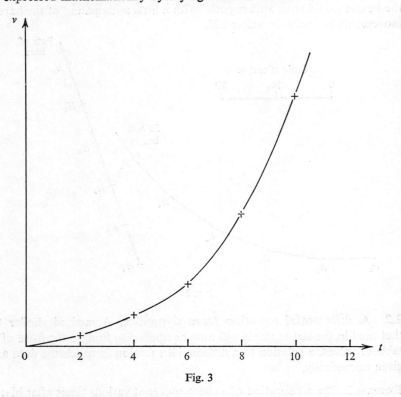

Fig. 3

(ii) The table gives the values of dv/dt, which is represented by the gradient of the graph, for $t = 0, 2, 4, 6, 8$ and 10. These are the points of the graph marked with a cross; but we do not know the precise positions of these points, since we have not yet found the corresponding values of v. (Indeed, when we have done this the problem is solved.)

If the acceleration were given by a known formula, we should try to find a function of which this was the derivative, using one of the standard techniques of integration. But with numerical data we can only hope for a numerical, approximate solution. The difficulty lies essentially in the fact that we are given only the instantaneous acceleration at various times; whereas to generate the graph we should like to know the average acceleration over a succession of time-intervals.

786

The simplest approximation that we can use is to replace the average acceleration over some short time-interval by the (known) value of the instantaneous acceleration at the beginning of the interval. For instance, we know that when $t = 6$ the acceleration is 90 m/s^2, and so we might estimate that the increase in speed of the rocket over the next two seconds would be about 180 m/s. Thus if the speed were known when $t = 6$, it could be estimated when $t = 8$.

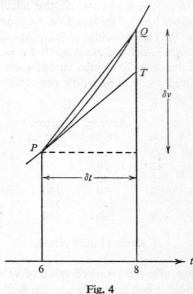

Fig. 4

This is illustrated in Figure 4, which shows an enlargement of a portion of Figure 3. The approximation is equivalent to taking the gradient of the chord PQ (which is measured by $\delta v/\delta t$) to be equal to the gradient of the tangent PT. Thus

$$\frac{\delta v}{\delta t} \quad \text{over the interval } 6 < t < 8$$

$$\simeq \frac{dv}{dt} \quad \text{at } t = 6$$

$$= 90 \quad \text{(from the given table);}$$

whence $\qquad \delta v = \dfrac{\delta v}{\delta t} \times \delta t \simeq 90 \times 2 = 180.$

This calculation can be summarized in the approximate equation

$$\delta v \simeq \left(\frac{dv}{dt}\right) \times \delta t,$$

the value of dv/dt being taken at the left end of the interval.

A similar calculation can be carried out over each of the time-intervals, and it is found that the increases in speed δv over the intervals

$$0 < t < 2, \quad 2 < t < 4, \quad ..., \quad 10 < t < 12$$

are 20, 40, 80, 180, 340, 520 m/s. But one further problem remains: the speed at the end of an interval cannot be estimated until the speed at the beginning of that interval is known. Thus for each interval we need a 'jumping-off' value from which to continue the calculation.

This is where the other item of information mentioned above comes in: that $v = 0$ when $t = 0$. This provides a jumping-off value for the first interval $0 < t < 2$, from which we estimate that $v = 20$ when $t = 2$. We can then use this value $v = 20$ as the jumping-off value for the next interval $2 < t < 4$; and so on. The whole calculation can then be tabulated as follows:

Interval	δt	Approx. $\delta v/\delta t$	Approx. δv	t	v
$0 < t < 2$	2	10	20	0†	0†
$2 < t < 4$	2	20	40	2	20
$4 < t < 6$	2	40	80	4	60
$6 < t < 8$	2	90	180	6	140
$8 < t < 10$	2	170	340	8	320
$10 < t < 12$	2	260	520	10	660
				12	1180

† Known initial values.

The final two columns give the required table of values for the speed at different times. From these can be drawn a graph such as Figure 3, and the speeds at other times can be estimated from this.

The method used in this example has the advantage of being very simple; it is an easy matter to provide a set of instructions for calculating successive entries in the table, and thus to write a flow diagram for the complete computation. If more values for the acceleration could be obtained the value of δt could be reduced, thereby improving the approximation; note that δt need not be constant throughout the calculation, though it is simpler if it is. Nevertheless, the general effect of the method is as shown in Figure 5; it is not unlike the traditional nightmare of trying to catch a train which has always left the station just before you arrive.

2.3   An improved technique. Figure 4 shows clearly that the root of the trouble lies in the use of the gradient of the tangent PT as an approximation to the gradient of the chord PQ, which is liable to introduce a considerable error. A better approximation, in general, would be to replace the gradient of PQ by that of the tangent at a point R in the middle of the interval (see Figure 6).

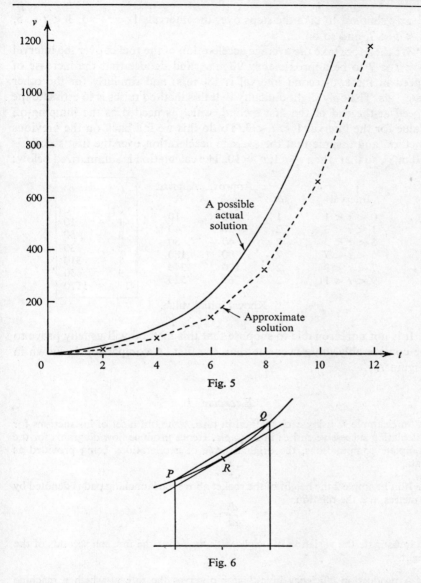

Fig. 5

Fig. 6

We shall illustrate the method by working Example 2 again using this alternative approximation. Whereas previously the acceleration of 90 m/s at $t = 6$ was used as an approximation to the average acceleration over the interval $6 < t < 8$, we now use it as an approximation to the average acceleration over an interval with $t = 6$ as the mid-point; and since in this example the instantaneous acceleration is given at $t = 2, 4, 6, ...,$ it is

789

clearly simplest to take the steps over the intervals $1 < t < 3$, $3 < t < 5$, $5 < t < 7$, and so on.

We therefore take the average acceleration of the rocket over the interval $5 < t < 7$ to be approximately 90 m/s², and deduce that the increase of speed in the two-second interval is 180 m/s; and similarly for the other intervals. The only slight difficulty that this method raises is to estimate the speed at the end of the first second, which is needed as the jumping-off value for the interval $1 < t < 3$. To do this we fall back on the previous method and assume that the average acceleration over the first second is 10 m/s², so that when $t = 1$, $v = 10$. The calculation is summarized below:

Interval	δt	Approx. $\delta v/\delta t$	Approx. δv	t	v
$0 < t < 1$	1	10	10	0†	0†
$1 < t < 3$	2	20	40	1	10
$3 < t < 5$	2	40	80	3	50
$5 < t < 7$	2	90	180	5	130
$7 < t < 9$	2	170	340	7	310
$9 < t < 11$	2	260	520	9	650
				11	1170

† Known initial value.

It is not unreasonable to suppose that this method will usually prove to be considerably more accurate than the first. A comparison is shown in Figure 7.

Exercise A

1. In Example 2, using each method in turn, write out a set of instructions for calculating successive entries in the table. Hence produce flow diagrams for the complete computations, the original table of accelerations being provided as data.

2. If in Example 2 the height of the rocket above the launching pad is denoted by h metres, use the relation

$$\frac{dh}{dt} = v$$

to investigate the variation of height with time over the first ten seconds of the flight.

3. A production efficiency investigator observes the rate at which a machine operator turns out a motor car component at various times after he starts work, and obtains the following figures:

Number of minutes after starting	10	30	50	70	90	110	130	150	170
Components per minute	3·8	4·7	5·2	5·4	5·5	5·4	5·3	5·0	4·4

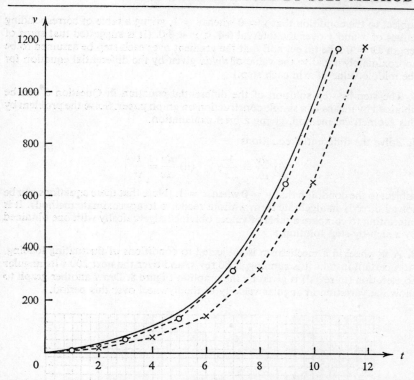

Fig. 7. × indicates points of the original step-by-step approximation. o indicates points of the improved step-by-step approximation. The continuous line is a possible solution curve consistent with the data.

From these data draw a graph of the total number of components he will produce for continuous shifts of work of various lengths. Use your graph to make a recommendation to the management about the duration of working periods in the factory, and justify your proposal.

4. A cyclist and his machine together have a mass of 100 kg, and are proceeding along a level road at 4 m/s. Seeing green traffic lights ahead the cyclist first of all puts on a spurt, then brakes as he realizes he will not make it. The net accelerating force at the wheels over the whole minute is as follows:

Time (s)	0	10	20	30	40	50	60
Force (N)	22	28	45	20	−3	−67	−148

Deduce a table of accelerations, and hence draw a graph of his speed during this period. From this use an approximate method of evaluating definite integrals to estimate the distance he travels in the complete minute.

5. Obtain a solution of the differential equation

$$\frac{dy}{dx} = \frac{1}{x}$$

791

subject to the condition that $y = 0$ when $x = 1$, giving a table of corresponding values of x and y over the interval $0.4 < x < 3.0$. (It is suggested that steps of length $\delta x = 0.2$ be taken, and that the gradient over each step be assumed to be approximately equal to the value of dy/dx given by the differential equation for the middle value of x in each step.)

6. The step-by-step solution of the differential equation in Question 5 can be obtained by means of a simple construction on graph paper. Solve the problem by this geometrical method, giving a brief explanation.

7. Solve the differential equations

$$\text{(i)} \quad \frac{dy}{dx} = \frac{1}{\sqrt{x}}, \qquad \text{(ii)} \quad \frac{dy}{dx} = \frac{1}{x^2}$$

subject to the condition that $y = 0$ when $x = 1$. (Note that these equations can be solved directly in algebraic form without recourse to approximate methods. It is interesting to compare a table of values obtained algebraically with one obtained by a step-by-step solution.)

8. A flywheel in a mechanism is subjected to conditions of fluctuating loading. At a certain instant it is running at 80 rev/s, and over the next 200 s its angular acceleration (in rev/s²) is given by the graph in Figure 8. Draw another graph to show the variation in angular velocity of the flywheel over this period.

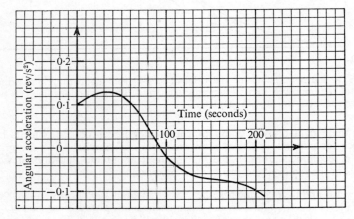

Fig. 8

2.4 General description of the method.

Before discussing some more differential equations it will be useful to review in general terms the method of solution so far described.

Let us suppose that we have a situation in which variables x, y are related so that y is a function of x. A typical member x of the domain is often referred to as the 'independent variable', and the corresponding member y of the codomain as the 'dependent variable'. We suppose further that information about the relationship between x and y is available in the form

792

of a differential equation, so that dy/dx is given in terms of either x, or y, or both. In its most general form the differential equation can be written

$$\frac{dy}{dx} = f(x, y).$$

The solution is the explicit display of y as a function of x, which we may write as

$$y = \phi(x).$$

If, as in most of the examples so far, this is found in graphical form, the graph is called a *solution curve* for the differential equation. The solution curve has the property that, for every point (x, y) on the curve, the value of $f(x, y)$ is exactly equal to the gradient of the curve at that point.

But with step-by-step methods we do not aim to find every point of the solution curve. Instead, we start from a jumping-off point P on the curve, and from this make a finite displacement $\begin{pmatrix} \delta x \\ \delta y \end{pmatrix}$, whose gradient is $\delta y/\delta x$, to obtain a further point Q (see Figure 9).

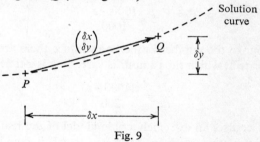

Fig. 9

In Example 2 we chose the increment in the independent variable (there denoted by t) to suit our convenience (in fact δt was taken as 2 for most of the calculation). This was because the differential equation gave the gradient as a function of this variable alone.

If, having selected δx, we could find $\delta y/\delta x$ exactly, then the increment δy could be found from

$$\delta y = \frac{\delta y}{\delta x} \times \delta x,$$

and the displacement vector

$$\mathbf{PQ} = \begin{pmatrix} \delta x \\ \delta y \end{pmatrix}$$

would be known exactly. In practice, however, we do not know $\delta y/\delta x$; and we therefore use the best approximation we can get. In the method of Section 2.3 we used for this the value of dy/dx given by the differential equation for the midway value $x + \frac{1}{2}\delta x$ of the horizontal step.

In this way an approximate displacement $\begin{pmatrix} \delta x \\ \delta y \end{pmatrix}$ is found. Using this we

793

can move from P to the next plotted point Q, which lies very near to the solution curve; and Q then becomes the jumping-off point for the next stage of the calculation.

2.5 The next example is somewhat different, since the differential equation gives the gradient in terms of the dependent variable rather than the independent variable.

Example 3. Devise a mathematical model for the rumour-spreading problem described in Section 1, and solve the appropriate differential equation.

We shall need some numerical information. Let us suppose that there are 1000 pupils in the school, and that each person who knows the rumour passes it on to five others every hour. At a time when z people have already heard the rumour, only a fraction $(1000-z)/1000$ of those who are told the rumour will be hearing it for the first time; and therefore each 'carrier' will add

$$5 \times \frac{1000-z}{1000}$$

pupils per hour to the number in the know. Since there are at that time z carriers, the rate at which the rumour is spreading is z times this number; that is

$$\frac{dz}{dt} = \frac{z(1000-z)}{200}.$$

(This is, of course, an extremely crude model of the real situation; you may find it interesting to discuss ways in which it could be improved. Notice also that we have represented a quantity which must be a whole number—the number of pupils in the know—by a variable z which we regard as increasing continuously through the real numbers; this is an assumption which is often made in physical applications, when the molecular structure of matter is ignored. Despite these limitations, the equation may give some kind of indication of what may be expected in practice.)

Some assumption must also be made about the initial situation; for obviously we cannot now start with $z = 0$. Let us suppose that the rumour is initiated in a 'cell' of ten pupils, so that $z = 10$ when $t = 0$.

Now if at this stage we try to proceed on the lines of the 'improved method' described in Section 2.3 we run into difficulty. Let us, for example, investigate the situation during the first hour, over the time-interval $0 < t < 1$. We need to find the rate of spread $\delta z/\delta t$ averaged over this period, and the assumption previously made is that this is given approximately by dz/dt at $t = \frac{1}{2}$. But now dz/dt is given not in terms of t but as a function of z; and we cannot find dz/dt when $t = \frac{1}{2}$ until we know z when $t = \frac{1}{2}$ —that is, until we have solved the differential equation!

794

We can get round this difficulty by choosing the steps δz rather than δt; that is, we ask the question 'how long will it be before (say) 50 people have heard the rumour?'. To answer this, we must find the average rate of spread $\delta z/\delta t$ over the interval $10 < z < 50$, and as usual we must make some approximation. It seems not unreasonable that the value of dz/dt given by the formula when $z = 30$ will be quite close: thus

$$\frac{\delta z}{\delta t} \simeq \frac{30(1000-20)}{200} = 145 \cdot 5.$$

This means that at this stage the rumour is spreading at a rate of about 145·5 people per hour. The time for the extra 40 people to hear it is therefore $40 \div 145 \cdot 5$, or 0·27 hours.

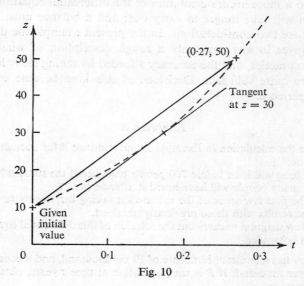

Fig. 10

This part of the calculation is illustrated in Figure 10. The time δt taken for the number of people in the know to increase from 10 to 50 is found from

$$\delta t = \delta z \div \frac{\delta z}{\delta t} \simeq 40 \div 145 \cdot 5 = 0 \cdot 27.$$

The calculation can now be continued from this new point on the graph. Let us consider the time taken for the rumour to spread to another 40 people, from $z = 50$ to $z = 90$. An approximation to the average rate is now given by the value of dz/dt found from the formula when $z = 70$, which is

$$\frac{70(1000-70)}{200} = 325 \cdot 5 \text{ people per hour;}$$

and for this increase we deduce that

$$\delta t = \delta z \div \frac{\delta z}{\delta t} \simeq 40 \div 325 \cdot 5 = 0 \cdot 12.$$

Thus 90 people will have heard the rumour after a further $0 \cdot 12$ hours, that is when $t = 0 \cdot 39$.

By continuing in this way a description can be built up of the passage of the rumour through the school.

2.6 Choice of size of step. It might be asked how, in the solution of Example 3, the particular value of the increment $\delta z = 40$ was selected. There is no specific rule governing the size of this number. Smaller steps will lead to a more accurate solution of the differential equation, but the calculation will take longer to carry out; and a balance must be struck between these two considerations. In the present example the differential equation gives in any case only a rough description of what may be expected in practice, and the accuracy afforded by taking fairly large steps is therefore quite sufficient. Decisions of this kind become easier with greater experience.

Exercise B

1. Tabulate the calculation in Example 3, and continue it far enough to answer the questions:

(a) How long will it be before 700 people have heard the rumour?

(b) How many people will have heard it after an hour?

Repeat the first few steps of the calculation taking increments $\delta z = 20$, and compare the results with those previously obtained.

Write a flow diagram to carry out the solution of this differential equation with the aid of a computer.

2. A country has a constant birth rate of 19 per thousand, and a constant death rate of 15 per thousand. If P is the population at time t years, obtain the differential equation

$$\frac{dP}{dt} = 0 \cdot 004P$$

describing the rate of growth of the population. If the total population in 1960 is 10 million, estimate when it will be 11 million. By continuing this calculation in steps of one million at a time, estimate when it will be 15 million.

3. The acceleration of a parachutist in free fall from an aircraft is given by

$$a = 10 - 0 \cdot 004v^2,$$

v being his speed; the units are metres and seconds. Explain why a formula of this kind might be expected, and state the value which it gives for his terminal velocity in free fall. Write this as a differential equation, and from it draw a graph showing the variation of v with t.

From this graph use the method of Section 2.3 to draw a graph of the distance fallen against time.

796

4. Water-tank tests suggest that the retardation experienced by an under-water projectile at different speeds will be:

Speed (m/s)	17	67	130
Retardation (m/s²)	3	47	200

If such a projectile is fired into water at a speed of 160 m/s, estimate the variation of speed with time subsequently.

5. The water in a kettle is brought to the boil and then allowed to cool. Its temperature $\theta°$ C at a time t minutes after the heat is turned off is governed by the differential equation

$$\frac{d\theta}{dt} = -0\cdot02(\theta - 15).$$

Explain the significance of this equation in physical terms. Estimate the time taken for the temperature to fall to 30° C.

3. FAMILIES OF CURVES

3.1 Consider the equation $y = kx.$

For a given value of k this equation clearly represents a straight line through the origin. Thus $y = 2x$, $y = 5x$, $y = -3x$ are all lines through the origin with gradients 2, 5, -3 respectively. The set of all these lines is an example of a *family* of lines.

It is obviously impossible on a figure to draw without confusion all the lines of a family; but a good idea can be conveyed by drawing a number of typical lines, as in Figure 11. Notice, however, that the y-axis (the line $x = 0$) is not a line of the set.

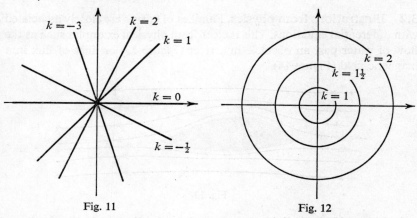

Fig. 11   Fig. 12

Figure 12 shows another example of a family, this time of circles with centre the origin. The circle of this family with radius k has equation

$$x^2 + y^2 = k^2;$$

and different positive values of k give different circles of the family.

797

We see then that an equation involving coordinates x, y and a variable number k may be expected to represent a family of curves. Such an equation can be put into the general form

$$F(x, y, k) = 0.$$

If a particular number is written for k, the resulting equation in x and y will correspond to one of the curves of the family. The number k is called a *parameter*.

Contour lines on a map afford a practical illustration of a family. With each point on the map, having coordinates (x, y), there is associated a height h above sea level of the corresponding point on the ground. Thus we have a function (denoted by ϕ, say) mapping (x, y) onto h; we write

$$h = \phi(x, y),$$

or $$\phi(x, y) - h = 0.$$

A particular value, such as $h = 100$, gives an equation

$$\phi(x, y) - 100 = 0$$

represented by a locus on the map—the 100 m contour line. The complete set of loci for different values of h gives the family of contours; h is the parameter, and the equation is

$$F(x, y, h) = 0,$$

where $F(x, y, h)$ stands for the expression $\phi(x, y) - h$.

3.2   Illustrations from physics. Families of curves are closely associated with differential equations. This is clear from physical examples such as the flow of water past an obstacle in a river (Figure 13) or lines of flux in a magnetic field (Figure 14).

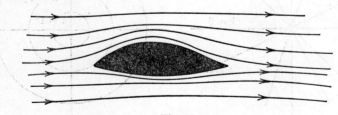

Fig. 13

In Figure 13 the individual curves of the family are the stream lines; these can be identified by introducing a small, light object into the stream and following its track, or by means of drops of coloured liquid. The stream lines have the property that their direction at each point is that of the flow at the point (Figure 15). Thus with each point (x, y) of the stream is associated a gradient. We express this relationship by means of a function f, and write

$$\frac{dy}{dx} = f(x, y).$$

This is the differential equation of the stream lines.

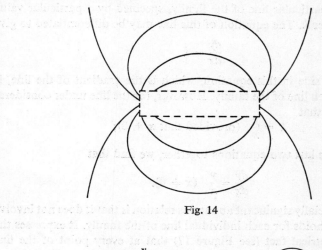

Fig. 14

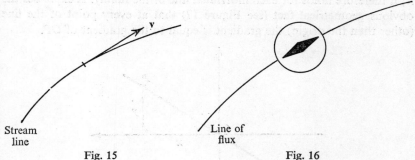

Stream
line

Line of
flux

Fig. 15   Fig. 16

Lines of magnetic flux in a plane can be traced by placing a small compass needle at various points; the direction of the needle indicates the direction of the magnetic flux at the point. This again leads to a differential equation of the same form.

We may notice in passing that with each point of a stream line is associated not only a direction but also the strength of the stream—that is, the velocity—at the point. Thus there is a function which associates with each point (which may be indicated by its position vector **r**) a velocity vector **v**. Such a function, whose domain and codomain are both sets of vectors, is known as a *vector field*. The differential equation of the stream lines is obtained by equating their direction at any point to the direction of the velocity vector associated with that point.

3.3 The differential equation of a family.

Differential equations can also be associated with families of the kind discussed in Section 3.1.

Example 4. Find a differential equation for the family of lines with equation

$$y = kx.$$

Consider a particular line of the family, specified by a particular value of the parameter k. The equation of this line may be differentiated to give

$$\frac{dy}{dx} = k.$$

Now the right side in this equation, which is the gradient of the line, is different for each line of the family. However, for the line under consideration, we know that

$$k = \frac{y}{x} \quad \text{(provided that } x \neq 0\text{)};$$

and putting the last two equations together, we find that

$$\frac{dy}{dx} = \frac{y}{x} \quad (x \neq 0).$$

What is especially significant about this relation is that it does not involve k; it therefore holds for each individual line of the family. It expresses the obvious geometrical fact (see Figure 17) that at every point of the line (other than the origin) the gradient is equal to the gradient of OP.

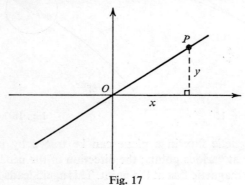

Fig. 17

It is of interest to see how this differential equation could also be obtained by an alternative method. The equation of any line of the family can be written in the form

$$y . \frac{1}{x} = k.$$

This can be interpreted as follows. For the line with parameter k there is a function mapping x onto y with domain the real numbers; and we can define from this a product function by combining it with the function

800

mapping x onto $1/x$, with domain the real numbers excluding zero. What the equation above says is that this product function, expressed by the relation

$$x \to y \cdot \frac{1}{x},$$

is in fact a constant function over the domain R^*. It follows that over this domain the function has zero derivative.

Now by the product rule for differentiation (Chapter 17, Section 3),

$$\frac{d}{dx}\left(y \cdot \frac{1}{x}\right) = \frac{dy}{dx} \cdot \frac{1}{x} + y \cdot \left(-\frac{1}{x^2}\right).$$

Therefore, for the line of the family with parameter k over the domain R^*,

$$\frac{dy}{dx} \cdot \frac{1}{x} + y \cdot \left(-\frac{1}{x^2}\right) = 0,$$

or

$$\frac{dy}{dx} = \frac{y}{x};$$

and since this differential equation does not involve k, it holds for each individual line of the family.

Example 5. Find a differential equation for the family of semicircles given by

$$x^2 + y^2 = k^2 \quad (y > 0).$$

(Notice that the equation $x^2 + y^2 = k^2$ by itself, although it defines a family of curves, does not define y as a function of x and therefore cannot define a differential equation involving dy/dx. This is because

$$x^2 + y^2 = k^2 \Rightarrow y = \pm\sqrt{(k^2 - x^2)}.$$

By including the condition $y > 0$ we specify a function, $x \to +\sqrt{(k^2 - x^2)}$, mapping the interval $\{x: -k < x < k\}$ onto the interval $\{y: 0 < y \leqslant k\}$. The points $x = \pm k$, $y = 0$ are excluded in order to make the function differentiable over the whole domain.)

It is simplest to proceed as in the alternative method used in Example 4. For the circle with parameter k there is a function mapping x to y with domain the interval $(-k, k)$; and from this we can form the composite function

$$x \to x^2 + y^2$$

with the same domain. What the equation states is that this composite function is a constant function over the interval $(-k, k)$, and therefore has zero derivative. Now

$$\frac{d}{dx}(x^2 + y^2) = \frac{d}{dx}(x^2) + \frac{d}{dx}(y^2)$$

$$= 2x + \frac{d}{dx}(y^2).$$

To differentiate the function $x \to y^2$, we note that this is a combination of the functions $x \to y$ and $y \to y^2$, and use the chain rule (Chapter 17, Section 2). This gives

$$\frac{d}{dx}(y^2) = \frac{d}{dy}(y^2) \times \frac{dy}{dx} = 2y\frac{dy}{dx},$$

so that

$$\frac{d}{dx}(x^2+y^2) = 2x+2y\frac{dy}{dx}.$$

Since this derivative is zero over the interval $(-k, k)$,

$$2x+2y\frac{dy}{dx} = 0,$$

whence

$$\frac{dy}{dx} = -\frac{x}{y} \quad \text{(since } y \neq 0\text{)}.$$

This will be recognized as the equation (1) of Section 1, for the graph whose tangent at every point P is at right-angles to OP. It is clear that every semicircle of the given family has this property.

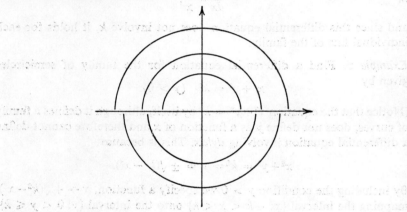

Fig. 18

Finally, it should be noticed that the condition $y > 0$ was introduced solely so that a differentiable function should be defined. The family of semicircles given by

$$x^2+y^2 = k^2 \quad (y < 0)$$

would also give rise to the same differential equation. In fact, the complete identification is between the differential equation

$$\frac{dy}{dx} = -\frac{x}{y}$$

and the union of the two families of semicircles

$$x^2+y^2 = k_1^2 \quad (y > 0) \quad \text{and} \quad x^2+y^2 = k_2^2 \quad (y < 0),$$

where k_1, k_2 are positive real numbers (see Figure 18).

3.4   Sketching families of curves. The next example deals with a family of curves which are not straight lines or circles.

Example 6. Sketch some typical members of the family of curves given by the equation
$$y = x^3 + kx^2.$$

The simplest curve of the family is that given by $k = 0$. The equation is then $y = x^3$, and the curve lies entirely in the first and third quadrants, with a horizontal point of inflexion at the origin.

For a general member of the family the y-coordinate differs from that of $y = x^3$ by an amount kx^2. Since x^2 cannot be negative, this means that when k is positive the curve lies above $y = x^3$ except at the origin, where the two graphs touch; and if k is negative it lies below $y = x^3$. We note also that the equation can be written
$$y = x^2(x+k),$$
so that the graph crosses the x-axis where $x = -k$. For large values of x, the absolute magnitude of x^2 is much smaller than that of x^3, so that the sign of y is ultimately the same as that of x^3: in fact, $y \to \infty$ as $x \to \infty$ and $y \to -\infty$ as $x \to -\infty$.

If particular numbers are substituted for x and y, a linear equation is obtained for k, except when $x = 0$. This shows that there is just one curve of the family through each point of the plane, other than points on the line $x = 0$. If $x = 0$ the equation for k has no solution unless also $y = 0$; and all curves of the family pass through the point $(0, 0)$.

These features of the family are illustrated in the sketch in Figure 19 (see p. 804).

Exercise C

In Questions 1–4 sketch some typical members of the family of curves given by the equations; obtain a differential equation (independent of the parameter k) satisfied by every curve of the family; and give a geometrical interpretation of the differential equation.

1. $y - 1 = k(x - 2)$.   **2.** $y = kx^2$.

3. $xy = k$ $(k \neq 0)$.   **4.** $x^2 - y^2 = k^2$ $(y > 0)$.

5. If y is a function of x, write expressions for the derivatives with respect to x of the following, in terms of x, y and dy/dx:

(i) y^3; (ii) $1/y$; (iii) $x^2 y$; (iv) xy^2; (v) x/y.

In Questions 6–9 find, by the methods of Examples 4 (alternative solution) and 5, the gradients of the given graphs at the points named.

6. $x^2 - 3y^2 = 1$ at $(2, 1)$.   **7.** $x^3 + y^3 = 3xy$ at $(\frac{2}{3}, \frac{4}{3})$.

8. $\dfrac{1}{x} + \dfrac{1}{y} = 1$ at $(\frac{1}{3}, -\frac{1}{2})$.   **9.** $xy(x+y) = 12$ at $(1, 3)$.

5-2

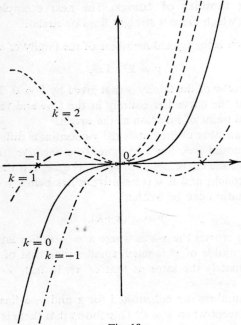

Fig. 19

10. Prove that all members of the family $y = x^3 + kx^2$, discussed in Example 6, satisfy the differential equation

$$x\frac{dy}{dx} = 2y + x^3.$$

Deduce that the stationary points of members of the family all lie on the curve $y = -\frac{1}{2}x^3$. Reproduce Figure 19 and show this curve on your diagram.

Prove also that all the points of inflexion of members of the family lie on the curve $y = -2x^3$. Show this curve on your diagram also.

11. Use the result of Example 6 (Section 3.4) to sketch some typical members of the family given by the equation

$$y^2 = x^3 + kx^2.$$

12. Sketch some typical members of the families of curves given by:

$$\text{(i) } x^3 + y = k; \qquad \text{(ii) } x^3 + \frac{1}{y} = k.$$

Find a differential equation for each family, and deduce that for each the stationary points all lie on the y-axis.

13. A particle is moving along a straight line and (with the usual notation) $dv/dt = a$ and $dx/dt = v$. Prove that

$$\frac{d}{dx}(\tfrac{1}{2}v^2) = v\frac{dv}{dx} = a.$$

Deduce the equation for *constant* acceleration

$$v^2 = u^2 + 2ax,$$

where x is the distance moved along the line from the point where the velocity is u.

14. For a particle in general three-dimensional motion, prove that

$$\frac{d}{dt}(\tfrac{1}{2}\mathbf{v}^2) = \mathbf{a}.\mathbf{v},$$

and deduce that

$$\mathbf{F}.\mathbf{v} = \frac{d}{dt}(\tfrac{1}{2}mv^2).$$

*15. Sketch some typical members of the family

$$y^2 = 4k(x+k),$$

choosing both positive and negative values of k. Explain why there are two members of the family through any point of the plane other than the origin.

Suggest restrictions which, for any particular k, would ensure that the equation defines y as a differentiable function of x. With this restriction applied, differentiate the equation with respect to x. Writing dy/dx as $\tan\psi$, prove that:

(i) $k = \tfrac{1}{2}y\tan\psi$,   (ii) $y = 2x\tan\psi + y\tan^2\psi$,

(iii) $y = x\tan 2\psi$.

Deduce that, for the two curves of the family through a point P, the tangents at P are at right-angles; and that the angle between OP and either tangent is equal to the angle which the tangent makes with the x-axis.

*16. Draw some typical curves of the family

$$x^2 + y^2 - 2kx = 0.$$

State any obvious geometrical properties of the family. If some suitable restriction is imposed to ensure that the equation defines y as a function of x, prove that

$$\frac{dy}{dx} = \frac{y^2 - x^2}{2xy}.$$

Describe also the family defined by

$$x^2 + y^2 - 2k'y = 0,$$

and find a similar expression for the derivative for any curve of this family.

Prove that, in general, through any point there passes one and only one member of each of the families. Show further that the two curves intersect at right-angles.

(*Hint.* If two curves cut each other at right-angles, what can be said about their gradients at the point of intersection?)

*17. Water is flowing across a plane, and the velocity of the flow at the point (x, y) is given by

$$\mathbf{v} = \begin{pmatrix} \dfrac{\alpha x}{x^2 + y^2} \\[2mm] \dfrac{\alpha y}{x^2 + y^2} \end{pmatrix}.$$

Write down the differential equation for the stream lines, and interpret it geometrically. Find also the magnitude of the stream velocity at (x, y), and deduce that the rate of flow of water across any circle centre the origin is $2\pi\alpha$. Describe the flow in physical terms.

*18. Investigate the flow of water across a plane if the stream velocity is given by

$$\mathbf{v} = \begin{pmatrix} -\alpha y \\ \alpha x \end{pmatrix}.$$

Prove that each particle of water describes a closed path in a period $2\pi/\alpha$.

*19. What would be represented in three-dimensional geometry by an equation of the form

$$F(x, y, z, k) = 0,$$

where k is a parameter? Illustrate your answer by discussing the family

$$x^2 + y^2 - z + k = 0.$$

4. FAMILIES DEFINED BY DIFFERENTIAL EQUATIONS

4.1 'Compass needle' diagrams. We have seen how each member of a family of curves may satisfy the same differential equation. We shall now investigate the reverse problem: given a differential equation, to find the family of curves associated with it.

Example 7. Investigate the family of curves defined by the differential equation

$$\frac{dy}{dx} = x + y.$$

We notice first that if any particular coordinates (x, y) are substituted into the right side, then the equation gives a value for dy/dx. For example, the substitution $x = 1$, $y = 2$ gives $dy/dx = 3$. This means that the particular member of the family of curves (if there is one) which passes through $(1, 2)$ has gradient 3 at that point. A similar calculation may be carried out for a selection of points and the results displayed in a table:

		Values of x				
		-2	-1	0	1	2
Values of y	2	0	1	2	3	4
	1	-1	0	1	2	3
	0	-2	-1	0	1	2
	-1	-3	-2	-1	0	1
	-2	-4	-3	-2	-1	0

Values of $\dfrac{dy}{dx} (= x + y)$

From this table a diagram can be drawn showing the direction of the tangents to the curves of the family which pass through the selected points, as in Figure 20. (In this figure the gradients have been plotted at intervals of $\frac{1}{2}$ in the x- and y-coordinates from $-2\frac{1}{2}$ to $+2\frac{1}{2}$.) We may liken this to the alignment, at different points, of a compass needle in a magnetic field, from which the lines of magnetic flux can be sketched (cf. Figure 16).

We notice at once that points on the line $x+y = 0$ have a special importance, since at every one of these points the corresponding solution curve has a zero gradient. Above this line the gradients of the solution curves are positive, and they increase the further away from the line one goes. Thus there are clearly solution curves of the form of Figure 21.

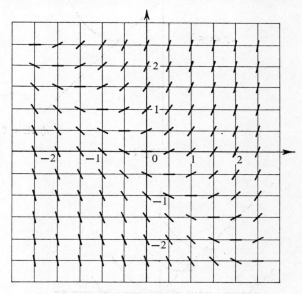

Fig. 20

But what happens to these solutions below the line $x+y = 0$? The gradient dy/dx is then negative and the curves must turn upwards. At first sight their subsequent behaviour is extremely perplexing. For suppose that a solution curve reaches the line $x+y = -2$; then it would have to cross it with gradient -2 (see Figure 22), and it is difficult to see how this part of the curve could join on to that already sketched.

Closer investigation reveals a similar difficulty about crossing the line $x+y = -1$. It would appear that every solution curve crosses this line with gradient -1; but this is the gradient of the line itself!

This is the clue to the apparent paradox. The line $x+y = -1$ is itself one of the solution curves (as is clearly shown by the 'compass needle' diagram, Figure 20), and no other solution curve crosses this line. Once we have seen this the rest of the evidence fits into place, and the complete

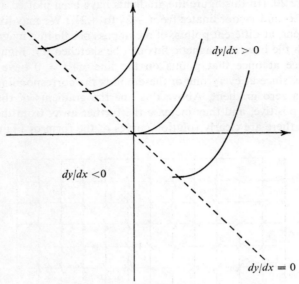

$dy/dx > 0$

$dy/dx < 0$

$dy/dx = 0$

Fig. 21

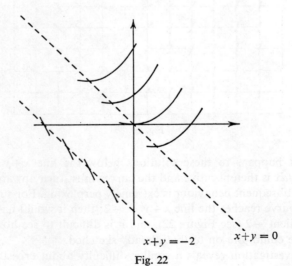

$x+y = -2$ $x+y = 0$

Fig. 22

family of solutions can be sketched: Figure 23 shows some typical solution curves.

(An argumentative person might still maintain that solutions of the form of Figure 24 could exist. They do not in fact, but it is necessary to use more sophisticated reasoning to establish this. One would be surprised if such a simple differential equation gave rise to a solution which was 'part curve, part straight line', since this is likely to involve discontinuity of the higher derivatives at the point of transition.)

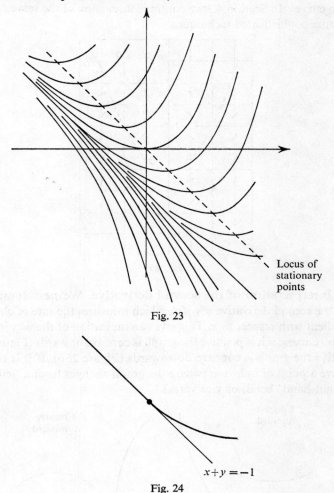

Fig. 23

Locus of
stationary
points

$x+y = -1$

Fig. 24

4.2   A more difficult example.

Example 8. Discuss graphically the solutions of the equation

$$\frac{dy}{dx} = y - x^2.$$

We begin as in Example 7 by drawing the 'compass needle' diagram (Figure 25). The curve shown with a broken line is the graph of $y - x^2 = 0$, which we denote by D_1; solutions which cross this curve have zero gradient at the point of transition.

At this stage we could already make some tentative attempts to sketch solution curves. In Section 4.3 we continue discussion of the same example using more sophisticated techniques.

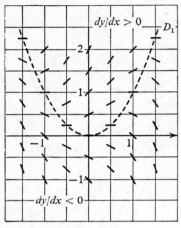

Fig. 25

*4.3   Interpretation of the second derivative. We next consider the sign of the second derivative d^2y/dx^2, which measures the rate of change of the gradient with respect to x. This gives an indication of the way in which the graph curves: if it is positive the graph is concave upwards (Figure 26 a), if negative the graph is concave downwards (Figure 26 b). If it is zero, we may have a point of inflexion (where the graph changes from a 'left-hand' to a 'right-hand' bend, or vice versa).

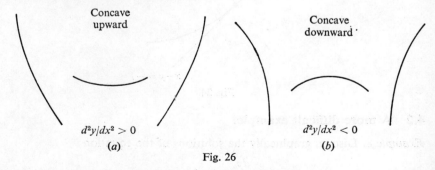

Fig. 26

Now along any solution curve of the differential equation, the relation

$$\frac{dy}{dx} = y - x^2$$

810

holds. Therefore, for variation along this curve,

$$\frac{d^2y}{dx^2} = \frac{dy}{dx} - 2x$$

$$= y - x^2 - 2x.$$

It follows that the solution curves will be concave upwards if $y > x^2 + 2x$, and concave downwards if $y < x^2 + 2x$. Figure 27 shows the graph of $y = x^2 + 2x$, labelled D_2, which separates the points of the plane at which the solution curves are concave upwards from those at which they are concave downwards. At any point where a solution curve crosses this graph it has an inflexion. Nevertheless, it is important to realize that some solution curves may never cross this graph; they may never meet it at all, or they may just touch it without crossing it.

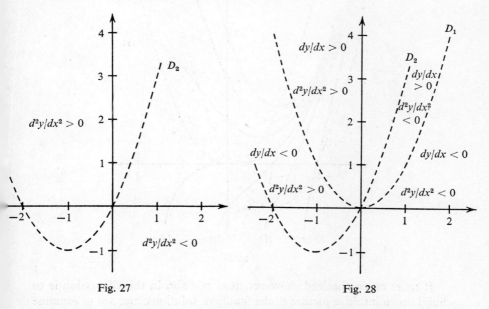

Fig. 27   Fig. 28

Combining Figures 25 and 27 we obtain Figure 28, from which we see that D_1 and D_2 divide the plane into four regions, each distinguished by a different pair of signs for dy/dx and d^2y/dx^2. We are now in a position to estimate the general shape of the solution curves; some typical ones are shown in Figure 29.

It is in fact the case that all curves of the family are initially, for large negative x, in the region between D_1 and D_2, with negative gradient and concave upwards. If such a curve cuts D_2 well to the left, it does so with a very steep gradient (since, when $d^2y/dx^2 = 0$, $dy/dx = 2x$); but there are no curves which lie completely below D_2 throughout their length.

The curves marked (*a*), (*b*) and (*c*) in due course cut D_2, after which they turn concave downwards. The curve marked (*d*) is similar, except that at the point of intersection with D_2 it also touches D_1; its point of inflexion is therefore also a stationary (horizontal gradient) point. The three remaining curves escape from the initial region by crossing D_1 rather than D_2; their gradients then become positive, but the curves are still concave upwards. The curve marked (*e*) in due course cuts D_2, beyond which it turns concave downwards; eventually therefore it must again cut D_1, beyond which its gradient becomes negative. Curves (*f*) and (*g*) never cut D_2, and are concave upwards throughout their length.

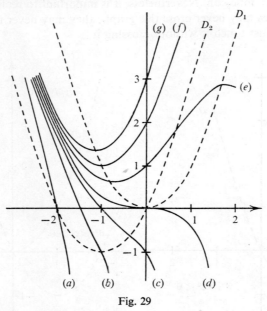

Fig. 29

It must be emphasized, however, that our aim in this discussion is to build up an intuitive picture of the family of solutions, and not to examine every corner in detail. Doubtful questions may be settled by step-by-step methods of solution (or in this case by an algebraic solution); but this would be less instructive, and probably far more laborious (see Section 6).

4.4   Boundary conditions and uniqueness of solutions. The discussion of the preceding sections suggests that, in general, a differential equation of the form

$$\frac{dy}{dx} = f(x, y)$$

will have one solution curve through each point of that part of the plane over which $f(x, y)$ is defined. Given one point through which the solution curve is required to pass, we have an equation for the parameter of the family of solutions; and having determined this parameter, the solution curve is fixed.

For example, the differential equation

$$\frac{dy}{dx} = \frac{y}{x} \quad (x \neq 0)$$

is satisfied by any line of the family $y = kx$. We can therefore find one line of the family to pass through the point (a, b), where $a \neq 0$, by choosing the particular value b/a for k. Then

$$y = \frac{b}{a} x$$

is the unique solution of the differential equation whose graph passes through the given point (a, b).

Differential equations of this kind are said to be of the *first order*, because they involve only the first derivative dy/dx. A condition imposed on a solution, such as requiring the graph to pass through a particular point, is called an *initial condition*, or *boundary condition*. Thus we see that the solution of a differential equation of the first order is determined in general by a single boundary condition.

If a differential equation involves also the second derivative (but no higher ones) it is said to be of the *second order*. A typical example of a differential equation of second order is

$$\frac{d^2x}{dt^2} + 5\frac{dx}{dt} + 4x = \cos t.$$

Let us suppose that, when $t = 0$, $x = 2$, and consider how we might develop the solution from this initial condition. Substitution of these values shows that, when $t = 0$, the derivatives are related by the equation

$$\frac{d^2x}{dt^2} + 5\frac{dx}{dt} + 8 = 1;$$

but we cannot determine the gradient dx/dt from this. Indeed, a solution can be found for which, at $t = 0$, dx/dt has any value we care to name. Thus there are infinitely many solution curves through the point. Such a differential equation requires two boundary conditions to fix a solution. These might be, for example, the specification of both x and dx/dt when $t = 0$; or two pairs of corresponding values of x and t, such as that $x = 2$ when $t = 0$ and $x = 1$ when $t = \pi$.

Second-order differential equations are usually associated with two-parameter families of curves; that is, with equations of general form

$$F(x, y, h, k) = 0.$$

813

Exercise D

In Questions 1–4, sketch some typical curves of the family of solutions of the given differential equation.

1. $\dfrac{dy}{dx} = y.$

2. $\dfrac{dz}{dt} = 2t - z.$

3. $\dfrac{dy}{dt} = y - 5.$

4. $\dfrac{dy}{dx} = xy - 1.$

5. Verify that $y = x^2 + 2x + 2$ satisfies the differential equation of Example 8. Reproduce the 'compass needle' diagram (Figure 25) and show this graph on it. How is this solution curve related to D_2?

In Questions 6–8 give the differential equation of the family of curves, and specify the solution satisfying the given boundary condition.

6. $xy^2 = k$; passes through the point $(2, -1)$.

7. $z = k \sin 2t - 1$; $z = 3$ when $t = \tfrac{1}{4}\pi$.

8. $y = kx + k^2$; passes through $(2, 3)$. (Explain the contradiction to the general rule.)

9. Find a differential equation, independent of h and k, satisfied by curves of the two-parameter family
$$y = kx^2 + h.$$
Find a solution of the differential equation whose graph passes through both $(0, -2)$ and $(1, 1)$.

10. Find a differential equation for the two-parameter family
$$z = h \sin 3t + k \cos 3t.$$
Find a solution for which $z = 2$ and $dz/dt = 5$ when $t = 0$.

5. FIRST-ORDER EQUATIONS:
ALGEBRAIC SOLUTION

5.1 Some particular examples. There are some differential equations for which it is possible to give the equation of the family of solutions in algebraic form. A few very simple examples will be discussed here; a later chapter deals with more powerful methods of tackling the problem.

Example 9. Solve the equation
$$\frac{dy}{dx} = x^2.$$

This is a straightforward integration problem; we are asked to find a primitive for the function $f(x) = x^2$. It was shown in Chapter 22 that
$$y = \tfrac{1}{3}x^3 + k$$

814

is a solution, whatever numerical value is assigned to k. If, therefore, we regard k as a parameter, this is the equation of the family of solutions of the differential equation.

Example 10. Solve the equation

$$\frac{dy}{dx} = y^2.$$

First method. This can be reduced to a problem similar to Example 9 by first finding the inverse function mapping y onto x, using the property that

$$\frac{dy}{dx} = 1 \bigg/ \frac{dx}{dy}.$$

Taking reciprocals of both sides of the differential equation, we obtain

$$\frac{dx}{dy} = \frac{1}{y^2} \quad (y \neq 0),$$

and we see that all that is required is to find the primitive $\int y^{-2} dy$. The solution is therefore

$$x = -\frac{1}{y} + k \quad (y \neq 0),$$

where k is a parameter. This can, if desired, be re-written in a form giving y in terms of x, as

$$y = \frac{1}{k-x}.$$

Second method. A slightly less obvious approach, but one which will be important in the next example, is to re-write the differential equation in the form

$$\frac{1}{y^2}\frac{dy}{dx} = 1 \quad (y \neq 0),$$

or

$$1 - \frac{1}{y^2}\frac{dy}{dx} = 0.$$

Now since y is a function of x, the left side of this equation can be written as

$$\frac{d}{dx}\left(x + \frac{1}{y}\right);$$

and the differential equation states that the composite function mapping x onto $x + y^{-1}$ has zero derivative. It is therefore a constant function, so that

$$x + \frac{1}{y} = k \quad (y \neq 0),$$

as before.

Example 11. Solve the equation

$$\frac{dy}{dx} = x^2 y^2.$$

This will yield to a combination of the methods used in Examples 9 and 10. Following the second method of the previous example, we re-cast the equation in the form

$$x^2 - \frac{1}{y^2}\frac{dy}{dx} = 0 \quad (y \neq 0),$$

which is the same as

$$\frac{d}{dx}\left(\tfrac{1}{3}x^3 + \frac{1}{y}\right) = 0.$$

The family of solutions therefore has equation

$$\tfrac{1}{3}x^3 + \frac{1}{y} = k \quad (y \neq 0).$$

*5.2 What is a 'solution'? A more rigorous discussion. In Example 10 we wrote the solution as

$$x + \frac{1}{y} = k \quad (y \neq 0).$$

Now let us consider the solution curve which passes through $(1, 1)$. There clearly is such a curve; its gradient at $(1, 1)$ is 1, and we could if we wished develop the solution step-by-step from this point. Its algebraic equation has the value $k = 2$ for its parameter.

Now let us attempt to extend our vision of the curve to either side of the known point. When $x = 1\tfrac{1}{4}$, $y = 1\tfrac{1}{3}$; when $x = 1\tfrac{1}{2}$, $y = 2$; when $x = 1\tfrac{3}{4}$, $y = 4$; and as x approaches 2, y becomes larger and larger. But there is a sense in which we cannot cross the line $x = 2$. Of course, the algebraic equation gives values for y if $x > 2$; but, as we have reached a discontinuity of the function mapping x onto y, no approximate numerical method would ever enable us to cross the line.

If we work to the left of the starting point there is less difficulty. For as x becomes large and negative, y remains positive and becomes smaller and smaller. For instance, when $x = 0$, $y = \tfrac{1}{2}$; when $x = -10$, $y = \tfrac{1}{12}$; and when $x = -100$, $y = \tfrac{1}{102}$.

Thus far we have achieved a solution curve shown in Figure 30, and, strictly, that is as far as we can go. Of course, if we were to start at the point $(3, -1)$ and proceed as above we should generate another curve for which $k = 2$. But, as in Example 5 (Section 3.3), we should consider the two curves separately as given by

$$x + \frac{1}{y} = 2 \quad (y > 0) \quad \text{and} \quad x + \frac{1}{y} = 2 \quad (y < 0).$$

The complete solution of the differential equation is the union of the two families

$$x + \frac{1}{y} = k_1 \quad (y > 0) \quad \text{and} \quad x + \frac{1}{y} = k_2 \quad (y < 0).$$

Similar remarks apply to the solution given in Example 11.

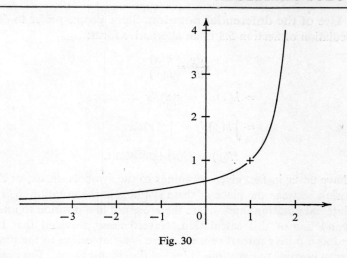

Fig. 30

5.3 Separating the variables. The method of Example 11 can be used to solve a variety of differential equations

$$\frac{dy}{dx} = f(x, y),$$

where the function $f(x, y)$ has the special form $g(x)/h(y)$. In Example 11, for instance, $g(x) = x^2$ and $h(y) = 1/y^2$. We then say that the differential equation has *separable variables*.

In this case the equation

$$\frac{dy}{dx} = \frac{g(x)}{h(y)}$$

can be arranged as $$g(x) - h(y)\frac{dy}{dx} = 0.$$

Now it may happen that g and h are functions for which primitives (denoted by G and H) can be found, so that $G' = g$ and $H' = h$. Then the equation becomes

$$G'(x) - H'(y)\frac{dy}{dx} = 0.$$

The left side of this equation is the derivative with respect to x of the function $G(x) - H(y)$; and we know that a function whose derivative is zero is a constant. We therefore deduce the equation

$$G(x) - H(y) = k$$

for the family of solutions.

*5.4 Use of the differential notation. Some people prefer to display the calculation of Section 5.3 in an alternative form:

$$\frac{dy}{dx} = \frac{g(x)}{h(y)}$$

$$\Rightarrow h(y)\,dy = g(x)\,dx$$

$$\Rightarrow \int h(y)\,dy = \int g(x)\,dx$$

$$\Rightarrow H(y) = G(x) + \text{constant}.$$

We have never in fact given meanings to the symbols dy, dx, or shown the relation between the place of these symbols in the notation dy/dx and in the integral notation; and we are therefore not in a position to interpret the second line of this calculation. Nevertheless, provided that this is regarded as a purely formal process, there is no objection to the practice.

It is even possible to cast straight integration in this mould. For example,

$$\frac{dy}{dx} = x^3$$

$$\Rightarrow dy = x^3\,dx$$

$$\Rightarrow \int dy = \int x^3\,dx$$

$$\Rightarrow y = \tfrac{1}{4}x^4 + k.$$

Exercise E

1. In Examples 10 and 11, write y as the subject of the equations, and verify by direct differentiation of the resulting formula that the solution is correct.

2. Find the solution curve of the equation

$$\frac{dy}{dx} = \sqrt{(xy)}$$

which passes through the point $(4, 1)$.

3. Give an equation for the solution curves of

$$\frac{dy}{dx} = \frac{x}{y}.$$

What geometrical fact is expressed by this equation? Illustrate the property with a sketch.

4. Can the method of separation of variables be applied to any of the differential equations in Questions 1–4 of Exercise D? If not, say what difficulty arises in each case.

5. A motor boat is travelling at 30 knots in still water when the engine cuts out. It is known that, when moving at v knots, the boat experiences a retardation due to water resistance of αv^2 knots/s. Write a differential equation for the speed at a time t seconds after the engine cuts out, and solve it.

It is observed that the speed drops to 10 knots in 15 seconds. Use this information to find the value of α, and hence find how long it takes for the speed to drop to 5 knots.

6. A motorist travelling at 15 m/s disengages gear and freewheels to rest. The retardation of the car has two components: a constant 0·08 m/s² due to friction in the working parts and road resistance, and retardation due to air resistance of 0·02v^2 m/s², where v is the speed in m/s. Find how long it takes for the car to freewheel to rest.

7. Solve the differential equations

$$\text{(i)} \quad \frac{dy}{dx} = \frac{y^2}{x^2}, \quad \text{(ii)} \quad \frac{dy}{dx} = \frac{y^2+1}{x^2+1}.$$

Express the solutions in the form $y = f(x)$, and then evaluate $f'(x)$ and verify the correctness of your solutions by direct substitution.

8. Describe the solution curves of the differential equation

$$\left(\frac{dy}{dx}\right)^2 - \frac{dy}{dx} = 0.$$

9. A spherical lump of ice melts at a rate λA cm³/s, where A is the surface area in cm²; it retains its spherical shape as it melts. Prove that its radius diminishes at a constant rate.

10. An oscillating body which can move in a straight line is pulled back towards its equilibrium position by a force which, when the body is a distance x from this position, produces in it an acceleration of amount $-n^2x$. Given that it is initially released at a distance r from its equilibrium position, find an expression for its velocity at a distance x, and deduce its maximum velocity in the course of an oscillation.

(*Hint.* Remember that dv/dt can be written as $v(dv/dx)$; see Exercise C, Question 13.)

6. FIRST-ORDER EQUATIONS:
NUMERICAL SOLUTION

6.1 It is not so easy to obtain a good approximate numerical solution to an equation of the general form

$$\frac{dy}{dx} = f(x, y)$$

as it was for the special cases of the kind discussed in Examples 2 and 3 (Sections 2.3 and 2.5), which were equivalent to the forms

$$\frac{dy}{dx} = f(x) \quad \text{and} \quad \frac{dy}{dx} = f(y).$$

The very inaccurate 'beagle and hare' technique (compare Example 1) can still be applied, but it is no longer possible to use the improved method outlined in Section 2.3. This relied upon knowing the value of dy/dx at points at which we knew only the value of x (or, in the application in Section 2.5, only the value of y). But the very nature of the equation

$$\frac{dy}{dx} = f(x, y)$$

shows that this is impossible in the more general case.

Example 12. Investigate by numerical methods the differential equation

$$\frac{dy}{dx} = y - x^2.$$

(Compare the graphical treatment in Sections 4.2 and 4.3, Example 8.)

We shall examine in detail the solution passing through the point $(0, 1)$. For a first indication of the form of this solution, let us proceed step-by-step, approximating to $\delta y/\delta x$ over each interval by the value of dy/dx (calculated from the differential equation) at the jumping-off point at the left end of this interval. This is in essence the method used in Example 1, Section 2.1. The calculation up to $x = 3$, taking steps of length $\delta x = 0\cdot5$, is as follows:

Interval	δx	Approx. $\dfrac{\delta y}{\delta x}$	Approx. δy	x	y
				0	1
$0 < x < 0\cdot5$	$0\cdot5$	1	$0\cdot5$	$0\cdot5$	$1\cdot5$
$0\cdot5 < x < 1\cdot0$	$0\cdot5$	$1\cdot25$	$0\cdot62$	$1\cdot0$	$2\cdot12$
$1\cdot0 < x < 1\cdot5$	$0\cdot5$	$1\cdot12$	$0\cdot56$	$1\cdot5$	$2\cdot68$
$1\cdot5 < x < 2\cdot0$	$0\cdot5$	$0\cdot43$	$0\cdot21$	$2\cdot0$	$2\cdot89$
$2\cdot0 < x < 2\cdot5$	$0\cdot5$	$-1\cdot11$	$-0\cdot55$	$2\cdot5$	$2\cdot34$
$2\cdot5 < x < 3\cdot0$	$0\cdot5$	$-3\cdot89$	$-1\cdot94$	$3\cdot0$	$0\cdot40$

It is suggested that, as a class project, similar calculations might be carried out with other starting points, such as $(0, 0)$, $(0, 0\cdot5)$, $(0, 1\cdot5)$, $(0, 2\cdot0)$ and so on; the various curves of the family of solutions should then be sketched. It is also of interest to investigate the effect of taking shorter steps (say $\delta x = 0\cdot2$) and to carry the computation backwards for negative x.

*6.2 Improving the accuracy of numerical solutions.

We go on to describe two methods by which, for a relatively small increase in the amount of computation, we may substantially improve the accuracy of the solution. Each method will be illustrated from the equation already discussed:

$$\frac{dy}{dx} = y - x^2$$

with initial point $(0, 1)$ and with steps $\delta x = 0\cdot5$.

820

First method. This is a development of the improved technique of Section 2.3, and uses as its basis two very accurate approximations:

(i) The gradient of a chord of a curve joining (x, y) to $(x+\delta x, y+\delta y)$ is very nearly equal, if δx is small, to the gradient of the curve at $x+\frac{1}{2}\delta x$. Geometrically, in Figure 31 the tangent at R is almost parallel to PQ.

(ii) Two solution curves of a family which are close to each other have, for given x, gradients which differ by only a small amount. That is, in Figure 32 the tangents at R and M are nearly parallel.

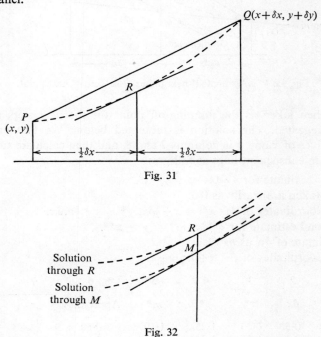

Fig. 31

Fig. 32

These two ideas are combined in Figure 33. We start at P, the point (x, y), and aim to find Q, the point on the solution curve through P with coordinate $x+\delta x$. As in Section 6.1, the differential equation gives the value of dy/dx at (x, y); denote this by m, the gradient of the tangent PT to the solution curve. On this tangent we mark M, whose coordinates are $(x+\frac{1}{2}\delta x, y+\frac{1}{2}m\delta x)$; write these as (x^*, y^*). Now there is a solution curve through M, and by substituting the coordinates (x^*, y^*) in the differential equation we can find the gradient of this curve at M, which we denote by m^*. By (ii) above, the gradient at R to the solution curve through P is approximately equal to m^*; and by (i) this is approximately equal to the

821

gradient PQ, which is the value of $\delta y/\delta x$ which we want to determine. We therefore make the step from P to P', with gradient m^*, and expect that P' will be very close to Q, and thus nearly on the solution curve through P.

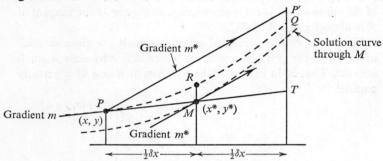

Fig. 33. P' is 'estimated' next point, Q is 'actual' next point.

P' is then taken as the jumping-off point for the next step, and the process repeated. The solution is tabulated below. We first enter the initial values of x and y in columns 7 and 8, and then calculate successive columns in subsequent lines as follows:

1. First estimate for $\delta y/\delta x$: $m = y - x^2$.
2. δx, taken arbitrarily as 0·5.
3, 4. Coordinates of M: $x^* = x + \frac{1}{2}\delta x$, $y^* = y + \frac{1}{2}m\delta x$.
5. Second estimate for $\delta y/\delta x$: $m^* = y^* - x^{*2}$.
6. Estimate of δy, as $m^*\delta x$.
7, 8. Coordinates of P': $x + \delta x$, $y + \delta y$.

1	2	3	4	5	6	7	8
m	δx	x^*	y^*	m^*	Approx. δy	x	y
1·00	0·5	0·25	1·25	1·19	0·59	0	1
1·34	0·5	0·75	1·92	1·36	0·68	0·5	1·59
1·27	0·5	1·25	2·59	1·03	0·51	1·0	2·27
0·53	0·5	1·75	2·91	−0·15	−0·07	1·5	2·78
−1·29	0·5	2·25	2·39	−2·67	−1·33	2·0	2·71
−4·87	0·5	2·75	0·16	−7·40	−3·70	2·5	1·38
						3·0	−2·32

This method can be very reliable—the first three estimates are within 0·01 of being correct. The fourth and subsequent ones are considerably less accurate. This is not only because errors tend to accumulate, but because for this particular differential equation the approximations (i) and (ii) on which the method is based cease to be satisfactory for values of x above about 2. (Notice the very large discrepancies between m and m^*.)

822

It will be found that the values for $x = 2$ onwards are considerably adjusted by taking smaller steps (see Exercise F, Question 9).

Second method. This uses a local approximation of the second degree, on the lines of Chapter 16, Section 5.

We may regard the method described in Sections 2.1 and 6.1 of the present chapter as the replacement of the solution curve by its local linear approximation at the left end of the interval. If the equation of the solution curve is

$$y = \phi(x),$$

then the increment δy has been calculated from

$$\delta y \simeq \phi'(x)\delta x.$$

If the second degree local approximation

$$\delta y \simeq \phi'(x)\delta x + \tfrac{1}{2}\phi''(x)(\delta x)^2$$

were used instead, we might expect to get a more accurate approximation to the solution curve.

Now $\phi'(x)$ is the gradient of the solution curve at P, and we know from the differential equation that in this example

$$\phi'(x) = y - x^2.$$

The second derivative is found by differentiating this with respect to x; remembering that y itself is a function of x:

$$\phi''(x) = \frac{dy}{dx} - 2x = y - x^2 - 2x.$$

The calculation now proceeds as follows:

$\phi'(x)$	$\phi''(x)$	δx	$\phi'(x)\delta x$	$\tfrac{1}{2}\phi''(x)(\delta x)^2$	Approx. δy	x	y
1·00	1·00	0·5	0·5	0·12	0·62	0	1
1·37	0·37	0·5	0·68	0·05	0·73	0·5	1·62
1·35	−0·65	0·5	0·67	−0·08	0·59	1·0	2·35
0·69	−2·31	0·5	0·34	−0·29	0·05	1·5	2·94
−1·01	−5·01	0·5	−0·50	−0·63	−1·13	2·0	2·99
−4·39	−9·39	0·5	−2·19	−1·17	−3·36	2·5	1·86
						3·0	−1·50

One might ask why these results differ so sharply from those obtained by the first method. It is noticeable that in several intervals the 'correction term' $\tfrac{1}{2}\phi''(x)(\delta x)^2$ is comparable in magnitude to the first term of the approximation; it is then reasonable to expect that the additional term in the cubic approximation, $\tfrac{1}{6}\phi'''(x)(\delta x)^3$, might not be negligible. If so, then this can be calculated in a similar way and used to refine the solution further. (In particular, notice that $\phi''(x)$ changes sign between $x = 1·0$ and $1·5$, indicating a point of inflexion in the solution curve; no quadratic approximation could show this feature.) Better results will also be achieved by taking smaller steps.

It would in any case be very unwise to deduce, on the basis of one example, that the first method is superior to the second. Indeed, a little analysis shows that if, for this differential equation, the starting point is $(0, c)$ and $c > 2$, then the second method is certainly superior (see Exercise F, Question 10).

Exercise F

The questions marked with an asterisk require the methods of Section 6.2.

1. Using the method of Section 6.1, taking steps $\delta x = 0.2$ over the interval $0 < x < 2$, estimate solutions of

$$\frac{dy}{dx} = x+y$$

with initial points $(0, 0)$, $(0, -1)$ and $(0, -2)$. Compare your results with the graphs drawn in Figure 23.

2. Devise a flow diagram for a step-by-step solution of the equation in Question 1. If a negative value were assigned to δx in the program, would it calculate correctly points to the left of the initial point? If not, what other modification would be necessary? Follow through your instructions for the solution through $(0, 0)$ for negative values of x, as far as $x = -2$.

3. Using the method of Section 6.1 (or, if you prefer, one of the more refined methods of Section 6.2) estimate the solution of the equation

$$\frac{dy}{dx} = xy-1$$

with initial point $(0, 1)$. Consider the interval $0 < x < 2$ with steps of length $\delta x = 0.2$.

Compare the result with your solution of Exercise D, Question 4.

(As a class project it would be interesting to work the solution with a number of different initial points.)

4. A graph has the property that the tangent at every point P has a gradient which is minus the gradient of OP. If the graph passes through $(2, 5)$, obtain a table of corresponding values of x and y over the interval $2 < x < 5$.

5. The speed of an object falling through a resisting medium is given by the formula $9.8(t-0.06x)$ m/s, where x metres is the distance moved in the first t seconds. From this information investigate the variation of x with t during the fall.

*6. Taking steps $\delta x = 0.2$ over the interval $0 < x < 2$, estimate the solution of the equation

$$\frac{dx}{dy} = y-x^2$$

which passes through $(0, 2.5)$. Use all three methods described in Section 6 and compare the results on a graph.

*7. Use one of the methods of Section 6.2 to improve your answers to Questions 1 and 2 of this Exercise.

*8. Apply the first method of Section 6.2 to the solution of

$$\frac{dy}{dx} = y,$$

with $y = 1$ when $x = 0$. Show that, with intervals $\delta x = 0\cdot1$, the solution is equivalent to multiplying the value of y by $1\cdot105$ at each stage, and deduce an equation satisfied by corresponding values of x and y. Show that this can be put into the form

$$y = c^x,$$

and state the value of c obtained by this method.

What would the solution be for the boundary condition $y = a$ when $x = 0$?

*9. For the Example discussed in Section 6.2:

(a) Use the cubic local approximation to improve the result obtained by the second method.

(b) By taking $\delta x = 0\cdot1$ in the interval $1\cdot5 < x < 2\cdot0$, improve the result obtained by the first method for $x = 2$.

*10. Consider the solution of the differential equation

$$\frac{dy}{dx} = y - x^2,$$

which passes through the point $(0, c)$. Show by using the methods of Section 6.2, with $\delta x = h$, that:

(a) M has coordinates $(\frac{1}{2}h, c + \frac{1}{2}ch)$;

(b) $m^* = c + \frac{1}{2}ch - \frac{1}{4}h^2$, and P' has coordinates $(h, c + ch + \frac{1}{2}ch^2 - \frac{1}{4}h^3)$.

(c) Show that the second method gives for the next point the coordinates $(h, c + ch + \frac{1}{2}ch^2)$.

(d) Prove that $d^3y/dx^3 = y - x^2 - 2x - 2$, and that this is also the value of d^ny/dx^n for $n > 3$.

(e) Deduce that, for positive x, d^ny/dx^n is positive for all n at points in the plane lying above the parabola $y = x^2 + 2x + 2$.

(f) Deduce that all solution curves cutting the y-axis at points above $(0, 2)$ 'bend upwards' for all positive values of x.

(g) Show that in this case the estimate for the 'next point' given in (c) is always too small, but that it is better than that given in (b).

(h) Prove that for solution curves cutting the y-axis below $(0, 2)$ the estimate given in (c) is always too large.

Miscellaneous Exercise

1. At 11 a.m. an orator mounted a soap-box and began to speak. His audience grew from nothing to a considerable size before the claims of lunch proved too strong for his hearers. The figures were as follows:

Time (minutes after 11 a.m.)	0	10	20	30	40	50	60	70	80	90
Rate of increase of crowd (per minute)	0	47	76	86	79	54	11	-50	-158	-227

Estimate when the crowd was greatest, and how many were then present. When did the orator find he was talking to himself?

2. A family of solution curves to a differential equation has an envelope C (that is, at each point of C there is a member of the family which touches C). Explain why C must also be a solution curve for the differential equation.

Illustrate this property with the following example. The lines

$$y = mx - \tfrac{1}{4}m^2$$

for different values of m all touch the parabola

$$y = x^2.$$

Show that the family of lines satisfies the differential equation

$$y - x\frac{dy}{dx} + \frac{1}{4}\left(\frac{dy}{dx}\right)^2 = 0,$$

and that the parabola is also a solution curve for this equation. How many solution curves pass through a general point (x, y) of the plane?

3. Sketch typical members of the family of lines

$$\frac{x}{k} + \frac{y}{1-k} = 1,$$

and find a differential equation for the family. Show that this equation is also satisfied by the solutions

$$y = x + 1 \pm 2\sqrt{x},$$

and suggest a reason for this.

4. Prove that every curve of the family $xy = k$ cuts every curve of the family $y^2 - x^2 = c$ at right-angles. Illustrate this property in a sketch.

5. Sketch the family of curves with equation

$$\frac{x^2}{1+k} + \frac{y^2}{k} = 1.$$

Prove that, in general, there are two members of the family through a given point of the plane, and that the gradients satisfy the equation

$$\left(x\frac{dy}{dx} - y\right)\left(x + y\frac{dy}{dx}\right) = \frac{dy}{dx}.$$

Hence prove that the two members of the family cut each other at right-angles.

6. Devise a step-by-step method for solving the differential equation of the second order

$$\frac{d^2x}{dt^2} + 5\frac{dx}{dt} + 4x = \cos t,$$

and carry through the solution with initial conditions $x = 2$ and $dx/dt = 0$ when $t = 0$, using steps $\delta t = 0.1$ and working through the interval $0 < t < 0.5$.

Can you adapt the second method of Section 6.2 to improve the accuracy of your solution?

7. Show that, if

$$\frac{dy}{dt} = 4z - y \quad \text{and} \quad \frac{dz}{dt} = -z - 4y,$$

then

$$\frac{d^2y}{dt^2} + 2\frac{dy}{dt} + 17y = 0.$$

This last equation describes the oscillation of a certain physical system, which is started in motion at time $t = 0$ with $y = 4$ and $dy/dt = 0$. Apply a step-by-step method of solution to the first pair of equations to investigate the motion of the system over the interval $0 < t < 2$.

8. The method of approximation to the solution, $y = \phi(x)$, of

$$\frac{dy}{dx} = f(x)$$

described in Section 2.3 is equivalent to replacing the exact increment

$$\delta y = \phi(x + \delta x) - \phi(x)$$

by the approximate increment

$$\delta_1 y = \phi'(x + \tfrac{1}{2}\delta x)\,\delta x.$$

Use Taylor's polynomial approximations to show that these two expressions have the same quadratic approximations, and compare the cubic and quartic approximations.

Another method of solving the differential equation would be to replace the average gradient over a step by the average of the gradients at the two ends of the step. Show that this is equivalent to replacing δy by

$$\delta_2 y = \tfrac{1}{2}\{\phi'(x) + \phi'(x + \delta x)\}\,\delta x.$$

Compare the quadratic, cubic and quartic approximations for δy and $\delta_2 y$. Show that $\delta_1 y$ is in general a slightly better approximation than $\delta_2 y$, and that

$$\tfrac{2}{3}\delta_1 y + \tfrac{1}{3}\delta_2 y$$

is a very good approximation. Explain the connection with Simpson's Rule for approximate integration.

28

PROGRAMMING

1. MACHINE CALCULATIONS

1.1 Stages of a calculation. Whenever an unsolved problem arises in mathematics, three quite distinct phases of activity are needed to solve it. The first two phases tend to be of low physical activity and high mental activity; the principles by which the solution is to be obtained have to be found or decided upon, and they have then to be organized for actual calculation. These two operations are called *numerical analysis* and *programming*.

The third phase, however, tends to be of high physical activity and low mental activity, and consists of applying the chosen method to the actual numbers in hand. It often proves to be no more than sheer drudgery, and it is not surprising that man has resorted to building machines which can assist in the boring task of simply manipulating numbers.

As time has progressed, these machines have become more and more sophisticated, and the manipulations which they can carry out completely unaided by human intervention have become more and more advanced. More recently, machines have been developed which can perform many thousands of simple repetitive operations every second, and, as the amount of labour needed to carry out the decisions of the first phase has become less and less of a barrier, there has been some 'feed-back' which has radically affected both numerical analysis and programming.

These numerical methods which have now entered the bounds of possibility are discussed in detail wherever they are relevant to the present course; and there is a brief mention, in the last section of this chapter, of recent developments in programming, whereby a machine is able to accept and interpret instructions not very different from the language in which mathematics is normally written.

1.2 Numbers in a machine. Whenever a machine is used as an aid to calculation, it has to have some physical means of representing every number with which it has to work. No machine can work with unknown variables; all it can do is to operate upon numbers which have previously been fed in, though it can obey some criterion which indicates when the work is complete. Thus, when a machine appears to be solving an equation, it is in fact simply manipulating different numbers, according to a pre-arranged scheme, until it finds one which is sufficiently close to the solution.

Several ways of representing numbers immediately spring to mind. In a desk calculator, a cash register, or a mileometer, the numbers involved are represented by the states of rotation of a series of wheels. In an electrical machine, a voltage level, a degree of magnetization, or a current can be used to represent a number; and, at a much lower level, the sand in an egg-timer represents a length of time (past or future), and the number of beads on one side of an abacus a quantity of money.

Such systems can be divided into two categories, and it is both convenient and expedient mathematically to distinguish them. The test is essentially whether they rely upon a *measuring* or a *counting* process—in fact, whether the physical variables used are quantities which vary continuously or discretely.

1.3   Analogue and digital devices. The first category, of *analogue* machines, includes all systems which represent a number by a continuously varying physical quantity, such as a length, a voltage, or a weight. They obtain the answer by measuring the representation of a number at the output.

The second category, of *digital* machines, includes all systems which represent a number by a physical quantity which varies discontinuously, such as the number of teeth on a cog-wheel, or the number of beads or counters. They obtain the answer by counting the number of these discontinuous elements at the output.

At this level, it is the digital machines which have influenced the principles of computation most. As a result, we shall be thinking entirely in terms of digital devices when we refer to machine processes. All the numerical analysis is presented so that the flow-diagrams produced can easily be adapted for application to an actual digital machine. To be able to organize calculations in this way is not only of immediate practical value, but it also often leads directly to a deeper understanding of the mathematical principles involved.

Now, the fastest and most efficient computers are electronically operated. The reasons for this are that voltages and currents can be changed more quickly, and with less power applied, than any mechanical devices.

It has also been found convenient to construct the electronic computer on a binary digital principle. We might, therefore, choose to use voltages so that, instead of allowing seven volts (say) to represent the number seven, we choose a critical voltage level only, below which the voltage represents the number 0, and above which it represents the number 1. Magnetic cores are in fact commonly used for a similar representation, in terms of the degree of magnetization.

Variations in level as the electrical signals are transmitted from place to place in the computer will then become of little importance, and the only penalty, as it were, is that the machine has to use the binary scale rather than the familiar denary scale. Luckily, however, the choice of number scale has no effect on the principles governing the method by which any particular problem is solved, and the only consequences which will affect our discussion spring from the fact that a modern general purpose computer is usually a digital, and not an analogue, machine.

Example 1. Which of these are analogue devices? Give reasons: (*a*) a mileometer; (*b*) a dial weighing machine.

(*a*) The number of miles travelled in a journey is represented in a mileometer by numbers engraved on a wheel. The wheels are rotated discontinuously; on a bicycle, for example, each revolution of the front wheel turns the register almost instantaneously through a fixed angle (usually 60°); while on a car, although the tenths are moving for much of the time, the movement starts only at the beginning of each completed tenth. The device is therefore not analogue, but digital.

(*b*) The reading on a dial weighing machine is indicated by a pointer which moves over a circular scale. The position of the pointer is controlled by a spring which is extended by the weight being measured. Since the spring extends continuously as increasing weight is applied, the pointer will rotate continuously over the dial scale. The device thus falls into the analogue category.

Exercise A

1. Which of these are analogue devices? Give reasons:

(*a*) a mechanical clock; (*b*) a water clock;
(*c*) a master-and-slave clock; (*d*) a spring balance;
(*e*) a beam balance; (*f*) a cyclometer;
(*g*) a speedometer; (*h*) a thermometer;
(*i*) an abacus; (*j*) a slide rule.

2. Is there any reason why an analogue or a digital device should be the more accurate?

3. The quadratic equation $x^2 + ax - b = 0$ may be solved (if a and b are positive) by using a modified Wheatstone's bridge. If the equation is re-written as

$$\frac{x}{1} = \frac{b}{x+a},$$

resistances of x (variable), 1, b, and $(x+a)$ are placed in the four arms; x is then adjusted until a balance occurs. Is the device analogue or digital:

(*a*) if x is contained in a resistance box;
(*b*) if x is part of a metre wire bridge?

4. Voltages of x, y, and z are applied to three resistances whose values are all r ohms, which are connected in parallel as shown in Figure 1. Using v to denote the voltage at P, write down expressions for the currents i_x, i_y, i_z in the three resistors.

If no current is drawn from P, what current will flow through the earthed resistor R? Obtain an expression for v in terms of x, y, and z.

Can this circuit be used as an adder? Is it an analogue or a digital device?

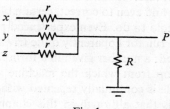

Fig. 1

2. COMPUTER OPERATIONS

2.1 Breakdown of a routine. Imagine that you employ a clerk in an engineering office, whose job it is to calculate the breaking strengths of various structures, and that you have provided him with a desk calculator and a book of instructions, which tells him what to do with the various figures with which he may be confronted. Before you read on, think how to break down the routine by which he works into five separate parts.

First, we can distinguish the *output*—the part that matters to you—which will be the answer to the problem set in a form in which you can understand it. Secondly, there must be the *input*, which must give all the data which the clerk will need for this problem. Thirdly, he will need *storage* space, to hold the various numbers with which he works as the problem proceeds. Fourthly, he needs an *arithmetic* unit, the desk calculator with which he carries out arithmetical instructions. Lastly, he has a *control* unit, the book of instructions, which tells him at every stage what to do next, and the brain which enables him to move from one instruction correctly to the next.

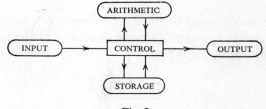

Fig. 2

He will work by moving backwards and forwards between these five elements, and Figure 2 represents the process.

831

Every computing system has these five elements, in some form or other, and the instructions which operate each of them must be given very precisely indeed. Unfortunately, a computer cannot tell, as a clerk might, when the instructions it receives are mistaken; and although routines have been devised to detect, and even to correct, certain types of error, basically it does just what it is told to do. Even experienced programmers will find that a program fails to run for apparently quite trivial reasons—a comma, or even a space, omitted; a number given in a form for which the machine is not prepared; a loop from which the machine will never emerge by itself, because one cycle is continually repeated without alteration.

The moral of this is that although in this chapter we are using flow diagrams only, and not a particular machine language, it must be a point of honour to get all instructions precisely right, and to have a program thoroughly checked before it is handed in. This is a precaution which will save a lot of disappointment—and expense—when you have programs actually run on a computer, and it is sensible to work in pairs, checking each other's programs without using your intelligence to avoid the errors in them. English, and particularly spoken English, is often a little imprecise, and errors in spelling and syntax, and even omission of some of the material, can easily be overlooked; in computing, however, any mistake may well make a whole program worthless.

2.2 Storage. In these next sections, therefore, we shall recall and clarify the conventions we have already made.

Storage locations are represented, at present, only by single capital letters, though we shall later extend the number of stores available, and develop systematic ways of dealing with large numbers of stores.

A typical instruction for substitution is

$$\boxed{A := B}$$

(read 'A is to be set equal to B' or 'A becomes B'), which transfers a 'carbon copy' of the contents of storage location B to storage location A. But we may also write, for example,

$$\boxed{A := 3}$$

or
$$\boxed{A := 2 \cdot 753}$$

to feed numbers directly into the stores.

832

2.3 Arithmetic. We shall, at present, admit only the four simple binary operations $+$, $-$, $\times$, and $\div$. Typical arithmetical operations will therefore be

$$\boxed{A := B+C}$$

$$\boxed{A := 2 \times A}$$

$$\boxed{C := C+1}$$

The multiplication sign should never be omitted in flow diagrams.

2.4 Input. We shall imagine that all numbers needed in the program are available, say on punched cards or on tape, in the order in which they are needed. Then the instruction

$$\boxed{\text{READ } A}$$

will put the next of these numbers into store A, destroying whatever was there before, and leave the machine ready to read the following number (if any). It is not possible to read in the same number a second time, unless it appears on the tape again; nor can we take a number out of order.

We shall also combine a series of 'READ' instructions into a single instruction, such as

$$\boxed{\text{READ } A, B, C}$$

which reads the next three numbers on the tape, and stores them in stores A, B, and C respectively.

It is often useful to end a set of numbers to be read (called a 'data tape' hereafter) with some number such as -999, which can then be used as a signal that there are no more numbers of that set to come.

2.5 Output. We shall continue to use the simple instruction

$$\boxed{\text{PRINT } A}$$

to display the contents of storage location A. It is convenient to imagine that if the output is integral, it will be printed exactly, but that if it is not it will be rounded to (say) six significant decimal digits. Numbers between 10^{-6} and 10^6 will then be displayed with a decimal point; larger and smaller numbers would need a power of 10 to be shown as well.

7   SAM 3

As a matter of fact, it takes a good deal of care with output formats to make sure that the right layout is obtained; for the moment, however, we shall simply assume that the instruction

$$\boxed{\text{PRINT } A, B, C}$$

causes A, B, and C to appear on the same line, and that each new PRINT instruction begins on a new line.

2.6 Control. The function of the control unit is to tell the computer which instruction to obey next. Normally, control passes from one instruction to the next below it, until the final instruction

$$\boxed{\text{STOP}}$$

is reached. If, however, the program needs a branch or a loop, we can use a decision box to ask a YES/NO question about the relative sizes of the contents of two stores (or of the contents of one store and a number). The symbols $=$, $>$, $\geqslant$, $<$, $\leqslant$, $\neq$ may be used. Examples are:

Control lines which re-enter the diagram to make a loop should join the main control line *between* two instruction boxes. There may be other instruction boxes en route, but arrows should always be used to indicate how control passes if it is not straight down the page.

2.7 Dry runs. It is very useful to represent the contents of the stores of a computer on paper, to see that a program runs correctly for simple numbers.

Example 2. Test this program, which should produce $x.y^n$, where n is a natural number.

834

Data tape: x, y, n.

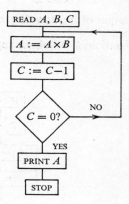

If we do a *dry run*, imagining that the data tape reads, say, 2, 3, 4, we can build up the following register of store contents. We hope to produce the answer 162:

A	B	C
2	3	4
6		3
18		2
54		1
162		0

This gives the correct answer, 2×3^4. It is, moreover, easy to see that it will give the correct answer to any problem of this type presented to the computer, though it should be realized that a computer can only handle actual numbers, and not variables. Thus, to evaluate $3 \cdot 47 \times 1 \cdot 25^7$, we should write '3·47, 1·25, 7' on the data tape. The program, in fact, is general, but its use is confined to particular cases.

The dry run can also be used to build up a program; but that is a matter for a later section.

Exercise B

In Questions 1–9, find the output of the flow-diagram, and explain the process which it has been carrying out.

(The student should do Questions 1–9 without any omissions.)

1.

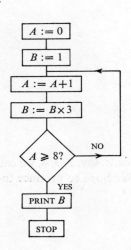

2.

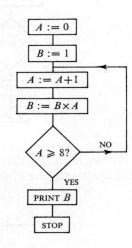

3.

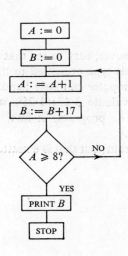

4.

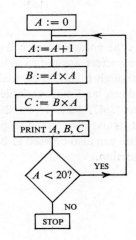

836

5.

6.

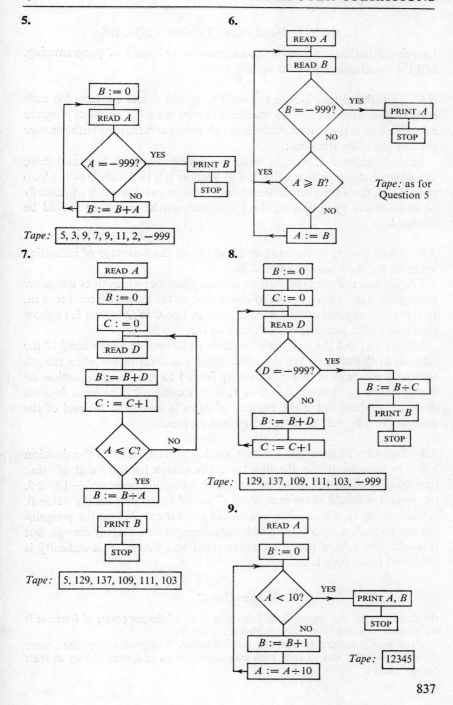

Tape: 5, 3, 9, 7, 9, 11, 2, −999

Tape: as for Question 5

7.

8.

Tape: 5, 129, 137, 109, 111, 103

Tape: 129, 137, 109, 111, 103, −999

9.

Tape: 12345

837

3. SOME SIMPLE TECHNIQUES

Exercise B indicates some of the commonest problems of programming, and the usual techniques for solving them.

3.1   Initial values. Notice the need to specify initial contents for each store. If this were not done, a number left over from the previous program might well be in the store already, and this would certainly make the answer printed out quite irrelevant.

In most cases, it is wise to write the (innermost) loop first, and then, using paper stores as in the dry run of Section 2.7, to decide how the loop should end. Only then should the initial values be considered; it will usually be quite clear, by following the loops backwards, how they should be assigned.

3.2   Data tapes. Questions 7 and 8 illustrate the two ways of indicating when all the data have been read in.

(*a*) We can end the tape with an arbitrary number which does not occur among the data, such as –999, to signal that all the data have been read in. In this case, we shall usually need a counter, like *C* in Question 8, to show how many data items have been read so far.

(*b*) We can put the number *n* of items to be read in at the head of the tape, as in Question 7. We shall then need a counter to see when the *n*th item has been read in. It may count up from 1 to *n*, as in this question, or it may count down from *n* to 0 or 1, as in Example 2. The latter is often more convenient, but if the number of items is needed at the end of the program it may well be better to use the former.

3.3   Equality. Except for the tape ending signals, none of the decision boxes in Exercise B uses the sign ' = '. The reason for this habit of using inequalities can easily be seen in Example 2, where if *n* were, say, −1 or 2·5, the program would never end, since *C* would never contain the value 0. An inequality in the decision box would at least ensure that the program did not contain a loop from which the computer could never emerge, but it would also ensure that the answer given was wrong. This difficulty is discussed more fully later.

Exercise C

(In this Exercise, the reader should develop some of the programs of Exercise B for himself to solve more complicated problems.)

Write flow diagrams to evaluate the following. Where necessary, data tapes should be written out in full, with numbers such as *n, i*, etc., shown in their correct places.

1. Adapt Question 2 of Exercise B to evaluate:
   (a) 12!; (b) $n!$; (c) $12! \div 8!$;
   (d) $12! \div (8!4!)$; (e) $\binom{n}{i}$. (See p. 759, Exercise G, Question 4.)

2. Adapt Question 3 of Exercise B to find the quotient and remainder:
   (a) when 1968 is divided by 37;
   (b) when 1968 is divided by 37, using only the operation $+$;
   (c) when p is divided by q, q being integral.

3. Adapt Question 6 of Exercise B to find, for a given set of numbers on tape:
   (a) the least;
   (b) the least and the greatest;
   (c) the range and the mean of extremes.

4. Adapt Questions 7 and 8 of Exercise B to find:
   (a) $1^2 + 2^2 + 3^2$ and $1 + 2 + 3$ simultaneously;
   (b) $a^2 + b^2 + c^2 + d^2$ and $a + b + c + d$ simultaneously;
   (c) the mean and variance of 1, 2, 3, 4, 5;
   (d) the mean and variance of n numbers given on tape;
   (e) the mean and variance of an unspecified number of numbers.

5. Adapt Question 9 of Exercise B to find:
   (a) the standard form† of any positive number;
   (b) the standard form of any number.

6. Write a flow diagram for $|k|$ (that is, k if $k \geqslant 0$, $-k$ otherwise).

7. Write flow diagrams to evaluate (modifying them in turn):
   (a) $(((2) \times y + 3) \times y + 1)$, where $y = 3$;
   (b) $4x^3 + 3x^2 + 2x + 1$, where $x = 1 \cdot 43$;
   (c) $a_n x^n + a_{n-1} x^{n-1} + \ldots + a_1 x + a_0$, writing out the data tape in full.

4. THE DESK CALCULATOR

A very simple digital device is the *desk calculator*, illustrated in Figure 3. Familiarity with it is not essential, but it will greatly help in the work of this chapter if a machine, or a set of machines, is available for demonstration and practice.

Most machines have three *registers* (or storage locations). We shall call them:

S, the *setting register*, where numbers are fed into it;

A, the *accumulator*, where numbers set in S can be added;

C, the *counter*, which indicates how many such additions there have been.

† I.e. the form $a \times 10^b$ where $1 \leqslant a < 10$ and $b \in Z$.

Fig. 3

By turning the handle in the positive direction, the operator can obey the pair of instructions

$$\begin{array}{l} A := A+S \\ C := C+1 \end{array}$$

and similarly, by turning it in the opposite, or negative, direction, he can obey

$$\begin{array}{l} A := A-S \\ C := C-1 \end{array}$$

In the latter case, if the contents of S are greater than the contents of A, the accumulator behaves as if it had one more figure available at the left, but a bell rings to indicate that there has been an *overflow*. The bell also rings if there is an overflow after an addition.

There is usually a gear which can be set to count in the opposite direction, so that if the handle is turned in the positive direction the effect is

$$\begin{array}{l} A := A+S \\ C := C-1 \end{array}$$

and if it is turned in the negative direction the effect is

$$\begin{array}{l} A := A-S \\ C := C+1 \end{array}$$

840

The calculator will also be equipped with levers which return the contents of the various stores to zero, and with a carriage shift, which allows, for $i = 0$ to 10, say, corresponding to the instructions above,

$$A := A \pm S \times 10^i$$
$$C := C \pm 10^i$$

to be carried out with a single turn of the handle. This, however, is only a device for speeding up calculations, and need not be taken further here; nor need the 'short-cutting' method used on an actual machine, which allows

$$A := A + S \times 187$$
$$C := C + 187$$

to be carried out by means of six turns of the handle; C is increased by 200, decreased by 10, and decreased by 3 successively. For our purposes, we can imagine that the handle is actually turned 187 times; there is no difference in principle.

Thus the machine has a means of putting in numbers, and three storage locations; it can be used to add, to subtract, and to count. The output of the machine, that is, the answer to be found, is read from one or more of the registers.

If further storage locations are needed, they will of course be *paper stores*—numbers written down by the operator, and used again as necessary; and similarly data must be tabulated on paper before the calculation can begin. Practice in this process should soon give the operator an insight into the techniques of programming.

Example 3. What does the following sequence of desk calculator operations do?

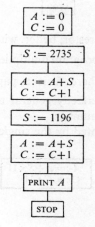

$$A := 0$$
$$C := 0$$

$$S := 2735$$

$$A := A + S$$
$$C := C + 1$$

$$S := 1196$$

$$A := A + S$$
$$C := C + 1$$

PRINT A

STOP

The effect of this progam is to find the sum, 3931, of the numbers fed into the machine. If both the *S* instructions had been replaced by

$$\boxed{\text{READ } S}$$

we should have a perfectly general program for adding two numbers together.

Notice that after the third instruction box the contents of *S* are still 2735, and that after the fifth instruction box the previous contents of *A* and *C* are lost by 'over-writing'; this reminds us of the 'carbon copy' convention.

What do the final contents of *C* tell us? Is either or both of the instructions in the first box dispensable?

Example 4. What does the following sequence of desk calculator operations do?

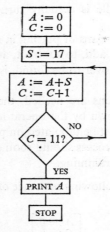

Experiment with paper stores, or, better, with a desk calculator, will soon convince the reader that the program multiplies 17 by 11. If $\boxed{S := 17}$ were replaced by $\boxed{\text{READ } S, X}$ (where *X* is a paper store), and $C = 11$? by $C = X$? this would be a perfectly general multiplication program, provided that *X* was a natural number.

This loop may be represented by the single pair of instructions

$$\boxed{\begin{array}{l} A := A + S \times 11 \\ C := C + 11 \end{array}}$$

Exercise D

(These are only specimen questions; the reader should invent many more.)

1. Write down flow diagrams to summarize the processes:
(a) $594 + 118 + 38$;   (b) $286 - 117 + 99$;   (c) $-210 + 547$.
Note the contents of each store at each stage.

2. Multiply two integers together, and summarize the process in a flow diagram. How can you proceed with non-integral numbers?

3. Find out how to divide integers to find the quotient and the remainder:
(a) by repeated addition;
(b) by repeated subtraction, and summarize the processes in flow diagrams.

4. Use a desk calculator to evaluate $1 \cdot 47^5$.

5. Use a desk calculator to evaluate $8!$.
Use a desk calculator and paper stores to evaluate the following, and write flow diagrams to summarize the process:

6. $11^2 + 13^2 + 15^2$.   **7.** $270(1 \cdot 05)^6$.

8. $\begin{vmatrix} 0 \cdot 175 & 0 \cdot 065 \\ 0 \cdot 31 & 0 \cdot 22 \end{vmatrix}$.   **9.** $(0 \cdot 184 \quad 0 \cdot 632) \begin{pmatrix} 0 \cdot 48 \\ 0 \cdot 17 \end{pmatrix}$.

10. $11^3 + 13^3 + 15^3$.

11. $1 \cdot 23x^4 - 2 \cdot 17x^2 + 1 \cdot 37x + 4 \cdot 41$ for $x = 2 \cdot 31$.

12. Build up simultaneously, by splitting the register A, the sums Σf, $\Sigma x f$, $\Sigma x^2 f$ from the table:

x	0	1	2	3	4	5
f	1	4	11	12	3	1

Carry this out, and apply Charlier's checks. Write flow diagrams for this purpose.

(The reason for the restriction to the simple *binary* operations in our flow diagrams should now be appreciated; a desk calculator can only perform one such operation at a time, and though a computer program, nowadays, may give instructions of great complexity, they must still be obeyed one binary operation at a time.)

5. COUNTERS

It is often necessary to count the number of times a particular loop has been cycled. As we have seen, this is very easily done by including an instruction

$$\boxed{C := C+1}$$

in the loop, and the counter register of the desk calculator shows very clearly how it operates. A decision box which decides on the course of action to be taken after examining the contents of C should therefore not be liable to error, because only integers are used.

Notice, in passing, that with an *analogue* device integers will not have this property. We should either have to use an inequality, or to specify that two numbers should be equal to a certain degree of accuracy. This may not be a serious problem—if, say, integers were represented by exact numbers of centimetres, equality 'to the nearest millimetre' would be ample for this sort of decision.

Now the problem with a *digital* device, such as a desk calculator, is in dealing with fractions. Suppose that we write

$$\boxed{C := C + \tfrac{1}{3}}$$

and hope to end a loop when it has been cycled twelve times. What should we put in the decision box? Check your answer on a desk calculator.

Unfortunately, even if we use 0·33333333 to represent $\tfrac{1}{3}$, after twelve such additions we only reach the total 3·99999996, so that if we write $C = 4$?, or even $C \geqslant 4$? in the decision box, the program will fail to give the right answer.

Similarly, even if we use

$$\boxed{C := C + 0 \cdot 1}$$

repeatedly on a computer, after twenty cycles the answer will not be precisely 2, in general, although on a desk calculator it will. There are several possible reasons for this—which it is not necessary for the programmer to appreciate in detail—depending on the digital nature of the computer. The two principal sources of error are in the rounding of numbers converted to binary (if the computer works that way) and in the possibility of small random errors in the last figure.

To overcome this difficulty, most computers distinguish between *integer* stores, which hold integers exactly, and *real* stores, which hold numbers which are not necessarily integers, and should not be relied upon for accuracy in the last significant figure.

We shall not draw the distinction in this text, but the reader is advised:

(*a*) always to use integers for counting when possible; and

(*b*) when integers are not being used, to put in decision boxes inequality signs with a suitable margin of error.

Thus, in the two cases suggested above, it would be wise if possible to use the instruction

$$\boxed{C := C + 1}$$

844

in each case, and to use $C \times \frac{1}{3}$ or $C \div 10$ for calculation; or, if for some reason this is very inconvenient, to write, for example,

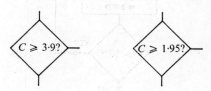

in the decision boxes. $C \geqslant 4$? and $C \geqslant 2$? are definitely wrong.

When a process is to continue until a number is very nearly zero, it is most inconvenient to have to consider positive and negative numbers separately. Indeed, one of the commonest errors in computer programs produced at school seems to be to put

for example, and for the program to end prematurely when A is, say, $-\frac{1}{2}$. We therefore write

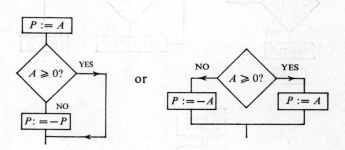

to make P the positive number numerically equal to A. This occurs so frequently that we allow the special instruction

$$P := \text{MOD}\,(A)$$

to summarize the process.

A correct decision, determining whether A is sufficiently close to zero, is then

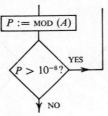

Exercise E

(A desk calculator should be used for this Exercise.)

1. Compare these flow diagrams. What is the answer in each case, and how many times is the loop cycled?

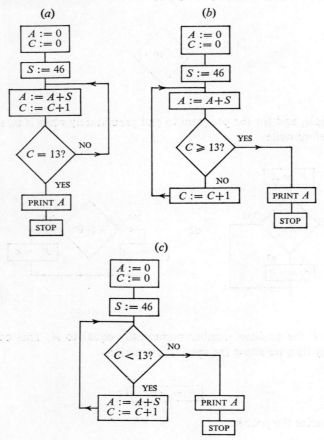

2. Adapt each of the flow diagrams of Question 1 to divide 598 by 46, and carry out each calculation to check your program.

3. Adapt each of the flow diagrams of Question 1 to divide 440 by $13\frac{1}{3}$, and carry out each calculation to check your program.

4. Calculate

$$1 - \frac{1}{1!} + \frac{1}{2!} - \frac{1}{3!} + \frac{1}{4!} - \frac{1}{5!} + \cdots$$

to within 0·001 of the true value, and summarize the process in a flow diagram.

5. Tabulate the values of $x^3 - 3x + 1$ for $x = 0, \frac{1}{5}, \frac{2}{5}, \ldots, 2$ and summarize the process in a flow diagram.

6. HARDER LOOPS

To build up a more complicated program, it is generally wise to start with the innermost loop, if there are to be several, and to work outwards, filling in the final and initial adjustments later. Programs to calculate the mean and the variance of a given set of numbers, and to evaluate $\cos x$ for small x, illustrate this well.

Example 5. Write a program to calculate the mean and variance of a given set of n readings.

We shall assume that the number n of readings is given at the head of the tape. We do not want to waste storage space by using n stores to hold the data, so we use one store only, and build up Σx and Σx^2 simultaneously, over-writing the store into which we read the data after each item has made its contribution.

We allot a store M to indicate how many readings are to come; S to hold the sum, and T to hold the sum of squares, so far; A to hold each reading in turn; and N to hold the number, n, of readings.

The main part of the program may be summarized as:

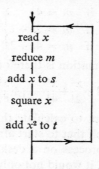

We write the program in three sections, and it is convenient to use *labels*, as in the diagram below, to keep the various parts of the program tidy,

and to give us a means of referring back to other parts of the program
without having to draw control lines. First, we write the section from (1)
to (2); then (unusually) up to (1); and finally from (2) to the end. The
process is self-explanatory.

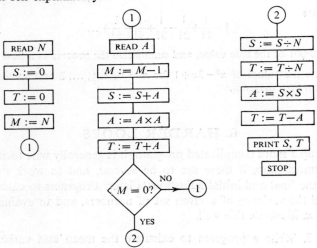

Example 6. Calculate cos *x*, for *x* = 1·0472; (*a*) to four decimal places;
(*b*) to four significant figures; (*c*) using four terms of the series.

We shall use a Taylor approximation for cos *x*, so that we need first to
consider the derivatives of cos *x* at *x* = 0.

Now,

$$f(x) = \cos x \Rightarrow f'(x) = -\sin x \Rightarrow f''(x) = -\cos x \Rightarrow f'''(x) = \sin x,$$

and so on, so that

$$f(0) = 1, \quad f'(0) = 0, \quad f''(0) = -1, \quad f'''(0) = 0$$

and, in general,

$$f^{(m)}(0) = \begin{cases} 1 & \text{if} \quad m = 4n \\ 0 & \text{if} \quad m = 2n+1 \\ -1 & \text{if} \quad m = 4n+2 \end{cases} \quad \text{for some } n \in N.$$

A typical Taylor approximation is therefore

$$1 - \frac{x^2}{2!} + \frac{x^4}{4!} - \frac{x^6}{6!} + \frac{x^8}{8!}.$$

The reader should attempt to calculate this, with *x* = 1·0472. He will
very quickly convince himself that to start afresh as he comes to each new
term is a most inefficient process on a desk calculator; and although it
would work on a computer, it would not only be very untidy but, because
of the large number of multiplications involved, also very wasteful of
computer time.

848

It would be an improvement on this to calculate x^2, and then by successive multiplication to build up and record x^4, x^6, x^8, and so on; and, similarly, to build up $2!$, $4!$, $6!$, $8!$, and so on. But it is probably better to devise a simple repetitive process which calculates each term from the last. Thus to calculate the term in x^6 from the term in x^4 we multiply by $-x^2$ and divide by 5×6; and in general our working may be expressed as follows:

*Increase n by 2.

Multiply the previous term by $-x^2/(n-1)n$

Add the new term to the sum.

Go back to *.

The essential numbers in this calculation are $-x^2$, $(n-1)$, and n, besides the values of the existing term and the existing sum. To make it possible to do the work on a desk calculator, using only one arithmetic operation at a time, we need to work roughly as follows:

$-x^2$	n	Term	Term/$(n-1)$	Term/$(n-1)n$	Sum
$-x^2$	4	$x^4/4!$	?	?	$1-x^2/2!+x^4/4!$
	6		$x^4/5!$		
				$x^4/6!$	
$-x^6/6!$					
					$1-x^2/2!+x^4/4!-x^6/6!$

Here the last entry in each column shows the current value of the expression named.

Now we must choose names for the stores which hold the five essential numbers. By increasing n first to 5 and then to 6, however, we can avoid having a separate store for n and for $(n-1)$; the store holding $-x^2$ we may call P, and the other three N, T, and S, respectively.

It is most important that these stores should hold the correct numbers at the end of each cycle; indeed, this is the essence of the calculation. But provided that this condition is fulfilled, we can use them as we like during the cycle, and store T can therefore be used for all the necessary working. The central part of the program may then be written:

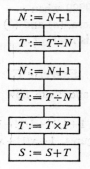

$$N := N+1$$
$$T := T \div N$$
$$N := N+1$$
$$T := T \div N$$
$$T := T \times P$$
$$S := S+T$$

ending with some sort of decision box, to tell the computer whether to begin another cycle or to move to the next part of the program.

In case (c), the decision depends on whether or not N contains the number 6. For different values of x, this is clearly the least useful of the three. In case (a), it is enough to insist that the absolute value of T is less than, say, 10^{-6}; this leaves plenty of margin for error, and, even on a desk calculator, it is advisable to retain six decimal places throughout the work; the final answer can then be rounded appropriately. But in case (b), the most generally useful, it is best to continue until the absolute value of T/S is less than, say, 10^{-6}; and because multiplication is easier than division (and if, for some value of x, S were to be zero at any stage, it would be impossible to form T/S), the best decision is based upon

$$\text{MOD }(T) < \text{MOD }(S) \times 10^{-6}.$$

It only remains to see what N, S, T and P should contain at the beginning of the first cycle; here, the contents must be 0, 1, 1, and $-x^2$, and it is easy to arrange for this. The program then appears as follows:

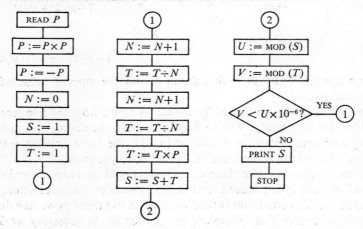

The answer can be achieved in five minutes on a desk calculator, reaching the conclusion 0·499999 when $n = 10$, and therefore giving the required answer as 0·5000. Here, (a) and (b) give the same result; why is (b) very much better when x is near $\frac{1}{2}\pi$?

Exercise F

Perform the following tasks, and write flow diagrams to summarize your working:

1. Sum, to four decimal places, $1 + 1/1! + 1/2! + 1/3! + \ldots + 1/8!$.

2. Sum, to four significant figures, $1 + x/1! + x^2/2! + x^3/3! + \ldots + x^8/8!$, where $x = 0.54$.

850

3. Use an appropriate Taylor approximation for $\sin x$ to compute $\sin 0.74$:
  (a) to four decimal places;
  (b) to four significant figures;
  (c) for five terms of the series.

4. Compute the compound interest on £1000 at $2\frac{1}{2}\%$ for 20 years.

5. Compute the total amount if I invest £50 at the beginning of each year for 20 years, at $2\frac{1}{2}\%$ compound interest.

6. Work out the values of $\binom{14}{i}$ for $i = 0$ to $i = 14$. (Compare p. 759, Question 4.)

7. Work out the binomial probabilities for $n = 6$, $p = \frac{1}{4}$ (that is, the terms of $(\frac{3}{4} + \frac{1}{4}t)^6$).

8. Given that $2\frac{1}{2}$ and 3 are the first two terms:
  (a) of an arithmetic progression,
  (b) of a geometric progression,
calculate the sum of the first fifteen terms of the series.

9. Tabulate the values of $1/(1+x^2)$ from $x = 0$ to $x = 1$ in steps of 0.1, and hence estimate the value of
$$\int_0^1 \frac{1}{1+x^2}\, dx.$$

10. Calculate the Fibonacci numbers, generated by $u_0 = 0$, $u_1 = 1$, and $u_{i+1} = u_i + u_{i-1}$, as far as u_{16}, and also the ratios u_{i+1}/u_i for values of i from 1 to 15.

11. Why can the relation $u_{i+1} = 1.99u_i - u_{i-1}$ be used to generate a table of sines at intervals of 0.1 radian? Carry out the process from 0 to 1.5 radians, and consider how accurate your later results will be.
  (*Hint.* Express $\sin(i+0.1) + \sin(i-0.1)$ in terms of $\sin i$.)

12. Convert the number 11876 to the binary scale, calculating first (a) the most significant, (b) the least significant digit. How do you suppose a computer working in the binary scale would handle decimal input?

7. BRANCHING

Decision boxes are used not only to complete loops, but also to allow for alternative courses of action. Most of the commercial applications of programming, which come under the name 'Data Processing', are concerned with applying simple alternative routines, such as the one in Example 8, to large numbers of input items. But it is also often necessary to build safeguards into general mathematical programs, such as the very simple one in Example 7.

Example 7. Write a flow diagram which will solve the equation $ax = b$ whenever possible.

The basic program is obvious. The interest lies only in allowing for the case $a = 0$. Let us suppose that there is a store E loaded with some output

8-2

which indicates that there is an error in the data, without allowing the computer to embark on the hopeless task of dividing by zero.

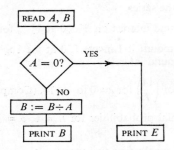

Example 8. Write a flow diagram to compute a quarter's electricity bill, if the first *n* units cost £0·0312 each (where *n* is a number which varies from consumer to consumer), and all subsequent units cost £0·0069 each.

Let us suppose that for each consumer the appropriate number *n*, and the number of units consumed during the quarter, are fed in on a data tape in that order. If a consumer uses more than *n* units, we can think of his bill as a charge of £0·0069 a unit plus a surcharge of £0·0243 × *n*. The only difficulty is to allow for smaller bills.

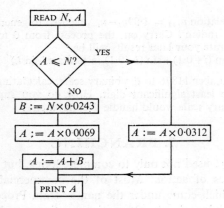

8. FUNCTIONS AND ROUTINES

If the *routine* of Example 8 were needed frequently in a more complicated task, it would be useful to be able to write a single instruction such as

CHARGE (N, A)

which would cause the computer to carry out the whole program without the need for the programmer to write it out more than once.

852

Similarly, in Section 5, we defined the simple *function* MOD (X), which we use whenever we need it.

Nowadays all computers have facilities for storing functions and routines so that programmers can call upon them when they need them, and they will also have a stock of *library* functions permanently available, of which some of the simplest are:

MOD (X); SQRT (X); INT (X) (the largest integer not greater than X).

SIN (X), COS (X) and their inverses ARCSIN (X), ARCCOS (X); LOG (X), ANTILOG (X).

It is important that the precise conditions under which these functions operate should be carefully defined, and in Exercise G this has been done.

Exercise G

1. Write a flow diagram to work out gas bills, given the number of therms supplied. The charge is £0·1685 for each of the first 26 therms, £0·1350 for each of the next 74, and £0·1080 thereafter.

2. Write a flow diagram to calculate the postage payable on a letter, given its weight. (Use INT (X), if you need it.)

3. Write a flow diagram:
    (*a*) to convert a time given in hours, minutes and seconds into seconds;
    (*b*) to reverse the process.

4. Christmas Day fell on a Monday in 1967. Write a flow diagram to print out the day on which it falls for the rest of the century. (Sunday = 1, Monday = 2, etc. Use INT ($X/7$) if you like.)

5. Write a flow diagram to print out wages slips. The input is: N the worker's number; H, the number of hours worked; R, the rate per hour; D, the deductions. The output is N, H, R, D, and W, the total wage. Work in pounds throughout; use 1, 40, 0·5, 5 for a dry run.

6. Modify the diagram of Question 5 to allow for K hours worked at a higher rate S.

7. Modify the diagram of Question 6 to print out the wages slips for all the workers in a factory, and to total H, K, D and W, and to print out the number of wage slips made out.

8. The Ruritanian tax laws are very simple. Non-taxable allowances for each person are 10 % of his gross income as earned income allowance: also ø200 as personal allowance. The first ø1000 of taxable income is taxed at 50 %, the rest at 80 %. Find the tax on incomes of ø200, ø250, ø500, ø1000, ø2000, and write a flow diagram to produce the tax, TAX (X), on any income øX.

9. In a Ruritanian factory, wages are paid weekly by computer. The input consists of the *annual* rate of pay; 8 % of a man's *gross* income is retained for the superannuation fund, and not for tax; and the output consists of gross weekly pay, superannuation and tax deductions, and net weekly pay. Give the output for annual rates of ø200, ø250, ø500, ø1000, and ø2000, and write a flow diagram to produce the wages slips.

10. Modify the flow diagram of Question 9 to sum each of the outputs for the whole factory, and to print out the totals at the end.

11. Write a program to put any number into standard form.

12. Given a function SQRT (X) which finds the square root of any number between 1 and 100, write a flow diagram to find the square root of any positive number.

13. Given a function ARCTAN (X) which finds the angle (in circular measure) whose tangent is X, where X lies between 0 and 1, write a flow diagram to find the angle between $-\frac{1}{2}\pi$ and $+\frac{1}{2}\pi$ with any given tangent.

14. Given a function COS (X) which finds the cosine of any angle X (in circular measure) between 0 and $\frac{1}{2}\pi$, write a flow diagram to find the cosine of any angle.

15. Modify the flow diagram of Question 14 to print a table of cosines of all angles between $0°$ and $360°$, at intervals of $10°$.

16. Write a flow diagram to print in standard form: (a) the sum, (b) the product, and (c) the quotient of two positive numbers given in standard form.

17. Write a program to solve the equation $ax^2+bx+c = 0$, printing '999' if there are not two distinct real roots.

18. Write a flow diagram, using the functions LOG (X) and ANTILOG (X), to evaluate
$$\left(1+\frac{1}{N}\right)^N$$
and use a table of logarithms for a dry run with $N = 1, 5, 10, 100, 1000$. Comment on the program and its results, and state what accuracy might be expected from a machine which works to eight decimal figures.

19. Write a flow diagram, using the function INT (X), to print out the smallest factor of a given number.

20. Modify the flow diagram of Question 19 to find all the prime factors of a given number. Why is this not in fact a useful program for discovering large prime numbers?

9. ITERATIVE PROCEDURES

In view of the high speed at which computers work, it is perhaps not surprising that mathematical processes involving iteration play a considerable part in the type of problem which such machines are used to solve. We have devoted a good deal of attention in earlier chapters to such processes, and here we need only a short consideration of how such processes can be expressed in flow diagrams.

The main part of the calculation clearly lies inside a loop. The initial guess is manipulated to provide a better guess; this second estimate is manipulated in exactly the same way to produce a better guess still, and so forth. In general, it is useful not to over-write the last two estimates—if only to see by how much the estimate has improved—and we can summarize the procedure thus:

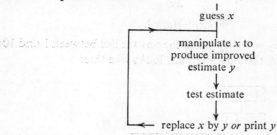

We have already seen (Example 6) how to end such a program, by taking a specified number of loops; by continuing until the correction is less than a specified number; or by continuing until the correction is less than a specified fraction of the present estimate; here, we need only consider how to make the initial guess.

It is one of the beauties of Newton's method of solving equations that almost any initial guess will lead us quite quickly to a solution. However, when there are several solutions (as in the case of a polynomial equation), or when it is not immediately obvious how the function behaves, it is often wise to start by applying a quite unsophisticated trial-and-error method, such as computing the values of $f(x)$ for small integral values of x, to find an initial estimate with some element of deliberate choice in it. In difficult cases, it may even be wise to find the roots of $f'(x) = 0$, because of the way in which they separate the roots of $f(x) = 0$. Here, we suppose that some sensible method has been found of making a first guess.

At this point, it is convenient to allow, purely as an abbreviation, instructions such as

$$A := A - (A \times A - B)/(2 \times A)$$

which can easily be broken down into a sequence of binary operations; this will allow the structure of the flow diagram to appear more clearly, and, although for a desk calculator this breaking down process is in fact necessary, it will save time in the initial stages of writing these flow diagrams.

Example 9. Write a flow diagram to find the square root of any number between 1 and 100, using Newton's method.

We can treat the problem as one of finding a solution of $x^2 - a = 0$, where a is a given number between 1 and 100. Now, Newton's method for solving $f(x) = 0$ is the iterative one of replacing an estimate x_i by x_{i+1}, where

$$x_{i+1} = x_i - \frac{f(x_i)}{f'(x_i)}.$$

In this case,

$$x_{i+1} = x_i - \frac{x_i^2 - a}{2x_i}$$

$$= \tfrac{1}{2}x_i + \tfrac{1}{2}(a/x_i).$$

If then we start with $x_1 = 3$, say (since the answer lies between 1 and 10), and continue from there, the flow diagram looks like this:

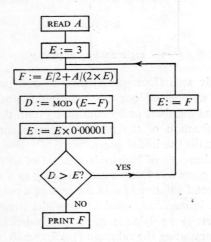

A diagram illustrates this process for the case when $A = 2$.

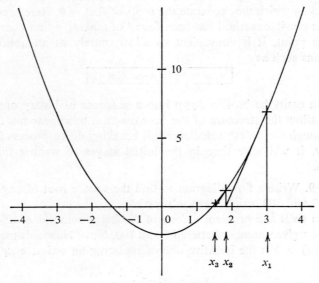

Fig. 4

It is interesting to see how the sequence develops on a desk calculator, retaining seven decimal places:

$$x_1 = 3{\cdot}0000000, \quad x_2 = 1{\cdot}8333333, \quad x_3 = 1{\cdot}4621203,$$

$$x_4 = 1{\cdot}4149984, \quad x_5 = 1{\cdot}4142138, \quad x_6 = 1{\cdot}4142136,$$

which entitles us to print the answer $1{\cdot}41421$. Only the first three approximations can be seen on the diagram above.

It would be more economical, in fact, to start with $x = 7$ than with $x = 3$; the mean value of $\sqrt{x}$ for this interval is $6{\cdot}727$.

Example 10. Investigate the sequence given by $x_1 = 3$, $x_{i+1} = \frac{1}{2}x_i + 1/x_i$.

In this case, we are solving an equation of the form $x = f(x)$, instead of $f(x) = 0$; but the flow diagram and the sequence generated are the same as in Example 9. The diagram illustrates the process '$y: = f(x); x: = y$', where $f(x) = \frac{1}{2}x + 1/x$.

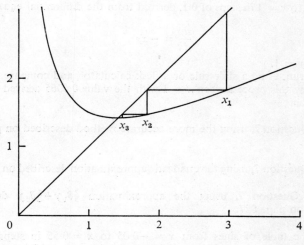

Fig. 5

Exercise H

Write flow diagrams to fulfil the following tasks:

1. Find the cube root of a positive number.

2. Find a root of $2x^2 + 3x - 4 = 0$ by Newton's method, and find and check the other root.

3. Use an iteration $x_{i+1} = a + b/x_i$ (where a, b are positive) to solve the equation $x^2 - 1\cdot5x - 2 = 0$. Draw a diagram, and find the first few terms of the sequence. (Find the positive root only; what happens if x_0 is negative?)

4. For angles less than $0\cdot1$ radians, $x - \frac{1}{6}x^3$ is regarded as a sufficiently accurate estimate of $\sin x$. Use an iteration $x_{i+1} = 0\cdot08 + \frac{1}{6}x_i^3$ to solve the equation $\sin x = 0\cdot08$, draw a diagram, and explain why the process works.

5. For angles less than $0\cdot1$ radians, $1 - \frac{1}{2}x^2 + \frac{1}{24}x^4$ is a good estimate of $\cos x$. Use an iteration $y_{i+1} = 2(1 - a) + \frac{1}{12}y_i^2$ to solve $\cos x = 0\cdot95$ by finding the value of x^2.

6. The cost of an electrical plant in thousands of pounds is reckoned to be about $(2 + n/80 + 230/n)$, where n is the number of units of a particular type used. Find the number n which minimizes this by systematic trial, and also by Newton's method. Compare the two processes.

Questions 7 to 10 refer to the methods of Chapter 27, Section 6.

7. Use the method described in Example 12, page 820, to tabulate values of y, from $x = 0$ to $x = 1$ in steps of $0\cdot1$, derived from the differential equation

$$\frac{dy}{dx} = -xy$$

if $x = 0 \Rightarrow y = 1$.

Do a dry run, using a slide rule or a desk calculator, and compare the value of y given by this process when $x = 1$ with the value $0\cdot6065$ derived from the exact solution.

8. Repeat Question 7, using the more accurate method described on pages 821 and 822.

9. Repeat Question 7, using the quadratic approximation described on page 823.

10. Repeat Question 7, using the approximation $\frac{2}{3}\delta_1 y + \frac{1}{3}\delta_2 y$ derived in Question 8 on page 827.

11. Copy the table of sines from $x = -0\cdot05$ to $x = 0\cdot55$ in steps of $0\cdot05$. Generate a table of cosines from $x = 0$ to $x = 0\cdot5$ in steps of $0\cdot1$:
   (*a*) by an approximate differentiation process;
   (*b*) by approximate integration, using the trapezium rule;
   (*c*) by approximate integration, using Simpson's rule, and
   (*d*) by a method analogous to Question 8.
   Compare each of these tables with the true values.
   Can you see why numerical integration is a better process than numerical differentiation?

10. MODIFICATION

We have frequently found it useful in our previous work to use the *suffix* notation x_1, x_2, x_3, a_{11}, a_{12}, and so forth, not only in iterative processes, but also in three-dimensional vector work, in matrix algebra, and in statistical calculations. The advantage of the notation is that we can talk generally about x_i, a_{ij}, and so forth, and allow i and j to take a whole range of different values successively.

One of the greatest advances in computer design was made when it was found possible to reproduce this convenient device by *modification* of the addresses of storage locations. If we adopt an address style $A(1)$, $A(7)$, $A(22)$, and so forth, where the suffixes are generally written in this way for convenience of typing, once we can make the computer interpret the address $A(I)$ as $A(1)$ when the contents of I are 1, and as $A(22)$ when the contents of I are 22, we shall find a number of advantages.

First, we can refer conveniently to many more stores (and the capacity of a modern computer is reckoned in thousands of stores) than was possible when we were restricted to single letters of the alphabet. Indeed, the possibility of double suffixes $A(I, J)$—in principle very little more difficult—makes the number of possible addresses almost unlimited.

But, more important, we can handle large amounts of data systematically by means of the loops with which we are already familiar. Thus if we want to read in a hundred data items, all we need to do is to write

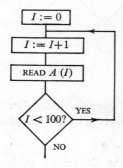

and clearly a similar system can be applied for summing, finding maxima, and so forth, with as many data items as are required.

A great value of this form of modification lies in its characteristic of retaining data items for subsequent use. In Example 5 above, for example, data items were read and added into S, and then over-written and lost for ever. Further calculations involving the data items—perhaps to apply a more efficient process—would require them all to be read again. Again, in the evaluation of a polynomial, especially if it is to be tabulated, as is so often required, it is useful to have the coefficients stored rather than to have to read the data again repeatedly.

Example 11. Tabulate the values of $a_n x^n + a_{n-1} x^{n-1} + \ldots + a_1 x + a_0$ for values of x from 0 to 1 in steps of 0·01, where $a_0, a_1, \ldots, a_n$ are given on tape in that order.

We use the nesting method suggested by Figure 2, on p. 70 of Book 1, as follows:

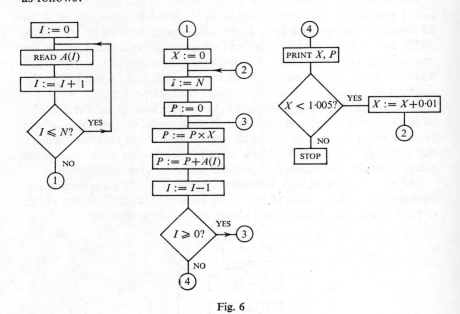

Fig. 6

Notice that in the 'read' loop the index I must increase, but that in the nesting process the coefficients are given in the opposite order, and I must decrease.

Example 12. Print out the frequency table for a population of N examination marks, given in a random order and expressed as integral percentages.

We shall use the store $A(I)$ to count the number of candidates who obtain I marks, and we shall use the store N to count how many more candidates are to come.

The first block of instructions sets the stores $A(I)$, $I = 0$ to 100, to zero; the second adds 1 to store $A(I)$ whenever the number I is read from the tape; and the third prints out the results.

860

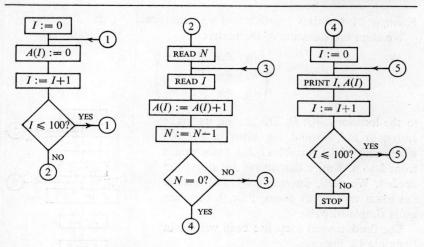

Example 13. Find the scalar product of two $n \times 1$ vectors.

We suppose that the vectors are already stored in $A(1)$ to $A(N)$ and in $B(1)$ to $B(N)$, where N is also the address of a store holding n. Then, with the obvious notation, we want to find

$$\sum_{i=1}^{i=n} a_i b_i.$$

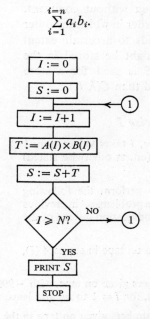

This simple program forms the basis of Example 14, which uses the slightly harder double suffix $A(1, 4)$, for instance.

Example 14. Multiply together two $n \times n$ matrices.

We store the elements of the matrix

$$\begin{pmatrix} a_{11} & a_{12} & a_{13} & \cdots \\ a_{21} & a_{22} & a_{23} & \cdots \\ a_{31} & a_{32} & a_{33} & \cdots \\ \cdots\cdots\cdots\cdots\cdots\cdots \end{pmatrix}$$

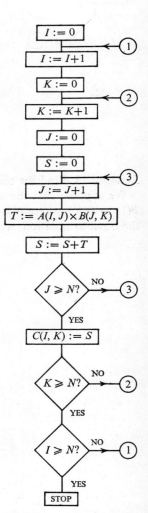

in the locations $A(I, J)$. The second matrix is stored in $B(J, K)$ and the third in $C(I, K)$, where each of the variables I, J, K takes values from 1 to n. Notice that so far $3n^2$ stores are needed. We shall, for simplicity, not include the READ and PRINT loops, though they are quite simple to write.

The fundamental loop has been written in Example 13, because

$$c_{ik} = \sum_{j=1}^{j=n} a_{ij} b_{jk}$$

is the abstract expression which describes the multiplication process.

The program is given without comment, except to say that the order in which the outer loops are taken depends to a certain extent on how the arrays might be stored in the computer, and that S is used for a store which is quicker to find than $C(I, K)$.

Exercise I

(Throughout this exercise, i takes values from 1 to m; j from 1 to n; k (unless otherwise stated) from 1 to p.)

Write flow diagrams to perform the following tasks, many of which solve problems set in previous exercises by the use of modification instead of the use of a data tape:

1. Store m numbers given on tape in stores $A(I)$, for $I = 1$ to m.

2. Store a series of numbers given on tape, with -999 as a signal that the series has ended, in stores $A(I)$, for $I = 1$ to m, and leave the number m in store M.

3. Store a series of mn numbers given on tape in the order

$$a_{11}, a_{12}, \ldots, a_{1n}, a_{21}, a_{22}, \ldots, a_{2n}, \ldots, a_{m1}, a_{m2}, \ldots, a_{mn},$$

in stores $A(I, J)$.

862

4. Print out the contents of the stores (a) in Question 1, (b) in Question 3. (See below.)

5. Find the most efficient method you can of storing in the stores $A(I)$ the numbers: (a) i, (b) $2i-1$, (c) i^2, (d) 2^i, (e) the integral part of the square root of i.

Questions 1–4 deal adequately with input and output; for the remaining questions, assume that (for example) the number a_i is already stored in $A(I)$, and that the answers are required in the stores stated; do not give orders for printing out, unless specifically asked to do so.

6. Store the sum $\sum\limits_{i=1}^{i=m} a_i$ in storage location S.

7. Store the largest of $\{a_i\}$ in store M.

8. Store the mean of $\{a_i\}$ in store M.

9. Store the greatest, the least, the range, and the mean of the greatest and least members of $\{a_i\}$ in stores G, L, R, M.

10. Store the number, the mean, and the variance of $\{a_i\}$ in stores N, M, V.

11. Store the deviations from the mean in the stores $B(I)$, the mean absolute deviation in M, and the standard deviation in S.

12. Sort $\{a_i\}$ into ascending order in the stores $B(I)$, by using Question 7 repeatedly, and store the median (assuming m odd) in Q.

13. Print out the values of

$$\sum_{i=0}^{i=m} a_i x^i / i!$$

for $x = 0$ to 1 by steps of 0·01.

14. If $\{a_i\}$ and $\{b_j\}$ are stored in ascending order of magnitude, merge them into a single list stored in ascending order in $C(K)$, for $k = 1$ to $k = m+n$.

15. If the elements of a $m \times n$ matrix are stored in $A(I, J)$, and of a $n \times p$ matrix in $B(J, K)$, store their product in $C(I, K)$.

*16. Sort $\{a_i\}$ into ascending order in the stores $B(I)$, given that $m = 16$, by using Question 14 repeatedly, with lists of length 1, 2, 4, 8 respectively.

17. Sort $\{a_i\}$ into ascending order by exchanging contents of consecutive stores until the smallest is in $A(m)$, and so forth.

18. Print out all the permutations of the natural numbers: (a) 1 to 3, (b) 1 to 4, (c) 1 to 5, and (d) 1 to 6.

19. If m is even and $\{a_i\}$ are the values of $f(x_i)$, where $x_i = p+i(q-p)/m$, use Simpson's rule to find the approximation to

$$\int_p^q f(x)\,dx.$$

(Here i takes values from 0 to m; $x_0 = p$, $x_m = q$.)

20. Find the coefficients of the quotient, and the remainder, when

$$a_m x^m + a_{m-1} x^{m-1} + \ldots + a_1 x + a_0$$

is divided by $(x-c)$.

863

*11. COMPUTER LANGUAGES

It is not necessary for this course to use any equipment more complicated than a desk calculator. The lessons learnt in preparing flow diagrams of this type are valuable in themselves, and the student should by now be familiar with all the most important ideas of programming.

Nevertheless, since many schools have the chance occasionally to use a computer, and since the flow diagrams of this chapter already come very close to a form that a computer can obey, it may be of interest to suggest some problems which have been solved successfully in schools with the use of a computer, and to translate a few programs into actual computer languages.

It is interesting to see how quickly computer languages have developed in the few years of their history. For the first computers, virtually the only facilities that the programmer could use were transfer (store locations being numbered), addition into one special store (an accumulator), comparison of two numbers, and (depending on the result of the comparison, or independently of it) a jump facility. It is in fact quite easy to break these operations down even further, and to work in terms of '.and' and 'or' and 'not' elements, or fewer still, but the work is excessively tedious, and quite unnecessary for the casual user in these days.

The next stage was the stage of autocodes, which would allow binary operations, such as ×, /, +, and −, with even a few 'library' functions, such as SQRT, permanently stored in the machine. Stores were named by convenient letters, or combinations of letters and figures, and a single instruction was enough to set in motion a whole sequence of operations which would previously have had to be coded one by one.

After this, the development of high-level languages began very rapidly, and in the early 1960s international conferences were held to standardize some of them. Elaborate 'compilers' were provided with most moderate-sized computers—a 'compiler' is a sort of electronic dictionary, which will translate the user's instructions, often very similar to those in this chapter, into machine instructions—and with them, routines for the detection, and, occasionally, the correction, of errors in the programs.

Two of the languages most commonly met with by schools in this country are introduced briefly in the Appendix to this volume; but it is emphasized that although the information given there is correct it is incomplete, and anyone intending to make use of a computer with such a compiler must find out about the local conventions, especially about input and output, and should study fuller accounts of the languages for himself.

The following exercise contains questions suitable for practice when a computer is available. Many occur elsewhere in the book: some involve

864

ideas from the Further Mathematics course. They are collected here for convenience. They vary greatly in difficulty, and appropriate selection should be made.

*Miscellaneous Exercise

Write computer programs to perform the following tasks: the following notes may help.

(*a*) Always get someone else to check your program carefully.

(*b*) It is sometimes interesting to print out some intermediate results, to show how the calculation has been going.

(*c*) Put no more than 'READ' and 'PRINT' for input and output, because you will certainly have to adapt them at a later stage.

(*d*) Write general programs, but choose particular data to feed in, preferably from problems you have solved previously by other methods.

Tabulation

1. Write a program to tabulate the squares and cubes of the natural numbers from 1 to 20.

2. Tabulate $1/i$ and $\sum_{r=1}^{r=i} 1/r$ for the natural numbers from 1 to 20.

3. Tabulate $n!$ and $\log n!$ for $n = 1$ to $n = 12$.

4. Print out the value of $(1 + 1/n)^n$ for $n = 1$ to $n = 20$.

5. Given a function $\text{SIN}(X)$, where X is in radians, print a table of sines, in degrees, from $0°$ to $90°$ in steps of $5°$.

6. Print out a table of areas of circles and volumes of spheres with radii from 1 to 10 cm.

7. Print out a table of values of the function $ax^2 + bx + c$ for x from 0.0 to 2.0 in steps of 0.1. (Consider what must be *added* at each step.)

8. Print out a table of values of a quartic function for the same values as in Question 7.

9. Use Newton's method to tabulate the square and cube roots of the numbers from 1 to 20, to four significant figures.

10. Use a Taylor approximation to tabulate $\sin x$ and $\cos x$ in steps of 0.1 from 0.0 to 2.0, to four decimal places.

Expansions in series

11. Find approximate values of e and of $1/e$ by summing the series
$$1 \pm 1/1! + 1/2! \pm 1/3! + 1/4! \pm \dots . \quad \text{(See p. 893.)}$$
How many terms are needed to achieve six-figure accuracy?

12. Use a Taylor approximation for $(1 + x)^{\frac{1}{2}}$ to find the square roots of numbers from 1 to 1.5 by steps of 0.05.

13. Use a Taylor approximation for $\tan^{-1} x$ to estimate $\tan^{-1}(\frac{1}{5})$. (See p. 482.)

14. Approximate to π by using the fact that $\frac{1}{4}\pi = 4 \tan^{-1}(\frac{1}{5}) - \tan^{-1}(\frac{1}{239})$.

15. Approximate to π by using the fact that

$$1^{-2} + 2^{-2} + 3^{-2} + \ldots + n^{-2} \simeq \frac{1}{6}\pi^2.$$

Number patterns

16. Print out the first fifteen rows of Pascal's Triangle.

17. Print out the first twenty terms of Fibonacci's sequence, generated by $u_1 = 1$, $u_2 = 1$, $u_{n+1} = u_n + u_{n-1}$, and the first twenty approximations to the Golden Section, u_{n+1}/u_n. (See Question 9, p. 38.)

18. The ancient Greeks approximated to $\sqrt{2}$ by the sequence p_n/q_n, where $p_1 = q_1 = 1$, $p_{n+1} = p_n + 2q_n$, $q_{n+1} = q_n + p_n$. Print out the first twenty values of p_n, q_n, and p_n/q_n, and compare them with the successive approximations of Newton's method, with $x_1 = 1$.

19. Print out all prime numbers less than 1000. (Test each odd number k for odd factors less than $\sqrt{k}$.)

20. An early method of generating 'pseudo-random' numbers was the mid-squares method. Thus, $2736^2 = 07485696$, and the successor to 2736 was 4856. Regarding this sequence as generating pairs of two-digit random numbers, starting with 27 36 48 56, print out forty such numbers and their mean and variance. (This is in fact a poor method; the sequences following the 5th and 30th sets of four numbers show why.)

Linear equations

21. Reduce three equations in three unknowns to echelon form, by row operations only, and hence solve the equations. (Use a check sum.) (See p. 594.)

22. Solve a set of 3×3 equations with identical left-hand sides by inversion and multiplication. (See Chapter 42.)

23. Solve by the method of relaxation:
    (*a*) two equations in two unknowns;
    (*b*) three equations in three unknowns. (See p. 599.)

Equations in one unknown

24. Solve $x^3 + x + 1 = 0$ by trial and error, working first in integers then in tenths, hundredths, etc., to four decimal places.

25. Solve the equation $x^2 = \cos x$ to four decimal places.

26. Find all three roots of $x^3 - 3x + 1 = 0$ to six decimal places.

27. Solve any quadratic equation, printing out the real and imaginary parts of any complex roots.

866

28. Find the solutions of a cubic equation by 'bracketing'—starting with the step of 1 needed to make the polynomial change sign, and halving the step successively, to six places of decimals. When will this method fail?

Integration

29. Approximate to π by using the Trapezium Rule to estimate

$$\int_0^1 \frac{4}{1+x^2}\,dx,$$

with twenty strips. What accuracy do you expect?

30. Repeat Question 29, using Simpson's Rule.

31. Repeat Questions 29 and 30, using a hundred strips.

32. Solve the differential equation $dy/dx = 1/x$, subject to the condition that $y = 0$ when $x = 1$, by taking steps of 0.1 over the interval $(0.4, 3.0)$ in x. (See p. 791, Question 5.)

33. If the acceleration (in m/s²) of a rocket at two second intervals after take-off is 0, 10, 30, 80, 160, 250, investigate how the speed and distance travelled vary over the first ten seconds.

34. A stone is projected with an initial velocity $\begin{pmatrix} 40 \\ 50 \end{pmatrix}$, in m/s, and it is subject to gravity, and (*a*) to no air resistance, (*b*) to a resistance $\frac{1}{100}mv^2$ directly opposing the velocity, (*c*) to a resistance $\frac{1}{20}mv^2$ directly opposing the velocity. Investigate its motion. (Write one program, with three values of k.)

35. Show that if $dy/dt = 4z - y$ and $dz/dt = -z - 4y$,

$$\frac{d^2y}{dt^2} + 2\frac{dy}{dt} + 17y = 0.$$

This describes the oscillation of a certain physical system, which is started in motion at time $t = 0$ with $y = 4$, $dy/dt = 0$. Investigate the motion.

Probability and statistics

36. Sort a set of (integral) marks, given in random order, into a grouped frequency table, and estimate their mean and variance.

37. Print out the Binomial frequencies, calculating their mean and standard deviation, for chosen values of n, a, b.

38. Two judges place ten candidates in order in a beauty contest. Kendall's Rank Correlation Coefficient, to measure the degree of agreement, depends on the number of agreements and disagreements between the judges over the ordering of the 45 pairs to be found among ten candidates; it is defined as

(number of agreements − number of disagreements)/45.

39. The Normal frequency function, where t is measured in s.d.'s from the mean, is $(2\pi)^{-\frac{1}{2}}.\exp(-\frac{1}{2}t^2)$. Tabulate its integral from 0 to 3, in steps of 0.1. (This gives a cumulative frequency function, CUM (X).)

40. Assuming that a function CUM (X), defined as in Question 39, with

$$\text{CUM } (0) = 0,$$

is available, and given that recruits to the Army have mean chest measurement 94 cm with S.D. 4·8 cm, estimate how many will have chest measurements under 85 cm, 85–90 cm, 90–95 cm, ..., over 105 cm.

41. The correlation coefficient between pairs of readings (x_i, y_i) is calculated as $s_{xy}/s_x s_y$, where s_x, s_y are the S.D.'s of the two separate populations, and s_{xy} is their covariance, calculated as

$$\Sigma x_i y_i/N - \Sigma x_i/N . \Sigma y_i/N.$$

42. Devise a method of estimating the sextiles of a population such as that of Question 41.

43. Write a program to find the mean, variance, skewness and kurtosis of a set of data, given in the form of a grouped frequency table. (See p. 346.)

Commercial

44. Find the letter post and the parcel post on a package of any admissible weight.

45. Find the amount to which £1000 grows when invested at compound interest:
(*a*) at $2\frac{1}{2}\%$ for 20 years;
(*b*) at 5% for 10 years.

46. Repeat Question 52, if the £1000 is invested:
(*a*) at £50 annually;
(*b*) at £100 annually.

47. Write a program to estimate the income tax payable, allowing for personal and other fixed allowances, earned income allowance, and the different rates of tax, on various incomes.

48. Write a wages program as in Exercise G, Question 10.

Sorting

49. Find the greatest and least of a set of numbers given on tape.

50. Merge two correctly ordered lists of data into a single list also in ascending order.

51. Sort a set of 16 numbers into ascending order by repeatedly applying Question 50.

52. Sort a set of 16 numbers into ascending order by exchanging consecutive pairs of numbers until the greatest is last, and repeating the process as often as necessary.

53. Arrange a matrix so that the greatest element is a_{11}, the greatest element not now in row 1 or column 1 is a_{22}, and so on.

Minimizing

54. Minimize (*a*) by trial and error, (*b*) directly by calculus a function $ax + b/x$. (What is the condition for the function to have a minimum?)

55. Maximize the function xy^2z^3, if x, y, z are positive numbers such that $x+y+z = 1$.

(Start at, say, $x = 0{\cdot}3$, $y = 0{\cdot}3$, $z = 0{\cdot}4$, and adjust x and y (making corresponding adjustments in z) as follows: taking steps of $0{\cdot}1$, increase or decrease x, keeping y constant, while the function increases; then increase or decrease y, keeping x constant. Repeat for steps of $0{\cdot}01$, $0{\cdot}001$, etc.)

56. Devise a method for solving a Linear Programming problem in two variables by trial and error. Then read an account of a method for solving such a problem by the simplex tableau method, and write a program to do so.

57. Given the matrix of distances between five towns in pairs, find the shortest 'round tour', starting and ending at the same point, and visiting each town just once.

Miscellaneous

58. Print out the natural numbers from 1 to 100, except that if the number contains a 7 or is divisible by 7 it is replaced by 999.

59. Print out the dates of Easter Day (from the information given in a Prayer Book about the method of calculation) from 1950 to 2000.

60. Given the date, find the day of the week for any day this century.

REVISION EXERCISES

25. BINOMIAL PROBABILITY FUNCTIONS

1. Assuming that boys and girls are born with equal probability, what is the probability that a family of six children has more boys than girls?

2. Three married couples went to a dance together. They decided that before each dance they would draw lots to determine partners. Mr A would draw first, followed by Mr B, leaving Mr C his partner. There were 24 dances.

(a) What is the probability that Mr A danced with his wife exactly three times?

(b) What is the probability that no husband danced with his wife all evening?

(c) What is the probability that each husband had the last dance with his own wife?

3. If the probability of rain on any given day is 1/3, what are the probabilities that in a given week

(a) there is no rain;

(b) there are exactly three consecutive dry days;

(c) there are at least two dry days?

4. If on average one person in fifty is left-handed, how many people would you need to have together in order to be 95 % certain of having at least one left-hander in the group?

With this group, what is the chance that there will in fact be just two left-handers?

5. Use the binomial theorem to calculate $10^{0.3}$ to three places of decimals by first calculating $1.024^{-0.1}$.

How can you quickly check the accuracy of your answer from the tables?

6. In the game of Scrabble, there are 44 vowels (counting the blanks) and 56 consonants. I pick out 7 letters at random; what is the chance that I get 3 vowels and 4 consonants?

(a) By considering the possible numbers of vowels drawn, prove that

$$\binom{44}{0}\binom{56}{7} + \binom{44}{1}\binom{56}{6} + \binom{44}{2}\binom{56}{5} + \ldots + \binom{44}{7}\binom{56}{0} = \binom{100}{7}.$$

(b) Generalize this argument to find the sum of

$$\binom{n}{0}\binom{m}{r} + \binom{n}{1}\binom{m}{r-1} + \binom{n}{2}\binom{m}{r-2} + \ldots + \binom{n}{r}\binom{m}{0}; \quad r < m, r < n.$$

26. PROBABILITY PARAMETERS

1. The output of a factory making radio valves is tested by selecting random samples of 5 valves and counting the number of defective valves in a sample. The following data are obtained:

Number of defectives in a sample of 5	0	1	2	3	4	5
Number of samples	35	15	9	0	1	0

On this evidence what do you suggest as the most likely proportion of defectives actually being turned out?

2. In a type of skittles at a fair, there are three pins to be knocked down. Each pin knocked over scores 1 point. It is as easy to fell two pins as it is to miss altogether, but it is twice as hard as this to fell a single pin, as also to knock down all three. Write down the probability generator for one throw.

Use this to give, as fractions, the probabilities of the various possible scores after three throws (the pins being put up after each throw), and also the 'expected' total score. If it costs 5 pence for three shies, will it be more remunerative for the showman to offer a prize of £0.12½ for a score of 6 or more, or a prize of £0.25 for a score of 7 or more?

3. For the probability model of Question 2, calculate (a) the variance, (b) the skewness, of the pattern of scores with three shies.

One might think that the game favoured an even total score; do you think this is so, and how could you test it?

4. A small boy is collecting car numbers. Suppose for the moment he is only interested in the last digit of the numbers. How many cars must he expect to note before he has collected the ten digits 0 to 9 in the correct order?

If, however, he merely notes down the digits in any order, so long as they are different from the ones he already has, how many must he expect to see now before he has a complete set of digits?

(*Hint*: when he has, say, three digits noted down, what is the probability of the next one he sees being different from these three? What then is the expected number of cars to be seen before he gets a new digit?)

5. Answer the two parts of Question 4 for the full numbers, 999 in all. Use the fact that $1+\frac{1}{2}+\frac{1}{3}+\frac{1}{4}+\frac{1}{5}+\ldots+(1/n)$ is approximately $\log_e n$.

6. It can be assumed that, for a binomial system with a large number of trials, 95 % of the outcomes will lie within two standard deviations of the mean. If I throw a die 1000 times, how many sixes ought to make me suspicious that the die is biased, if my suspicions are aroused by events with a probability of less than 0·05?

27. INTRODUCTION TO DIFFERENTIAL EQUATIONS

1. Sketch some solution curves of the differential equation

$$\frac{dy}{dx} = 1 - \frac{1}{x+y},$$

noting the locus of turning points and where the gradient is discontinuous.

2. Given that $dy/dx = xy-4$, find d^2y/dx^2 in terms of x and y. Hence show the regions of the plane in which the solution curves of this differential equation satisfy the inequalities

(a) $dy/dx > 0$, $d^2y/dx^2 > 0$;　　(b) $dy/dx > 0$, $d^2y/dx^2 < 0$;

(c) $dy/dx < 0$, $d^2y/dx^2 > 0$;　　(d) $dy/dx < 0$, $d^2y/dx^2 < 0$.

Sketch some of the solution curves.

871

3. Use a step-by-step method, with $0 \cdot 2$ as the step-length, to estimate the value of y when $x = 1$, given that

$$dy/dx = 1 + y^2 \quad \text{and} \quad y = 0 \quad \text{when} \quad x = 0.$$

Compare your value of y with the exact value when $x = 1$.

Can you suggest a way of improving your estimate? (O.C.)

4. Write a flow diagram for carrying out a step-by-step solution of the simultaneous differential equations

$$dy/dx = -z, \quad dz/dx = y, \quad \text{given} \quad y = 1 \quad \text{and} \quad z = 0 \quad \text{at} \quad x = 0.$$

Carry out the solution with a step-interval of $0 \cdot 2$, until y becomes zero. When would you expect this to happen?

5. Solve the differential equation

$$dy/dx + y^2(x-1)^2 = 0,$$

giving the general solution and also the solution for which $y = 1$ when $x = 0$. Sketch a graph showing the relation of this solution to the others.

6. Find a differential equation for the family of curves

$$y = kx + x^2 + k^2, \quad \text{where } k \text{ varies.}$$

Verify that $y = 3x^2/4$ satisfies the differential equation, but is not a member of the family. Explain this with a sketch of the family and the curve $y = 3x^2/4$.

28. PROGRAMMING

1. Use a desk calculator to find the total sum credited to an investor on 31 December 1974, if he invests £60 on 1 January 1968 and thereafter at six-monthly intervals, and if 2 % of the existing sum is added as interest on 30 June and 3 December each year.

2. Write a flow diagram to print out the series of rational approximations to $\sqrt{2}$ (known to the ancient Greeks) given by $r_n = p_n/q_n$, until $q_n \times q_{n-1} > 10^5$, where

$$p_{n+1} = p_n + 2q_n \quad \text{and} \quad q_{n+1} = p_n + q_n \quad \text{and} \quad p_1 = q_1 = 1.$$

3. Write a flow diagram to print out the probabilities of throwing just i sixes in a series of eight throws of a fair die, for $i = 0, 1, 2, ..., 8$.

Modify your diagram to print out the probabilities of throwing not more than i sixes, under the same conditions.

4. Draw up a flow diagram to print out the number of mathematics periods to be taught each week in a large school, under the following conditions.

The school is organized in eight forms, and children must be taught in sets drawn wholly from one form. In forms 1 to 5, they spend five periods a week on mathematics, and the sets must not be larger than 25; in forms 6 to 8, they spend eight periods a week, and the sets must not be larger than 15. The input is to be given in pairs of numbers (x, y), where x is the form number, and y the number of children in that form reading mathematics.

5. Write a flow diagram to solve the equations

$$ax + by = c \quad \text{(I)}$$
$$dx + ey = f \quad \text{(II)}$$

by taking (0, 0) as the initial estimate, and continuing to derive new estimates for x and y from the previous estimates, using equations (I) and (II) respectively, until both estimates agree with the previous estimates to within 10^{-4}. (x must be estimated first from the line whose gradient is numerically greater.)

6. Write a program to tabulate the values of v and h at intervals of 0·1 second, until $h < 0$, given that

$$v = \frac{dh}{dt} \quad \text{and} \quad \frac{dv}{dt} = g - kv^2.$$

When $t = 0$, $h = 0$ and $v = u$; read the numbers g, k, u from tape, and use the approximation

$$f(t+h) \simeq f(t) + h \cdot f'(t).$$

29

EXPONENTIAL AND LOGARITHMIC FUNCTIONS

1. THE EXPONENTIAL LAW

1.1 When a sum of money is invested at compound interest, the interest in a particular year is a given fraction of the amount at the beginning of the year; and therefore the total sum invested is multiplied by a fixed proportion each year. For example, if the rate of interest is 4 %, the increase in the capital is 0·04 times its value at the beginning of the year, so that the capital at the end of the year is 1·04 times as much as at the beginning. It follows that after t years the capital is multiplied by $(1·04)^t$. We say that it increases exponentially, because the number of years appears in the exponent, or index, in the formula.

In this example the actual addition of interest is made just once a year; the capital does not grow continuously right through the year. There are, however, examples (particularly from science) where a quantity increases continuously—or so nearly continuously that we cannot distinguish the difference—at a rate which is proportional to its value at the time. Now this is a property which we can express mathematically by a differential equation. If x is a measure of the quantity at time t, its rate of increase is dx/dt; the fact that this is proportional to x is written

$$\frac{dx}{dt} = cx,$$

where c is a constant of proportion (the 'growth factor'). This is known as the *exponential law of growth*.

1.2 This differential equation is of a form which can be tackled by separating the variables, since it can be written as

$$\frac{1}{x}\frac{dx}{dt} = c.$$

Now if a primitive ϕ could be found for the reciprocal function $1/x$, so that

$$\phi'(x) = \frac{1}{x},$$

then the left side of this differential equation could be re-cast as follows:

$$\frac{1}{x}\frac{dx}{dt} = \phi'(x)\frac{dx}{dt} = \frac{d}{dt}\phi(x).$$

874

It would then be a simple matter to complete the solution:

$$\frac{d}{dt}\phi(x) = c$$

$$\Rightarrow \phi(x) = k + ct.$$

2. THE NATURAL LOGARITHM

2.1 We see then that solving the differential equation for the exponential law of growth is closely bound up with the problem of integrating the reciprocal function; and we shall now pursue this line of attack further.

There is, of course, a general rule for integrating powers of x:

$$\int x^m \, dx = \frac{x^{m+1}}{m+1} + k.$$

Unfortunately this breaks down when m has the value -1, so that it cannot be used to solve this problem. Instead, we shall approach it from a quite different point of view, through the definite integral

$$\int_1^a \frac{1}{x} \, dx.$$

This integral has a value (for $a > 0$) which depends on the number a, and it therefore defines a function of a.

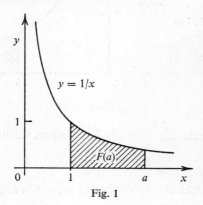

Fig. 1

We shall write

$$F(a) = \int_1^a \frac{1}{x} \, dx,$$

and begin by establishing an important property of this function. At this stage we shall take $a > 1$; then $F(a)$ measures the area under the graph of $y = 1/x$ (a rectangular hyperbola) over the interval $1 < x < a$ (see Figure 1).

875

2.2 Consider the effect of applying to the graph in Figure 1 the linear transformation with matrix
$$\mathbf{T} = \begin{pmatrix} b & 0 \\ 0 & 1/b \end{pmatrix}.$$

This transformation is the combination of a 'stretch' of ratio $b:1$ parallel to the x-axis and a 'squash' of ratio $1/b:1$ parallel to the y-axis.

We can easily show that $\mathbf{T}$ transforms the graph $y = 1/x$ into itself. For any point on the graph has coordinates of the form $(t, 1/t)$, where t is some number; and
$$\begin{pmatrix} b & 0 \\ 0 & 1/b \end{pmatrix} \begin{pmatrix} t \\ 1/t \end{pmatrix} = \begin{pmatrix} bt \\ 1/bt \end{pmatrix}.$$

Therefore
$$\left(t, \frac{1}{t}\right) \overset{\mathbf{T}}{\to} \left(bt, \frac{1}{bt}\right),$$

and the image point $(bt, 1/bt)$ also lies on the graph $y = 1/x$ (see Figure 2). We note also that
$$(1, 0) \overset{\mathbf{T}}{\to} (b, 0) \quad \text{and} \quad (a, 0) \overset{\mathbf{T}}{\to} (ab, 0),$$

so that the region under the graph over the interval $1 < x < a$ transforms into the region under the graph over the interval $b < x < ab$.

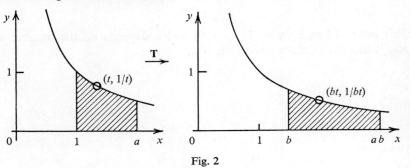

Fig. 2

Now the transformation $\mathbf{T}$ clearly leaves areas unaltered, since
$$\det \mathbf{T} = b \cdot \frac{1}{b} = 1.$$

It follows that the areas of the two shaded regions in Figure 2 are the same; that is, that
$$\int_1^a \frac{1}{x}\, dx = \int_b^{ab} \frac{1}{x}\, dx.$$

The left side of this equation is $F(a)$; and the right side can also be written in terms of the function F, since
$$\int_b^{ab} \frac{1}{x}\, dx = \int_1^{ab} \frac{1}{x}\, dx - \int_1^b \frac{1}{x}\, dx$$
$$= F(ab) - F(b).$$

by the additive property of area. It follows that

$$F(a) = F(ab) - F(b).$$

or

$$F(a) + F(b) = F(ab).$$

2.3 If $0 < a < 1$, the interpretation of $F(a)$ as an area needs to be modified, as does also the proof of the result $F(a) + F(b) = F(ab)$. This remains true, though, and the methods of Chapter 23 provide a justification which is independent of the value of a:

Substituting $x = bt$,

$$\int_b^{ab} \frac{1}{x}\, dx = \int_1^a \frac{1}{bt}\, b\, dt = \int_1^a \frac{1}{t}\, dt = F(a).$$

Now

$$\int_b^{ab} \frac{1}{x}\, dx = \int_1^{ab} \frac{1}{x}\, dx - \int_1^b \frac{1}{x}\, dx \quad \text{even if } a < 1,$$

so $F(a) + F(b) = F(ab)$ follows as before.

2.4 The relationship established at the end of the preceding section is one with which we are already familiar. It is in fact the fundamental property of logarithms, which justifies their use as a computational device for multiplying two numbers a and b (see Chapter 6).

What we have shown, therefore, is that the integral

$$\int_1^a \frac{1}{x}\, dx$$

can be used as a logarithm. It is called the *natural logarithm* of the number a, and is normally† denoted by

$$\log a.$$

2.5 Values of the natural logarithm (which is also sometimes called a hyperbolic or Napierian logarithm) have been tabulated.‡ It is usual to give values of $\log x$ only over the interval $1 < x < 10$, together with logarithms of powers of 10; logarithms of other numbers can then be found by applying the law

$$\log a + \log b = \log (ab).$$

For example,

$$\log 13 = \log 10 + \log 1\cdot 3$$
$$= 2\cdot 3026 + 0\cdot 2624$$
$$= 2\cdot 565;$$
$$\log 0\cdot 05 + \log 100 = \log 5$$
$$\Rightarrow \qquad \log 0\cdot 05 = 1\cdot 6094 - 4\cdot 6052$$
$$= -2\cdot 996.$$

† Some writers, particularly on the continent, use the symbol ln a for the natural logarithm of a.

‡ See, for example, *S.M.P. Advanced Tables*.

Exercise A

(In this exercise, care must be taken not to assume that the natural logarithm function has properties which other logarithms are known to possess.)

1. (a) Explain why $\log 1 = 0$.

   (b) If $0 < b < 1$, explain why
$$\int_1^b \frac{1}{x}\,dx$$
is negative, and interpret it in terms of an area under the graph of $y = 1/x$. Is the proof of Section 2.2 valid if $0 < b < 1$?

   (c) Can you ascribe a meaning to $\log(-2)$?

2. Show that the areas under the graph of $y = 1/x$ over the intervals $\frac{1}{2} < x < 1$, $1 < x < 2$, $2 < x < 4$, $4 < x < 8$, etc., are equal. Illustrate with a diagram, generalize and prove your result.

3. From the fundamental property of logarithms, deduce that

   (a) $\log(a/b) = \log a - \log b$;

   (b) $\log(1/a) = -\log a$.

4. Use Simpson's Rule to obtain approximations to $\log 2$, $\log 2 \cdot 5$ and $\log 3$. Deduce approximate values for:

   (a) $\log 5$;   (b) $\log 10$;   (c) $\log 2\frac{2}{3}$;   (d) $\log 2\frac{7}{9}$.

   A number e is defined by the equation $\log e = 1$. Explain why there is only one such number, and use (c) and (d) to estimate its value.

5. (a) Use Figure 1 to prove that $\log 2 > \frac{1}{2}$; and hence, by the method of induction, prove that
$$\log 2^n > \tfrac{1}{2}n.$$

   (b) Deduce (using also the result of Question 3 (b)) that
$$\log 2^{-n} < -\tfrac{1}{2}n.$$

6. (a) Sketch the area represented by $\log 1 \cdot 2$ and show that
$$0 \cdot 16 < \log 1 \cdot 2 < 0 \cdot 2.$$

   (b) If α is a positive number, show that $\alpha/(1+\alpha) < \log(1+\alpha) < \alpha$. Find a corresponding result if α is a number between -1 and 0.

7. Use the natural logarithm tables to find the values of

   (a) $\log 350$;   (b) $\log 0 \cdot 75$;   (c) $\log \sqrt{5}$.

8. Use natural logarithm tables to carry out the following calculations:

   (a) $38 \cdot 9 \times 5 \cdot 23$;   (b) $81 \cdot 7 \div 9 \cdot 52$;   (c) $(0 \cdot 076)^2$;   (d) $\sqrt[3]{0 \cdot 5}$.

   What is the advantage of using ordinary logarithms (to base 10) rather than natural logarithms to perform arithmetical calculations?

9. Use the method of induction to establish the result
$$\log(a^n) = n \log a$$
for any natural number n. Show how this result can be used to answer Question 2.

878

10. Suggest the appropriate domain and codomain for the function log, defined by the mapping $x \to \log x$.
Explain why the function:
(a) is increasing;
(b) is continuous;
(c) tends to infinity as x tends to infinity;
(d) tends to minus infinity as x tends to $0+$.
Sketch the graph of the function.

11. (a) Write a flow diagram for computing the natural logarithm of any number greater than 2, given $\log 2 = 0.6931$ and a table of values of logarithms over the interval $1 \leqslant x < 2$.

(You may use the instruction $\boxed{B := \log A}$ if $1 \leqslant A < 2$.)

(b) How should your flow diagram be modified to cope with numbers of any magnitude?

12. From the definitions $a^{r/s} = \sqrt[s]{(a^r)}$ and $a^{-m} = 1/a^m$ extend the result of Question 9 to any positive or negative rational number n.

3. LOGARITHMS TO BASE e

3.1 We showed in Section 2.4 that the natural logarithm *can be used* as a logarithm; that is, it possesses the property

$$\log a + \log b = \log (ab)$$

which justifies the use of logarithms as an aid to computation. This prompts the question whether we can say that the natural logarithm, defined by the integral, *is* a logarithm in the sense in which the word is used in Chapter 6. In other words, is there a number q for which logarithms to base q are the same as natural logarithms, so that

$$\log_q a = \log a?$$

Now if there is such a number, it is easy to see how to find it. For one property of all logarithms is that the logarithm of the base itself is equal to 1; that is,
$$\log_q q = 1.$$

It follows that we must look for a number whose natural logarithm is 1.

We proceed as follows. It is clear from Figure 3 that the area under $y = 1/x$ over the interval $1 < x < 2$ lies between the areas of two rectangles, both of width 1 and of heights $\frac{1}{2}$ and 1 respectively. Therefore

$$\log 2 < 1$$

and $$\log 2 > \tfrac{1}{2}.$$

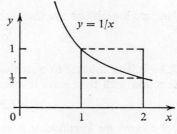

Fig. 3

From the second inequality it follows that

$$\log 4 = \log 2 + \log 2 > \tfrac{1}{2} + \tfrac{1}{2} = 1.$$

Putting these results together

$$\log 2 < 1 < \log 4;$$

and since $\log a$, the area under $y = 1/x$ from 1 to a, increases continuously with a, there must be a number between 2 and 4 whose natural logarithm is 1.

This number is always denoted by the letter e, so that

$$\log e = 1.$$

e can be found approximately by interpolation between known values of the logarithm (see Exercise A, Question 4). More precisely, the value of e is about 2·7183. It is in fact an irrational number, and cannot therefore be given exactly in decimal notation. The simplest way of calculating it is to use the formula given in Section 8.2.

3.2 From the property $\log a + \log b = \log (ab)$

for natural logarithms, proved in Section 2.2, we can deduce exactly as in Chapter 6 that, for any rational number n,

$$\log (a^n) = n \log a.$$

(See Exercise A, Questions 9 and 12.) In particular

$$\log (e^n) = n \log e = n.$$

This means that the natural logarithm is the function which maps the number e^n onto the number n. It is therefore the inverse of the 'exponential function' which maps n onto e^n. Symbolically,

$$\boldsymbol{y = \log x \Leftrightarrow x = e^y.}$$

We have now achieved the identification which we have been aiming at.†
This last statement recalls the definition of logarithms given in Chapter 6:

$$y = \log_e x \Leftrightarrow x = e^y.$$

Natural logarithms are therefore *the same as* logarithms to base e:

$$\log x = \log_e x.$$

3.3 It is of interest to note that, since natural logarithm and exponential function with base e are inverse, the general result

$$x = f^{-1}(f(x)) = f(f^{-1}(x))$$

† Strictly, the identification is not complete until irrational exponents have been discussed (see Section 7).

880

gives $x = e^{\log x}$ (for all $x > 0$)

and $y = \log(e^y)$ (for all y).

These relationships are often useful.

Exercise B

1. Write down the values of:
    (a) $\log(e^2)$;   (b) $\log(1/e)$;   (c) $\log(\sqrt{e})$.

2. Use tables of natural logarithms to evaluate:
    (a) $\log(2e)$;   (b) $e^{1\cdot3}$;   (c) $\sqrt{e}$;   (d) $\log(2+e)$;
    (e) e^e.

3. Simplify, where possible:
    (a) $e^{\log x^2}$;   (b) $\log(3e^x)$;   (c) $e^{3\log x}$;   (d) $\log(e^x.e^y)$;
    (e) $\log(2+e^x)$;   (f) $e^{1+\log x}$;   (g) $e^{\log x - \log y}$.

4. Make x the subject of the following formulae:
    (a) $y = 2e^{3x}$;   (b) $y = 2 + e^{3+x}$;   (c) $y = 7 + 5\log x$;
    (d) $\log y = 2 + \log x$;   (e) $y = \frac{1}{2}(e^x + e^{-x})$.

5. What is the connection between $\log x$ and $\log_{10} x$? Draw graphs of the two functions on the same diagram, and explain how one could be transformed into the other.

6. Give the values of the following integrals:

    (a) $\displaystyle\int_1^e \frac{1}{x}\,dx$;   (b) $\displaystyle\int_{1/e}^1 \frac{1}{x}\,dx$;   (c) $\displaystyle\int_{e^n}^{e^{n+1}} \frac{1}{x}\,dx$.

4. THE LOGARITHMIC FUNCTION

4.1 So far we have concentrated our attention on the arithmetical aspects of the natural logarithm—as a measure of the area under the graph of the reciprocal function over a specific interval. If, however, we think of the extremity a of the interval as a variable, then we are led to consider the function
$$a \to \log a$$

mapping the domain of positive real numbers onto the codomain of the real numbers. In particular, it will be of interest to differentiate this function. Its graph is shown in Figure 4.

At this stage it may help to make a change in the notation used. Let r stand for the reciprocal function
$$r: x \to 1/x,$$

whose graph is the rectangular hyperbola shown in Figure 1. We note that this sets up a continuous mapping of the positive real numbers onto the positive real numbers. We can now write

$$\log a = \int_1^a r;$$

or, what is the same thing,

$$\log x = \int_1^x r.$$

The notation is illustrated in Figure 5.

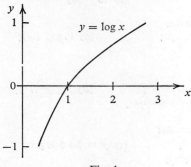

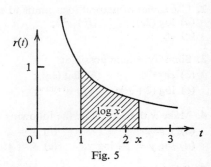

Fig. 4   Fig. 5

In this form we are reminded of the Fundamental Theorem proved in Section 4.2 of Chapter 22: that if f is a continuous function, and

$$\phi(x) = \int_1^x f,$$

then $\phi' = f.$

Applying this to the natural logarithm integral, it follows directly that

$$\log' = r;$$

that is, $\dfrac{d}{dx} \log x = \dfrac{1}{x}.$

From this, we can obtain many other results concerning logarithms.

Example 1. Differentiate $\log 3x$.

First method. Using the chain rule for differentiating composite functions

$$\frac{d}{dx} \log 3x = \frac{1}{3x} \cdot 3 = \frac{1}{x}.$$

Second method. Since
$$\log 3x = \log 3 + \log x,$$

and $\log 3$ is a constant whose derivative is zero,

$$\frac{d}{dx} \log 3x = 0 + \frac{d}{dx} \log x = \frac{1}{x}.$$

4.2 Since the derived function for the natural logarithm is the reciprocal function, we can state that the logarithm is a primitive of the reciprocal:

$$\int \frac{1}{x} dx = k + \log x.$$

Exercise C

1. After simplifying first where possible, differentiate:

(a) $\log x^2$;   (b) $\log 1/x$;   (c) $\log(1+x^2)$;

(d) $\log 5x^3$;   (e) $\log \sin x$.

2. Differentiate:

(a) $x \log x$;   (b) $\dfrac{\log x}{x}$;   (c) $x^2 \log 3x$.

3. What are the gradients of the graph of $y = \log x$ (Figure 4) at $(1, 0)$ and $(e^3, 3)$?

4. With the same axes, sketch the graphs of $\log x$ and $\log 3x$, and illustrate

$$\frac{d}{dx}(\log x) = \frac{d}{dx}(\log 3x).$$

State two different transformations which map the first graph onto the second.

5. Write down the derivative with respect to x of $\log f(x)$. Use your answer to find the following indefinite integrals:

(a) $\displaystyle\int \frac{3}{4+3x} dx$;   (b) $\displaystyle\int \frac{2x}{x^2-1} dx$;   (c) $\displaystyle\int \frac{\cos x}{\sin x} dx$.

6. Evaluate to 3 significant figures:

(a) $\displaystyle\int_2^3 \frac{1}{2x+1} dx$;   (b) $\displaystyle\int_0^a \frac{x}{a^2+x^2} dx$;   (c) $\displaystyle\int_0^{\frac{1}{4}\pi} \tan x \, dx$.

7. Use the methods of substitution or integration by parts to find the following indefinite integrals:

(a) $\displaystyle\int \frac{x}{(4x+1)^2} dx$;   (b) $\displaystyle\int x^2 \log x \, dx$;   (c) $\displaystyle\int \frac{x^3}{x^2+1} dx$.

8. (a) Differentiate $\log(\sec x + \tan x)$ with respect to x, and re-cast your answer in the form of a statement about an indefinite integral.

(b) Find $\int \csc x \, dx$ by a similar method.

9. Find $(d/dx)(\log \tan x)$, simplifying your answer as much as possible. Show how $\int \csc x \, dx$ can be deduced, and demonstrate that your answer is equivalent to that found in Question 8.

10. Suggest a suitable domain and codomain for the function $x \to \log(-x)$. Evaluate $d/dx \log(-x)$.

11. Which of the following statements is correct:

$$\int \frac{1}{x-a}\,dx = k + \log(x-a), \quad \int \frac{1}{x-a}\,dx = k + \log(a-x)?$$

Comment on your answer, and evaluate

$$\int_1^4 \frac{1}{x-6}\,dx.$$

12. Verify that, with boundary condition $y = 0$ when $x = 1$, the exact solution of the differential equation

$$\frac{dy}{dx} = \frac{1}{x} \quad \text{is} \quad y = \log x.$$

Use an approximate method of solution, with steps of length $x = 0.05$, to estimate the values of $\log 1.2$, $\log 1.25$ and $\log 0.9$. From your answers deduce successively the values of:

$\log 1.5, \quad \log 1.8, \quad \log 2, \quad \log 8, \quad \log 10, \quad \log_{10} 2, \quad \log_{10} 3, \quad \log_{10} 5.$

13. Interpret $\log a/(a-1)$ in terms of the graphs of (a) the reciprocal function and (b) the logarithm function. What is the limit of this expression as a tends to 1?

14. A Mercator chart is to be constructed whose scale at the equator is that of a globe of radius R. The principle of construction is that all lines of latitude on the chart have the same length, and the scale along the meridians is adjusted so that at each point it is the same as the scale along the appropriate circle of latitude. If on the chart the circle of latitude θ is at a distance x from the equator, obtain the differential equation

$$\frac{dx}{d\theta} = R \sec \theta.$$

Use the result of Question 8 to construct a grid for such a Mercator chart with $R = 1$ inch or $R = 2$ cm.

15. Use the chain rule to find the derivative of $\log(x^n)$, where n is a rational number. Hence show that

$$\frac{d}{dx}\{\log(x^n) - n \log x\} = 0$$

and use this to prove that

$$\log(x^n) = n \log x.$$

What assumptions have been made in the course of the proof? How are these justified?

5. THE EXPONENTIAL LAW (RESUMED)

We showed in Section 1 that the differential equation

$$\frac{dx}{dt} = cx$$

can be solved in the form

$$\phi(x) = k + ct,$$

884

where $\phi(x)$ is a primitive of $1/x$. We now know that $\log x$ is such a primitive, from which we deduce (for $x > 0$)

$$\frac{dx}{dt} = cx \;\Leftrightarrow\; \log x = k + ct.$$

Now since $\log x$ is the same as $\log_e x$, this last equation can be re-cast in the form

$$x = e^{k+ct}$$

But

$$e^{k+ct} = e^k . e^{ct},$$

so that we may write

$$x = A e^{ct},$$

where a new symbol A has been introduced for the number e^k. We notice that, as in the compound interest formula (Section 1.1), the letter t appears in the exponent; this justifies the use of the term 'exponential law of growth' to describe this differential equation.

The result

$$\frac{dx}{dt} = cx \;\Leftrightarrow\; x = A e^{ct}$$

is a very important one, and has many applications.

Example 2. A tank with capacity 50 litres is full of a liquid chemical, and it is desired to flush the chemical out with water. The water is fed into the tank through a pipe at a rate of 100 litres per minute, mixes (we suppose instantaneously) with the chemical, and the mixture is drained off through another pipe at the same rate. Find a formula for the amount of the chemical remaining in the tank after t minutes, and find the time that must elapse before this amount drops to (i) 0·5 litres, (ii) 0·005 litres.

If there are x litres of liquid chemical in the tank after t minutes, then the liquid in the tank contains a proportion $x/50$ of the chemical. Since 100 litres of liquid are led off per minute, the rate at which the chemical is being evacuated is

$$\frac{x}{50} . 100 \text{ litres per minute,}$$

or $2x$ litres per minute. The differential equation connecting x and t is therefore

$$\frac{dx}{dt} = -2x.$$

We have shown that the solution of this has the form

$$x = A e^{-2t}.$$

There is also the boundary condition, that when $t = 0$, $x = 50$. The constant A must therefore have value 50, so that

$$x = 50 e^{-2t}.$$

Substitution of $x = 0.5$ in this relation leads to the equation

$$e^{-2t} = 0.01,$$

whence $-2t = \log (0.01) = -\log 100 = -4.6,$

so that $t = 2.3.$

This means that the amount of chemical drops to 0.5 litres, one-hundredth of its original value, in 2·3 minutes; and therefore, since the law is exponential, it drops to one-hundredth of *this* amount, that is to 0·005 litres, in a further 2·3 minutes, which is 4·6 minutes after the process begins.

Exercise D

1. Give the solution of the differential equation

$$\frac{dy}{dx} = 3y$$

for which $y = 5$ when $x = 2$. Write the solution in three different forms:

$$y = e^{px+q}, \quad y = Ae^{rx}, \quad y = Bs^x,$$

where numerical values are substituted for A, B, p, q, r and s.

2. Repeat Question 1 for the differential equation

$$\frac{dy}{dx} = -\tfrac{1}{2}y$$

with the boundary condition $y = 3$ when $x = 0.8$.

3. Where in Example 2 is the assumption of instantaneous mixing introduced into the mathematical formulation?

4. A bicycle wheel is set spinning at a rate of 40 revolutions per minute, and slows down under the action of the friction at the bearings. The effect of this is to produce a retardation of $2z$ revolutions per minute per minute, where z is the rate of rotation in revolutions per minute. At what rate is it rotating one minute after it is set in motion?

5. A child makes his way to school at a speed which is proportional to the distance he still has to cover. He leaves home, 0·8 km away from school, running at 10 km/h. How long will it be before he has gone nine-tenths of the way?

6. The population P of a colony of insects t days after the beginning of an experiment is determined by the differential equation

$$\frac{dP}{dt} = 0.5P.$$

Solve this equation, and deduce the actual percentage increase in the population (*a*) during the first day, (*b*) during the tenth day.

7. The rate at which the temperature of the bath water drops is proportional to the amount by which this temperature exceeds that of the surrounding atmosphere, which may be taken to remain constant at 15 degrees. If it takes 10 minutes for the temperature to fall from 40 to 35 degrees, calculate the constant of proportion, and find how long it would take for the temperature to fall from 55 to 45 degrees.

8. Solve the differential equation

$$\frac{dy}{dx} = \frac{y}{x}$$

with boundary condition $y = b$ when $x = a$.

9. A bullet fired from a rifle at a muzzle velocity of 1000 m/s experiences a retardation due to air resistance of $0.002v^2$ m/s², where v is the speed in m/s. What will its speed be when it has travelled a distance of 1500 m?
   (*Hint:* $a = v.dv/dx$.)

10. Differentiate $\log (a + bv^2)$, and deduce an expression for

$$\int \frac{v}{a + bv^2} dv.$$

A motorist travelling at 15 m/s disengages gear and freewheels to rest. The retardation of the car has two components: a constant 0.08 m/s² due to friction in the working parts and road resistance, and retardation due to air resistance of $0.02v^2$ m/s², where v is the speed in m/s. Find how far the car travels in freewheeling to rest. (Compare Chapter 27, Exercise E, Question 6.)

11. The way in which compound interest, say on £1000 at 4 % per annum, is calculated varies in different commercial applications.
   (*a*) Interest of 4 % on the previous capital may be added on at the end of each year.
   (*b*) Interest of 2 % on the previous capital may be added on at the end of each half-year.
   (*c*) Interest of 1 % on the previous capital may be added on at the end of each quarter.
   (*d*) The interest may be supposed to be added on 'continuously', so that the rate at which the capital grows in £ per year is 4 % of the instantaneous value of the capital.
   Calculate, for each of these situations, the sum invested at various times over a five-year period; express the results in formulae, and draw the corresponding graphs.
   Generalize this problem by considering a sum of money invested at $(100r)$ % per annum, the interest being added on either n times a year or continuously. Deduce that, when n is large,

$$\left(1 + \frac{r}{n}\right)^n \simeq e^r.$$

12. Use a calculating machine to compute 1.2^5, 1.1^{10} and 1.05^{20}. Comment on your answers. (Compare Question 11. It is useful to have a machine with back transfer.)

13. Use the result of Exercise A, Question 6, to prove that

$$\frac{r}{1+r/n} < \log\left(1+\frac{r}{n}\right)^n < r$$

for positive r and n; and hence derive the result in the last part of Question 11.

14. In Section 5 the symbol A was substituted for e^k, which is essentially a positive number; but $x = Ae^{ct}$ is a solution of the differential equation also if A is negative. Explain the apparent discrepancy.

(*Hint*: See Exercise C, Question 10.)

6. THE EXPONENTIAL FUNCTION

6.1   An exponential function is one which maps a number x onto the power q^x, so that x is the exponent (or index) to which the base q is raised. We have seen that this function has for its inverse the logarithm to base q.

The inverse of the natural logarithm is often referred to as '*the* exponential function', and for the present we shall denote it by the symbol exp; thus

$$y = \exp x \Leftrightarrow x = \log y.$$

We shall examine a few properties of this function.

6.2   Clearly the graph of $y = \exp x$ is related to that of $y = \log x$ by interchanging x and y; that is, by reflection in the line $y = x$. The two graphs are shown in Figure 6.

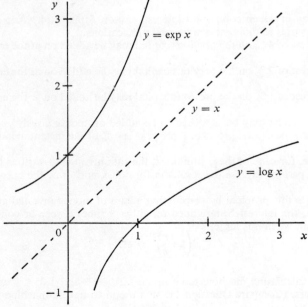

Fig. 6

6.3 The derived function for the exponential function can be found by using the method of differentiation described in Chapter 17:

$$y = \exp x \Rightarrow \log y = x$$

$$\Rightarrow \frac{1}{y}\frac{dy}{dx} = 1$$

$$\Rightarrow \frac{dy}{dx} = y$$

$$\Rightarrow \frac{dy}{dx} = \exp x.$$

Thus the exponential function has the property that its derivative is always equal to its local value:

$$\frac{d}{dx}\exp x = \exp x.$$

An immediate extension, using the chain rule, is

$$\frac{d}{dx}\exp(cx) = c \,.\, \exp(cx),$$

which brings us back again to the property of the exponential law of growth.

7. IRRATIONAL EXPONENTS

7.1 The reader may well ask what is the point of introducing the notation $\exp x$ for the inverse of the natural logarithm. Is this not precisely the same as e^x, in the notation with which we are already familiar? The answer to this question highlights a subtle but important distinction, which we must now examine in greater depth.

The natural logarithm, defined as an integral, maps the positive real numbers onto the real numbers. Since it is a continuous increasing function, its inverse

$$x \to \exp x$$

maps the domain of real numbers onto the positive real numbers.

On the other hand, the expression e^x (and more generally q^x) has been defined only when x is a rational number. Indeed the notation was used originally only for positive integral powers. In Chapter 6, the notation was extended, by means of the definitions

$$q^{r/s} = \sqrt[s]{(q^r)} \quad \text{and} \quad q^{-m} = 1/q^m,$$

to exponents which are positive or negative rational numbers. But as yet we have not assigned any meaning to expressions such as 2^π or $e^{\sqrt{2}}$. The function

$$x \to e^x$$

889

can be regarded at present only as a mapping of the domain of rational numbers into the positive real numbers.

It is not really satisfactory to retain two distinct notations for functions which are in essence so similar. (Although, because of its familiarity, index notation is normally retained for the general function, the symbol exp is sometimes preferred when printing complicated expressions; thus $\exp\left(-\dfrac{x^2}{2\sigma^2}\right)$ is more easily read than $e^{-x^2/2\sigma^2}$.)

We therefore decide to extend the meaning of the expression e^x so as to preserve the identification
$$e^x = \exp x,$$

when x is any real number. That is, we *define* e^x for general real x by means of the equivalence
$$y = e^x \Leftrightarrow x = \log y.$$

With this definition, the notations $\exp x$ and e^x are now interchangeable.

The important result of Section 6·3 can now be written
$$\frac{d}{dx}(e^x) = e^x,$$

and it clearly follows that
$$\int e^x\,dx = k + e^x.$$

*7.2   We still have to extend the meaning of the general exponential expression q^x. This can simply be done by requiring that the identity
$$x \log q = \log(q^x),$$

known to be true for rational values of x (see Exercise A, Question 12), remains true when x is irrational. We therefore *define*, for any real x and positive real q,
$$q^x = \exp(x \log q).$$

Notice that this includes the definition of e^x as a special case.

*7.3   When a definition is extended it is, of course, necessary to investigate whether properties which were true with the more restricted definition remain true in the general situation. We shall now look from this point of view at two important properties of exponentials which are known to be true for rational exponents. The proofs must depend on the more general definitions given above.

(i) $q^a . q^b = q^{a+b}$.

From the definition $q^a = \exp(a \log q)$,

it follows that $\log(q^a) = a \log q,$

and similarly for b. Therefore

$$\log(q^a . q^b) = \log(q^a) + \log(q^b)$$
$$= a \log q + b \log q$$
$$= (a+b) \log q$$
$$= \log(q^{a+b}).$$

Since the natural logarithm has a unique inverse, we deduce that

$$q^a . q^b = q^{a+b}.$$

(ii) $(d/dx)(x^n) = nx^{n-1}$.

By definition $x^n = \exp(n \log x)$.

Differentiating, using the chain rule,

$$\frac{d}{dx} x^n = \exp(n \log x) . \frac{n}{x}$$
$$= x^n . nx^{-1}$$
$$= nx^{n-1}, \quad \text{using the result of (i)}.$$

This proves that the rule for differentiating powers of x remains valid when the index is irrational.

Exercise E

1. Differentiate:

(a) e^{3x};   (b) e^{x^2};   (c) e^{-x};   (d) xe^x.

2. Evaluate:

(a) $\displaystyle\int_0^1 e^{2x} dx$;   (b) $\displaystyle\int_{-1}^1 e^{x+3} dx$.

3. With the same axes, sketch graphs of e^x, e^{-x}, e^{2x}. Write down the gradient of each graph at the point where $x = 0$.

4. Find the coordinates of the maximum point and the point of inflexion on the graph of xe^{-x}. Sketch the graph, and discuss its behaviour as x tends to infinity.

5. Simplify and differentiate $\log(x^n e^{-x})$, where $n \geqslant 1$, and $x > 0$. Find the turning point on the graph of $y = \log(x^n e^{-x})$, and sketch the graph. Explain informally why $x^n e^{-x} \to 0$ as $x \to \infty$.

6. Find $\displaystyle\int_0^a xe^{-x} dx$, and its limit (if any) as $a \to \infty$.

7. Find whether or not the area under the graph of $y = x^2 e^{-3x}$ (where x is restricted to positive values) is bounded.

8. Evaluate $d/dx \exp(-\tfrac{1}{2}x^2)$, and find the inflexions on the graph of

$$y = \exp(-\tfrac{1}{2}x^2).$$

Sketch the graph.

9. If u, v and y are differentiable functions of x such that
$$\log y = \log u + \log v,$$
obtain an equation connecting their derivatives by differentiating this relation with respect to x; and deduce the product rule given in Section 3.2 of Book 2, Chapter 17.

10. Use a method similar to that in Question 9 to find a formula for $(d/dx)(u^v)$, where u and v are differentiable functions of x and u is positive.

11. Prove that $(d/dx)q^x = q^x \log q$.

12. Investigate whether the relation
$$(q^a)^b = q^{ab}$$
remains valid when either a or b or both are irrational.

13. Prove that $\log_{10} 2$ is an irrational number. Generalize this result.

14. Without using the explicit form for the solution, prove that if $y = \phi(x)$ is a solution of
$$\frac{dy}{dx} = y,$$
then $y = \phi(cx)$ is a solution of
$$\frac{dy}{dx} = cy.$$

15. In Section 3.2 we claimed to have proved that natural logarithms are the same as logarithms to base e. What had we in fact proved at this stage?

16. Find the minimum point on the graph
$$y = x^x.$$
Sketch the graph, with domain the positive real numbers.

8. POLYNOMIAL APPROXIMATIONS

8.1 The method of local approximation by polynomials described in Chapter 16 can be applied to the logarithmic and exponential functions, and provides a useful means of computing values of these functions.

We shall apply the general form for such approximations (see Chapter 16, Section 5.3)
$$f(p+\alpha) \simeq f(p) + f'(p)\alpha + \frac{f''(p)}{2!}\alpha^2 + \ldots + \frac{f^{(n)}(p)}{n!}\alpha^n,$$
where α is small.

8.2 For the exponential function it will be sufficient to find an approximation to the function at 0, since around any other point p of the domain the form of the function is merely a 'scaled up' version of its value around 0, by virtue of the relation
$$\exp(p+\alpha) = \exp p . \exp \alpha.$$

We therefore write $p = 0, f = \exp$ in the general formula. Since

$$\exp' = \exp,$$

it follows that
$$\exp'' = \exp, \quad \exp''' = \exp, \quad \text{and so on.}$$

Therefore all the derivatives at 0 have the value $\exp 0$, or 1, and we deduce immediately the polynomial approximation for $\exp \alpha$, or e^{α},

$$e^{\alpha} \simeq 1 + \alpha + \frac{\alpha^2}{2!} + \frac{\alpha^3}{3!} + \dots + \frac{\alpha^n}{n!}.$$

Because the denominators in the successive terms $(2!, 3!, 4!, \dots)$ increase very rapidly, this turns out to be a very effective approximation even for comparatively large values of α. A particularly important result is obtained by taking α to be 1, giving

$$e \simeq 1 + \frac{1}{1!} + \frac{1}{2!} + \frac{1}{3!} + \dots + \frac{1}{n!}.$$

(The second term has been written as $1/1!$ to bring out the essential pattern.) It can in fact be shown that the limit of the sum on the right as n tends to infinity is exactly e, so that by taking enough terms this expression can be used to compute the value of e to any desired degree of accuracy.

It can be seen by direct differentiation that

$$\frac{d}{d\alpha}\left(1 + \alpha + \frac{\alpha^2}{2!} + \dots + \frac{\alpha^n}{n!}\right) = 1 + \alpha + \frac{\alpha^2}{2!} + \dots + \frac{\alpha^{n-1}}{(n-1)!},$$

so that this polynomial approximation has a derivative which differs from the values of the polynomial itself only by the last term $\alpha^n/n!$. It follows that if α is small this polynomial has the property that its derivative is *very nearly* equal to the value of the polynomial—a result which is *exactly* true for the exponential function itself.

8.3 Taylor's approximation can be used similarly for the natural logarithm. Again it will suffice to find an approximation around the particular value 1; the more general approximation around p can then be found by using

$$\log(p + \beta) = \log p + \log\left(1 + \frac{\beta}{p}\right).$$

We therefore write $p = 1, f = \log$ in the general formula. Successive derived functions are

$$f'(x) = \frac{1}{x}, \quad f''(x) = -\frac{1}{x^2}, \quad f'''(x) = \frac{2}{x^3}$$

and more generally
$$f^{(r)}(x) = (-1)^{r-1} \cdot \frac{(r-1)!}{x^r};$$

so that $f(1) = 0,\ \ f'(1) = 1,\ \ f''(1) = -1,\ \ f'''(1) = 2,$
$$f^{(r)}(1) = (-1)^{r-1}.(r-1)!.$$

Substitution in the formula for Taylor's approximation gives

$$\log(1+\alpha) \simeq \alpha - \tfrac{1}{2}\alpha^2 + \tfrac{1}{3}\alpha^3 - \ldots + (-)^{n-1}\frac{\alpha^n}{n},$$

for small α.

Figure 7 shows a comparison between the graph of the function and its fifth degree polynomial approximation over the interval $-1 < x < 1\cdot5$. It is important to notice the divergence from the logarithmic curve of the approximating polynomial graph for values of x beyond 1, a divergence

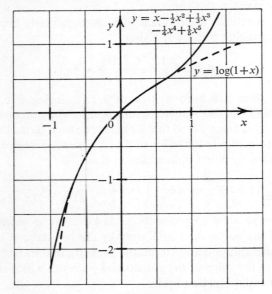

Fig. 7

which will indeed be more accentuated as more terms are taken. This means that, if we want to compute values of the natural logarithm, the polynomial approximation furnishes quite an efficient method for values of α which are comfortably within the interval $-1 < \alpha < 1$; but it will give quite misleading results outside this interval.

Example 3. Find $\log 1\cdot3$.

The fourth degree polynomial approximation with $x = 0\cdot3$ gives

$$\log 1\cdot3 \simeq 0\cdot3 - \frac{(0\cdot3)^2}{2} + \frac{(0\cdot3)^3}{3} - \frac{(0\cdot3)^4}{4}$$
$$= 0\cdot3 - 0\cdot045 + 0\cdot009 - 0\cdot002025$$
$$= 0\cdot261975.$$

Discussion of the error involved in this approximation is deferred until Section 8.4; meanwhile, the size of the last term suggests that the answer should be rounded to 0·262. Higher degree polynomial approximations will give more accurate answers if desired.

Example 4. Suggest methods of computing log 2·5.

It is useless to apply a polynomial approximation directly with $\alpha = 1\cdot5$, since this is outside the interval $-1 < \alpha < 1$. We must therefore resort to a less direct method. For example, we may note that

$$\log 2\cdot5 = -\log\frac{1}{2\cdot5} = -\log 0\cdot4$$

$$= -\log(1-0\cdot6),$$

for which the formula derived above gives the approximate value

$$-\left\{(-0\cdot6)-\tfrac{1}{2}(-0\cdot6)^2+\tfrac{1}{3}(-0\cdot6)^3\ldots+(-1)^{n-1}\frac{(-0\cdot6)^n}{n}\right\}$$

$$= 0\cdot6+0\cdot18+0\cdot072+\ldots+\frac{(0\cdot6)^n}{n}.$$

The value of n can be selected according to the closeness of the approximation sought.

A refinement on this method is to observe that

$$0\cdot4 = 0\cdot8\times0\cdot5,$$

so that $\qquad \log 2\cdot5 = -\{\log 0\cdot8+\log 0\cdot5\}$

$$= -\log(1-0\cdot2)-\log(1-0\cdot5).$$

The two logarithms on the right can then be evaluated in the way described above. Since 0·2 and 0·5 are both less than 0·6, equivalent accuracy may be achieved by taking fewer terms.

*8.4 For the approximation to $\log(1+\alpha)$ it is possible to be more specific about the magnitude of the error by approaching the problem from a different point of view. We shall illustrate this by finding the order of magnitude of the error involved in Example 3.

The calculation depends on the fact that

$$(1-x+x^2-x^3)(1+x) = 1-x^4,$$

which can be rearranged to give

$$1-x+x^2-x^3 = \frac{1}{1+x}-\frac{x^4}{1+x},$$

or $\qquad\qquad \frac{1}{1+x} = 1-x+x^2-x^3+\frac{x^4}{1+x}.$

Since the expressions on the left and right sides have equal values for all x, the integrals of each over the interval $0 < x < 0\cdot3$ must be the same.

895

Now

$$\int_0^{0\cdot3} \frac{1}{1+x} dx = \left[\log(1+x) \right]_0^{0\cdot3} = \log 1\cdot3;$$

and

$$\int_0^{0\cdot3} (1-x+x^2-x^3)\,dx = \left[x - \tfrac{1}{2}x^2 + \tfrac{1}{3}x^3 - \tfrac{1}{4}x^4 \right]_0^{0\cdot3}$$

$$= 0\cdot3 - \tfrac{1}{2}(0\cdot3)^2 + \tfrac{1}{3}(0\cdot3)^3 - \tfrac{1}{4}(0\cdot3)^4.$$

Therefore

$$\log 1\cdot3 = 0\cdot3 - \tfrac{1}{2}(0\cdot3)^2 + \tfrac{1}{3}(0\cdot3)^3 - \tfrac{1}{4}(0\cdot3)^4 + \int_0^{0\cdot3} \frac{x^4}{1+x} dx,$$

and we see that the error involved in the Taylor approximation is exactly the value of the final integral.

Now this integral cannot be computed precisely, but an estimate of its value can be obtained by observing that, over the interval $0 < x < 0\cdot3$,

$$1\cdot3 > 1+x > 1,$$

so that

$$\frac{x^4}{1\cdot3} < \frac{x^4}{1+x} < x^4.$$

Thus

$$\int_0^{0\cdot3} \frac{x^4}{1\cdot3} dx < \int_0^{0\cdot3} \frac{x^4}{1+x} dx < \int_0^{0\cdot3} x^4 dx.$$

The values of the first and last integrals are

$$\frac{(0\cdot3)^5}{6\cdot5} = 0\cdot000374 \quad \text{and} \quad \frac{(0\cdot3)^5}{5} = 0\cdot000486$$

so that the error in Taylor's approximation lies within these bounds. In Example 3 the Taylor approximation to four terms was shown to be 0·261975, so we can now assert that the correct value lies between 0·261975+0·000374 and 0·261975+0·000486. That is,

$$0\cdot262349 < \log 1\cdot3 < 0\cdot262461;$$

or in another form, $\log 1\cdot3 = 0\cdot262405$, with a maximum possible error of 0·000056 either way.

Exercise F

1. Work out the value of e to 5 decimal places in the way suggested in Section 8.2. (Consider carefully how to avoid tiresome calculation.)

2. Evaluate $\sqrt{e}$ and $1/\sqrt{e}$ to 4 decimal places, and check by multiplying your answers together.

3. Draw graphs of

$$y = 1+x, \quad y = 1+x+\frac{x^2}{2!}, \quad y = 1+x+\frac{x^2}{2!}+\frac{x^3}{3!} \quad \text{and} \quad y = e^x$$

over the interval $-2 \leqslant x \leqslant 2$.

896

4. Evaluate to 4 decimal places
  (a) log 1·1; (b) log 0·8; (c) log 1·44.
Use four figure tables to check your answers.

5. The sixth and seventh degree approximations to $\log(1+x)$ are called $P(x)$ and $Q(x)$. Copy and complete the following table and compare the graphs of $P(x)$, $Q(x)$, $\log(1+x)$ as in Figure 7.

x	-1	-0.5	0	0.5	1	1.5
$P(x)$	-2.45		0		0.62	
$Q(x)$	-2.59		0		0.76	2.28
$\log(1+x)$	—		0			

6. (a) Discuss what degree polynomial approximation to $\log(1+x)$ would be needed to evaluate log 2 by substituting 1 for x.
  (b) Find log 2 to 4 decimal places, using a more convenient method.

7. Compute $\log\frac{49}{50}$ to 4 decimal places. Given that log 10 = 2·3026, use this and the answer to Question 6 to find $\log_{10}7$.

8. Show that the square of

$$1+x+\frac{x^2}{2!}+\frac{x^3}{3!} \quad\text{agrees with}\quad 1+2x+\frac{(2x)^2}{2!}+\frac{(2x)^3}{3!}$$

as far as the term in x^3. What is the significance of this result?

9. Write down cubic polynomial approximations to e^{α} and $e^{-\alpha}$ for small α, and multiply them together. Explain the result.

10. Write a flow diagram for computing the value of $e^{0.85}$ to 6 decimal places.

11. Write a flow diagram to compute a table of logarithms over the interval $1 \leqslant x \leqslant 1.5$, by steps of 0·01, to 4 decimal places.

12. Apply Taylor's formula with a general value of p to find an approximation to $\exp(p+\alpha)$ for small α, and show how this could be derived from the special form with $p = 0$.

13. Apply Taylor's formula with a general value of p to find an approximation to $\log(p+\beta)$ for small β, and show how this could be derived from the result in Section 8.3.

14. Follow through the argument of Section 8.4 to estimate the magnitude of the error involved in using three terms of the Taylor approximation to compute log 1·04. Between what bounds can you be sure that the value lies?

15. Repeat Question 14 for the calculation of log 0·9 using four terms of the Taylor approximation.

16. (a) Use the Taylor approximations and the relation

$$q^x = \exp(x \log q)$$

to evaluate the fifth root of 1·1 to four decimal places.
  (b) Check your answer by using instead a Taylor approximation to $(1+y)^m$.

*9. THE HYPERBOLIC FUNCTIONS

9.1 A function f whose domain is the set of all real numbers can be written as the sum of an even function $\frac{1}{2}\{f(x)+f(-x)\}$ and an odd function $\frac{1}{2}\{f(x)-f(-x)\}$ (see Chapter 5, Exercise G). If this process is applied to the exponential function we obtain a pair of *hyperbolic functions*, denoted by the symbols cosh and sinh:

$$\cosh x = \tfrac{1}{2}\{e^x+e^{-x}\}, \quad \sinh x = \tfrac{1}{2}\{e^x-e^{-x}\}.$$

The reason for the notation is that these functions have certain properties similar to those of the circular functions cos and sin. When complex numbers have been studied in more detail it will be found that there is indeed a close connection between the corresponding circular and hyperbolic functions.

We note first the important relations

$$\cosh x + \sinh x = e^x \quad \text{and} \quad \cosh x - \sinh x = e^{-x},$$

from which we deduce that

$$(\cosh x + \sinh x)(\cosh x - \sinh x) = e^x . e^{-x},$$

or $$\cosh^2 x - \sinh^2 x = 1.$$

This is analogous to the familiar result for circular functions

$$\cos^2 x + \sin^2 x = 1.$$

Analogues for the addition formulae for sine and cosine can be obtained by noting that

$$e^{a+b} = e^a . e^b = (\cosh a + \sinh a)(\cosh b + \sinh b),$$

$$e^{-a-b} = e^{-a} . e^{-b} = (\cosh a - \sinh a)(\cosh b - \sinh b).$$

Hence

$$\cosh (a+b) = \tfrac{1}{2}\{e^{a+b}+e^{-a-b}\} = \cosh a \cosh b + \sinh a \sinh b,$$

$$\sinh (a+b) = \tfrac{1}{2}\{e^{a+b}-e^{-a-b}\} = \sinh a \cosh b + \cosh a \sinh b.$$

These results are very similar to the corresponding formulae for circular functions, but with certain differences of sign.

9.2 The graphs of $y = \cosh x$ and $y = \sinh x$ are easily drawn from those of $y = e^x$ and $y = e^{-x}$ (see Figure 8). It will be noticed that, for large x, both graphs approximate to that of $y = \tfrac{1}{2}e^x$.

The function sinh sets up a one-one mapping of the real numbers onto the real numbers. There is therefore an inverse function, denoted by $\sinh^{-1}$, which also maps the real numbers onto the real numbers.

Rather more care is needed with the function cosh, which maps the real numbers onto the interval $y \geqslant 1$, since this mapping is not one-one.

898

Indeed, for each number of the range other than 1 itself there are *two* members of the domain of which it is the image, one positive and the other negative. This mapping does not therefore establish an inverse function. To overcome this difficulty, we adopt the usual device of restricting the domain of the mapping.

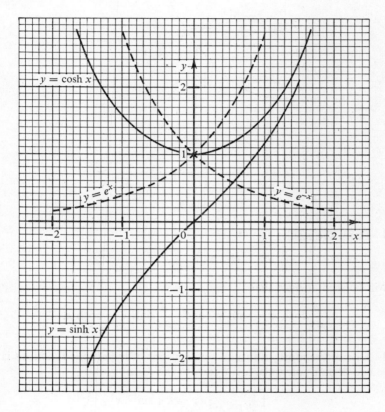

Fig. 8

It will be noticed that the function cosh does effect a one-one mapping of the *non-negative* real numbers onto the interval $y \geqslant 1$ (see Figure 9); and so this mapping defines an inverse function, denoted by $\cosh^{-1}$, whose domain is the set of real numbers from 1 upwards and whose range is the set of non-negative real numbers.

We therefore use the symbol $\cosh^{-1} y$ (where $y \geqslant 1$) to stand for the unique non-negative number x such that

$$\cosh x = y.$$

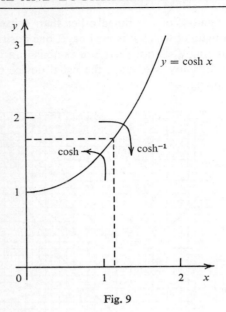

Fig. 9

9.3 From the results

$$\frac{d}{dx}e^x = e^x \quad \text{and} \quad \frac{d}{dx}e^{-x} = -e^{-x}$$

it will be seen at once that

$$\frac{d}{dx}\cosh x = \sinh x \quad \text{and} \quad \frac{d}{dx}\sinh x = \cosh x.$$

9.4 One of the most important applications of hyperbolic functions is to evaluate certain integrals, analogous to the form

$$\int \frac{1}{\sqrt{(1-x^2)}}\,dx = k + \sin^{-1} x$$

already established.

(i) To find

$$\int \frac{1}{\sqrt{(1+x^2)}}\,dx$$

we make the substitution $\qquad x = \sinh u,$

suggested by the property $1 + \sinh^2 u = \cosh^2 u$ (see Section 9.1). Then

$$\frac{dx}{du} = \cosh u$$

and $\qquad\qquad \sqrt{(1+x^2)} = \sqrt{(\cosh^2 u)}$

$$= +\cosh u,$$

900

since the positive square root is implied by the notation and $\cosh u$ is always positive. It follows that

$$\int \frac{1}{\sqrt{(1+x^2)}} \, dx = \int \frac{1}{\cosh u} . \cosh u \, du$$

$$= \int 1 . du$$

$$= k+u$$

$$= k+\sinh^{-1} x.$$

(ii) We evaluate

$$\int \frac{1}{\sqrt{(x^2-1)}} \, dx$$

in a similar manner. We now make the substitution

$$x = \cosh u.$$

To be quite specific we take u to be positive, so that

$$u = \cosh^{-1} x;$$

$\sinh u$ is then positive, and therefore

$$\sqrt{(x^2-1)} = \sqrt{(\cosh^2 u - 1)}$$

$$= \sqrt{(\sinh^2 u)}$$

$$= +\sinh u.$$

The calculation is completed as before:

$$\int \frac{1}{\sqrt{(x^2-1)}} \, dx = \int \frac{1}{\sinh u} . \sinh u \, du$$

$$= \int 1 . du$$

$$= k+u$$

$$= k+\cosh^{-1} x.$$

9.5 Values of $\cosh x$ and $\sinh x$ can, of course, be computed directly from the definitions and a table of values of the exponential function. We shall now establish a pair of important formulae by which values of the inverse functions $\cosh^{-1}$ and $\sinh^{-1}$ can be computed from tables of natural logarithms.

(i) To evaluate $\cosh^{-1} y$ (where $y > 1$), we write

$$\cosh^{-1} y = x,$$

whence $\qquad y = \cosh x = \tfrac{1}{2}\{e^x+e^{-x}\} = \dfrac{e^x}{2}+\dfrac{1}{2e^x}.$

Multiplying by $2e^x$ and rearranging the terms,

$$(e^x)^2 - 2ye^x + 1 = 0.$$

901

This is a quadratic equation for the unknown e^x, and the usual method of solution gives
$$e^x = y \pm \sqrt{(y^2 - 1)}.$$

Now from the definition of $\cosh^{-1} y$ (see Section 9.2) we know that x must be positive, so that e^x must be greater than 1. Since the product of the roots of the quadratic equation for e^x is 1, one root must be greater than 1 and one less than 1 (for both are certainly positive). It follows that
$$y + \sqrt{(y^2 - 1)} > 1 \quad \text{and} \quad y - \sqrt{(y^2 - 1)} < 1;$$
and therefore that the solution relevant to our problem is
$$e^x = y + \sqrt{(y^2 - 1)},$$
whence
$$x = \log\{y + \sqrt{(y^2 - 1)}\}.$$

This proves the formula we are seeking:
$$\cosh^{-1} y = \log\{y + \sqrt{(y^2 - 1)}\}.$$

(ii) A similar method can be used for the function $\sinh^{-1}$. Writing
$$\sinh^{-1} y = x,$$
we arrive at the quadratic equation
$$(e^x)^2 - 2ye^x - 1 = 0$$
with solutions
$$e^x = y \pm \sqrt{(y^2 + 1)}.$$

Now the solution with the minus sign can certainly be discarded, since e^x is always a positive number and $y - \sqrt{(y^2 + 1)}$ is negative whatever the value of y. Therefore
$$e^x = y + \sqrt{(y^2 + 1)},$$
whence
$$\sinh^{-1} y = \log\{y + \sqrt{(y^2 + 1)}\}.$$

Exercise G

1. Evaluate: $\cosh 2$, $\sinh 2$, $\cosh^{-1} 2$, $\sinh^{-1} 2$.

2. Find results for hyperbolic functions analogous to the following:
   (a) $\cos 2x = 2\cos^2 x - 1 = 1 - 2\sin^2 x$;
   (b) $\int \sin^2 x \, dx = k + \frac{1}{2}(x - \sin x \cos x)$;
   (c) $y = A \sin nx + B \cos nx \Rightarrow \dfrac{d^2 y}{dx^2} = -n^2 y$.

3. Solve the equation
$$3 \cosh x + 4 \sinh x = 10.$$

4. Find polynomial Taylor approximations for $\cosh(p + \alpha)$ and $\sinh(p + \alpha)$, where α is small; and show how they could have been derived from the special cases when $p = 0$.

5. Sketch the graphs of $y = \sinh^{-1} x$ and $y = \cosh^{-1} x$.

6. Prove that
$$(\cosh x + \sinh x)^n = \cosh nx + \sinh nx,$$
and that
$$(\cosh x - \sinh x)^n = \cosh nx - \sinh nx.$$

7. Prove that the area contained between the graphs $y = \sinh x$ and $y = \cosh x$, the y-axis and the line $x = k$ (where $k > 0$) is always less than 1, whatever the value of k.

8. Obtain the results of Section 9.4 by differentiating the equations
$$\sinh y = x \quad \text{and} \quad \cosh y = x$$
with respect to x, paying careful regard to signs where necessary.

9. Use arguments from dimensions to extend the results of Section 9.4 to integrals of the form
$$\int \frac{1}{\sqrt{(b^2 + a^2 x^2)}}\,dx \quad \text{and} \quad \int \frac{1}{\sqrt{(a^2 x^2 - b^2)}}\,dx$$
and verify your answers by direct differentiation, using the results of Question 8.

10. Obtain the derivative of $\cosh^{-1} x$ by differentiating $\log\{x + \sqrt{(x^2 - 1)}\}$.

11. Prove that, for all values of t, the point P with coordinates $(a\cosh t, a\sinh t)$ lies on the rectangular hyperbola $x^2 - y^2 = a^2$. Describe how P moves on the hyperbola as t increases through the set of real numbers. Are all points of the hyperbola expressible in this form?

If A is the point $(a, 0)$, what is the area of the region bounded by OA, OP and the arc AP of the hyperbola? Compare your results with the corresponding ones for the point $(a\cos t, a\sin t)$ on the circle $x^2 + y^2 = a^2$. (This analogy explains the use of the term 'hyperbolic functions' to describe cosh and sinh.)

Miscellaneous Exercise

1. Differentiate $e^{-\frac{1}{2}x^2}$.

You are given that, if
$$f(x) = \frac{1}{\sqrt{(2\pi)}}\, e^{-\frac{1}{2}x^2}, \quad \text{then} \quad \int_{-\infty}^{\infty} f(x)\,dx = 1.$$

Deduce that
$$\int_{-\infty}^{\infty} x f(x)\,dx = 0, \quad \int_{-\infty}^{\infty} x^2 f(x)\,dx = 1,$$
$$\int_{-\infty}^{\infty} x^3 f(x)\,dx = 0, \quad \int_{-\infty}^{\infty} x^4 f(x)\,dx = 3;$$
and evaluate the next two integrals in the sequence.

2. Find the maximum point on the graph of
$$y = \frac{\log x}{x},$$
and sketch the graph. Deduce that there is only one pair of different positive integers a, b such that
$$a^b = b^a.$$

903

3. In a model of an economic situation the cost of living index is supposed to increase continuously, at a rate proportional to its value at the time. The formula for the rate of increase is $0.04C$ points per year, where C is the current index. If the index is chosen to have the value 100 at a particular date, what will it be t years later? By what percentage will it have increased

(a) at the end of a year;

(b) at the end of 10 years?

In the same model the wage rate index is supposed to increase at a rate $0.06W$ points per year, where W is the current index. An index of 'real purchasing power' is defined by the expression W/C. Obtain a differential equation describing how this third index varies with time.

4. Evaluate

$$\int_4^6 \left(ax + b - \frac{1}{x} \right)^2 dx.$$

It is desired to make this integral as small as possible by choosing appropriate values of a and b. Write down two equations which a and b must satisfy to achieve this, and solve them. Explain why you might expect the function $x \to ax + b$, with these values of a and b, to give the 'best' linear approximation to the reciprocal function $x \to 1/x$ over the interval $4 < x < 6$. (See Book 2, Chapter 16, Section 4.1.)

5. Use the Newton–Raphson approximation to solve the equation

$$x \cosh x = 1.$$

6. By drawing appropriate graphs, find as accurately as you can the number $h \, (\neq 0)$ for which

$$\int_0^h \frac{1-x}{1+x^2} \, dx = 0.$$

7. A matrix of the form

$$\begin{pmatrix} \cosh a & \sinh a \\ \sinh a & \cosh a \end{pmatrix}$$

will be called an E-matrix, and denoted by the symbol $E(a)$.

(a) Prove that the product of two E-matrices is an E-matrix. What isomorphism is suggested by your calculations?

(b) Prove that the transformation represented by an E-matrix leaves invariant rectangular hyperbolas of the form $x^2 - y^2 = \pm k^2$.

(c) What is the determinant of $E(a)$? What property of the hyperbolas referred to in (b) does this suggest?

(d) Do E-matrices constitute a group?

(e) Can you suggest an analogous set of matrices whose elements are circular functions?

8. A function f is given to have the property that, for all x and u in its domain,

$$f(x) + f(u) = f(xu).$$

By differentiating this relation with respect to u for a particular value of x, and then making the substitution $u = 1$, prove that f must be a primitive of a function of the form p/x. Prove also, from the original relation, that $f(1) = 0$. Deduce that

$$f(a) = \int_1^a \frac{p}{x} \, dx.$$

904

9. Let p be any positive number, and write

$$L(a) = \int_1^a \frac{p}{x}\, dx.$$

(a) Prove that $L(a)+L(b) = L(ab)$.

(b) Prove the existence of a number q such that $L(q) = 1$; and that $q = \epsilon^{1/p}$.

(c) Prove that $L(x)$ is the same as $\log_q x$.

(d) If q', p' are related to each other in the same way as q, p, prove that

$$\log_q a = \frac{p}{p'}\log_{q'} a, \quad \text{and} \quad \frac{p}{p'} = \log_q q'.$$

SUMMARY OF IMPORTANT RESULTS

$$\log a = \int_1^a \frac{1}{x}\, dx:$$

$$\log a + \log b = \log (ab); \quad \log (a^n) = n \log a.$$

$$\log x = \log_e x.$$

$$y = \log x \iff x = e^y \quad \text{or} \quad \exp y.$$

$$\frac{d}{dx}\log x = \frac{1}{x}.$$

$$\frac{d}{dx}(e^x) = e^x.$$

$$\frac{dx}{dt} = cx \iff x = A e^{ct}.$$

$$q^x = \exp (x \log q).$$

For small α
$$\begin{cases} e^\alpha \simeq 1+\alpha+\dfrac{\alpha^2}{2!}+\dfrac{\alpha^3}{3!}+\ldots+\dfrac{\alpha^n}{n!}, \\[2mm] \log (1+\alpha) \simeq \alpha-\tfrac{1}{2}\alpha^2+\tfrac{1}{3}\alpha^3-\ldots+(-1)^{n-1}\dfrac{\alpha^n}{n}. \end{cases}$$

$$\cosh x = \tfrac{1}{2}\{e^x+e^{-x}\}, \quad \sinh x = \tfrac{1}{2}\{e^x-e^{-x}\}.$$

$$\cosh^2 x - \sinh^2 x = 1.$$

$$\int \frac{1}{\sqrt{(x^2-1)}}\, dx = k+\cosh^{-1} x, \quad \int \frac{1}{\sqrt{(1+x^2)}}\, dx = k+\sinh^{-1} x.$$

$$\cosh^{-1} y = \log \{y+\sqrt{(y^2-1)}\}, \quad \sinh^{-1} y = \log \{y+\sqrt{(y^2+1)}\}.$$

30

CURRENT ELECTRICITY

1. DIRECT CURRENT ELECTRICITY

1.1 We have seen in the case of mechanics that a mathematical model requires a choice of postulates and laws as the basis for subsequent theory, calculations and predictions. If the postulates accord with the physical situation, we shall expect the predictions to tally with the results of appropriate experiments. Inevitably, though, the mathematical model does not represent the physical situation perfectly, and it would be surprising, for instance, if the prototype of a new aircraft behaved exactly as predicted at the drawing board stage.

Mechanics is one example of a good mathematical model, and another, perhaps better, is provided by Current Electricity. Basic to the model are the definitions of potential difference (p.d.), electric current, resistance and electromotive force (e.m.f.), together with the units in which they are measured. All this is assumed in this chapter, and also the symbols and conventions used when drawing a circuit diagram.

These various assumptions will be clarified as we proceed; for the moment we can list our basic suppositions as follows:

1. A *battery* produces a positive potential difference between its positive and negative terminals; if the terminals are not otherwise connected, this is called the electromotive force (e.m.f.) of the battery. We shall assume for the moment that this remains the same even when the terminals are connected by a conductor and a current is taken from the battery.

2. *Ohm's Law.* When a potential difference, V volts, is applied across a conductor, a current, I amperes, flows in the conductor, and the ratio of these quantities, V/I, is constant if the temperature is kept constant. This ratio is defined as the *resistance, R* ohms, of the conductor, so that

$$V = IR.$$

3. A *resistor* is a conductor of electricity which possesses appreciable resistance. By contrast we shall assume that the wires or metal strips which make up most of an electrical circuit have zero resistance.

The resistance of a conductor depends on its temperature; for most common materials, such as the filaments of light-bulbs and the elements of electric heaters, it increases with temperature. Unless, however, we make statements to the contrary we shall assume that resistances remain constant.

4. *Kirchhoff's First Law.* At any node (that is, a junction of wires, etc.)

906

the total current entering it equals the total current leaving it. In Figure 1, $x = y+z$.

5. The notation V_{AB} is used for the p.d. between two points, A and B respectively, of a circuit. Voltages are additive; that is,

$$V_{AC} = V_{AB} + V_{BC}.$$

Note that $\qquad\qquad V_{BA} = -V_{AB}.$

Thus in Figure 1, using property 2, $V_{AB} = xR_1$, $V_{AD} = xR_1 + zR_3$. It follows that round any closed loop of a circuit, the sum of the products (current × resistance) is equal to the net e.m.f. in that loop. This result is known as *Kirchhoff's Second Law*.

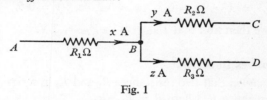

Fig. 1

6. *Units and symbols*. The unit of current is the *ampere*. This is in fact defined in terms of the mechanical force induced between two long thin straight current-bearing wires, but a full discussion of this involves more physical knowledge than we are assuming here. The abbreviation for ampere is A.

The charge carried by 1 ampere in 1 second is the *coulomb* (C). The unit of potential difference is the *volt* (V), and is defined in terms of work. A full definition must be left until work has been discussed. When a potential difference of 1 volt drives a current of 1 ampere through a resistor, its resistance is 1 *ohm* (Ω), and the power consumed is 1 *watt* (W).

We now give three examples to illustrate the meaning of these assumptions.

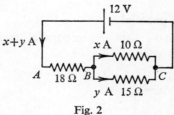

Fig. 2

Example 1. A 12-volt battery is connected up with three resistors as shown in Figure 2. Find the current through each part of the circuit. (The long part of the battery symbol is the positive terminal.)

In Figure 2 three points have been marked A, B, C. Then

$$V_{AC} = V_{AB} + V_{BC}, \quad \text{and} \quad V_{AC} = 12 \text{ V},$$

the e.m.f. of the battery.

When showing the currents on the diagram, Kirchhoff's First Law has been used.

Now Ohm's Law ($V = IR$) applied to each resistor in turn gives

$$V_{AB} = 18(x+y) \text{ V}, \quad V_{BC} = 10x \text{ V}, \quad V_{BC} = 15y \text{ V}.$$

It follows that $\qquad 10x = 15y, \quad \text{i.e. } 2x = 3y.$

Also, since $\qquad V_{AB} + V_{BC} = V_{AC} = 12 \text{ V},$

we have $\qquad 18x + 18y + 10x = 12,$

giving $\qquad 18x + 12x + 10x = 12,$

$$\Rightarrow x = \tfrac{12}{40} = 0 \cdot 3, \quad y = 0 \cdot 2, \quad x+y = 0 \cdot 5.$$

As a check, we then find that $V_{AB} = 9 \text{ V}$, $V_{BC} = 3 \text{ V}$.

1.2   Resistances in series.

It is easily shown that two resistances R_1 and R_2 in series are equivalent to a single resistance R, where $R = R_1 + R_2$.

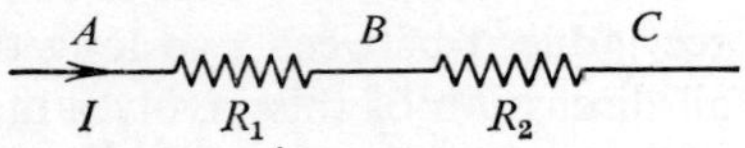

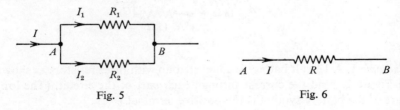

Fig. 3 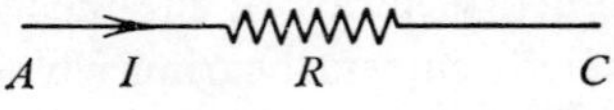   Fig. 4

From Figure 3:   From Figure 4:

$$V_{AC} = V_{AB} + V_{BC} \qquad\qquad V_{AC} = IR.$$

$$= IR_1 + IR_2.$$

So $\qquad\qquad\qquad\qquad IR = IR_1 + IR_2,$

$$\Rightarrow R = R_1 + R_2.$$

1.3   Resistances in parallel.

In the same way, two resistances in parallel (as in Figure 5) are equivalent to a single resistance.

Fig. 5   Fig. 6

In this case $\qquad\qquad I = \dfrac{V_{AB}}{R}, \quad$ from Figure 6,

and
$$I = I_1 + I_2 = \frac{V_{AB}}{R_1} + \frac{V_{AB}}{R_2} \quad \text{from Figure 5.}$$

It follows that
$$\frac{1}{R} = \frac{1}{R_1} + \frac{1}{R_2}.$$

The results of Sections 1.2 and 1.3 can be extended to apply to three or more resistors in series or in parallel.

$$R = \Sigma R_i \quad \text{in the series case,}$$

and
$$\frac{1}{R} = \Sigma \frac{1}{R_i} \quad \text{in the parallel case.}$$

Example 1 (alternative solution). Applying the above formulae, the 10- and 15-ohm resistors are equivalent to one of resistance $R\,\Omega$ where

$$\frac{1}{R} = \frac{1}{10} + \frac{1}{15} = \frac{3+2}{30} = \frac{1}{6},$$

i.e. $R = 6$. So an equivalent circuit is as shown in Figure 7. This in turn is equivalent to that shown in Figure 8, and Ohm's Law applied to this simple circuit gives the current as 0·5 A.

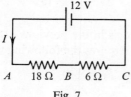

Fig. 7

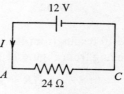

Fig. 8

Figure 7 then gives $V_{AB} = 9$ V and $V_{BC} = 3$ V, but the original circuit diagram is required to give the currents through the 10- and 15-ohm resistors. (As before, $V_{BC} = 10x$ V $= 15y$ V and hence $x = 0·3$ and $y = 0·2$.)

Example 2. Find the currents in each part of the circuit shown in Figure 9.

Figure 9 looks very complicated, but successive use of the results for resistors in series and parallel quickly simplifies the problem.

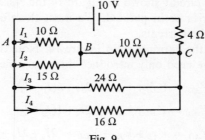

Fig. 9

909

Equivalent circuits are:

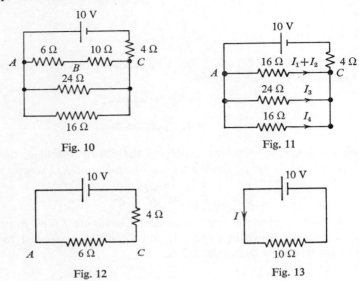

Fig. 10

Fig. 11

Fig. 12

Fig. 13

Figure 10 results from the same working as in the previous example. Proceeding from Figure 11 to Figure 12 requires the following working:

$$1/R = \tfrac{1}{16} + \tfrac{1}{24} + \tfrac{1}{16} = \tfrac{8}{48} = \tfrac{1}{6}$$

$$\Rightarrow R = 6\,\Omega.$$

It follows that $I = 1$ A from Figure 13,

and therefore $V_{AC} = 6$ V from Figure 12.

Hence $I_4 = \tfrac{6}{16}$ A, $I_3 = \tfrac{6}{24}$ A, $I_1 + I_2 = \tfrac{6}{16}$ A from Figure 11,

so that $V_{AB} = \tfrac{36}{16}$ V from Figure 10,

and $I_1 = \tfrac{36}{160}$ A, $I_2 = \tfrac{36}{240}$ A from Figure 9.

Example 3. In the circuit shown in Figure 14 the resistors cannot be said to be either in series or in parallel. We must therefore work from first principles to find the currents.

First, we put in the currents as in Figure 14. Note that by using Kirchhoff's First Law we need only introduce three variables.

Now $\quad 10 = V_{AD} = V_{AB} + V_{BD} = 2I_1 + 6(I_1 - I_3),$

and $\quad 10 = V_{AD} = V_{AC} + V_{CD} = 2I_2 + 1(I_2 + I_3),$

and $\quad 10 = V_{AD} = V_{AB} + V_{BC} + V_{CD} = 2I_1 + 2I_3 + 1(I_2 + I_3).$

910

Three equations involving three unknowns should be sufficient.
We have

$$8I_1 \quad -6I_3 = 10,$$
$$3I_2 + I_3 = 10,$$
$$2I_1 + I_2 + 3I_3 = 10.$$

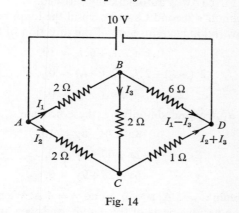

Fig. 14

Solving in the usual way we get

$$I_1 = 2 \text{ A}, \quad I_2 = 3 \text{ A}, \quad I_3 = 1 \text{ A}.$$

1.4 Loop currents.

Figure 15 repeats the circuit of Figure 14. We saw earlier that currents in each part of the circuit can be expressed in terms of three variables; the currents in AB, AC and BC were chosen then, but other triads would have done equally well. The number 3 is the number of regions of the plane enclosed by the circuit, and this is an invariant of the circuit provided that it is drawn without any two wires crossing over one another. Check that Figure 16 is an alternative way of drawing the same circuit.

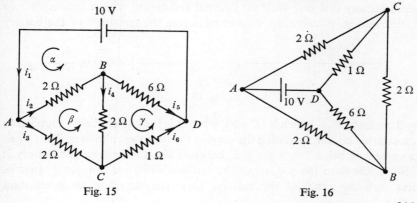

Fig. 15   Fig. 16

One way of specifying the currents is in terms of the loop currents α, β and γ as shown in Figure 15.

From these we find the currents in the various branches to be

$$i_1 = \alpha, \quad i_2 = \alpha - \beta, \quad i_3 = \beta, \quad i_4 = -\beta + \gamma, \quad i_5 = \alpha - \gamma, \quad i_6 = \gamma.$$

and Kirchhoff's First Law is automatically satisfied.

Applying Kirchhoff's Second Law to each of the loops round which the loop currents flow (taking careful note of the direction of these currents), we obtain

$$0 . i_1 + 2 . i_2 + 6 . i_5 = 10,$$
$$2 . (-i_2) + 2 . i_3 + 2 . (-i_4) = 0,$$
$$2 . i_4 + 1 . i_6 + 6 . (-i_5) = 0.$$

Substituting for α, β, γ and simplifying, these become

$$8\alpha - 2\beta - 6\gamma = 10,$$
$$-2\alpha + 6\beta - 2\gamma = 0,$$
$$-6\alpha - 2\beta + 9\gamma = 0.$$

Solving, we obtain $\alpha = 5$ A, $\beta = 3$ A and $\gamma = 4$ A. We have now found the currents in the various parts of the circuit, and they are easily seen to be in agreement with our previous results.

In summary, this method, which can be applied to any circuit consisting of resistors and batteries, involves first specifying loop currents for each of the enclosed regions of the network, and then writing down the equations given by Kirchhoff's Second Law for each of the enclosed loops. (If the circuit diagram cannot be drawn so that no wires cross, the same method still applies, but the number of loop currents required is not quite so obvious.)

1.5 Internal resistance of a battery.

In practice, a battery has an internal resistance, and behaves like an ideal battery (i.e. one with no internal resistance) with a resistance r in series with it. A voltmeter connected across the terminals of the battery

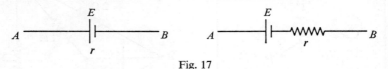

Fig. 17

will measure V_{AB}, which is $(E - Ir)$, where I is the current being supplied to an external circuit, including the current through the voltmeter. Thus when a current is being taken the p.d. between the terminals of the battery is always less than the p.d. when the terminals are not connected; that is, less than the e.m.f. of the battery. This latter is taken to be constant (though in practice it decreases as the battery 'runs down'), but the actual p.d. between the terminals depends on the current in the circuit, and it is important to distinguish it from the e.m.f. For example, in this simple circuit (Figure 18)

$$IR = E - Ir$$

$$\Rightarrow \quad I = \frac{E}{R+r}$$

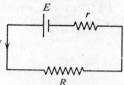

so that the e.m.f. of the battery is E but the p.d. across the battery terminals is

$$\frac{ER}{R+r}.$$

Fig. 18

Exercise A

1. The battery in Figure 19 has e.m.f. V and negligible internal resistance.

    (a) Find V if $I = 4$ A, $R = 20\ \Omega$.
    (b) Find R if $V = 90$ V, $I = 0.3$ A.
    (c) Find V if $I = 0.02$ mA and $R = 4$ MΩ.
    (1 mA (milliamp) = 10^{-3} A; 1 MΩ (megohm) = $10^{6}\ \Omega$.)

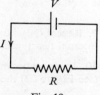

Fig. 19

2. A battery of e.m.f. 12 V and internal resistance 1 Ω is connected to a 5 Ω resistor. What current flows and what is the p.d. across the battery?

3. A battery of e.m.f. 12 V and internal resistance 1 Ω is connected to two resistances in parallel, of 12 Ω and 18 Ω. Find the current through each resistor.

4. When a battery is connected to a 7-ohm resistor, a current of 0.2 A flows. When a 5-ohm resistor is placed in series with the other, the current is reduced to 0.12 A. Find the e.m.f. and internal resistance of the battery.

5. Repeat Question 4 if the currents are I_1 and I_2 when the *total* external resistances are R_1 and R_2.

    If the currents in Question 4 are correct (i.e. an accurate ammeter has been used in the experiment) but there may be up to a 5 % error in the values of the resistances, find the maximum possible errors in the calculated values of the e.m.f. and internal resistance.

6. (a) Find the current through each resistor in the circuit shown in Figure 20.
    (b) What would happen if the switch A were closed?

7. Reproduce the circuit of Figure 14. Call the current supplied by the battery x, and let y and z be the currents in the branches AC and CD. Express the currents in each of the other branches in terms of x, y, z, and then form three independent equations in x, y, z. Solve these equations.

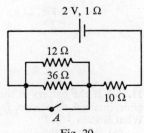

Fig. 20

8. (*a*) If the batteries in the circuit shown in Figure 21 supply *x* and *y* A, as shown, write down V_{AB} in three different ways, and hence find *x* and *y*.

(*b*) By the same method, find the *total* current if the 3·6-ohm resistor is replaced by one of *R* Ω.

(*c*) The two batteries could be replaced by a single battery of e.m.f. *E* V and internal resistance *r* Ω. What are the values of *E* and *r*?

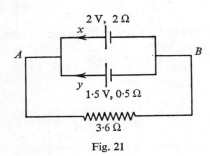

Fig. 21

9. Repeat Question 8(*b*) and (*c*) if the two batteries have e.m.f.'s E_1 and E_2 and internal resistances r_1 and r_2.

10. In an experiment to find the e.m.f. and internal resistance of a battery (see Figure 22) the following results were obtained:

R:	2	3	4	5	6
I:	0·78	0·56	0·45	0·37	0·31

Compare the answers given: (*a*) by drawing the graph of *IR* against *I*, and (*b*) the graph of 1/*I* against *R*.

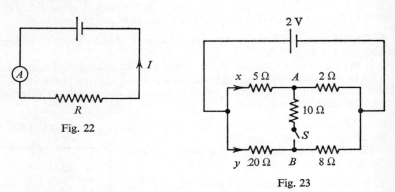

Fig. 22

Fig. 23

11. (*a*) If the battery in the circuit shown in Figure 23 has e.m.f. 2 V and negligible internal resistance, find the currents *x* and *y* when the switch *S* is open. What is then V_{AB}?

(*b*) What is the effect of closing *S*?

914

12. (a) Repeat Question 11(a) if the 8-ohm resistor is replaced by one of resistance 20 Ω.

(b) Find the current in the 10-ohm resistor when S is closed (use three loop currents).

(c) Would you expect your answer to (b) to be larger, smaller or the same if the 5 Ω and 2 Ω resistors are replaced by ones of resistance 500 Ω and 200 Ω? Calculate the current now.

(d) If you understand the theory of a Wheatstone Bridge, consider under what circumstances this circuit will give most accurate values for a resistance.

13.

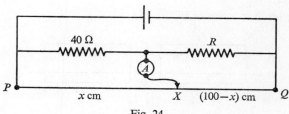

Fig. 24

The Metre Bridge whose circuit is shown in Figure 24 is used to find an unknown resistance R. A is an ammeter with a central zero (i.e. it records positive and negative currents) and PQ is a uniform wire of resistance 1 Ω per cm length. It is 100 cm long. The point X is found for which the current through the ammeter is zero.

Then

$$\frac{R}{40} = \frac{100 - x}{x} = \frac{100}{x} - 1 \quad \text{(see Question 11)}.$$

(a) Find R when $x = 57$ cm and also when $x = 57 \cdot 5$ cm.

(b) Find dR/dx when $x = 57$ cm.

(c) Interpret each symbol of the statement $\delta R \simeq dR/dx \cdot \delta x$ in terms of this circuit, and so check that your answers to (a) and (b) are consistent.

2. MATRIX METHODS

The fact that the solution of network problems usually involves linear equations suggests that matrix methods might be useful. The next exercise explores this idea.

Exercise B

1. Here we focus attention on one small part of the circuit only. We may think of the box on the left as containing batteries as well as other components, and refer to A and B as the input terminals, I_0 and V_0 as the input current and voltage.

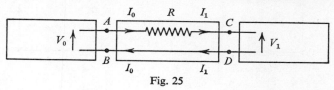

Fig. 25

The box on the right may contain other resistors in an unspecified arrangement. I_1 and V_1 are the output current and voltage of this 'four terminal network'. It is clear that

$$V_0 = V_1 + I_1 R, \quad \text{i.e.} \quad \begin{pmatrix} V_0 \\ I_0 \end{pmatrix} = \begin{pmatrix} 1 & R \\ 0 & 1 \end{pmatrix} \begin{pmatrix} V_1 \\ I_1 \end{pmatrix}.$$
$$I_0 = \quad I_1,$$

Form the product of the matrices

$$\begin{pmatrix} 1 & R_1 \\ 0 & 1 \end{pmatrix} \quad \text{and} \quad \begin{pmatrix} 1 & R_2 \\ 0 & 1 \end{pmatrix}.$$

Interpret the result in terms of Figure 26.

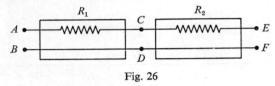

Fig. 26

2. (*a*) Show that, for Figure 27,

$$\begin{pmatrix} V_0 \\ I_0 \end{pmatrix} = \begin{pmatrix} 1 & 0 \\ 1/S & 1 \end{pmatrix} \begin{pmatrix} V_1 \\ I_1 \end{pmatrix}.$$

(*b*) Simplify

$$\begin{pmatrix} 1 & 0 \\ 1/S_1 & 1 \end{pmatrix} \begin{pmatrix} 1 & 0 \\ 1/S_2 & 1 \end{pmatrix},$$

and explain the result.

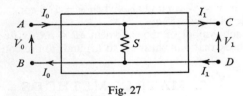

Fig. 27

3. By forming the product of three matrices of the types established in Questions 1, 2, find the single matrix corresponding to the resistances of Figure 28. If the output and input voltages are 0 and 12, find the output and input currents. Compare with Section 1.1, Example 1.

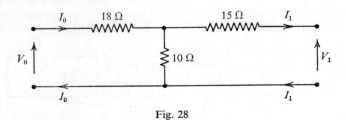

Fig. 28

4. The circuit of Figure 29 can be thought of as having *loops* l and m, and *branches* 1, 2, 3. Write down equations expressing each branch current in terms of the loop currents, and express these in the form $\mathbf{i} = \mathbf{MI}$, where

$$\mathbf{I} \text{ is } \begin{pmatrix} I_l \\ I_m \end{pmatrix}, \quad \mathbf{i} \text{ is } \begin{pmatrix} i_1 \\ i_2 \\ i_3 \end{pmatrix},$$

and $\mathbf{M}$ is a 3×2 matrix containing only the numbers 1, 0, -1.

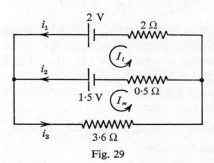

Fig. 29

If v_1, v_2, v_3 are the voltage drops (potential differences) across the resistances in each branch, in the same sense as the currents, find a matrix R such that

$$\mathbf{v} = \begin{pmatrix} v_1 \\ v_2 \\ v_3 \end{pmatrix} = \mathbf{Ri}.$$

If
$$\mathbf{e} = \begin{pmatrix} 0.5 \\ 1.5 \end{pmatrix},$$

that is a vector giving the net e.m.f.'s in each loop, explain why $\mathbf{e} = \mathbf{M'v}$, where $\mathbf{M'}$ is the transpose of $\mathbf{M}$, i.e. the 2×3 matrix with the rows and columns of $\mathbf{M}$ interchanged.

Hence show that $\mathbf{e} = \mathbf{M'RMI}$, and by finding the inverse of the matrix product $\mathbf{M'RM}$ find I_l and I_m.

2.1 Matrix methods—an example. Exercise A, Question 8 and Exercise B, Question 4, were concerned with the same problem. It may seem that the second method only succeeded in making an easy question difficult. In developing matrix techniques for networks, what we are seeking is a routine which—with the aid of a computer maybe—would enable us to cope with complicated network problems in a systematic way. The techniques of Exercise B, Questions 1–3, can only be applied to a limited range of networks, but the method of Question 4 is more generally applicable. We now discuss this in detail.

The example we choose to illustrate the method is that of Section 1.4.

We may specify the currents in terms of the loop currents α, β and γ by means of the matrix equation

$$\begin{pmatrix} i_1 \\ i_2 \\ i_3 \\ i_4 \\ i_5 \\ i_6 \end{pmatrix} = \begin{pmatrix} 1 & 0 & 0 \\ 1 & -1 & 0 \\ 0 & 1 & 0 \\ 0 & -1 & 1 \\ 1 & 0 & -1 \\ 0 & 0 & 1 \end{pmatrix} \begin{pmatrix} \alpha \\ \beta \\ \gamma \end{pmatrix}.$$

The 6×3 matrix is an incidence matrix called a *tie-set matrix*, and shows the connection between the loops chosen and the branches of the network.

The matrix equation is written $\mathbf{i} = \mathbf{MI}$. Here $\mathbf{i}$ is the branch current vector, and $\mathbf{I}$ is the vector of loop currents.

Now if the voltage drops across the resistances in each branch are written v_1, v_2, v_3, v_4, v_5, v_6, then

$$v_1 = 0, \quad v_2 = 2i_2, \quad v_3 = 2i_3, \quad v_4 = 2i_4, \quad v_5 = 6i_5, \quad v_6 = i_6.$$

These equations can be written

$$\begin{pmatrix} v_1 \\ v_2 \\ v_3 \\ v_4 \\ v_5 \\ v_6 \end{pmatrix} = \begin{pmatrix} 0 & 0 & 0 & 0 & 0 & 0 \\ 0 & 2 & 0 & 0 & 0 & 0 \\ 0 & 0 & 2 & 0 & 0 & 0 \\ 0 & 0 & 0 & 2 & 0 & 0 \\ 0 & 0 & 0 & 0 & 6 & 0 \\ 0 & 0 & 0 & 0 & 0 & 1 \end{pmatrix} \begin{pmatrix} i_1 \\ i_2 \\ i_3 \\ i_4 \\ i_5 \\ i_6 \end{pmatrix},$$

or $\mathbf{v} = \mathbf{Ri}$.

Combining the equations $\mathbf{v} = \mathbf{Ri}$ and $\mathbf{i} = \mathbf{MI}$, we get $\mathbf{v} = \mathbf{RMI}$; this expresses the voltage drop in the resistances in each branch in terms of the three loop currents.

The third and last set of equations comes from equating the sum of the voltage drops in each loop with the net e.m.f. in that loop.

In this example

$$10 = v_1 + v_2 + v_5$$
$$0 = -v_2 + v_3 - v_4$$
$$0 = v_4 - v_5 + v_6;$$

i.e.
$$\begin{pmatrix} 10 \\ 0 \\ 0 \end{pmatrix} = \begin{pmatrix} 1 & 1 & 0 & 0 & 1 & 0 \\ 0 & -1 & 1 & -1 & 0 & 0 \\ 0 & 0 & 0 & 1 & -1 & 1 \end{pmatrix} \begin{pmatrix} v_1 \\ v_2 \\ v_3 \\ v_4 \\ v_5 \\ v_6 \end{pmatrix}.$$

This matrix equation is written $\mathbf{e} = \mathbf{M'v}$. Note that $\mathbf{M'}$ is the transpose of $\mathbf{M}$, the result of interchanging rows and columns.

Finally, we combine $\mathbf{e} = \mathbf{M'v}$ and $\mathbf{v} = \mathbf{RMI}$ to get $\mathbf{e} = \mathbf{M'RMI}$. We know $\mathbf{e}$, $\mathbf{M'}$, $\mathbf{R}$, $\mathbf{M}$ and wish to find the vector $\mathbf{I}$. This is $(\mathbf{M'RM})^{-1}\mathbf{e}$.

Performing these operations

$$\mathbf{M'RM} = \begin{pmatrix} 8 & -2 & -6 \\ -2 & 6 & -2 \\ -6 & -2 & 9 \end{pmatrix}$$

$$\Rightarrow (\mathbf{M'RM})^{-1} = \begin{pmatrix} 0\cdot5 & 0\cdot3 & 0\cdot4 \\ 0\cdot3 & 0\cdot36 & 0\cdot28 \\ 0\cdot4 & 0\cdot28 & 0\cdot44 \end{pmatrix}$$

$$\Rightarrow \mathbf{I} = \begin{pmatrix} \alpha \\ \beta \\ \gamma \end{pmatrix} = \begin{pmatrix} 5 \\ 3 \\ 4 \end{pmatrix}.$$

In a simple example, this method seems unduly laborious. The point is that the equation $\mathbf{e} = \mathbf{M'RMI}$ applies, however complicated the network; $\mathbf{e}$ and $\mathbf{R}$ are written down very easily and the procedure for writing down $\mathbf{M}$ is straightforward. Standard matrix methods complete the calculation. As so often in applied mathematics, the formulation of the equations is the difficult job, and their solution is a routine matter.

2.2 Summary of the procedure. In any problem such as that in the last section, the procedure is as follows:

1. Show the loop currents on a diagram; they should all have the same sense—either all clockwise or anticlockwise.

2. Label the branches 1, 2, 3, ...

3. Write down the vector $\mathbf{e}$, containing the net e.m.f.'s in each loop. Use the sign convention determined by (1).

4. Write down the matrix $\mathbf{R}$. This has the branch resistances down the leading diagonal in the order adopted in (2), and zeros elsewhere.

5. Write down the matrix $\mathbf{M}$. Each row corresponds to a branch and each column to a loop. If a branch forms a part of two loops, $+1$ and -1 (in either order) should be placed in the corresponding places in its row. If a branch forms part of one loop only, $+1$ or -1 (it does not matter which) should be placed in the appropriate place in its row. All other elements are zero. (The arbitrary decisions about signs correspond to arbitrary assignments of directions to the branch currents.)

6. Simplify and solve the equation $\mathbf{e} = \mathbf{M'RMI}$ to give the loop currents.

Exercise C

1. Repeat Exercise A, Question 6(a), using the methods of Section 2.

2. Make up a network with two loops like Figure 29, and find the loop currents.

3. Repeat the example of Section 2.1, using Figure 16.

4. Work out the matrix **M′RM** for the circuit of Figure 30, but do not invert it.

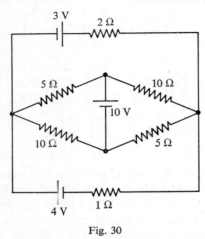

Fig. 30

3. POWER

3.1   Forms of energy. Electricity carries energy. The immense increase in the use of electricity in this century stems from the ease with which it does this. Energy is used to produce the electricity, and we turn this energy back into useful work when we switch on an electric fire, or a washing-machine, or a refrigerator, or a light. Energy comes in various forms, and they are all interchangeable, directly or indirectly. Heat, light, mechanical energy, atomic energy, chemical energy, electrical energy are some of the many forms that energy can take.

The commonest ways of producing electrical energy are the chemical battery, and the dynamo or generator. The chemical battery turns chemical energy directly into electrical energy. In a power station, atomic energy or chemical energy is turned into heat, which is then converted into mechanical energy, and finally into electrical energy.

We measure these various kinds of energy in terms of their mechanical equivalents. Mechanical energy is easily measured: when a force moves the body which it is applied to, energy is expended which is proportional to the force and the distance it moves in the direction in which it is being applied. The energy expended when 1 newton moves through 1 metre is called 1 joule:

$$1 \text{ joule (J)} = 1 \text{ newton} \times 1 \text{ metre} = 1 \text{ N m}.$$

This will be understood more clearly when the chapter on Work and Energy is reached (Chapter 39).

Electrical energy is measured in terms of the mechanical energy into which it can be converted, that is, its value in joules at the standard rate of exchange. This is in fact used to define the volt: 1 volt is the p.d. through which 1 coulomb must fall to expend 1 joule of energy. Formally,

$$1 \text{ volt (V)} \times 1 \text{ coulomb (C)} = 1 \text{ joule (J)}.$$

3.2 Power consumed in resistors.

We are usually interested in *power*, which is defined as the *rate of consuming energy*, or of doing work. A powerful man can dig a plot of land quickly—that is, at a great rate. If energy is being expended at 1 joule per second, the power being developed is 1 *watt* (W). A current therefore of I amperes falling through a p.d. of V volts carries a charge of I coulombs per second through this p.d. and does IV joules of work per second; that is, its power is $P = IV$ watts. Comparing the units, we may say

$$1 \text{ watt (W)} = 1 \text{ J/s} = 1 \text{ V C/s} = 1 \text{ VA},$$

or

$$1 \text{ volt} \times 1 \text{ ampere} = 1 \text{ watt} = 1 \text{ newton} \times 1 \text{ metre}/1 \text{ second}.$$

This fall in p.d. will usually take place in a resistor, and the power developed will be turned into heat energy. Of course electric motors use the power in other ways.

In Example 1, the 12 V battery supplied a current of 0·5 A, thereby supplying a power of $0·5 \text{ A} \times 12 \text{ V} = 6 \text{ W}$. Of this total, the 10-ohm resistor was consuming $0·3 \text{ A} \times 3 \text{ V} = 0·9 \text{ W}$. Work out the power consumed by the other two resistors, and check that the total power consumed is equal to the total power being supplied. This power would appear in the form of heat. The power consumed by an electric radiator is much greater (several kilowatts, i.e. thousands of watts), and the heat and light produced is evident.

Combination of the two formulae $V = IR$ and $P = IV$ gives two useful variations: $P = I^2R$ and $P = V^2/R$. With these formulae great care must be taken to use the appropriate current and p.d., i.e. those relevant to the component under consideration.

Example 4. A battery of e.m.f. 12 V and internal resistance 2 Ω is connected to two resistors as in Figure 31. What power is consumed by the 24-ohm resistor if the switch at C is (*a*) open, and (*b*) closed?

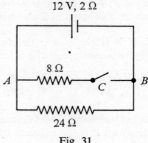
12 V, 2 Ω
8 Ω
A
C
B
24 Ω
Fig. 31

(*a*) $I = \dfrac{12 \text{ V}}{(2+24)\,\Omega} = 0·46 \text{ A}.$

Power in 24-ohm resistor $= I^2R$

$$= (0·46)^2 \times 24 \text{ W}$$

$$= 5·1 \text{ W}.$$

(*b*) The two resistors are equivalent to a single resistance of $R\,\Omega$ where

$$\frac{1}{R} = \frac{1}{8} + \frac{1}{24} = \frac{1}{6}$$

$$\Rightarrow R = 6.$$

The total current is now

$$\frac{12\,V}{(2+6)\,\Omega} = 1{\cdot}5\,A,$$

and

$$V_{AB} = 1{\cdot}5\,A \times 6\,\Omega$$

$$= 9\,V.$$

Power consumed in the 24-ohm resistor is

$$V^2/R = 9^2/24\,W$$

$$= 3{\cdot}4\,W.$$

This demonstrates (though the figures are not realistic) why car lights become dimmer while the self-starter is being operated. Note that if there were no internal resistance, the power in each case would be $12^2/24\,W$, that is, 6 W.

Exercise D

1. When a p.d. of V V is applied to a resistance $R\,\Omega$, a current of I A flows. Find the power dissipated in the resistance if:
    (*a*) $I = 5$, $V = 200$;   (*b*) $I = 3$, $R = 7$;   (*c*) $V = 230$, $R = 20$.

2. A 1-kilowatt electric radiator is designed for use with 230-volt mains. Find the resistance of the element. One day, the mains voltage drops, and the current through the element drops to 4 A. If the resistance of the element is then 5 % less than before, what power does the fire now consume?

3. A 2-volt battery with internal resistance $2\,\Omega$ is connected to two 30-ohm resistors in parallel. Find the power dissipated in each.

4. A battery of e.m.f. E and internal resistance r supplies current to a resistance R. Find expressions for the total power supplied by the battery, and the power dissipated in the external resistance.

5. If P is the power developed in the resistance R of the circuit shown in Figure 32, complete the following table, and draw the graph of P against R.

$$R{:}\ \ 0\ \ 6\ \ 12\ \ 18\ \ 24\ \ 36$$
$$P{:}$$

6. In Question 5 find a formula for P in terms of R, and then find the value of R for which P is a maximum by differentiation.

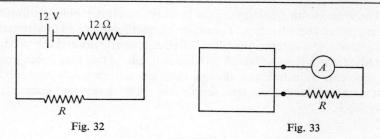

Fig. 32   Fig. 33

7. It is expected that a home-made 'power pack' (represented by the rectangle in Figure 33) will behave like a battery with internal resistance. An ammeter and resistor were connected across its terminals as shown, and when R was varied, the following results were obtained:

R:	10	20	30	40	50
I:	2·8	2·15	1·7	1·45	1·25
$P = I^2R$:					

(a) Copy and complete the table and draw the graph of P against R.
(b) Can you guess the apparent internal resistance of the power pack?
(c) Carry out *one* further calculation to corroborate your answer to (b).

4. MAXIMUM POWER TRANSFER

The last three questions of Exercise D suggest a result of considerable importance. We are often concerned with designing equipment so that the maximum power is developed in it.

Example 5. We shall prove that in the simple circuit shown in Figure 34 the battery will deliver maximum power to the resistor if R is exactly equal to the internal resistance.

$$I = \frac{E}{R+r},$$

so the power dissipated in the external resistance is given by

$$P = \frac{E^2R}{(R+r)^2}.$$

Fig. 34

This is a maximum when $$\frac{dP}{dR} = 0,$$

that is, when $$\frac{E^2(R+r) - 2E^2R}{(R+r)^3} = 0$$

$$\Rightarrow (R+r) - 2R = 0$$

$$\Rightarrow R = r.$$

923

There are innumerable examples in which maximum energy transfer is an important consideration. The design of microphones and loudspeakers, the gearbox of a car, the 'coupling' of electronic circuits and the 'feeding' of radio transmitting aerials all provide problems of this type (often known as problems in matching), though they are not so easily expressed in mathematical terms. A few simple electrical cases are indicated in Exercise E.

Exercise E

1. A 2-volt, 1-ohm battery is connected to two resistors in series, of resistances $4\,\Omega$ and $R\,\Omega$. What value of R makes the power consumed in that resistor a maximum?

2. Two 2-volt, 1-ohm batteries are connected in parallel to a resistance R (see Figure 35). What value of R makes the power consumed in it a maximum?

3. Find a formula for the power consumed by R, and the value of R which makes this a maximum (see Figure 36).

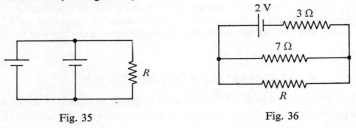

Fig. 35   Fig. 36

4. (*a*) Find a formula for the current through R (see Figure 37).

(*b*) The components within the dotted rectangle are equivalent to a single battery of e.m.f. E' and internal resistance r'. What are E' and r'?

(*c*) What value of R gives maximum power in the external circuit?

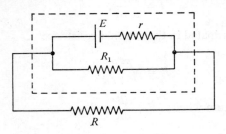

Fig. 37

5. An electric motor (represented by the rectangle in Figure 38) is driven by a 12-volt battery. The total resistance of the circuit is $3\,\Omega$, and the motor produces a 'back-e.m.f.' V (that is, a voltage opposing the battery) which depends upon the

924

speed at which the motor is working. Find, in terms of V, the power supplied by the motor, assuming it to be 90 % efficient, and the back-e.m.f. that makes this a maximum.

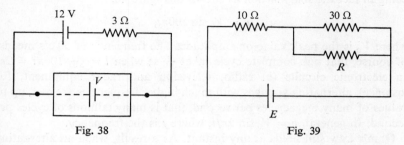

Fig. 38   Fig. 39

6. For a given E in the circuit shown in Figure 39 find the values of R which minimize the power consumed:

    (a) by R;

    (b) by the 10-ohm resistor;

    (c) by the 30-ohm resistor.

7. The potential difference across a non-linear resistance is given by $V = 9I^2$, where I A is the current through it. It is connected in series with a constant resistance ($R\,\Omega$) and a 12-volt battery of negligible internal resistance.

    (a) Obtain an expression for P, the power dissipated in the R-ohm resistor, in terms of I only, and hence find the values of I and R making this a maximum.

    (b) Express P in terms of R only, find dP/dR, and hence check your answers to (a).

    (c) Find the maximum value of I, and the corresponding value of R.

5. ALTERNATING CURRENT AND VOLTAGES

5.1 Sinusoidal voltages. So far we have considered only Direct Current (d.c.), that is current of constant magnitude flowing in one direction round a circuit. The domestic power supply is 50 cycles per second Alternating

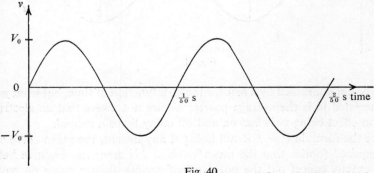

Fig. 40

Voltage. This causes an Alternating Current (a.c.) which flows first in one direction, then in the other. The voltage is a function of time, the function being in fact the *sine function* as shown in Figure 40.

$$v = V_0 \sin 100\pi t,$$

where V_0 is the peak value or amplitude. The frequency of 50 c/s means, of course, that one complete cycle takes $\frac{1}{50}$ s; when $t = \frac{1}{50}$, $100\pi t = 2\pi$. In electronic circuits (in radio, television and radar equipment, for instance), alternating voltages with much higher frequencies are met, up to values of many megacycles per second, that is many millions of cycles per second. In general, $v = V_0 \sin 2\pi f t$, where f is the frequency.

Ohm's Law still holds at any instant. As a result, when an alternating voltage is applied to a resistor, an alternating current flows, having the same frequency as the voltage and being *in phase* with it (see Figure 41). This means that the positive peaks occur simultaneously. $V_0 = I_0 R$, of course.

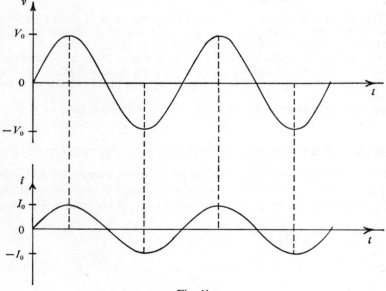

Fig. 41

The power consumed by a resistor is also a function of time, but what we are interested in is the average power; we are not aware that an electric fire is in effect being switched on and off many times a second.

Since the formula $P = I^2 R$ still holds at any instant, the mean value of i^2 is required (notice that the mean value of i is zero; the negative half cycles exactly cancel out the positive half cycles). Before going on, you

926

should draw or sketch graphs of $y = \sin x$ and $y = \sin^2 x$. The result will then be obvious.

If
$$i = I_0 \sin 2\pi ft,$$
$$i^2 = I_0^2 \sin^2 2\pi ft$$
$$= \tfrac{1}{2}I_0^2 (1 - \cos 4\pi ft).$$

Now the mean value of $\cos 4\pi ft$ taken over a complete cycle is zero, so the mean value of i^2 is $\tfrac{1}{2}I_0^2$. This shows that an a.c. with peak value I_0 is equivalent, from the power point of view, to a d.c. of $I_0/\sqrt{2}$. This is called the *Root Mean Square* (r.m.s.) value of the a.c. In the same way, the root mean square of an alternating voltage is $V_0/\sqrt{2}$; then, using r.m.s. values, $V = IR$ and the formulae $P = IV = I^2R = V^2/R$ also hold, provided that the current and voltage are in phase. When we talk of the mains voltage being 230 V, we mean that the r.m.s. voltage is 230. The peak value is $230\sqrt{2} = 325$ V.

You will remember that we have used the idea of a root mean square before, when defining standard deviation as a measure of spread. The average deviation from the mean is always zero, just as here the average current is zero.

5.2   The use of alternating current. It may seem to be an unnecessarily complicated procedure to use alternating current, but in fact it is much easier and cheaper to produce electricity in this form. It is also more immediately usable for running electric motors, and is just as useful for heating and lighting; it is also rather safer than direct current when used in the home.

Suitably generated alternating currents are also used to produce radio waves which are converted back into alternating currents in the domestic television set or radio receiver, and there used to create the picture and the sound which we observe. This is done by superposing alternating currents of much lower frequencies corresponding to the sounds being transmitted; the whole system of communication and reproduction of sound by electrical means depends on the use of a.c.

But the overriding reason for the use of a.c. is the ease with which it can be transformed; the current can be reduced at the price of increased voltage, and vice versa. This process we now examine.

5.3   Transformers. The circuit symbol for a transformer is shown in Figure 42.

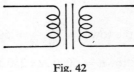

Fig. 42

If two separate coils of wire are wound round an iron core, an alternating voltage applied to one causes an alternating voltage to be induced in the other. This is because of the alternating magnetic field produced by the current in the first (primary) coil. The size of the e.m.f. in the other (secondary) coil depends upon the ratio of the number of turns in the two coils. We use the symbols n_p, n_s, V_p, V_s, I_p, I_s, where p and s indicate the primary and secondary variables, and the n's are the number of turns on the transformer. Then in a 'perfect' transformer

$$\frac{V_s}{V_p} = \frac{n_s}{n_p}.$$

(Here we are again considering a mathematical model which does not reproduce exactly conditions found in practice.)

If the voltage is stepped up, there must be a corresponding decrease in current, otherwise there would be a power gain. Assuming negligible power loss in our perfect transformer

$$I_s V_s = I_p V_p.$$

When electrical power is carried over long distances as in the National Grid system, it is important to reduce as far as possible the power losses in the cables. This is $I^2 R$, where R is the resistance of the cables; it is therefore desirable to have the current as small as possible, and this requires high voltages. At the power stations, 'step up' transformers increase the voltage to 132000 V, and then 'step-down' transformers are required in the areas where the electricity is to be used.

Example 6. A long cable of resistance 5 Ω feeds the local transformer of a small town. Here the voltage is stepped down to 250 V by a transformer with 95 % efficiency. The town behaves like a 0·05-ohm resistor at peak loading; what is the minimum grid voltage if the power loss in the cable is then to be less than 1 kilowatt? (Figure 43.)

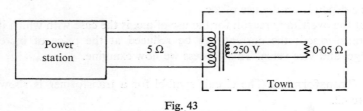

Fig. 43

Total current taken by the town $= \dfrac{250 \text{ V}}{0\cdot05 \text{ }\Omega} = 5000 \text{ A.}$

Power consumed in the town $= 5000 \text{ A} \times 250 \text{ V} = 1\cdot25 \times 10^6 \text{ W.}$

928

Power supplied to transformer $= 1 \cdot 25 \times 10^6 \times \frac{100}{95}$ W

$$= 1 \cdot 32 \times 10^6 \text{ W}$$

$$= IV,$$

where I = current in the cable, V = voltage in the grid.

Power loss in the cable $= I^2 \times 5 \, \Omega < 1000$ W

giving $I < 14 \cdot 1$ A

and $V > \dfrac{1 \cdot 32 \times 10^6 \text{ W}}{14 \cdot 1 \text{ A}} = 9 \cdot 36 \times 10^4$ V.

Notice that there is a slight difference between the grid voltages at the power station and town ends. These 'lost volts' ($14 \cdot 1 \times 5 = 70 \cdot 5$ V at the most) are negligible compared with the 93 600 V.

Exercise F

1. (a) What is the peak value of an a.c. whose r.m.s. value is 3 A?

(b) An a.c. is given by the formula $i = 10 \sin 2\pi ft$. What is its r.m.s. value?

2. An a.c. of I A, where $I = 2 \sin 100\pi t$, flows in a 5-ohm resistor. What power is dissipated as heat?

3. Sketch the graph of $y = 1 + 2 \sin x$ for $0 \leqslant x \leqslant 4\pi$.

With the same axes, sketch the graph of $y = (1 + 2 \sin x)^2$, and from this guess the mean value of $(1 + 2 \sin x)^2$ taken over a complete cycle.

4. A current of magnitude $(A + B \sin \omega t)$ passes through a resistance R. (A, B and ω are constants.) Find the value of the mean power developed.

5. (a) Simplify $\cos (\theta - \phi) - \cos (\theta + \phi)$.

(b) When an a.c. $i = I_0 \sin \omega t$ flows through an appliance, the corresponding p.d. is $v = V_0 \sin (\omega t + \epsilon)$.

Express the power consumed at time t as the difference of two cosines, and hence find the mean power. What happens when $\epsilon = \frac{1}{2}\pi$?

6. Sketch with the same axes, the graphs of:

(a) $i = \sin t$;   (b) $i = 2 \cos t$;   (c) $i = \sin t + 2 \cos t$.

What is the maximum value of i in (c)?

7. (a) Express $2 \sin t + 3 \sin (t + \frac{1}{3}\pi)$ first in the form $A \sin t + B \cos t$, then in the form $C \sin (t + \epsilon)$.

(b) Show that the sum of any two alternating currents of the same frequency (but not necessarily in phase) is an alternating current.

8. Sketch with the same axes the graphs of:

(a) $i = \sin t$;   (b) $i = \frac{1}{3} (\sin 3t)$;   (c) $i = \sin t + \frac{1}{3}(\sin 3t)$.

What do you deduce about alternating currents?

9. A high-frequency voltage, $V = V_0 \sin 10^5 \pi t$, is *modulated* by making its amplitude V_0 vary slowly with time, so that $V_0 = V_1 \sin 10^3 \pi t$.

(*a*) Sketch the graph of V against t.

(*b*) Show that $V = V_2 (\cos 2\pi f_1 t - \cos 2\pi f_2 t)$, giving the values of the frequencies f_1 and f_2, and of V_2 in terms of V_1.

(*c*) Explain why a wide band of frequencies is required to transmit high-pitched notes faithfully in this way.

10. A transformer steps the voltage down from 200 V to 5 V, and the secondary circuit contains only a 10-ohm resistor. Find the primary and secondary currents, assuming no power loss in the transformer.

11. A town (with local voltage 250 V) takes a maximum winter load of 10^7 watts. The supply is provided by a loss-free transformer fed from a power station through a long cable of resistance $2\,\Omega$. Find the power loss in the cable if the voltage across the primary of the transformer is (*a*) 2500 V, and (*b*) 25 000 V.

12. What is the effective load resistance of the town in Question 11? How many 1-kilowatt electric radiators all in parallel would have the same effect?

13. A loss-free step-up transformer has a turns ratio (and hence a voltage ratio) of 10. It is connected to a dynamo producing 4 V, and the secondary load is a 200-ohm resistance. Find the current supplied by the dynamo, and the effective load (i.e. the resistance which would draw the same current from the dynamo if there was no transformer).

14. Repeat Question 12, where the transformer has turns ratio t and the load has resistance R.

15. The output amplifier stage of a radio has internal resistance $5000\,\Omega$. A transformer matches this to a loudspeaker of resistance $3\,\Omega$. What turns ratio is required in the transformer? Is it used as a step-up or a step-down transformer? (By matching, we mean that there is maximum power transfer.)

16. In a radio circuit, the output voltage is $Af/\sqrt{(B^2+f^2)}$, where A and B are constants and f is the frequency. If this is applied to a load of resistance R, show in a graph how the power varies with f. For what values of f is the power greater than 0·9 times the maximum power?

31

APPLICATIONS OF FIRST-ORDER DIFFERENTIAL EQUATIONS

The mathematical treatment of situations in science may produce equations to be solved, formulae to be manipulated, or numerical data to be handled statistically. There are three stages in a typical problem—formulation, solution, and interpretation of results. In this chapter we are particularly concerned with the first stage, but also investigate one new method of solving certain differential equations.

1. FORMULATION OF PROBLEMS

In practice this is the most difficult stage. The problem must be put into mathematical form—symbols are introduced and the laws of science used to produce equations. It is at this stage that approximations may be necessary, and these should be made explicit if possible. Numerical data must be collected, and mathematical considerations may dictate what experiments are to be conducted to provide these data. This is best discussed in terms of a specific example.

Example 1

Problem. You are given a particular conical funnel. Investigate how the time taken for it to empty depends upon the initial height of liquid in the funnel.

The time, which we shall call T, clearly depends upon the initial height h_0 and a number of other factors—the shape of the funnel, the density, viscosity and surface tension of the liquid, gravitational acceleration, temperature and so on. We start by confining our attention to the two variables T and h_0, and attempt to keep the others fixed. In particular, the same liquid will be used throughout.

A series of experiments might then be conducted to give a table of values of (h_0, T) and these would be displayed in a graph. If a graph of $\log T$ against $\log h_0$ turned out to be a straight line, a power law relationship would be suggested.

Alternatively, we may think we know the appropriate physical law. Let us postulate that the rate of flow is proportional to the pressure difference at the orifice, and that this pressure difference is proportional to the depth of liquid.

13-2

In symbols, $dV/dt \propto p$, and $p \propto h$. (At time t, call the depth of liquid h, the volume of the liquid in the vessel V, and the pressure difference at the orifice p.) Together these imply

$$\frac{dV}{dt} \propto h,$$

that is

$$\frac{dV}{dt} = -kh,$$

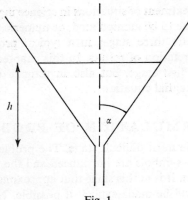

Fig. 1

where k is a constant. The rate of flow of liquid equals the rate at which V is *decreasing*. Since we know that dV/dt is negative, it is convenient to put in the minus sign above; k is then a positive constant.

The differential equation contains three variables V, t, h and cannot be integrated in this form. However, V can be eliminated if we use the formula

$$V = \tfrac{1}{3}\pi r^2 h$$

$$= \tfrac{1}{3}\pi (h \tan \alpha)^2 \, h$$

$$= \tfrac{1}{3}\pi \tan^2 \alpha \,.\, h^3$$

Then

$$\frac{dV}{dt} = \tfrac{1}{3}\pi \tan^2 \alpha \,.\, 3h^2 \frac{dh}{dt}, \qquad (1)$$

giving

$$\pi \tan^2 \alpha \,.\, h^2 \frac{dh}{dt} = -kh,$$

i.e.

$$h\frac{dh}{dt} = -k' \quad \text{where} \quad k' = k/\pi \tan^2 \alpha.$$

Integrating, we get

$$\tfrac{1}{2}h^2 = -k't + A,$$

where the constant $A = \tfrac{1}{2}h_0^2$, if $h = h_0$ when $t = 0$.

932

The solution curve is a parabolic arc as in Figure 2, and

$$T = \frac{h_0^2}{2k'}$$

$$= \frac{\pi \tan^2 \alpha \, h_0^2}{2k}.$$

If experiment confirms that $T \propto h_0^2$, this strengthens confidence in the original postulates.

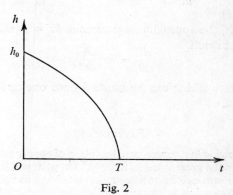

Fig. 2

Alternative derivation. It is sometimes useful to look at this in a different way. If the depth is reduced by a small amount δh in a short time interval t, V is the volume of the layer of liquid shaded in Figure 3. This is approximately disc-shaped, and in any case

$$\pi r^2 \delta h > \delta V > \pi (r - \delta r)^2 \delta h$$

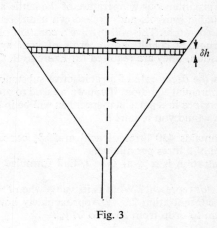

Fig. 3

(using the obvious notation). This gives

$$\pi r^2 \frac{\delta h}{\delta t} > \frac{\delta V}{\delta t} > \pi r^2 \frac{\delta h}{\delta t} - 2\pi r \, \delta r \frac{\delta h}{\delta t} + \pi (\delta r)^2 \frac{\delta h}{\delta t}.$$

If we now take the limit as $t \to 0$, we get

$$\pi r^2 \frac{dh}{dt} \geqslant \frac{dV}{dt} \geqslant \pi r^2 \frac{dh}{dt}.$$

Hence
$$\frac{dV}{dt} = \pi r^2 \frac{dh}{dt} = \pi \tan^2 \alpha . h^2 \frac{dh}{dt}$$

as in equation (1).

In other words, the approximate statement $\delta V \simeq \pi r^2 \delta h$ gives rise in the limit to the exact result
$$\frac{dV}{dt} = \pi r^2 \frac{dh}{dt}.$$

The intermediate working can be omitted once one understands that all of this is implied.

Exercise A

1. A crystal is growing in a concentrated solution of copper sulphate. Would you expect it to remain the same shape as it grows? On what will its rate of change of volume depend? Form a differential equation involving its volume V and time t. What further information is required before the differential equation can be integrated?

2. Water is being boiled in an electric kettle. If there were no heat losses, the temperature of the water would rise 10 deg C each minute. Actually the kettle takes 9 minutes to boil starting at the room temperature of 15 °C. We should like to know how long it would take if water from the hot tap (at 40 °C) is put in the kettle initially, but at this stage we shall be content merely to express the problem in symbols.

(*a*) What factors affect the instantaneous rate of loss of heat? In what way does it depend upon the instantaneous temperature of the kettle and water?

(*b*) Introduce suitable symbols and write down a differential equation connecting time and temperature. This will involve a constant of proportionality k.

(*c*) Write the boundary conditions in terms of your symbols. Keep your answers to this question. They are required for Exercise B, Question 6.

3. Upon what does the decay rate of a radioactive substance depend? Express your answer as a differential equation. If you were asked to predict what the mass of a radioactive substance in a particular specimen will be in 30 days' time, what further information would you require?

4. A large tank contains 450 litres of acid at 50 % concentration. Water is pumped in at a rate of 9 litres per minute.

(*a*) If the concentration is x % at time t, find formulae for x and dx/dt in terms of t.

(*b*) What does dx/dt represent? What is its value when $t = 50$ minutes?

(*c*) When is the concentration 25 %? Approximately how long does it take for the concentration to drop from 26 % to 24 %?

5. The volume and surface area of a crystal in the shape of a regular octahedron whose edges each have length x are given by the formulae

$$V = \tfrac{1}{3}\sqrt{2}\, x^3, \quad A = 2\sqrt{3}\, x^2.$$

If x increases by a small amount, δx, express the consequent small increase δV approximately in terms of x and δx. If $\delta V \simeq A.\delta z$, what is δz in terms of δx? Interpret your last answer by considering the shell added to the outside of the crystal.

6. In Question 5, show that if the volume of the crystal grows at a rate proportional to its surface area, then the graph of x against t is a straight line. Would a similar result be true of crystals of different shapes?

2. SOLUTION OF FIRST-ORDER DIFFERENTIAL EQUATIONS

Just as there are various techniques for evaluating integrals of special types, and also approximate numerical methods of wider applicability, so also with differential equations. Numerical methods were discussed in Chapter 27 and also exact methods when the variables are separable. This will suffice for the next exercise, and then in Section 3 another important method is discussed. Meanwhile, another worked example is included, illustrating the main points covered so far.

Example 2. A 500 litre tank contains acid at 10 % concentration. Acid at 5 % concentration is pumped in at a rate of 10 litres per minute, and at the same time an equal amount is run off. When will the concentration be down to 8 %?

Suppose that the concentration is x % after t minutes; then $x = 10$ when $t = 0$. It helps to think of the dilute acid as $5x$ litres of 'concentrated' acid and $(500-5x)$ litres of water. Now $\tfrac{5}{100} \times 10$ litres of concentrated acid enter the tank each minute and $(x/100) \times 10$ litres leave it—or rather, $(x/100) \times 10$ is the instantaneous rate, in litres per minute, at which concentrated acid is being run out. dx/dt is interpreted as the overall rate of increase of concentrated acid in the tank, and is given by the equation

$$\frac{d}{dt}(5x) = \frac{5}{100} \times 10 - \frac{x}{100} \times 10 = \frac{1}{10}(5-x).$$

The mathematical model is now completed. The initial condition is $x = 10$ when $t = 0$, and we wish to find the value of t when $x = 8$. It has been assumed that perfect mixing has taken place, and since no information is available about the shape of the tank, the positions of the inflow and outflow pipes, or any methods of stirring, this is the only possible assump-

935

tion. We now solve the differential equation by an exact method, but must remember to treat the final answer as *approximate*.

$$\frac{dx}{dt} = \frac{1}{50}(5-x) \Rightarrow \frac{1}{5-x}\frac{dx}{dt} = \frac{1}{50} \tag{1}$$

$$\Rightarrow -\log|5-x| = t/50 + A$$

$$\Rightarrow |5-x| = e^{-t/50-A}$$

$$\Rightarrow |5-x| = A'e^{-t/50}$$

$$\Rightarrow x = 5 \pm A'e^{-t/50}. \tag{2}$$

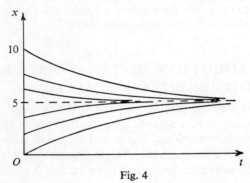

Fig. 4

The solution curves are all exponential with $x = 5$ as an asymptote, as one would expect. The initial conditions determine, as always, which curve is appropriate to this problem. Note that e^{-A} has been replaced by A', and this must be positive; however, equation (2) could also be written $x = 5 + Be^{-t/50}$, where B can take any value, positive or negative.

Since $x = 10$ when $t = 0$,

$$10 = 5 + A',$$

giving

$$A' = 5,$$

and

$$x = 5 + 5e^{-t/50}.$$

To find when $x = 8$, we have

$$8 = 5 + 5e^{-t/50},$$

giving

$$t = 50 \log 5/3$$

$$= 25 \cdot 5.$$

The concentration will thus be reduced to 8 % after 25·5 minutes.

On this occasion the answer is obtained more quickly using the square bracket notation. The working after equation (1) would then be

$$\left[-\log|5-x|\right]_{10}^{8} = \left[\frac{t}{50}+A\right]_{0}^{T}$$

$$\Rightarrow -\log 3 + \log 5 = (T/50 + A) - A$$

$$\Rightarrow T = 50 \log 5/3.$$

Exercise B

1. A cup of coffee is cooling in a room at a temperature of 15 °C. Initially, the temperature of the coffee is 98 °C, and 1 minute later it is 94 °C. Find its temperature after 20 minutes assuming that the rate of cooling is
   (a) proportional to the excess temperature, and
   (b) proportional to the 5/4th power of the excess temperature.
   (*Hint*: In each case, find the constant of proportionality by taking the rate of cooling as 4 degrees per minute when the excess temperature is 81 °C.)

2. The volume of a large spherical snowball decreases as it melts at a rate proportional to its surface area at any instant. Express this statement in symbols. What is the constant of proportionality if a snowball of radius 30 cm takes 10 days to melt? After how many days will (a) the radius be halved, and (b) the volume be halved?
   Discuss briefly the main assumptions made in forming the mathematical model. Which are least reasonable?

3. A radioactive substance decays at a rate proportional to its mass. When its mass is 20 mg, the decay rate is 1 mg per day.
   (a) t days later the mass is m; find a formula for m in terms of t.
   (b) What is its half-life (that is, after how long is its mass 10 mg)?
   (c) How long does it take to decay from 12 mg to 3 mg?
   (d) What is the rate of decay after 10 days?

4. A radioactive substance has half-life h days. Find a formula for its mass m in terms of t, the time, if its initial mass is m_0. What is the initial decay rate?

5. A 250 litre tank contains a mixture of 150 litres of blue paint and 100 litres of yellow paint. 10 litres of blue paint and 15 litres of yellow paint are pumped in each minute while 25 litres of the mixture are pumped out.
   (a) After how long would you expect there to be 125 litres of each paint in the tank?
   (b) If it was found in practice to take (i) a shorter or (ii) a longer time, what would be possible explanations?
   (c) Will the 500th and 1000th litres pumped out be significantly different in colour?

6. Integrate the differential equation obtained in Exercise A, Question 2(b). Show that the problem posed in that question requires the root of the equation $8.5k = 1 - e^{-9k}$. Obtain this approximately (e.g. by a graphical method) and so complete the solution.

7. One of the products of fission of a radioactive substance A is another radioactive substance B. 1 unit of mass of B results from the fission of 2 units of mass of A. The decay rates are

$$\frac{m_1}{100}, \quad \frac{m_2}{500} \text{ mg per day}$$

(where m_1 and m_2 are the masses of A, B in mg).
   (a) Use this data to form two differential equations.
   (b) Start with 20 mg of A. Find m_1 in terms of t, and show that m_2 cannot be found as an explicit function of t by the methods discussed so far.
   (c) Draw rough sketches of the graphs of m_1 and m_2 against t, and show that m_2 has a maximum value when $m_2 = 2.5m_1$.

937

3. LINEAR DIFFERENTIAL EQUATIONS
WITH CONSTANT COEFFICIENTS

In Chapter 27, we set about finding exact solutions to differential equations
of the form

$$\frac{dy}{dx} = f(x) \cdot g(y).$$

Exercise B, Question 7, introduced a new type which we now investigate.
These are equations of the form

$$\frac{dy}{dx} + ay = f(x).$$

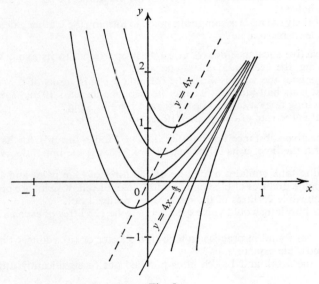

Fig. 5

Example 3. Solve the equation

$$\frac{dy}{dx} + 3y = 12x.$$

The methods of Chapter 27 enable us to sketch the family of solution
curves as in Figure 5. The main points considered are:

(i) $dy/dx = 0$ at all points on the line $y = 4x$.

   $dy/dx > 0$ at every point below $y = 4x$.

   $dy/dx < 0$ at every point above $y = 4x$.

(ii) $\dfrac{d^2y}{dx^2} = 12 - 3\dfrac{dy}{dx}$

   $= 3(4 - 12x + 3y).$

938

At all points on $4-12x+3y = 0$,

$$\frac{dy}{dx} = 4, \quad \frac{d^2y}{dx^2} = 0,$$

so this line is one member of the family. Above this line the curves are all concave upwards; below they are concave downwards.

In this process we have discovered one special member of the family of solution curves, the straight line $y = 4x-4/3$. This can be checked by substituting in $dy/dx+3y$, the left-hand side of the differential equation.

If $y = 4x-\frac{4}{3}$, $\frac{dy}{dx}+3y = 4+3(4x-\frac{4}{3}) = 12x$,

as required.

Now Chapter 29 contained many equations of the same form as

$$dy/dx+3y = 0,$$

and we know that $y = Ae^{-3x}$ is a solution of this for all values of A.

In other words, substitution in the left-hand side of the equation of

$$y = Ae^{-3x} \quad \text{gives } 0,$$
$$y = 4x-\tfrac{4}{3} \quad \text{gives } 12x.$$

It follows therefore from the *linearity* of the equation—and we shall study the meaning of this more closely in the next section—that substitution of the sum of these two,

$$y = 4x-\tfrac{4}{3}+Ae^{-3x} \quad \text{gives} \quad 12x+0 = 12x.$$

We should expect this to be the complete answer, different values of the constant A giving different members of the family of solutions. We shall prove this in the next section.

The complete solution is thus the sum of two parts. The first part, $(4x-\frac{4}{3})$, which produces $12x$ on the right-hand side of the equation, is peculiar to this particular equation and is called the *Particular Integral*, usually abbreviated to PI. It is found by trial, as in Example 4 which follows. The second part of the complete solution yields zero on the right-hand side; being the complete solution of

$$\frac{dy}{dx}+3y = 0$$

it will be the same for all differential equations of the form

$$\frac{dy}{dx}+3y = f(x),$$

whatever the form of the function f. It is called the *Complementary Function*, abbreviated to CF, and it will always contain an arbitrary constant A, which has to be determined in a practical problem by the initial conditions.

To find Particular Integrals requires a little ingenuity. We have to ask ourselves what type of function will give rise on differentiation to a function f such as appears on the right-hand side. Now polynomials give rise to polynomials, exponential functions give rise to functions of the same kind, sines give rise to cosines and cosines to sines. Accordingly, if f is a polynomial we try a polynomial for the PI; if f is an exponential function we try a multiple of this function for the PI; if f is a sine or cosine we try a combination of sine and cosine for the PI. Exercise C, Question 10, gives a number of examples of this procedure.

Example 4. Find the solution of $(dx/dt)+2x = 7e^{-3t}$ for which $x = 5$ when $t = 0$.

To obtain a PI, we try to find a number K so that $y = Ke^{-3t}$ satisfies the equation.

We require $\quad -3Ke^{-3t}+2Ke^{-3t} = 7e^{-3t}$, i.e. $K = -7$.

We conclude that $x = -7e^{-3t}$ is a Particular Integral.

Solving $dx/dt+2x = 0$ by separation of variables (or by inspection) gives $x = Ae^{-2t}$ as the Complementary Function.

The complete solution is therefore $x = Ae^{-2t}-7e^{-3t}$. The boundary condition $x = 5$ when $t = 0$ gives $A = 12$, and the corresponding solution is

$$x = 12e^{-2t}-7e^{-3t}.$$

The equation of Example 2,

$$\frac{dx}{dt}+\frac{1}{50}x = \frac{1}{10},$$

is solved very quickly by this method. The PI is $x = 5$, and the CF is $Ae^{-t/50}$; both can be written down without working.

Note that the CF contains a negative exponent and, whatever the value of A, will be very small for large values of t. For this reason the CF is called the *transient term*; this situation will recur in all our applications. The PI represents what remains when the CF is zero; this is the *steady state* solution after the transient disturbances due to the starting conditions have died away.

4. LINEARITY

The success of the method of Section 3 depends upon the linearity of the differential equations. It is now useful to make explicit what we mean by this term, which has previously only been used informally. The idea of a linear mapping of the number line, and a linear transformation of position vectors in two or more dimensions, is familiar. It is now helpful to view differentiation as a transformation applied to functions.

940

$$x \to ax$$

is the general linear transformation of one variable.

$$\begin{pmatrix} x \\ y \end{pmatrix} \to \begin{pmatrix} ax+by \\ cx+dy \end{pmatrix}$$

is the general linear transformation of vectors in two dimensions, which we may write

$$\begin{pmatrix} x \\ y \end{pmatrix} \to \mathbf{M} \begin{pmatrix} x \\ y \end{pmatrix}, \quad \text{where } \mathbf{M} = \begin{pmatrix} a & b \\ c & d \end{pmatrix}.$$

Now two of the properties of matrices used in earlier chapters are:

(i) $\mathbf{M(X_1+X_2)} = \mathbf{MX_1+MX_2}$ where $\mathbf{X_1}$ and $\mathbf{X_2}$ are column vectors;

(ii) $\mathbf{M}(\lambda\mathbf{X}) = \lambda\mathbf{MX}$, where λ is a scalar.

These properties are those which define premultiplication by a matrix as a *linear operation*. Generally, if X, X_1, X_2 are any elements and M is any operator satisfying these two properties, we say that M is a *linear operator*.

Consider now the operation of differentiation with respect to x. Let us write it as D, so that

$$D(x^3) = \frac{d(x^3)}{dx} = 3x^2, \quad \text{and} \quad Df(x) = f'(x).$$

Now $D[f(x)+g(x)] = D[f(x)]+D[g(x)]$ and $D[\lambda f(x)] = \lambda D[f(x)]$. These results can be established by going back to the definition of derivatives (see Chapter 7, p. 208), and we accept them without question whenever differentiating expressions like x^3+7x^2. This could be set out as follows:

$$\begin{aligned} D(x^3+7x^2) &= D(x^3)+D(7x^2) \\ &= D(x^3)+7D(x^2) \\ &= 3x^2+7.2x \\ &= 3x^2+14x. \end{aligned}$$

So differentiating is a linear operation. Next it can be shown (see Exercise C, Question 4) that the combination, by successive application, of two linear operations is another linear operation, so $D.D$ (D^2) is linear.

We can now, for example, write

$$\frac{d^2y}{dx^2}+8x\frac{dy}{dx}-3y \quad \text{as} \quad (D^2+8xD-3)y,$$

and it is easily shown that the contents of the bracket form a linear operator. Denoting this by the letter T, we have

$$T(x^3) = 6x+8x.3x^2-3x^3 = 6x+21x^3,$$
$$T(x^5) = 20x^3+8x.5x^4-3x^5 = 20x^3+37x^5.$$

It follows from the linearity properties that

$$\begin{aligned} T(3x^3+x^5) &= 3(6x+21x^3)+(20x^3+37x^5) \\ &= 18x+83x^3+37x^5. \end{aligned}$$

941

An equation like $T(y) = 0$ is called a *linear differential equation* if T is linear. In this case it is

$$\frac{d^2y}{dx^2} + 8x\frac{dy}{dx} - 3y = 0.$$

4.1 The PI, CF method continued. In Section 3, we saw how to obtain a one-parameter family of solutions to a first-order linear differential equation. It remains to show that all possible solutions have been included.

Consider again Example 4. Having found that $x = -7e^{-3t}$ is a PI, we could put $x = z - 7e^{-3t}$ and eliminate x in favour of z.

$$\frac{dx}{dt} + 2x = 7e^{-3t}$$

$$\Rightarrow \left(\frac{dz}{dt} + 21e^{-3t}\right) + 2(z - 7e^{-3t}) = 7e^{-3t}$$

$$\Rightarrow \qquad\qquad \frac{dz}{dt} + 2z = 0.$$

The solution of this equation, $z = Ae^{-2t}$, is the CF. Then

$$x = z - 7e^{-3t} = Ae^{-2t} - 7e^{-3t},$$

as before.

4.2 Proof in general notation. The justification of the method in general can be set out as follows.

Suppose we wish to solve $T(x) = f(t)$, where T is any linear differential operator.

First, one solution $x = u(t)$ is found if possible by trial. This means that $T(u(t)) = f(t)$.

Now substitute $x = u(t) + z$. Then

$$T(u(t) + z) = f(t)$$

$$\Rightarrow T(u(t)) + T(z) = f(t), \quad \text{using the first linearity property,}$$

$$\Rightarrow T(z) = 0.$$

If this has solution $z = v(t)$,

$$x = u(t) + z,$$

$$x = u(t) + v(t).$$

Exercise C

1. For the 'linear function' $f: x \to ax + b$, write down $f(2)$, $f(5)$, $f(7)$. Does $f(7) = f(5) + f(2)$? Does the function possess the linearity properties?

942

2. Which of the following are linear transformations?:

(a) $\begin{pmatrix} x \\ y \end{pmatrix} \rightarrow \begin{pmatrix} x \\ 0 \end{pmatrix}$;

(b) $\begin{pmatrix} x \\ y \end{pmatrix} \rightarrow \begin{pmatrix} -y \\ 5x \end{pmatrix}$;

(c) $\begin{pmatrix} x \\ y \end{pmatrix} \rightarrow \begin{pmatrix} x+2 \\ y+3 \end{pmatrix}$;

(d) $\begin{pmatrix} x \\ y \end{pmatrix} \rightarrow 2x+3y$;

(e) $\begin{pmatrix} x \\ y \end{pmatrix} \rightarrow \sqrt{(x^2+y^2)}$.

3. If T is a linear transformation of the plane into itself, show that

$$T\begin{pmatrix} 0 \\ 0 \end{pmatrix} = \begin{pmatrix} 0 \\ 0 \end{pmatrix}.$$

4. If T and U are any two linear transformations, show that TU is a linear transformation.

5. Which of the following mappings possess the linearity properties?:

(a) $x \rightarrow t + \dfrac{dx}{dt}$;

(b) $x \rightarrow x + \dfrac{dx}{dt}$;

(c) $x \rightarrow x \dfrac{dx}{dt}$;

(d) $y \rightarrow \left(\dfrac{dy}{dx}\right)^2$;

(e) $y \rightarrow \dfrac{dx}{dy}$;

(f) $y \rightarrow e^x \dfrac{d^2y}{dx^2}$.

6. Show that $x = \cos 3t$ is a solution of $\ddot{x} + 9x = 0$. Is $x = 5\cos 3t$ a solution? Can you find a quite different solution to this equation?

7. Show that $x = 1/t$ is a solution of $\dot{x} + x^2 = 0$. Is $x = 6/t$ also a solution?

8. Show that

$$y = \frac{1}{x+2} \quad \text{and} \quad y = \frac{1}{3x-1}$$

are both solutions of

$$y \frac{d^2y}{dx^2} - 2\left(\frac{dy}{dx}\right)^2 = 0.$$

Is

$$y = \frac{1}{x+2} + \frac{1}{3x-1}$$

a solution?

9. Show that if $y = f(x)$ and $y = g(x)$ are solutions of a linear differential equation $T(y) = 0$, so is $y = Af(x) + Bg(x)$, where A and B are any two numbers.

10. Find values of K and L for which:
(a) $x = Kt + L$ is a solution of $\dot{x} + 4x = 7t$;
(b) $x = Ke^t$ is a solution of $\dot{x} + 4x = 7e^t$;
(c) $x = K \sin t + L \cos t$ is a solution of $\dot{x} + x = 4 \cos t$;
(d) $x = Ke^{2t}$ is a solution of $5\dot{x} - 6x = e^{2t}$;
(e) $x = Kte^{2t}$ is a solution of $\dot{x} - 2x = 5e^{2t}$;
(f) $x = Kt^2 + L$ is a solution of $\dot{x} + 2tx = t^3$.

11. In each part of Question 10, find the complementary function, and hence write down the complete solution.

12. Is $\dot{x}+x = x^2$ a linear equation? Show that

$$x = \frac{1}{1-e^t}$$

is a solution (*a*) by differentiating immediately, and (*b*) by making t the subject of the equation and then differentiating. Can you find the general solution of this differential equation?

13. Solve:

 (*a*) $\dot{x}+3x = 9$;   (*b*) $2\dot{x}+5x = 4e^{-3t}$; (*c*) $\dot{x}+2x = t^2$;

 (*d*) $\dot{x}+5x = x^2$;   (*e*) $\dot{x}+x = \sin 3t$;   (*f*) $\dot{x}-4x = e^{4t}$;

 (*g*) $\dot{x}+x = 1/x$;   (*h*) $3\dot{x}-x = t+e^t$;   (*i*) $t\dot{x}+3x = 5t^2$;

 (*j*) $\dot{x}-x = te^t$;   (*k*) $\dot{x}+3x = tx$;   (*l*) $\dot{x} = x-t+4$.

14. *Write down* the general solutions of:

 (*a*) $\dot{x}-2x = 12$;   (*b*) $\dot{x}+8x = 10$;   (*c*) $3\dot{x}-5x = 4$.

15. (*a*) Solve $\dot{x}+3x = 24$ given that $x = 5$ when $t = 0$.
  (*b*) Solve $\dot{x}+2x = 8t$ given that $x = 0$ when $t = 0$.
  (*c*) Solve $\dot{x}+2x = 2\sin 3t+3\cos 3t$ given that $x = 2$ when $t = 0$.
For each part, sketch the solution curve for $t \geqslant 0$.

16. Show that $x = 2t^2$ is a solution of $2t\dot{x}+x = 10t^2$, and that $x = 1/\sqrt{t}$ is a solution of $2t\dot{x}+x = 0$. Does it follow that $x = 2t^2+5/\sqrt{t}$ is a solution of

$$2t\dot{x}+x = 10t^2?$$

17. Show that $x = t$ is a solution of $\dot{x}+x^2 = t^2+1$, and that $x = 1/(t+3)$ is a solution of $\dot{x}+x^2 = 0$. Can you write down the general solution of the first differential equation?

5. SOME APPLICATIONS

With the new functions we have learnt about in Chapter 29 and the new techniques we have acquired in this Chapter, we are now able to construct mathematical models to assist in the solution of a greater variety of physical problems. We shall consider a few miscellaneous applications in this section, and devote the next to a more thorough study of electrical circuits.

5.1 Air resistance. So far in our treatment of the motion of bodies through the air we have neglected the effects of air resistance. This makes our equations very much simpler, but removes our conclusions further from reality. Air resistance in fact is a highly complicated affair, and depends on a variety of circumstances: the speed of the moving body, its shape, whether or not it is spinning, whether the air is calm or turbulent, damp or dry, dense or rare, and so on. For small bodies and slow speeds it is roughly proportional to the speed; but as the speed rises the resistance rises much more rapidly, and is now roughly proportional to the square of the speed—in fact, this is an underestimate. These two cases, resistance proportional to speed, and resistance proportional to the square of the speed, give easily soluble models for motion in a straight line.

Example 5. If a cricket ball is dropped from a height, its maximum speed is 30 m/s. Find the greatest height to which it will rise if it is thrown vertically upwards with a speed of 20 m/s. Assume that air resistance varies as the square of the speed of the ball relative to the air.

It is often easier to solve such problems in general terms, inserting the numerical constants at a later stage. Let us then call the terminal velocity u, and suppose the ball has risen a height x in time t, and that its speed is then v. The air resistance is now given by kv^2, where $ku^2 = mg$, since at the terminal velocity the resistance is just equal to the weight of the ball.

The equation of motion is therefore

$$m\frac{dv}{dt} = -mg - mg\frac{v^2}{u^2};$$

that is,

$$\frac{dv}{dt} = -g\left(1 + \frac{v^2}{u^2}\right).$$

We need to integrate this equation to find the displacement. To do so, it is convenient to turn it into a differential equation connecting v with x, and this is done by using the chain rule, which tells us that

$$\frac{dv}{dt} = \frac{dv}{dx} \times \frac{dx}{dt} = v\frac{dv}{dx}.$$

The equation now becomes

$$v\frac{dv}{dx} = -\frac{g}{u^2}(u^2 + v^2),$$

which can be integrated by separation of the variables.

This gives

$$\int \frac{2v\,dv}{u^2 + v^2} = \frac{-2gx}{u^2};$$

$$\Rightarrow \log(u^2 + v^2) = -2gx/u^2 + c.$$

The constant c can be found from the initial condition, $v = 20$ when $x = 0$. Inserting the value of u, we obtain finally

$$\log(v^2 + 30^2) = \log(20^2 + 30^2) - 19 \cdot 6x/30^2.$$

When $v = 0,$ $\dfrac{19\cdot 6x}{30^2} = \log(400 + 900) - \log(900)$

$$= \log\frac{1300}{900},$$

that is
$$x = \frac{900}{19 \cdot 6} \times \log 1 \cdot 44$$

$$= 16 \cdot 7 \text{ m approximately.}$$

In the absence of air resistance the ball would rise to a height of about 20 metres.

5.2 Chemical reactions. The rate at which a chemical reaction proceeds depends upon the nature of the reaction, the temperature and pressure under which it takes place, and so on. But for a given reaction, if temperature and pressure are kept constant, the rate is governed by the *Law of Mass Action*, which states that

> Under constant physical conditions, the rate of a chemical reaction is proportional to the product of the concentrations of the reacting molecules.

This amounts to saying that the rate is proportional to the probability of two molecules A and B of the reactants coming within range in the mass of inert material. The *concentration* is simply the number of molecules in a given volume, but since a molecule is minute, it is more usually expressed in moles/litre, a *mole* being that quantity of reactant which has a mass m g, where m is the so-called 'molecular weight'; that is, the mass of one molecule on the scale on which an atom of carbon-12 has mass 12 units. A mole is thus always the same number of molecules ($6 \cdot 023 \times 10^{23}$).

Example 6. Consider an artificially simple example. Suppose two compounds X and Y are reacting in solution to form Z. To form 3 g of Z requires 1 g of X and 2 g of Y. To begin with 50 g of X are present, and 40 g of Y. At the end of 10 minutes 15 g of Z have been formed. Give a general formula for the mass z of Z formed after t minutes, and predict the mass of Z formed after 25 minutes reaction.

If z g of Z have been formed in time t min, then $z/3$ g of X and $2z/3$ g of Y have been removed from solution. The concentrations will be proportional to the masses of the reacting substances, so that the law of mass-action gives
$$\frac{dz}{dt} = k\left(50 - \frac{z}{3}\right)\left(40 - \frac{2z}{3}\right) = A(150 - z)(60 - z),$$

where A is a constant.

This is an equation with separable variables, and it gives
$$At = \int \frac{dz}{(150 - z)(60 - z)}.$$

To integrate this, we must separate the rational form
$$\frac{1}{(150 - z)(60 - z)}$$

into two fractions. Since

$$\frac{1}{60-z} - \frac{1}{150-z} = \frac{90}{(60-z)(150-z)},$$

we have

$$90At = \int \frac{dz}{60-z} - \int \frac{dz}{150-z}$$

$$= \log(150-z) - \log(60-z) + c.$$

(We know that $z < 60$.) Now $z = 0$ when $t = 0$; this means that

$$c = -\log 150 + \log 60 = -\log 2 \cdot 5.$$

Hence

$$\frac{150-z}{60-z} = 2 \cdot 5 e^{Bt},$$

where $B = 90A$, another constant. To find B, we use the fact that $z = 15$ when $t = 10$; this gives

$$\tfrac{135}{45} = 2 \cdot 5 e^{10B},$$

that is

$$e^{10B} = \tfrac{6}{5} \quad \text{so that} \quad e^{tB} = (\tfrac{6}{5})^{t/10}.$$

Finally, our formula is

$$\frac{150-z}{60-z} = 2 \cdot 5(\tfrac{6}{5})^{t/10}.$$

When $t = 25$,

$$\frac{150-z}{60-z} = 2 \cdot 5 \times 1 \cdot 2^{2 \cdot 5} = 3 \cdot 94$$

and

$$z = (60 \times 3 \cdot 94 - 150)/2 \cdot 94 = 29 \cdot 4.$$

Just over 29 g of Z will have been formed in 25 minutes.

Exercise D

1. The acceleration of a sphere falling through a liquid is $(30 - 3v)$ cm/s² where v is its speed in cm/s.

(a) Sketch the graph of v against t.

(b) What is the maximum possible velocity? Is this ever reached?

(c) If the sphere starts from rest, how fast will it be travelling at time t, and how far will it then have fallen?

2. Verify that

$$\frac{1}{50-v} + \frac{1}{50+v} = \frac{100}{2500-v^2}.$$

The acceleration of a parachutist in free fall from an aircraft is given by the formula

$$a = 10 - 0 \cdot 004v^2,$$

v being his speed; the units are metres and seconds.

Write and solve differential equations for his speed:

(a) as a function of time;

(b) as a function of distance.

3. Formulate a differential equation as in Example 5 for a cricket ball falling under gravity through air producing a resistance kv^2, in terms of its terminal velocity u.

Solve this equation to find the displacement x in terms of the velocity v. Hence, find the velocity with which the cricket ball of Example 5 will eventually land.

4. Find, for the cricket ball of Example 5:
(a) the time taken to reach the highest point;
(b) the time to return to the ground. (Compare Question 2.)

5. A tank has a square base of side a, and vertical sides. It initially contains a liquid to a depth b. There is a small pipe leading from the bottom of the tank and when a tap in this is opened, the tank empties. Find the time taken for the tank to empty in terms of b and λ, where λ is the rate at which the height, h, of liquid in the tank decreases initially, assuming:
(a) that dh/dt is proportional to h, and
(b) that dh/dt is proportional to $\sqrt{h}$.
Which hypothesis is more likely to be correct?

6. Water flows from the tank in Question 5 into an identical tank, which itself empties into a third tank. Assume that the rate of flow through the pipe at the bottom of the first tank is $k_1 h_1$ and through the other pipe is $k_2 h_2$ (where h_1 and h_2 are the depths of water in the first two tanks, and k_1 and k_2 are different constants).
(a) Obtain differential equations involving dh_1/dt and dh_2/dt, and hence find h_1 and h_2 as functions of t, assuming that initially $h_1 = b$ and $h_2 = 0$.
(b) Sketch the graph of h_2 against t, and find the maximum value of h_2.

7. Continue the working of Exercise B, Question 7, finding m_1 and m_2 as functions of t. After how long will both m_1 and m_2 be less than 1 mg? How would the apparatus of Question 6 have to be altered for its mathematical model to be isomorphic to the model in this question?

8. In a reaction of the same type as in Example 6, the initial concentrations (in moles/litre) of X and Y are the same. If one molecule of X reacts with one of Y to form one of Z, show that the concentration z of Z obeys the law

$$\frac{dz}{dt} = k(c-z)^2, \quad \text{where } k, c \text{ are constants,}$$

and find a formula for z at time t in terms of k and c. Sketch the graph of z against t.

9. Example 6 was worked on the assumption that one molecule of X and one molecule of Y (of twice the mass) reacted to form one molecule of Z. Suppose on the other hand that the masses of the molecules of X and Y are equal, and that one of X and two of Y are needed to react to form one molecule of Z. Formulate the differential equation in this case, inserting constants as far as possible, but do not attempt to solve it.

10. A car is started from rest under a force which is proportional to the time against a resistance proportional to the velocity.
(a) Show that the appropriate differential equation is of the form
$$dv/dt + kv = at.$$

948

(b) Integrate this equation.

(c) Show that $v = \frac{1}{2}at^2$ for small values of t, and find an approximation to v at any time, linear in k, provided kt is small.

(d) Find the dimensions of a/k^3, and give a physical meaning to this quantity in terms of the situation when $kt = 2$.

11. If $x = ze^{2t}$, express dx/dt in terms of t, z, dz/dt. Use this substitution to solve $dx/dt - 2x = 5e^{2t}$, then compare your answer with Question 10(e) in Exercise C.

12. Solve $\dot{x} + ax = be^{-at}$ where a, b are constants.

13. A tank A contains a mixture of 250 litres of blue paint and 250 litres of yellow paint. Blue paint is pumped into A at 15 l/min, and paint is pumped out at the same rate into a tank B, which initially contains a mixture of 300 litres of blue paint and 200 litres of yellow paint. Paint is pumped out of B at the same rate. Assuming perfect mixing in each tank, when will the paint in B be yellower than that in A?

The next question should be answered before proceeding to Section 6.

14. (a) Draw the graph of $y = e^{-x}$ for positive x, plotting the points where $x = 0, 1, 2, 3, 4, 5$. For what values of x is (i) $y < 0.05$, (ii) $y < 0.01$?

(b) In Question 1, $v = 10 - 10e^{-3t}$. For what values of t is (i) $v > 9.5$, (ii) $v > 9.9$? Compare your answers with those for (a).

(c) If $v = Be^{-t/a}$, where a, B are constants, for what values of t is
$$(i)\ v < 0.05B, \qquad (ii)\ v < 0.01B?$$

6. APPLICATIONS TO ELECTRIC CIRCUITS

6.1   Inductance. When a current flows in a coil of wire, a magnetic field is set up. The forces resulting from such a field make it possible to design an electric motor. Also, a *changing* magnetic field causes an e.m.f. in a wire; this is the physical law associated with generators or dynamos. These two important phenomena apply simultaneously when a *variable* current flows in a coil of wire. A variable magnetic field results, and this induces an e.m.f. in the coil. Notice that when a constant current flows, there is no induced e.m.f.

The size of the induced e.m.f. is a function of the rate of change of current, and we shall be concerned only with coils for which (under normal operating conditions) this function is linear.

Then
$$e_L \propto \frac{di}{dt}, \quad \text{and we can write} \quad e_L = -L\frac{di}{dt}.$$

L is a positive constant and is called the *inductance* of the coil. The minus sign indicates the fact that the induced e.m.f. opposes the change of current. If the current is increasing, di/dt is positive, and the induced e.m.f. opposes the applied e.m.f.; when the current is falling, the situation is reversed. We use the symbol e_L for the induced e.m.f. to avoid confusion with the constant e.

The value of the constant L depends upon the size and shape of the coil, and is approximately proportional to the number of turns of wire in the coil, provided it is closely wound.

6.2   Inductance in a simple circuit.

This circuit shows an e.m.f. E (which is taken to be constant in the first instance) applied to two separate components in series. The left-hand one (note the circuit symbol) is assumed to have inductance L and negligible resistance; we call it an inductor. This is, of course, a theoretical concept never actually realized in practice. Similarly, it is assumed that the resistor is non-inductive; to reduce inductance, wire resistors have half their turns wound clockwise, and half anticlockwise.

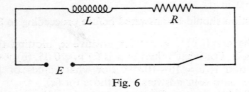

Fig. 6

The equation for the circuit (with the switch closed) is

$$E + e_L = iR,$$

giving

$$L\frac{di}{dt} + Ri = E.$$

This is exactly the same type of differential equation as has been considered earlier in the chapter. The complementary function is $Ae^{-Rt/L}$ and this is independent of the applied voltage. The particular integral is E/R.

The complete solution is therefore

$$i = \frac{E}{R} + Ae^{-Rt/L}.$$

The constant A depends upon the initial conditions. If we suppose that t is measured from the instant that the switch is closed, $i = 0$ when $t = 0$, and $A = -E/R$. The solution curve is then as shown in Figure 7.

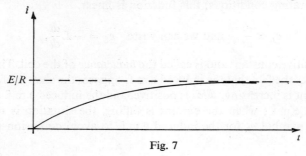

Fig. 7

950

Note that the particular integral gives the steady-state current, and the complementary function is negligible when t is large. In the steady state, L has no effect, and it is as if a battery were connected across the resistor alone.

6.3 Capacitance.

At this stage we shall introduce one more type of component, a capacitor or condenser. The circuit symbol is shown in Figure 8, and this indicates its nature. The simplest sort of capacitor consists of two metal plates separated by an air gap. Note that this means immediately that no direct current can flow in a part of a circuit containing a capacitor.

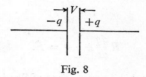

Fig. 8

If by any means a positive charge, q, is created on one of the plates, an equal and opposite negative charge will be attracted to the other plate, thus setting up a potential difference V between the plates. In all cases with which we are concerned, q is proportional to V, and we can write

$$q = CV, \quad \text{where } C \text{ is a constant.}$$

C is called the *capacitance* of the capacitor, and depends only upon its construction. To obtain large values of C, the area of the plates must be large and the distance between them small, so a common type consists of two sheets of metal foil separated by a thin non-conducting sheet (for example, waxed paper), the whole being rolled up into a cylinder for convenience.

In Figure 9, suppose that initially the capacitor is uncharged, and consequently the potential difference, V_C, across it is zero.

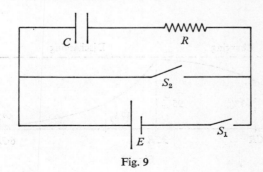

Fig. 9

951

When the switch S_1 is closed, the battery begins to pump negative charge onto the right-hand plate, and positive charge onto the left-hand plate of the capacitor. Now the rate of flow of charge is what is meant by an electric current; this current gradually increases the magnitude of the charges $+q$ and $-q$ on the capacitor, and hence increases V_C. This opposes E, and so the current is reduced. The capacitor therefore charges up at an ever-decreasing rate until V_C exactly balances E.

This is clearer when expressed mathematically:

$$E - V_C = iR,$$

that is

$$E - q/C = iR.$$

But

$$i = \frac{dq}{dt},$$

so

$$R\frac{dq}{dt} + \frac{1}{C}q = E.$$

This equation is identical in form to that of Section 6.2, and the solution curve therefore has the same shape. This represents the charging process described above. The particular integral $q = CE$ gives the final charge, and the complete solution is $q = CE - CEe^{-t/CR}$.

If S_1 is now opened, the capacitor remains charged until, for instance, S_2 is closed; then a current flows briefly while discharging takes place. As the charge decreases, so V_C decreases and the current decreases proportionally.

The relevant equation is now

$$R\frac{dq}{dt} + \frac{1}{C}q = 0,$$

and the solution is $q = Ae^{-t/CR}$. Taking t to be measured from the instant discharging begins, A is the initial charge, that is, CE (see Figure 10).

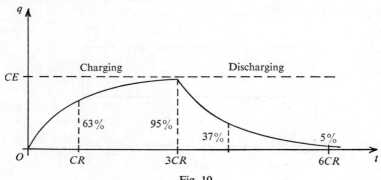

Fig. 10

6.4   Time constants. We can consider the capacitor of Section 6.3 to be fully charged when say, $q = 0.99CE$. This gives $e^{-t/CR} = 0.01$,

$$t = 5CR.$$

Thus the 'time taken to charge up'—a loose phrase whose meaning should be clear—is proportional to CR, which is called the *time constant*, of the circuit. Exercise D, Question 13, showed that the capacitor would be 63 % charged after CR seconds, 95 % charged after $3CR$ seconds, 99.3 % charged after $5CR$ seconds.

Similarly, the time constant of the circuit in Section 5.2 is L/R. This means the current can be considered to have reached its maximum value after about $5L/R$ seconds.

6.5   Units. The units in which L and C are usually measured are determined by the defining equations

$$e_L = -L\frac{di}{dt}, \quad q = CV, \quad i = \frac{dq}{dt}.$$

Now if q is measured in coulombs, and t in seconds, i will be given in amperes, since
$$1 \text{ ampere} = 1 \text{ coulomb/second.}$$

If the negative induced e.m.f. e_L is measured in volts, then L will be given in *henries* (H):
$$1 \text{ henry} = 1 \text{ volt second/ampere.}$$

If V, the p.d. between the plates of the capacitor, is also measured in volts, then C will be given in *farads* (F):
$$1 \text{ farad} = 1 \text{ coulomb/volt.}$$

Both henries and farads are large units, and it is more usual to meet inductances measured in *millihenries* (mH = 10^{-3} henry) and capacitances in *microfarads* (μF = 10^{-6} farad).

We have seen that both L/R and CR have the dimension of time. This means that if we take the dimension of resistance $\mathbf{R}$ as fundamental, we can attribute the dimensions of $\mathbf{R}.\mathbf{T}$ to inductance, and $\mathbf{R}^{-1}.\mathbf{T}$ to capacitance. In fact
$$1 \text{ henry} = 1 \text{ ohm second.}$$
and
$$1 \text{ farad} = 1 \text{ second/ohm.}$$

6.6   Approximations. As always, several approximations are involved in the simple mathematical treatment of circuits.

1. We assume that all the components are exactly *linear*, that is, $v \propto i$ for resistors, $e \propto di/dt$ for inductors, $q \propto v$ for capacitors.

2. We neglect stray inductance and capacitance. The connecting wires of any circuit are bound to have a little inductance, and any two parts of a circuit behave together like a small capacitor.

3. The concepts of a 'pure' inductor (without resistance or capacitance) and a 'pure' resistor are entirely theoretical.

Nevertheless, experiment shows that these approximations are usually fully justified, though difficulties arise when working with very high frequency voltages and currents.

6.7 Applications of simple circuits in electronics.

The following exercise aims to show how even the simplest possible circuit can have a variety of effects, and so serve a variety of purposes. Some of these are:

1. Coupling one stage (for example, of an amplifier) to another without distortion.

2. Blocking direct voltages while transmitting alternating voltages.

3. Producing a spike waveform for a radar transmitter or a synchronizing pulse for a television set.

4. Cutting down one alternating voltage more than another as required in the tone control of a radio or gramophone.

5. Smoothing a variable voltage, as required when alternating voltages are used to produce steady direct voltages.

6. Generating the time-base of an oscilloscope or television set.

See if you can decide, after doing each question or group of connected questions, which of these practical uses is being hinted at.

Exercise E

1. Find expressions for i in terms of t for the circuit of Section 6.3 both for charging and discharging. Give sketches of the corresponding graphs.

2. The input voltage for the circuit of Figure 11 (a) is a 'square wave', a periodic discontinuous function of time whose graph is shown in Figure 11 (b). This is equivalent to the circuit of Section 5.4 with S_1 closed for a period a, then S_2 closed but S_1 open for the next period b.

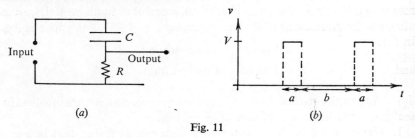

(a)   (b)

Fig. 11

If the time constant CR is about equal to a, and $b = 10a$, sketch
(a) the q, t graph;
(b) the i, t graph;
(c) the output voltage waveform.

954

3. Repeat Question 2 if $CR = a = b$. Consider the first two periods only.

4. Repeat Question 2 if (*a*) $CR = 0.01a$, (*b*) $CR = 100a$. In each case assume that *b* is about 1000*a*.

5. In Figure 12, the symbol to the right of the capacitor represents a type of valve which provides an almost instantaneous discharge when the voltage across it exceeds a certain value (in this respect it resembles a spark gap). *C* therefore charges up exponentially, then discharges and starts again.

Sketch the output waveform, and explain the effect of varying the value of *R*.

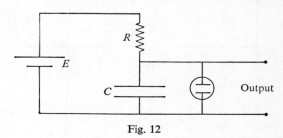

Fig. 12

6. Show that $i = 2 \sin \omega t + 5 \cos \omega t$ is the equation of an alternating current. What is its amplitude? What is its frequency?

7. (*a*) If
$$\left. \begin{array}{l} ax - by = m \\ bx + ay = n \end{array} \right\}, \quad \text{show that} \quad (a^2 + b^2)(x^2 + y^2) = m^2 + n^2.$$

(*b*) Find the amplitude of *i* if $i = H \sin \omega t + K \cos \omega t$ is a solution of
$$R\frac{di}{dt} + \frac{1}{C}i = A\omega \cos \omega t.$$

8. If an alternating e.m.f. of amplitude 5 V and frequency $1000/2\pi$ c/s is applied to the circuit of Figure 11 (*a*), show (using your answer to Question 7) that
$$\frac{5000}{\sqrt{[10^6 R^2 + (1/C^2)]}}$$
is the amplitude of the steady state current. The complementary function gives a 'transient' term, so you need only consider the particular integral.

9. (*a*) If $C = 10^{-6}$ F, $R = 10^3$ Ω, calculate the output voltage in Question 8.

(*b*) Repeat the calculation if the frequency is $3000/2\pi$ c/s and all the other values are unchanged.

(*c*) Using your answer to Question 7, sketch the graph of the amplitude of *i* against ω; consider *A*, *R*, *C* as constants. If the input had consisted of the sum of two alternating voltages of equal amplitude but different frequencies, what can you say about the output in the steady state?

10. If the input voltage in Figure 11 (*a*) is $A + B \sin \omega t$, write down a differential equation involving *q*, the charge on the capacitor, and hence find the equation of the output voltage.

Repeat, if the same input is applied to the circuit of Figure 13.

11. Show, by means of a sketched waveform, what you think the effect of the circuit in Figure 13 would be if the input voltage waveform was the result of full wave rectification, shown in Figure 14. (Do not attempt to answer this question quantitatively.)

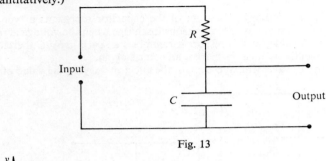

Fig. 13

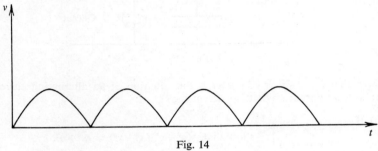

Fig. 14

12. In Figure 15 if the input voltage is $A + B \sin \omega t$, write down a differential equation involving i, and hence find the equation of the output voltage. (Compare with Question 10.)

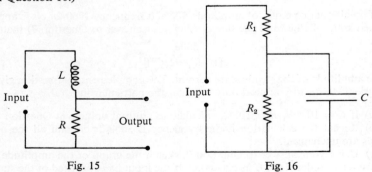

Fig. 15   Fig. 16

13. In Figure 16, if the charge on the capacitor is q, explain why the current through R_1 is

$$\frac{dq}{dt} + \frac{q}{CR_2}.$$

Then write down a differential equation involving q if the input voltage is $A \sin \omega t$.

956

14. In Figure 17, if i is the current through the resistor, find a differential equation involving i and t.

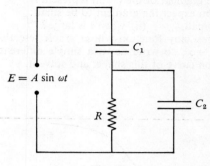

Fig. 17

15. (a) If $i = I_0 \sin(\omega t + \epsilon)$ is expressed in the form $i = A \sin \omega t + B \cos \omega t$, what are the values of A and B in terms of I_0 and ϵ?

(b) Show that there is an isomorphism between the addition of alternating currents of the same frequency and the addition of the position vectors of points of a plane, in which $I_0 \sin(\omega t + \epsilon)$ corresponds to the position vector of the point with *polar* coordinates (I_0, ϵ).

Miscellaneous Exercise

1. Solve:

(a) $(2-x)\dot{x} = 3 + 2t$;

(b) $(2-t)\dot{x} = 3 + 2x$;

(c) $(2-t) + \dot{x} = 3 + 2x$;

given that $x = 2$ when $t = 1$ in each case.

2. The solution curve in Question 1(a) is an ellipse. Find the coordinates of the points at which the tangents are parallel (i) to the x-axis, and (ii) to the t-axis.

3. Use a simple step-by-step method, proceeding by intervals $x = 0.2$, to construct a table of values over the interval $1 \leqslant x \leqslant 2$ for the solution of the differential equation

$$\frac{dy}{dx} + y = \frac{1}{x},$$

satisfying the condition that $y = 0$ when $x = 1$.

What is the complementary function for this differential equation?

Another solution curve of this differential equation passes through the point $(1.6, 2.3)$. Use the result of the first part, together with your knowledge of the complementary function, to find the points of this curve corresponding to $x = 1$ and $x = 2$.

4. Figure 18 is a graph showing the growth of the number, n, of bacteria in a culture.

(*a*) What does the gradient of the graph represent?

(*b*) Why would you expect the gradient to be small:
 (i) when n is small, (ii) when t is large?

(*c*) Can you suggest any function whose graph resembles this one? Your answer is probably 'no', so write down a simple differential equation which would have a solution curve of this shape, and solve it.

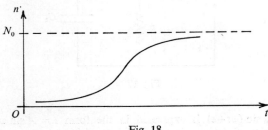

Fig. 18

5. Show that $x = A \sin bt + B \cos bt$ is a solution of $\ddot{x} + b^2 x = 0$, for all A, B.

6. Find by trial two simple independent solutions of $\ddot{x} = b^2 x$. Hence write down a solution containing two undetermined constants.

7. If $x = z e^{-at}$, write down an expression for $\dot{x}$ in terms of t, z, $\dot{z}$ and show that $\ddot{x} = (\ddot{z} - 2a\dot{z} + a^2 z) e^{-at}$.

Use this substitution to eliminate x in each of the following equations, and hence find solutions to each containing two undetermined constants.

(*a*) $\ddot{x} + 2a\dot{x} + a^2 x = 0$;

(*b*) $\ddot{x} + 2a\dot{x} + (a^2 + b^2) x = 0$;

(*c*) $\ddot{x} + 2a\dot{x} + (a^2 - b^2) x = 0$.

8. Use Question 7 to write down or derive, the complete solution of
$$p\ddot{x} + q\dot{x} + rx = 0.$$
Distinguish between the different cases that may arise.

9. Find particular integrals of:

(*a*) $\ddot{x} - 4x = 10$;

(*b*) $\ddot{x} + 6\dot{x} = e^{-2t}$;

(*c*) $\ddot{x} - 3\dot{x} + x = 7t$;

(*d*) $\ddot{x} + 5x = \sin 3t$;

(*e*) $\ddot{x} + 2\dot{x} + 5x = \cos t$;

(*f*) $\ddot{x} - \dot{x} = t e^{-t}$.

10. Write down the complete solution of the differential equation in Question 9(*d*).

11. In Figure 19, show that the current i satisfies the differential equation
$L\dfrac{d^2i}{dt^2} + \dfrac{i}{C} = A\omega\cos\omega t.$

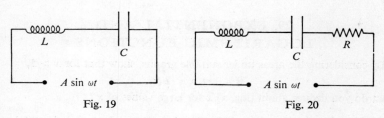

Fig. 19   Fig. 20

*12. In Figure 20, find a differential equation satisfied by the current i, and show that the steady state current (given by the PI) has amplitude

$$\frac{A}{\sqrt{\left[R^2 + \left(L\omega - \dfrac{1}{\omega C}\right)^2\right]}}.$$

What input frequency gives the greatest current? This is called the *resonant* frequency.

REVISION EXERCISES

29. EXPONENTIAL AND LOGARITHMIC FUNCTIONS

1. By considering the areas under suitable graphs, show that for $x > 1$,

$$0 < \log_e x < 2\sqrt{x}.$$

What do you deduce about $(\log_e x)/x$ for large values of x?

2. Find the maximum value of the function $f: x \rightarrow x^2 e^{-x}$ and the total area between the curve $y = f(x)$ and the positive x-axis.

3. (i) Find an expression for $\sinh^{-1}(\frac{12}{5})$ as a logarithm and hence evaluate it.
 (ii) If $\tanh x$ is defined as $\sinh x/\cosh x$:
  (a) prove that $-1 < \tanh x < +1$;
  (b) express $\tanh^{-1} y$ as a logarithm;
  (c) show that $\tanh^{-1} \frac{1}{3} = \frac{1}{2} \log_e 2$.

4. (a) Differentiate $y e^x$ with respect to x.
 (b) Solve the differential equation

$$dy/dx + y = e^x, \quad \text{given that} \quad y = 0 \quad \text{when} \quad x = 0.$$

 (c) Solve the differential equation

$$dy/dx + x = e^x, \quad \text{given that} \quad y = 0 \quad \text{when} \quad x = 0. \qquad \text{(O.C.)}$$

5. (a) Show that if $y = x^x$, then $\log_e y = x \log_e x$. Hence find dy/dx.
 (b) Use the result of (a) to find the derivative of $f: x \rightarrow x^{x^x}$.
 (c) Differentiate $\log (\log \sin x)$.

6. A snowman melts at the rate of $a(v+b)$ m³/s, where v is its volume after t seconds, and a and b are constants. One snowman melts in one-third of the time taken by a second snowman, whose volume initially is $7b$ m³. Find the initial volume of the first snowman.

30. CURRENT ELECTRICITY

1. In the circuit shown, with resistances P, Q, R, S and e.m.f.'s E and F, no current passes through the resistance S. Prove that

$$PE = (P+Q)F. \qquad \text{(O.C.)}$$

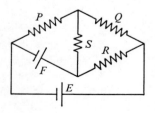

2. A 12-volt car battery with internal resistance 1 Ω, has a lighting circuit of total resistance 6 Ω permanently connected across its terminals. It is required to connect an additional resistance R temporarily across the terminals, without disconnecting the lights, to take maximum power through R. Find R, and the resulting loss of power in the lighting circuit.

3. 12 wires, each of resistance 1 Ω, are joined to form the edges of a cube. Find the equivalent single resistance when current enters and leaves the cube at opposite corners.

4. A network consists of the edges of a pentagon and its five diagonals. Choose a *tree* of branches of the network—that is, a connected set of branches without any closed loops. Show that there are always the same number of edges which cannot be fitted into such a tree, and find this number. How many independent meshes are there in the network? Write down a tie-set matrix for the ten triangular meshes and the ten branches. How many independent rows does it have?

5. In modern VHF transmission, the frequency and not the amplitude of the a.c. is varied. To illustrate the effect of this, sketch the graph of

$$v = V_0 \sin \{2\pi(10 + \sin \pi t)t\}.$$

6. The resistance on the mains side of a model-railway power-pack is 1000 Ω. It is designed to deliver 12 V to the track with no locomotive in circuit, when connected to 240 V mains. If the resistance of a locomotive is about 12 Ω and there is no power loss in the transformer, what number of locomotives can be run simultaneously to take up maximum power?

Point out some of the inadequacies of this idealized model of the situation.

31. APPLICATIONS OF DIFFERENTIAL EQUATIONS

1. Solve the differential equation

$$(1 - x^2)\frac{dy}{dx} - xy = x, \quad \text{given} \quad y = 1 \quad \text{when} \quad x = 0,$$

   (*a*) by substituting $z = y\sqrt{(1 - x^2)}$ for y;
   (*b*) by substituting $u = y + 1$ for y.

2. A motorist travelling at 15 m/s disengages gear and freewheels to rest. The retardation of the car has two components: a constant 0·03 m/s² due to friction, and a retardation of 0·0192 v^2 m/s² due to air-resistance, where v m/s is the speed after t s. Find how long it takes to come to rest, and how far it travels in doing so.

3. In a pathological investigation of the spread of infection in a culture, it is found that the time-rate at which the area of the infected part spreads is directly proportional to the product of the infected area and the uninfected area. Initially one half of the area is infected, and it is found that the intitial rate of spread is such that, if it remained constant thereafter, the culture would be completely infected in 24 hours. Set up a differential equation relating x, the infected proportion of the total area, to time t and deduce that after 12 hours about 73 % of the culture is infected. (O.C.)

4. In making a mathematical model of the formation of a raindrop by condensation, it is thought that in the early stages the mass of the drop will increase at a rate proportional to its surface area. Show that for a spherical drop this means that the radius increases uniformly with time.

After a time the drop begins to fall, and to account for the increased rate of growth a small term proportional to t is added to the constant of proportionality. Show that

$$\frac{dm}{dt} = m^{\frac{2}{3}}(a + bt).$$

If the first phase takes 30 s for a drop to grow from the initial dust speck to a diameter of 0·1 mm, when the second phase begins, and then after a further 30 s the diameter has become 0·3 mm, what time does the model predict for the diameter to grow to 1 mm?

5. A particle, moving in a straight line, is subject to a resistance of kv^n per unit mass, where v is its speed at time t. Show that if $n < 1$, the particle will come to rest at a distance

$$u^{2-n}/\{k(2-n)\}$$

from the point of projection, after a time

$$u^{1-n}/\{k(1-n)\},$$

where u is its initial speed.

Discuss what happens when $n = 1$, and when $1 < n < 2$.

6. An electron is emitted from the origin along the x-axis with velocity u, and is subject to a varying electric field which causes it to be acted on by a force $F(x)$ per unit mass in the positive direction of Ox.

Prove that $(dx/dt)^2 = f(x)$, where

$$f(x) = u^2 + \int_0^x 2F(\xi)\,d\xi.$$

Consider the case when $F(x) = -2u^2 x(a^2 - x^2)/a^4$ $(a > 0)$. Give a sketch of the graph of $y = f(x)$; find x as a function of t, and describe what happens as $t \to \infty$.

$$\left[\int \frac{dx}{a^2 - x^2} = \frac{1}{2a} \log \left| \frac{a+x}{a-x} \right| . \right]$$

32

RELATIVE MOTION

So far in our analysis of motion we have considered the situation with respect to a fixed frame of reference—the origin and axes of Cartesian coordinates, or the origin and central direction of polar coordinates. Everyday experience leads us to conclude that all motion is 'relative', and that by changing from one frame to another which is moving relative to it the motion of a body will be differently described. When we say that a frame of reference is 'fixed', as we often do, all we imply is that we are *principally* concerned with this particular frame of reference. In the first part of this chapter we shall consider how the motion of a body relative to one frame of reference corresponds to its motion relative to another. We shall restrict our attention almost entirely to cases where the frames of reference are *not* rotating relative to one another. Under this restriction we can safely talk of motion relative to an origin without bringing in the direction of the axes of reference, which we can conveniently suppose to be the same for all the origins of the different frames of reference in the problem.

1. RELATIVE DISPLACEMENT

1.1 Relative displacement. Figure 1 shows the displacements of a particle α from A to A' and of another particle β from B to B', both relative to a frame of reference with origin O; and we can imagine these displacements to take place in some interval of time.

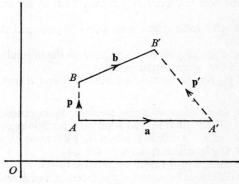

Fig. 1

Using the small letters shown to denote the various vectors we have
$\mathbf{a} + \mathbf{p}' = \mathbf{p} + \mathbf{b}$, since they are each equal to $\mathbf{AB}'$. Transposing this equation
we get
$$\mathbf{p}' - \mathbf{p} = \mathbf{b} - \mathbf{a}.$$

This equation is illustrated in Figure 2 where the vector marked with the
double arrow is both $\mathbf{p}' - \mathbf{p}$ and $\mathbf{b} - \mathbf{a}$. Now $\mathbf{p}$ and $\mathbf{p}'$ are the position vectors
of β relative to α at the beginning and end of the time interval, so that
$\mathbf{p}' - \mathbf{p}$ is the displacement of β relative to α in this interval. Over the same
interval, $\mathbf{b} - \mathbf{a}$ is the (vector) difference between the displacements of β
and α relative to O. (It is worth noticing that any point fixed relative to O
could replace O in the above analysis.)

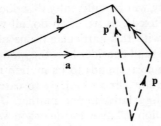

Fig. 2

We have shown that:

*The displacement of B relative to A is the displacement of B minus
the displacement of A;*

where the last two displacements are reckoned relative to some common
frame of reference.

Exercise A

1. At 1 p.m. a man B is at a cross-roads and a man A is 4 km away on the road
to the south. In the next ten minutes A moves 2 km to the north and B $1\frac{1}{2}$ km
to the east. Draw:

(*a*) B's position relative to A at 1 p.m. and 1.10 p.m. and show B's displacement relative to A.

(*b*) Draw B's and A's displacements relative to the ground. Check that their
vector difference is the vector found in (*a*).

Repeat (*a*) and (*b*) for the next ten minutes if A and B continue at the same
average speed.

2. An aircraft, A, in position A_1 sights another, B, in position B_1 5 km away
on a bearing 060°. When A has moved 3 km on a north-westerly course relative
to the air, it is at A_2, and B is then in position B_2, 7 km away on a bearing of 100°.

(*a*) What is B's displacement relative to the air?

(*b*) What is the change in B's position relative to A?

(*c*) What is the difference between the displacements of A and B relative to the
air and how is this related to the result of (*b*)?

3. In a sailing race boat A is 1 cable to the east of B, and C is 1 cable to the east of A. In the next minute A moves 1 cable north, B 1 cable west and C 1 cable south. Find the displacement of B relative to A and of C relative to A. Hence find the displacement of B relative to C. Check your result by finding directly the displacement of B relative to C.

1.2   Notation for relative displacement. Figure 3 shows a grid fixed in relation to some frame of reference. Relative to this a point P is displaced from P_1 to P_2. Now whatever origin O is chosen for this frame of reference, the displacement relative to O $(OP_2 - OP_1)$ is represented by a vector equivalent to P_1P_2.

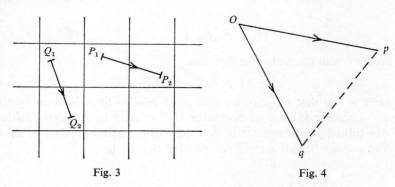

Fig. 3   Fig. 4

We shall now adopt the notation **op** for this vector; so that **op** represents the displacement of P relative to O (see Figure 4). It is easy to see that the actual location of O is not important, and we can usefully think of the letter o as standing for the whole frame of reference, and not to be confused with the particular origin O.

If point Q undergoes a displacement from Q_1 to Q_2 relative to O, then this will be represented by the vector **oq**, equivalent to Q_1Q_2. Now we know that the displacement of P relative to Q is the displacement of P relative to O minus the displacement of Q relative to O; that is,

$$\mathbf{qp} = \mathbf{op} - \mathbf{oq}.$$

A consideration of the following situation will illustrate this notation.

Relative to the earth's surface a man A moves east from A_1 to A_2 while a man B, originally S.S.E. of A, moves north from B_1 to B_2.

Figure 5 illustrates these displacements; notice that the actual positions of the two men are not given.

If the frame of reference fixed relative to the earth is denoted by e then **ea** and **eb** in Figure 6 represent the displacements of A and B relative to the earth respectively. Consequently **ab** represents the displacement of B relative to A and **ba** represents the displacement of A relative to B.

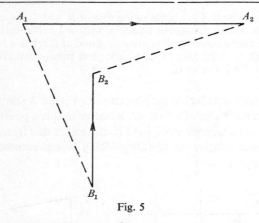

Fig. 5

Figure 6 also illustrates the fact that

$$\mathbf{ab} = \mathbf{A_2B_2} - \mathbf{A_1B_1}.$$

That is to say that the displacement of B relative to A is given by the vector-difference (final position-vector of B relative to the final position of A) − (initial position-vector of B relative to the initial position of A).

Now let us consider a more complicated situation.

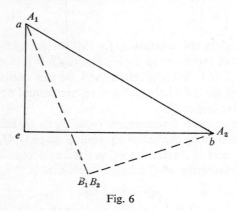

Fig. 6

A helicopter from an aircraft carrier is flying on a southerly course at 90 km/h through the air; the carrier is moving west relative to the sea at 30 km/h; the sea is moving south-east at 3 km/h relative to the sea bed; and the air is moving north-east at 22·5 km/h relative to the sea. How are all these movements related?

We shall assume that the velocities involved are constant and consider the relative displacements in the course of an hour. First, we denote the frame of reference fixed relative to the sea bed by e. Relative to e the sea is displaced, in one hour, 3 km to the south-east; this is represented by **es**, where s can be taken to denote either a definite particle of the sea or the whole frame of reference fixed relative to the sea surface. In the same way the displacement of the air relative to the sea is given by **sa**, where **sa** represents a shift of 22·5 km to the north-east; and likewise for the other displacements involved.

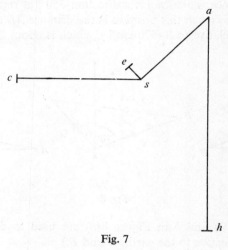

Fig. 7

Now if, for example, we are interested in the displacement of the helicopter relative to the carrier we can read this directly from the figure, where it is shown by the vector **ch**.

2. RELATIVE VELOCITY

In the example we have just been considering, the displacements were made in a fixed time (1 hour) at constant speeds. It is therefore possible to interpret Figure 7 as a relative velocity diagram, since by relative velocity we shall mean the rate of change of relative displacement. We may indeed adopt the same notation for relative velocities as we had for relative displacements, provided we are clear—and make it clear—which we are discussing. This notation will be used in the figures for many of the following examples although the working will be independent of it. It is important to realize that the relative velocity diagram does not in any way show the relations between simultaneous *positions*.. As usual we indicate velocity vectors by arrows with solid heads.

Example 1. Aircraft A is 20 km west of aircraft B. A is flying at 300 km/h on course 040° and B at 400 km/h on course 290°. What is the closest approach of A to B, and after how long is it reached?

967

The initial geographical situation relative to the ground is shown in Figure 8(*a*). In Figure 8(*b*) v_A and v_B represent the velocity of *A* and *B* relative to the ground, and therefore $v_A - v_B$ is the velocity of *A* relative to *B*, which by measurement is 570 km/h in direction 080°. The displacement diagram *relative* to *B* is shown in Figure 8(*c*), where *A* is *A*'s initial position, *AK* its course and *N* its nearest approach to *B*. By measurement the nearest distance is 3·5 km (in a direction 350°, at right angles to *AK*). The time taken to reach this position is the distance *AN* (19·5 km) divided by *A*'s velocity relative to *B* (570 km/h), which is about 2·1 minutes.

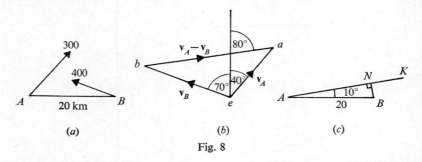

(a) (b) (c)

Fig. 8

(The letters *e*, *a* and *b* in Figure 8(*b*) are used to denote frames of reference fixed relative to the earth, *A* and *B*.)

Example 2. To a man cycling at 16 km/h along a straight road the wind appears to come from 60° to his left, and when he increases speed to 24 km/h, from 45° to his left. Find the true ground wind velocity.

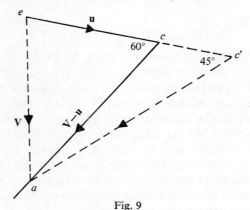

Fig. 9

The apparent wind is, of course, the wind relative to the man. If the ground wind is **V**, then the apparent wind is **V**−**u**, where **u** is the man's velocity. The direction of **V**−**u** is 60° when **u** = 16 km/h, and 45° when

$\mathbf{u} = 24$ km/h. If ec and ec' represent the two velocities of the man, and the point a is the intersection of lines through c and c' at angles of 60° and 45° to $\mathbf{u}$, then ea represents the ground wind $\mathbf{V}$. By measurement this is about 20 km/h from 103° to his left.

(The letters e, c, c' and a are used to denote frames of reference fixed relative to the earth, the cyclist at his two speeds, and the air.)

Example 3. A destroyer is heading for a port which lies 70 nautical miles away in a direction 120°. If her speed through the water is 12 knots and there is a tidal stream setting 350° at 3 knots, how long will she take to reach port if present conditions continue?

Triangle esd is a velocity triangle where $\mathbf{t}$ and $\mathbf{u}$ represent the velocities of the sea and the destroyer relative to the sea bed and $\mathbf{v}$ the velocity of the destroyer relative to the sea. Now we know the magnitude and direction of $\mathbf{t}$, the direction of $\mathbf{u}$ (towards the port) and the magnitude of $\mathbf{v}$ (12 knots). The diagram can therefore be drawn by marking the direction to the port ep, then the vector $\mathbf{t}$ and lastly, with a compass, finding the point d on ep at the scaled distance from s to represent 12 knots. By measurement u is found to be about 10 knots, so the destroyer is making good this speed

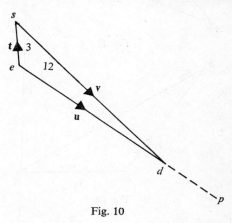

Fig. 10

relative to the sea bed towards port. She will therefore arrive in 7 hours. It is worth observing that the ship does not head directly towards her destination but at an angle offset by about 10° between $\mathbf{u}$ and $\mathbf{v}$.

Even when the velocities are not constant we can draw the same sort of relative velocity diagram. At the beginning of Chapter 19 we defined the velocity of a point P as $d\mathbf{r}/dt$, where $\mathbf{r}$ is the position vector of P from the origin O. We must now interpret this as the velocity *relative* to O. Remembering that

$$\frac{d\mathbf{r}}{dt} = \lim_{\delta t \to 0} \left(\frac{\delta \mathbf{r}}{\delta t}\right),$$

where $\delta\mathbf{r}$ is now the displacement of P relative to O in the interval δt, we see that the relative velocity is the rate of change of the displacement of P relative to O (as we have already assumed at the beginning of this section). It should be noticed that any point fixed in the frame of reference with O as origin will serve instead of O in the definition of relative velocity.

Now suppose particles B and C are moving in some way relative to a point A. Let $\mathbf{r}_1, \mathbf{r}_2$ be the position vectors of B and C relative to A, and $\mathbf{r}_{12}$ the position vector of C relative to B.

Then as
$$\mathbf{r}_1 + \mathbf{r}_{12} = \mathbf{r}_2,$$

we have
$$\mathbf{r}_{12} = \mathbf{r}_2 - \mathbf{r}_1.$$

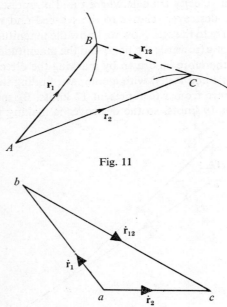

Fig. 11

Fig. 12

This is true for all times under consideration; we may therefore differentiate with respect to time, and obtain
$$\dot{\mathbf{r}}_{12} = \dot{\mathbf{r}}_2 - \dot{\mathbf{r}}_1.$$

In words: the velocity of C relative to B is the velocity of C relative to A minus the velocity of B relative to A.

This may be restated more simply in the two following ways: either

   (i) **velocity of C relative to B = velocity of C – velocity of B,**

or

   (ii) **velocity of C = velocity of B + velocity of C relative to B,** where it is understood that the velocities of B and C are relative to some common frame of reference.

These statements are illustrated in the relative velocity diagram of Figure 12 where the vectors represent the instantaneous values of the velocities.

Exercise B

1. A man walking at 6 km/h has the wind directly behind him. If the rain is falling at 30 km/h at 30° from the vertical, how should he hold his umbrella to give himself maximum protection?

2. An aircraft is flying high at an air speed of 500 km/h on a compass course of 350°. At this height the air is moving at 100 km/h in the direction 100°. What is the aircraft's track and speed relative to the ground?

3. The aircraft in the previous question is flying above a layer of cloud at the level of which the air is moving at 30 km/h in direction 180°. What is the aircraft's velocity relative to the cloud layer?

4. A low-flying aircraft passes directly over a car which is travelling at 50 km/h and appears to the driver to be moving at right-angles to his direction. If the ground speed of the aircraft is 200 km/h, after how long will it be 8 km away from the car?

5. A ship steering west has a speed of 15 knots through the water. If there is a tidal stream of 4 knots setting to the south-west, what is her track and speed relative to the land?

6. At a certain time two skaters are 15 m apart and on 'converging' courses each making an angle of 35° with the line joining them. One is moving at 10 m/s; what is the speed of the other if at their closest they are 2 m apart? (Two answers.)

7. At an anti-missile-missile launching base an enemy missile of speed 3000 km/h is detected 1200 km away on a course which would bring it to a distance of 135 km at its closest. If at that instant an a-m-m is launched and its speed is 1800 km/h, what are its possible courses for interception and how long would it take to intercept? What would be its least speed to intercept? Will there always be two possible intercepting courses if its speed is greater than this least speed?

8. A man sets out to swim a river in which the current runs uniformly at 1·6 m/s. He wants to land as close as possible to the point nearest to him on the opposite bank. In what direction should he be heading if his speed through the water is 1·2 m/s?

9. A boat whose speed through the water is 3 m/s points directly across an estuary 100 m wide. It is carried downstream by a current whose speed at different distances from the bank is given in the following table:

Distance (m)	0	10	20	30	40	50	60	70	80	90	100
Speed (m/s)	0	1·5	3	3·5	4	4·5	4	3·5	3	1·5	0

By taking the average speed of the current over the first 10 m from the bank to be 0·75 m/s, over the next 10 m to be 2·25 m/s and so on, sketch the path of the boat across the estuary. (Use graph paper.)

971

10. A train is travelling due east at 75 km/h and the wind is blowing from the north-east at a ground speed of 30 km/h. What is the direction in which the smoke trail lies? Show that at the same speed there are two possible directions in which the train could move for the trail to lie in a north–south direction. Which would give the thicker trail? Find also the speed of advance of the line of the trail. (Assume that the smoke particles are brought immediately to rest relative to the air, and so remain.)

11. An aircraft carrier steaming 090° at 20 knots sends out a helicopter with orders to remain on a bearing from the carrier of 060° and to return in two hours. If the helicopter's air speed is 60 knots and the wind relative to the sea is blowing to the south at 15 knots, after what time does the helicopter alter course to return?

12. An ant crawls from the centre at 2·5 cm/s along a radius of a 30 cm record which is rotating at 1 rad/s. Show on a diagram the positions of the ant at $\frac{1}{2}$ s intervals. Find the tangents to the ant's path at these points by drawing velocity triangles, and then sketch in the path.
  (a) What is the polar equation of the path?
  (b) Find formulae for its speed and direction at any time t s after it sets out.

13. Two particles are moving in concentric circular paths centre O and in the same sense, the inner one A, 3 m from O, at an angular velocity of 4 rad/s and the outer one B, 5 m from O, at an angular velocity of 2 rad/s. What is the angular velocity of the line AB when O, A, B are in a straight line and when $\angle OAB$ is a right angle?
  (*Hint.* Consider the motion relative to a rotating frame of reference in which O and A are fixed.)
  Note that the irregular motion of the planets relative to the earth arises in a similar manner.

14. A is 90 m from a cross-roads, strolling towards it at 0·6 m/s, while B, who is on the other road 120 m from their intersection, walks briskly away from it at 1·5 m/s. Find:
  (a) the velocity of B relative to A,
  (b) the angular velocity of AB.
By considering the components of the velocities of A and B along and perpendicular to AB, find the rate of increase of the distance AB. Also write down the radial and transverse components of the velocity of B relative to A.

*15. P and Q are points fixed in a body which is rotating with angular velocity ω. What is the velocity of Q relative to P if the distance PQ is d? By considering the velocities of P and Q in relation to the instantaneous centre, draw a vector triangle to show the velocity of Q relative to P and from it deduce your previous result (see Chapter 19, Section 8).

*16. An upright circular ring rolls without slipping along a straight line. Where is the instantaneous centre? If the join of the point of the contact between the ring and the line to a point P of the ring makes an angle θ with the vertical, show that the direction of the velocity passes through the top point of the ring for all possible θ. What is the speed of P in terms of θ if the angular velocity of the ring is ω? State also the relation between θ and ψ, where ψ is the gradient of the tangent to the locus of P (which is a cycloid). Compare Chapter 17, Section 4.2.

972

3. RELATIVE ACCELERATION

In Figure 13 r_1 and r_2 are the position vectors of points B and C relative to some point A, and r_{12} is the position vector of C relative to B. Then at any time

$$r_{12} = r_2 - r_1.$$

Since this is true for all values of t, we may differentiate and obtain

$$\dot{r}_{12} = \dot{r}_2 - \dot{r}_1,$$

and again

$$\ddot{r}_{12} = \ddot{r}_2 - \ddot{r}_1.$$

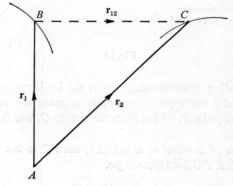

Fig. 13

In words:

The acceleration of C relative to B is the acceleration of C minus the acceleration of B (where the last two accelerations are relative to some common frame of reference).

This is exactly analogous to the result for relative velocities; as before it is often useful to restate the rule in the slightly different form:

The acceleration of C is the acceleration of B added to the acceleration of C relative to B.

We now give some examples to illustrate this relationship.

Example 4. A runs at a steady speed of 6 m/s round a circular track of radius 24 m. What is his acceleration relative to a car C moving due east with an acceleration of 0.67 m/s^2, where their directions of motion are inclined at 45° to one another? (Figure 14(a).)

If O is the centre of the circle, A's acceleration is purely along AO (since the speed is constant) and of magnitude

$$\frac{6^2}{24} = 1.5 \text{ m/s}^2.$$

973

In Figure 14(*b*) the acceleration of *A* relative to *C* is shown as the vector difference between the accelerations of *A* and *C*. By drawing and measurement or by calculation it will be found to be approximately 2 m/s² in a direction 300°.

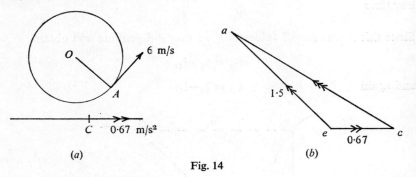

(*a*)　　　　　　　　　　　　　　　　　　　　　　(*b*)

Fig. 14

Example 5. A curling stone moving across the ice is retarding at 0·3 m/s². If it is rotating at 3 rad/s (with negligible angular acceleration) find the acceleration of the point *P*, 10 cm from the centre *O*, which has the greatest forward speed.

If the direction of motion is along *AB*, then *P* is the point shown in Figure 15(*a*) with ∠ *POB* a right-angle.

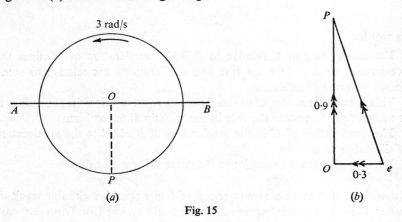

(*a*)　　　　　　　　　　　　　　　　　　　　　　(*b*)

Fig. 15

Relative to *P*, *O* moves in a circle, and therefore the acceleration of *P* relative to *O* is given by

$$\mathbf{a} = \omega^2\mathbf{r}$$

$$= 0.9 \text{ m/s}^2 \text{ along } \mathbf{PO}.$$

The acceleration of *O* is 0·3 m/s² along **BA** (since it is retarding).

974

Now the acceleration of P is the acceleration of O + the acceleration of P relative to O; from a scale drawing (Figure 15(b)) this is approximately 0·95 m/s² in a direction making 72° with **BA**.

Exercise C

Numerical problems can often be best solved by drawing.

1. Describe in general terms the variation in the acceleration of a link of a bicycle chain as the bicycle is ridden at constant velocity. What additional acceleration components are brought in when the bicycle accelerates?

2. On a racing circuit, at a particular instant, a car A is moving east at 30 m/s round a bend which is an arc of a circle of radius 120 m, and is 'accelerating' along its track at 1·5 m/s²; while another car B on a straight part of the course running north-east is slowing down to a corner at 3 m/s². What is the acceleration of A relative to B? At what rate in degrees per second is A altering its direction?

3. At the beginning of the stroke an oarsman, stationary relative to the boat and with his back inclined at 30° to the vertical, gives his slide an acceleration of 6 m/s² (relative to the boat) and his body an angular acceleration of 8 rad/s². If his shoulders move in a circular arc of radius 0·7 m relative to the slide, what is the acceleration of his shoulders at this instant if the boat is retarding at 8 m/s²?

4. A rod OA, of length a, is pivoted at O and to it is hinged a rod AB of length b. OA and OB make angles θ and ϕ respectively with a fixed direction. The system moves in a plane so that $\dot\theta$, but not $\dot\phi$, is constant. In separate sketches show in terms of θ, ϕ and their derivatives the acceleration of (a) A, (b) B relative to A, and (c) B.

5. A circular ring, of radius a, moves in a vertical plane with a clockwise angular velocity ω, and its centre moves horizontally to the right with speed v. What is the velocity of the lowest point of the ring? Find the condition for the ring to be rolling without slipping on a horizontal surface. If the ring is rolling in this way, and its centre has speed v and acceleration f, what is the acceleration of the lowest point (a) relative to the centre, and (b) relative to the ground?

6. An upright disc rolls without slipping along a horizontal line. Starting from rest it has an acceleration a. Show that at any time there is a point of the disc which has no acceleration.

7. A bomb explodes on the way down, scattering pieces in all directions with speeds up to 80 m/s. Within what region of space do all the pieces lie after an interval of t s?

8. A thread is held taut as it is unwound from a fixed reel of radius a and centre O. The free end of the straight part is P and the point of contact where the thread comes off the reel is T; the length TP is denoted by p, and the radius OT makes an angle θ with a fixed direction Ox. Express the coordinates of P relative to perpendicular axes Ox, Oy in terms of a, p, θ.

The thread is unwound so that $\dot\theta$ has a constant value. Find the Cartesian components of the acceleration of P (note that $\dot p \neq 0$), and show that they agree with the acceleration obtained by considering the acceleration of T and the acceleration of P relative to T.

Verify that the direction of the acceleration of P is along the reflection of PO in the line PT.

33

MOMENTUM AND IMPULSE

The theory of motion of a particle was introduced in Chapter 19 on Kinematics without any consideration of the causes of the motion. These causes were discussed in Chapter 24 (Introduction to Mechanics) and it is now appropriate to combine these two topics and consider motion as the effect of specific forces. In our examples we shall be concerned with a *simple* description of a physical problem and unless otherwise stated we shall ignore the effects of frictional and other forces.

1. THE IMPULSE–MOMENTUM EQUATION

1.1 The vector equation of motion of a particle of mass m is usually written in the form

$$F = m\mathbf{a}.$$

This implies an equivalence between two *vectors*; the vector sum of the system of forces acting on the particle, and the mass-acceleration vector of the particle. In this equation we must be careful to define consistent units for force, mass and acceleration.

1.2 It was explained in Chapter 19 that when the acceleration $\mathbf{a}$ is constant, the following equation relates the initial and final velocities:

$$\mathbf{v} = \mathbf{u} + t\mathbf{a}, \quad \text{where} \quad \mathbf{v} = \mathbf{u} \quad \text{when} \quad t = 0.$$

Figure 1 shows a vector diagram of this equation.

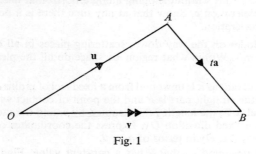

Fig. 1

Although the acceleration is constant the motion is not necessarily one-dimensional and the particle may move along a curve as t increases. For example, a projectile moves in two dimensions under a constant gravitational force.

976

1.3 If the quantities $\mathbf{F}$, m and $\mathbf{a}$ are all constant then we may combine the two equations

$$\begin{cases} \mathbf{F} = m\mathbf{a}, \\ \mathbf{v} = \mathbf{u} + t\mathbf{a}, \end{cases}$$

to give
$$m\mathbf{v} = m\mathbf{u} + mt\mathbf{a},$$

or
$$m\mathbf{v} = m\mathbf{u} + t\mathbf{F}.$$

This implies the enlargement by the scale factor m of the vector triangle of Figure 1, giving the triangle shown in Figure 2.

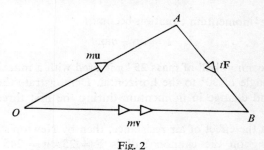

Fig. 2

1.4 Note on diagrams. We adopt a consistent scheme for the arrowheads indicating vectors in diagrams. Forces are denoted by plain arrows ($\longrightarrow$); velocities by solid arrowheads ($\rightarrow$); and momenta (or impulses) by open triangular arrowheads ($\rightarrowtail$). Doubling the arrowhead denotes that the vector is obtained as the sum or difference of the remaining vectors.

1.5 Units. The quantity $t\mathbf{F}$ is called the *impulse* of the force $\mathbf{F}$. If the force is measured in newtons, and t is measured in seconds, then the unit of impulse is the newton second (N s).

The quantity $m\mathbf{v}$ is called the *momentum* of the particle at the instant when its velocity is $\mathbf{v}$. It follows from the equation $m\mathbf{v} = m\mathbf{u} + t\mathbf{F}$ that the units of impulse and momentum are equivalent:

$$1 \text{ kg m/s} = 1 \text{ N s}.$$

1.6 Impulse–momentum equation. By writing the equation

$$m\mathbf{v} = m\mathbf{u} + t\mathbf{F}$$

in the form
$$t\mathbf{F} = m\mathbf{v} - m\mathbf{u}$$

we can equate the change in momentum $m\mathbf{v} - m\mathbf{u}$, with the impulse $t\mathbf{F}$ applied to the particle.

16   SAM 3

977

This equation will be called the 'Impulse–Momentum Equation' and the remainder of the chapter will be devoted to applying the equation to a variety of situations.

1.7   Impulse. Under certain conditions neither **F** nor t of the Impulse–Momentum equation are known. For example, a change in momentum can be observed when a ball hits a cricket bat, but the force and the time of impact are difficult to measure. Under these circumstances we can compute the total impulse from the change of momentum, and we label it with the single letter **I**.

The impulse–momentum equation becomes

$$I = m\mathbf{v} - m\mathbf{u}.$$

Example 1. A cannon ball of mass 25 kg is fired with a muzzle velocity of 30 m/s at an angle of 30° to the horizontal. Demonstrate the equality of the impulse and change in momentum during the first three seconds of flight.

If we neglect the effect of air resistance, then by Newton's Second Law the force acting on the cannon ball is $\mathbf{F} = 25 \times \mathbf{g} = 245$ N vertically downwards (see Figure 3(*a*)). Consequently the impulse for the time interval of 3 s is 735 N s vertically downwards.

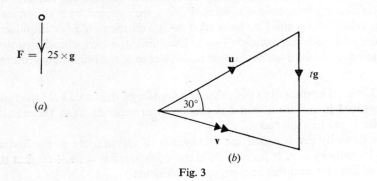

(*a*)

(*b*)

Fig. 3

To obtain the change in momentum, the velocity **v** may be found in the usual way from Figure 3(*b*):

$$\mathbf{v} = \mathbf{u} + t\mathbf{g} \quad \text{at time } t.$$

Enlargement by scale factor m gives

$$m\mathbf{v} = m\mathbf{u} + mt\mathbf{g}.$$

Therefore, as $m = 25$ kg,

$$m\mathbf{v} - m\mathbf{u} = 25 \text{ kg} \times 3 \text{ s} \times 9{\cdot}8 \text{ m/s}^2 \text{ vertically downwards}$$

$$= 735 \text{ N s vertically downwards}.$$

Hence $m\mathbf{v} - m\mathbf{u}$, the change in momentum of the cannon ball, is equal to the impulse as calculated above.

Example 2. A billiard ball travelling at 1 m/s hits a cushion along a line making an angle of 60° with it. The billiard ball maintains contact for 0·1 s, during which time the cushion exerts a constant force perpendicular to the side of the table of 1·4 N.

If the mass of the billiard ball is 120 g, calculate its velocity just after impact.

Two methods are given for the solution of this problem. The first is based on the impulse–momentum triangle, Figure 4; the second is an algebraic method based entirely on the impulse–momentum equation.

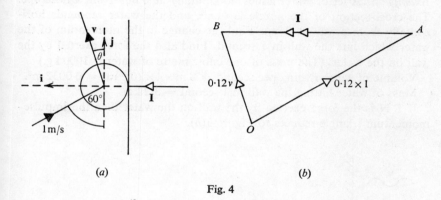

(a)   (b)

Fig. 4

Method (i). Figure 4(*a*) gives the impulse and momentum system for the billiard ball and Figure 4(*b*) is the appropriate impulse–momentum triangle.

AB (representing the impulse) $= 1\cdot4 \times 0\cdot1$ N s perpendicular to the cushion.

By measurement or calculation, $0\cdot12v = 0\cdot07$ N s and $O\hat{B}A = 59°$.

Therefore the final velocity of the billiard ball is 0·58 m/s at an angle of 31° with the cushion.

Method (ii). Take unit vectors **i** and **j** as shown in Figure 4(*a*), and let $\mathbf{v} = \begin{pmatrix} \dot{x} \\ \dot{y} \end{pmatrix}$ m/s. The impulse–momentum equation gives

$$0\cdot12 \begin{pmatrix} \dot{x} \\ \dot{y} \end{pmatrix} - 0\cdot12 \begin{pmatrix} -\sin 60 \\ \cos 60 \end{pmatrix} = 1\cdot4 \begin{pmatrix} 1 \\ 0 \end{pmatrix} 0\cdot1$$

that is

$$\begin{cases} \dot{x} + \tfrac{1}{2}\sqrt{3} = \tfrac{14}{12}, \\ \dot{y} - \tfrac{1}{2} = 0; \end{cases}$$

$$\begin{cases} \dot{x} = 0\cdot3, \\ \dot{y} = 0\cdot5. \end{cases}$$

This gives
$$\tan \theta = \frac{0 \cdot 3}{0 \cdot 5} \text{ leading to } \theta = 31°$$

and
$$v = \sqrt{\{(0 \cdot 5)^2 + (0 \cdot 3)^2\}}$$
$$= 0 \cdot 58.$$

The velocity is therefore 0·58 m/s at an angle of 31° with the cushion. Alternatively, we can write the answer in the vector form

$$\text{velocity} = \begin{pmatrix} 0 \cdot 3 \\ 0 \cdot 5 \end{pmatrix} \text{ m/s.}$$

Example 3. A jet of water issues horizontally at 8 m/s from a hosepipe. The cross-section of the nozzle is 4 cm², and the water rebounds horizontally from a wall at 2 m/s. Find the change in the momentum of the water which hits the wall in 1 second. Find also the force exerted by the wall on the water. (The mass of one cubic metre of water is 1000 kg.)

Volume of water issuing per second = $8 \text{ m} \times 4 \times 10^{-4} \text{ m}^2 = 0 \cdot 0032 \text{ m}^3$.

Mass of water hitting the wall in 1 second = 3·2 kg.

If F N is the force exerted by the wall on the water then the impulse–momentum triangle reduces to Figure 5(*b*).

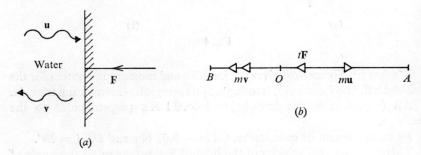

Fig. 5

The impulse–momentum equation gives

$$3 \cdot 2 \times 2 + 3 \cdot 2 \times 8 = F \times 1.$$

Hence the change in momentum during 1 second is 32 s N. This is equal to the force, F N, exerted by the wall on the water, multiplied by the time (1 s); therefore the force is 32 N.

By the interaction principle the force exerted by the water on the wall must be equal in magnitude but opposite in direction to F.

Example 4. A cricket ball of mass 150 g having velocity

$$\begin{pmatrix} 20 \\ -2 \\ 2\cdot3 \end{pmatrix} \text{m/s}$$

is hit by a cricket bat. If the subsequent velocity is

$$\begin{pmatrix} -1 \\ 12 \\ 0 \end{pmatrix} \text{m/s,}$$

what is the impulse applied to the ball? If the contact lasts for 10^{-2} seconds what is the force exerted by the ball on the bat?

Applying the impulse–momentum equation in component form

$$I = 0\cdot150 \begin{pmatrix} -1 \\ 12 \\ 0 \end{pmatrix} - 0\cdot150 \begin{pmatrix} 20 \\ -2 \\ 2\cdot3 \end{pmatrix} \text{N s}$$

$$= 0\cdot150 \begin{pmatrix} -21 \\ 14 \\ -2\cdot3 \end{pmatrix} = \begin{pmatrix} -3\cdot15 \\ 2\cdot1 \\ -0\cdot35 \end{pmatrix} \text{N s.}$$

If the impulse lasts for 10^{-2} s, then $I = F \times (\frac{1}{100} \text{ s})$, where F is the force exerted by the bat; and therefore

$$F = \begin{pmatrix} -315 \\ 210 \\ -35 \end{pmatrix} \text{N.}$$

Hence the magnitude of F is $35\sqrt{(81+36+1)}$ N acting in the direction.

$$\begin{pmatrix} -9 \\ 6 \\ -1 \end{pmatrix}$$

that is, by the interaction principle, the force exerted by the ball on the bat is 380 N in the direction

$$\begin{pmatrix} 9 \\ -6 \\ 1 \end{pmatrix}.$$

Exercise A

1. Calculate, in second-newtons, the momentum of each of the following:
   (a) a cable car of mass 1 tonne travelling at 3 m/s;
   (b) a boat of mass 300 tonnes travelling at 3 m/s;
   (c) a railway truck of mass 6 tonnes travelling at 50 km/h;
   (d) a go-kart of mass 50 kg travelling at 100 km/h;
   (e) a lorry weighing 3 tonnes travelling at 100 km/h;
   (f) a bullet of mass 30 g travelling at 500 m/s.

2. A ship of 4000 tonnes is moving at 0·03 m/s against a pier. Calculate the momentum of the ship in N s. Find the force of resistance (assumed constant) exerted by the pier if it takes 5 s for the ship to come to rest. The time taken is increased to 25 s by hanging rubber tyres from the pier; what would be the new force (again assumed constant)?

3. A ball bouncing against a wall receives an impulse of 1·1 N s perpendicular to the wall which gives it a final momentum of 0·6 N s at 30° to the wall. Draw a vector triangle and find the initial momentum of the ball.

4. The momentum of a cricket ball before hitting a bat is 1·7 N s, and the directions of motion before and after impact are at 60° and 45° with the face of the bat (see Figure 6).

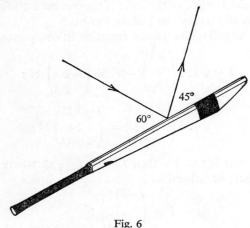

Fig. 6

Draw the impulse–momentum triangle and use this to estimate the final momentum of the ball and the impulse applied to it.

The mass of the cricket ball is 150 g; what are the speeds before and after impact?

5. A bullet of mass 30 g is travelling at 500 m/s when it ricochets from a piece of armour plate at 375 m/s and is deflected through 90°. Find the impulse on the bullet.

If the time of contact is of the order of 10^{-4} s, estimate the average force on the armour plate.

6. A pitching machine gives a standard impulse of 2·8 N s to a ball. The average mass of the balls used is 225 g and their speeds before and after the impulse average 6 m/s and 10 m/s respectively.

Find through what angle the balls are turned by the machine.

7. A ball of mass 0·8 kg strikes a wall. Unit vectors **i** and **j** are chosen as shown in the diagram (Figure 7). If

$$\mathbf{u} = \begin{pmatrix} 5 \\ -12 \end{pmatrix} \text{ m/s} \quad \text{and} \quad \mathbf{v} = \begin{pmatrix} 3 \\ 4 \end{pmatrix} \text{ m/s,}$$

calculate the impulse on the ball due to the impact. Using graph paper draw the impulse–momentum triangle.

982

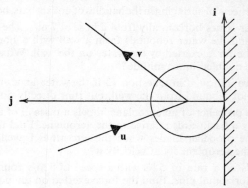

Fig. 7

8. A 150 g ball with velocity

$$\begin{pmatrix} 2 \\ -2 \\ 1 \end{pmatrix} \text{ m/s}$$

is in contact with a bat for $\frac{1}{40}$ s, as a result of which its new velocity is

$$\begin{pmatrix} -1 \\ 0{\cdot}4 \\ 2 \end{pmatrix} \text{ m/s}.$$

Calculate the average force exerted by the ball on the bat.

9. A ball-bearing of mass 25 g is deflected through 90° when it hits a flat metal barrier. Its initial velocity is 5 m/s at an angle of $\tan^{-1} \frac{4}{3}$ with the metal barrier. Find the impulse on the ball-bearing and its velocity after impact.

(Take $\mathbf{i}$ in the direction of the barrier and $\mathbf{j}$ normal to the barrier; note that the momentum must be constant in the direction of $\mathbf{i}$ over the time interval of the impulse.)

10. A particle of mass 100 g is attached to a fixed point O on a smooth horizontal table by an inelastic string of length 1 m. It is projected from a point A, 0·5 m from O, with a velocity of 2 m/s perpendicular to OA.

Find the impulse in the string when it becomes taut and, assuming it then remains taut, find the final velocity of the particle.

11. An impulse of

$$\begin{pmatrix} 3 \\ -9 \\ 6 \end{pmatrix} \text{ s N}$$

causes the final momentum of a 3 kg ball to be

$$\begin{pmatrix} 6 \\ 3 \\ 9 \end{pmatrix} \text{ s N}.$$

Calculate the ball's initial velocity, giving the magnitude and direction.

12. Discuss the effects of springing in the handles of cricket bats, hockey sticks, etc.

13. A jet of water issues horizontally from a hose at 7 m/s. The cross-section of the jet is 4 cm² and the water rebounds from a wall with a horizontal velocity of 1 m/s. Find the force exerted by the water on the wall. What is this force if the velocities are doubled in magnitude?

14. Find the force indicated in Question 13 if the water issues from the hose at 9 m/s and does not rebound from the wall, but runs directly downwards.

15. In time t the propeller of an aeroplane impels a mass m of air (originally at rest) at a velocity u backwards relative to the aeroplane. Find the force exerted by the air on the propeller blades when the aircraft is travelling forwards at velocity v. Can the aeroplane fly at velocity u?

16. Water travels at a rate of 5 l/s with a speed of 8 m/s round a right-angle bend in a rigid horizontal pipe. Find the force exerted on the pipe by the water. What would happen if the pipe were flexible?

2. THE IMPULSE OF A VARIABLE FORCE F

So far we have only considered questions involving a constant force. Clearly this is a considerable simplification and we widen the approach in the following Example, where **F** is variable in magnitude but constant in direction.

Example 5. A man hauls a bucket of water, of total mass 10 kg, from the depths of a well, His effective pull starts at 125 N and decreases uniformly at the rate of 5 N/s. Find the velocity of the bucket after 3 s.

Figure 8(a) gives the force diagram, from which it can be deduced that the resultant force is initially 27 N upwards, decreasing uniformly at the rate of 5 N/s during the three seconds. This is illustrated in Figure 8(b).

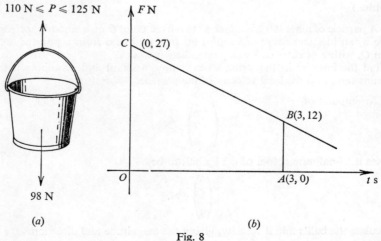

(a)

(b)

Fig. 8

984

As F is variable the impulse-momentum equation as we have used it is no longer applicable. However, it we divide the three-second interval into smaller units we can obtain an approximate answer by assuming that F is constant in these intervals. If we take three intervals, each of 1 second duration, then let

$$0 \leqslant t < 1, \quad F_0 = 27, \quad \mathbf{u} = 0, \quad \mathbf{v} = \mathbf{v}_1;$$
$$1 \leqslant t < 2, \quad F_1 = 22, \quad \mathbf{u} = \mathbf{v}_1, \quad \mathbf{v} = \mathbf{v}_2;$$
$$2 \leqslant t \leqslant 3, \quad F_2 = 17, \quad \mathbf{u} = \mathbf{v}_2, \quad \mathbf{v} = \mathbf{v}_3.$$

Thus we have the three impulse–momentum equations:

$$27 = 10v_1 - 10.0,$$
$$22 = 10v_2 - 10v_1,$$
$$17 = 10v_3 - 10v_2.$$

If we add the equations the right-hand side gives the change in momentum of the bucket

$$66 = 10v_3 - 10.0$$
$$\Rightarrow \quad v_3 = 6 \cdot 6,$$

giving 6·6 m/s as an approximation to the final velocity of the bucket. The left-hand side is, of course, the area shaded in Figure 9 which is superimposed on Figure 8. This gives a clear hint as to the interpretation of the impulse of the force in these circumstances; it is the area under the graph of F plotted against t.

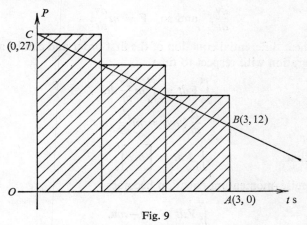

Fig. 9

To solve the problem exactly we calculate the area under the force-time graph, which is the area of $OABC$. This represents, therefore, an impulse of magnitude
$$\tfrac{1}{2}(27 + 12).3 \text{ s N.}$$
$$= \tfrac{1}{2}.39.3 \text{ s N.}$$

Now applying the impulse–momentum equation

$$\tfrac{1}{2}.39.3 = 10.v$$

$$\Rightarrow v = 5.85,$$

and the final velocity is 5.85 m/s.

We can justify our method in the following way; if at time t_i the value of F is F_i then for an interval of time δt_i the impulse–momentum equation gives

$$\mathbf{F}_i.(\delta t_i) = m\mathbf{v}_i - m\mathbf{u}_i$$

where $\mathbf{v}_i$ and $\mathbf{u}_i$ are respectively the final and initial velocities for this time interval. It follows that $\mathbf{u}_{i+1} = \mathbf{v}_i$. Adding the equations for all the intervals δt_i ($i = 1, 2, ..., n$)

$$\Sigma \mathbf{F}_i(\delta t_i) = m\mathbf{v} - m\mathbf{u},$$

where $\mathbf{v}$ and $\mathbf{u}$ are the velocities when $i = n$ and 0 respectively. As n increases indefinitely the left-hand side of the equation approaches the limit $\int_0^t \mathbf{F}\,dt$. Hence

$$\int_0^t \mathbf{F}\,dt = m\mathbf{v} - m\mathbf{u}.$$

This form of the impulse–momentum equation may also be obtained as follows: In Section 1.1. Newton's Second Law was quoted in the form

$$\mathbf{F} = m\mathbf{a}.$$

Although F and a are no longer constant a may still be written in the form

$$\frac{d\mathbf{v}}{dt}, \quad \text{and so} \quad \mathbf{F} = m\frac{d\mathbf{v}}{dt}.$$

This is a linear differential equation of the first order and can be solved by direct integration with respect to time

$$\int_0^t \mathbf{F}\,dt = \int_0^t m\frac{d\mathbf{v}}{dt}\,dt.$$

Since

$$\frac{d}{dt}(m\mathbf{v}) = m\frac{d\mathbf{v}}{dt}$$

it follows that

$$\int_0^t \mathbf{F}\,dt = \Big[m\mathbf{v} \Big]_0^t,$$

i.e. the impulse–momentum equation becomes

$$\int_0^t \mathbf{F}\,dt = m\mathbf{v} - m\mathbf{u},$$

where $\int_0^t \mathbf{F}\,dt$ is called the impulse of the force F.

Note that the only restriction applied in this proof is that the mass is constant. The previous result, with F constant, is now seen as a special case of this general equation.

986

Example 6. In this example we consider the case where **F** is variable in both magnitude and direction.

A ball is acted upon by a variable force **F** for 1 second. The force-time table below gives four readings taken during this time. Find the approximate change in momentum of the ball.

t (s)	0·1	0·4	0·7	0·9
F (N)	$\begin{pmatrix} 1 \\ 0{\cdot}1 \end{pmatrix}$	$\begin{pmatrix} 4 \\ 1{\cdot}6 \end{pmatrix}$	$\begin{pmatrix} 7 \\ 4{\cdot}9 \end{pmatrix}$	$\begin{pmatrix} 9 \\ 8{\cdot}1 \end{pmatrix}$

As an approximation we take the known value of **F** when $t = 0\cdot1$ s as the constant value for the interval $0 \leqslant t \leqslant 0\cdot2$ s, and so on.

$$\Sigma \mathbf{F}_i \delta t_i = 0\cdot2 \begin{pmatrix} 1 \\ 0{\cdot}1 \end{pmatrix} + 0\cdot4 \begin{pmatrix} 4 \\ 1{\cdot}6 \end{pmatrix} + 0\cdot2 \begin{pmatrix} 7 \\ 4{\cdot}9 \end{pmatrix} + 0\cdot2 \begin{pmatrix} 9 \\ 8{\cdot}1 \end{pmatrix}$$

$$= \begin{pmatrix} 5 \\ 3{\cdot}26 \end{pmatrix}.$$

Hence an estimate of the change in momentum of the ball during this time interval is

$$\begin{pmatrix} 5 \\ 3{\cdot}26 \end{pmatrix} \text{ s N.}$$

Exercise B

1. A ball of mass 90 g strikes a wall at right-angles when moving at 8 m/s and rebounds with a speed of 6 m/s. Assuming that the thrust between the ball and the wall increases uniformly with the time up to a maximum, and then decreases at the same rate, find the maximum thrust in newtons, if the total time of contact is 0·002 s.

2. A particle of mass m moves so that its acceleration **a** at time t is given by $\mathbf{a} = -4t\mathbf{i}$. When $t = 0$ its velocity is $\mathbf{u} = 32\mathbf{i}$. Find when it first comes to rest and the impulse of the force from $t = 0$ until then.

3. A train of mass 800 tonnes commences to climb a hill at a speed of 120 km/h. The engine exerts a constant pull of 135 000 N up the gradient, and the total resistance R due to all causes, including gravity, is directed parallel to the track and increases with time according to the following table:

R (N)	180 000	195 000	220 000	260 000	315 000	380 000
t (s)	0	5	10	15	20	25

Estimate the speed of the train after 25 seconds.

4. In starting to move a horse-drawn tram of mass 4000 kg the pull exerted by a horse is initially 1050 N. This pull decreases uniformly with time until after 10 seconds the pull is 350 N. Draw the force–time graph and hence find the velocity of the tram at 2-second intervals.

5. A car started from rest and accelerated for 60 s. Measurements of the resultant propulsive force were recorded:

P (N)	1050	650	480	260	170	130	80
t (s)	0	10	20	30	40	50	60

Estimate the speed of the car in km/h at the end of the 60 s if it had mass 1 tonne. Comment on the performance.

6. A particle is acted on by a variable force

$$\mathbf{F} = \begin{pmatrix} 2t \\ \sin 2t \end{pmatrix} \text{N.}$$

Construct a table of values of $\mathbf{F}$ for $t = 0\cdot1, 0\cdot3, 0\cdot5, 0\cdot7, 0\cdot9$ s. Hence estimate the change in momentum of the particle during one second. Obtain the exact value by integration.

3. COMPONENTS

If we form the scalar product of a unit vector $\mathbf{n}$ with a force $\mathbf{F}$ then the result is $\mathbf{F}.\mathbf{n} = F\cos\theta$, where F is the magnitude of $\mathbf{F}$ and θ is the angle between the vectors. This is the *resolved part* of the force $\mathbf{F}$ in the direction of $\mathbf{n}$.

Taking the scalar product of $\mathbf{n}$ with both sides of the impulse–momentum equation we have $\qquad t(\mathbf{F}.\mathbf{n}) = m\mathbf{v}.\mathbf{n} - m\mathbf{u}.\mathbf{n}.$

This implies that the change in momentum of the particle resolved in a particular direction is equal to the resolved part of the impulse in that direction.

When $\mathbf{F}.\mathbf{n} = 0$, i.e. when $\mathbf{n}$ is perpendicular to $\mathbf{F}$,

$$m\mathbf{v}.\mathbf{n} - m\mathbf{u}.\mathbf{n} = 0,$$

or $\qquad\qquad\qquad\qquad m\mathbf{v}.\mathbf{n} = m\mathbf{u}.\mathbf{n}.$

In this case the momentum of the particle is unchanged in the direction of $\mathbf{n}$. Since m is constant it follows that the velocity of the particle is constant in a direction perpendicular to that of the impulse.

The impulse–momentum triangle for the flight of the cannon ball in Example 1 is illustrated in Figure 10. As the impulse was in the vertical direction we may choose $\mathbf{n}$ in the horizontal direction and write

$$t(m\mathbf{g}.\mathbf{n}) = 0$$

$$m\mathbf{u}.\mathbf{n} = mu\cos 30°,$$

$$m\mathbf{v}.\mathbf{n} = mv\cos\phi.$$

Using $\qquad\qquad\qquad\qquad m\mathbf{v}.\mathbf{n} = m\mathbf{u}.\mathbf{n}.$

$$mv\cos\phi = mu\cos 30°,$$

$$v\cos\phi = 50\sqrt{3} \text{ ft/s.}$$

988

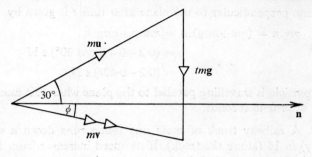

Fig. 10

Example 7. A particle of mass 50 g is projected at a speed of 8 m/s at an angle of 60° to the horizontal, from the foot of a plane inclined at 30° to the horizontal. Its trajectory is in the plane containing the line of greatest slope through the point of projection.

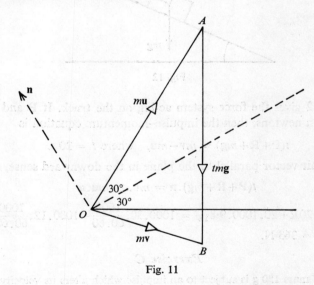

Fig. 11

What is its initial momentum perpendicular to the plane? What is its momentum perpendicular to the plane after t seconds? When is the particle travelling parallel to the plane?

The impulse–momentum triangle is shown in Figure 11.

If **n** is a unit vector in a direction perpendicular to the plane then the initial momentum perpendicular to the plane is $m\mathbf{u}.\mathbf{n}$, which is

$$0.05 \text{ kg} \times 8 \text{ m/s} \times \cos 60° = 0.2 \text{ s N}.$$

Momentum perpendicular to the plane after time t is given by

$$m\mathbf{v}.\mathbf{n} = (m\mathbf{u}+mt\mathbf{g}).\mathbf{n} = m\mathbf{u}.\mathbf{n}+mt\mathbf{g}.\mathbf{n}$$
$$= (0{\cdot}2-0{\cdot}49t \cos 30°) \text{ s N}$$
$$= (0{\cdot}2-0{\cdot}42t) \text{ s N.}$$

Hence the particle is travelling parallel to the plane when this momentum is zero, i.e. after 0·48 seconds.

Example 8. A railway truck of mass one tonne runs down a slope of 1 (vertically) in 16 (along the track). If its speed increases from 12 km/h to 30 km/h in 20 seconds, find the (constant) resistance to motion.

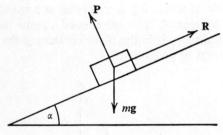

Fig. 12

Figure 12 gives the force system acting on the truck. If $\mathbf{P}$ and $\mathbf{R}$ are measured in newtons, then the impulse–momentum equation is

$$t(\mathbf{P}+\mathbf{R}+m\mathbf{g}) = m\mathbf{v}-m\mathbf{u}, \quad \text{where } t = 20 \text{ s.}$$

If $\mathbf{n}$ is a unit vector parallel to the plane in the downward sense, then

$$t(\mathbf{P}+\mathbf{R}+m\mathbf{g}).\mathbf{n} = m\mathbf{v}.\mathbf{n}-m\mathbf{u}.\mathbf{n}$$

$$\Rightarrow -20R+20.1000.9{\cdot}8\tfrac{1}{16} = 1000.30.\frac{1000}{60.60}-1000.12.\frac{1000}{60.60}$$

$$\Rightarrow R = 363 \text{ N.}$$

Exercise C

1. A ball of mass 150 g is subject to an impulse which alters its velocity from

$$\begin{pmatrix} -4 \\ 6 \end{pmatrix} \text{ m/s} \quad \text{to} \quad \begin{pmatrix} 12 \\ 2 \end{pmatrix} \text{ m/s.}$$

Write down the impulse–momentum equation and form the scalar product with each of the following vectors

$$\begin{pmatrix} 1 \\ 0 \end{pmatrix}, \quad \begin{pmatrix} 0 \\ 1 \end{pmatrix}, \quad \begin{pmatrix} 3 \\ 4 \end{pmatrix}, \quad \begin{pmatrix} 4 \\ 3 \end{pmatrix}, \quad \begin{pmatrix} 1 \\ 4 \end{pmatrix}, \quad \begin{pmatrix} -4 \\ 1 \end{pmatrix}.$$

In which direction is the momentum constant, and what is the momentum in that direction during the impulse?

2. Find the directions in which the momentum is constant during the impulse in Questions 7, 8 and 10 of Exercise A.

3. An engine exerts a constant tractive force of 9.10^4 N on a train of total mass 300 tonnes, moving against a resistance of 6.10^4 N along a horizontal track. Find the increase in velocity after 25 seconds.

4. If the power unit of the engine in Question 3 is shut off when it is travelling at 50 km/h, how long will the train take to come to rest?

5. A car starts to climb a hill of 1 in 14 at 84 km/h. The gear and throttle have been set so that on level ground the tractive force of the engine balances the resistances to motion. Assuming these forces remain constant, how soon will the car stop?

6. A particle of mass 40 g is attached to a fixed point O by a string of length 10 cm. It is dropped from a point A in such a way that the velocity of the particle as the string becomes taut is 1·4 m/s vertically downwards, and the string makes an angle of 60° with the downward vertical. Find the impulse in the string, assuming it remains taut.

7. Repeat Question 3 when the tractive force is P newtons, the total mass is M tonnes, the resistance is R newtons and the time is t s, the directions being the same as those in Question 3.

If the power unit is shut off at V km/h, how long will the train take to come to rest?

4. CONSERVATION OF MOMENTUM

4.1 Systems of particles and bodies. We have so far discussed the momentum of a single particle and it is now appropriate to investigate how the Impulse–Momentum Equation can be applied to systems of particles and solid bodies.

First, consider a mass m_1 subject to an impulse $\mathbf{I}_1$ which changes its velocity from $\mathbf{u}_1$ to $\mathbf{v}_1$. It follows that

$$\mathbf{I}_1 = m_1\mathbf{v}_1 - m_1\mathbf{u}_1.$$

Similar equations may be written for the action of impulses $\mathbf{I}_2$, $\mathbf{I}_3$, ..., etc., on other particles of masses m_2, m_3, ..., etc. If we have n particles we may summarize the effects of these impulses by the equations:

$$\mathbf{I}_i = m_i\mathbf{v}_i - m_i\mathbf{u}_i \quad (i = 1 \ldots n).$$

and we may think it worth while to add these equations together giving

$$\Sigma\mathbf{I}_i = \Sigma m_i\mathbf{v}_i - \Sigma m_i\mathbf{u}_i. \tag{1}$$

If the particles are independent of each other then there is little more to be said, but if they interact with one another then the terms in the above equation need closer examination.

At this stage it is relevant to recall the interaction principle which postulates that if the total force exerted by a particle A on a particle B is

991

P and if the total force exerted by the particle B on the particle A is **Q** then $\mathbf{P}+\mathbf{Q} = 0$ and **P** and **Q** are collinear.

Consider the left-hand side of equation (1) as applied to the following situation: A particle of mass m_1 moving with velocity $\mathbf{u}_1$ hits a particle of mass m_2 which is initially at rest. After impact the particles move with velocities $\mathbf{v}_1$ and (see Figure 13) $\mathbf{v}_2$ respectively. As the duration of impact must be the same for both particles it follows from the interaction principle that the impulses $\mathbf{I}_1$ and $\mathbf{I}_2$ acting on m_1 and m_2 respectively must satisfy the equation $\mathbf{I}_1+\mathbf{I}_2 = 0$. Applying equation (1) to these two particles we get

$$\mathbf{I}_1+\mathbf{I}_2 = m_1\mathbf{v}_1+m_2\mathbf{v}_2-m_1\mathbf{u}_1,$$

or

$$0 = m_1\mathbf{v}_1+m_2\mathbf{v}_2-m_1\mathbf{u}_1,$$

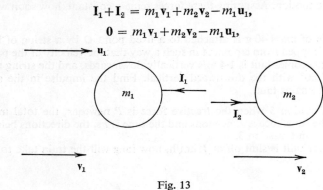

Fig. 13

In general collinear forces **P, Q** for which the equation $\mathbf{P}+\mathbf{Q} = 0$ is true may be regarded as internal forces acting on the system of particles under discussion (the remaining forces being regarded as external forces.) As $\mathbf{P}+\mathbf{Q} = 0$ is true for all internal forces under these circumstances it follows that for any time interval the impulses of **P** and **Q** must sum to zero.

Thus where many interactions occur the resulting impulses on the left-hand side of equation (1) sum to zero. In particular, if the system of particles is a body (a ball, rod, ship, etc.), then each $\mathbf{I}_i$ will, after simplification, contain the impulses of external forces only. In turn these will sum together to give the resultant impulse acting on the body. This accounts for the left-hand side of equation (1) for a system of particles.

In order to simplify the right-hand side of equation (1) we consider a general system of particles. Let the position vector of the point where the ith particle is situated be $\mathbf{r}_i$. Then at time t

$$\mathbf{v}_i = \frac{d}{dt}(\mathbf{r}_i).$$

As the mass of the particle, m_i, is supposed constant, we have

$$m_i\mathbf{v}_i = m_i\frac{d}{dt}(\mathbf{r}_i) = \frac{d}{dt}(m_i\mathbf{r}_i).$$

Finally
$$\frac{d}{dt}(\Sigma m_i \mathbf{r}_i) = \Sigma \frac{d}{dt}(m_i \mathbf{r}_i) = \Sigma m_i \mathbf{v}_i.$$

From an earlier theorem on centroids (Chapter 9, Section 5.2) we can define a position vector $\bar{\mathbf{r}}$ such that
$$\Sigma m_i \mathbf{r}_i = (\Sigma m_i)\bar{\mathbf{r}}$$
$$= M\bar{\mathbf{r}};$$

where $M = \Sigma m_i$ is the total mass of the system. The position vector $\bar{\mathbf{r}}$ defines a point, called the centre of mass of the system, which is independent of the origin of coordinates.

Consequently
$$\frac{d}{dt}(\Sigma m_i \mathbf{r}_i) = \frac{d}{dt}(M\bar{\mathbf{r}})$$
$$= M\bar{\mathbf{v}},$$

where $\bar{\mathbf{v}}$ is the velocity of the centre of mass of the system. A similar argument leads to the definition of $M\bar{\mathbf{u}}$.

Hence, for a system of particles of total mass M, equation (1) simplifies to
$$\mathbf{I} = M\bar{\mathbf{v}} - M\bar{\mathbf{u}}, \tag{2}$$

where $\mathbf{I}$ is the resultant external impulse and $\bar{\mathbf{u}}$ and $\bar{\mathbf{v}}$ are the initial and final velocities of the centre of mass of the system.

If now the system forms a *rigid body*—that is, if the distances between pairs of particles are always the same—its motion from one position to another could be effected by an isometric transformation. Since it can be shown that the centre of mass of the system occupies a fixed position relative to the system, the motion of the centre of mass is effected by the same isometric transformation. If we confine our attention to translations—that is, if we ignore the possibility of rotation, (reflection being of course physically impossible)—then the position of the centre of mass fixes the body completely, and we can regard the body simply as a particle of mass M located at the centre of mass and moving with it. There is in fact an obvious similarity between equation (2) which refers to bodies, and the impulse–momentum equation for a particle.

In the same way we can now extend equation (2) to deal with a number of bodies. By summation this leads to the impulse–momentum equation:
$$\Sigma \mathbf{I}_i = \Sigma M_i \mathbf{v}_i - \Sigma M_i \mathbf{u}_i, \tag{3}$$

where $\Sigma \mathbf{I}_i$ may be written as $t\Sigma \mathbf{F}_i$ if appropriate, and M_i is the mass of the body whose centre of mass has initial and final velocities $\mathbf{u}_i$, $\mathbf{v}_i$, etc.

In solving problems we may take as our 'system' *all* the bodies involved, or alternatively *some* of them considered in isolation from the rest, as in the following example.

Example 9. A bullet of mass 25 g which is given an impulse of 15 N s by a rifle, comes to relative rest in a block of wood of mass 700 g. What is then the velocity of the wood and bullet?

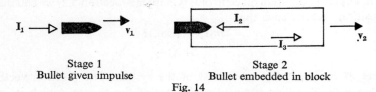

Stage 1
Bullet given impulse

Stage 2
Bullet embedded in block

Fig. 14

The left-hand side of equation (3) is $\Sigma \mathbf{I}_i = \mathbf{I}_1 + \mathbf{I}_2 + \mathbf{I}_3$. The interaction principle gives $\mathbf{I}_2 + \mathbf{I}_3 = \mathbf{0}$, implying $\mathbf{I} = \mathbf{I}_1$.

The right-hand side of equation (3) contains the terms

$$\Sigma M\mathbf{v} = 0\cdot025\mathbf{v}_2 + 0\cdot7\mathbf{v}_2$$

$$\Sigma M\mathbf{u} = \mathbf{0}$$

(both bullet and block initially at rest). Hence equation (3) gives

$$15 = 0\cdot725\mathbf{v}_2$$

$$\Rightarrow 20\cdot7 = \mathbf{v}_2;$$

i.e. the block moves with a velocity of 20·7 m/s along the line of impulse.

Note that the final combined velocity is obtained without finding the intermediate velocity of the bullet. We can also solve this problem by considering two systems: that of the bullet and that of the block.

For the first part of the bullet's motion (stage 1 above) equation (3) gives

$$15 = 0\cdot025v_1$$

or $$v_1 = 600 \text{ m/s}$$

along the line of impulse.

For the second part of the bullet's motion (stage 2 above) equation (3) gives

$$I_2 = 0\cdot025v_2 - 0\cdot025 . 600.$$

As this equation contains two unknowns more information is required. For the system consisting of the block only, equation (3) gives

$$\mathbf{I}_3 = 0\cdot7\mathbf{v}_2.$$

This also contains two unknowns, but we know that $\mathbf{I}_2 + \mathbf{I}_3 = \mathbf{0}$. Hence

$$v_2 = 20\cdot7 \text{ m/s}$$

as before and $$I_3 = -I_2 = 14\cdot5 \text{ N s.}$$

4.2 Conservation of linear momentum. Now let us return to equation (1) and form the scalar product of both sides with a unit vector **n**.

$$\mathbf{n}.(\Sigma\mathbf{I}) = \mathbf{n}.(\Sigma m\mathbf{v}) - \mathbf{n}.(\Sigma m\mathbf{u}).$$

Therefore the change in momentum of the system of bodies resolved in a particular direction is equal to the sum of the resolved parts of the system of impulses in that direction.

This equality is useful in its own right, but there are two important special cases when $\mathbf{n}.\Sigma\mathbf{I} = 0$. This will occur when either

(i) $\Sigma\mathbf{I} = 0$,

or   (ii) $\Sigma\mathbf{I} \neq 0$, and

$\mathbf{n}$ is in a direction perpendicular to the quantity $\Sigma\mathbf{I}$. In both cases equation (4) can be rewritten in the form

$$\mathbf{n}.(\Sigma m\mathbf{v}) = \mathbf{n}.(\Sigma m\mathbf{u})$$

which indicates that during the application of the impulses the total momentum of the system is unchanged in the direction of $\mathbf{n}$. In case (i) this may be in any direction; in case (ii) it must be in the direction at right-angles to that of $\Sigma\mathbf{I}$. This information is summarized in *The Principle of Conservation of Linear Momentum*:

> **For a system of bodies moving with prescribed velocities, the Linear Momentum of the system is conserved in the direction perpendicular to the total impulse, or in any direction if the total impulse is zero.**

It must be realized that the 'system' of this statement need not necessarily imply the whole system of bodies that could be considered.

4.3 Two body systems. Two bodies of masses m_1 and m_2 collide. Just before impact their velocities are $\mathbf{u}_1$ and $\mathbf{u}_2$ and immediately after impact their velocities are $\mathbf{v}_1$ and $\mathbf{v}_2$ respectively.

Taking our system to be the two bodies, we neglect external effects. (In many cases there will be no effective external forces, but even if there are, we shall usually assume that the time of impact is sufficiently short for their impulses to be negligible compared with those of the very large forces called into play by the impact itself.) The interaction principle then implies that there is no resultant impulse, hence momentum is conserved in every direction, i.e.

$$m_1\mathbf{u}_1 + m_2\mathbf{u}_2 = m_1\mathbf{v}_1 + m_2\mathbf{v}_2.$$

Figure 15(b) represents this diagrammatically. The dotted diagonal can be seen to represent the total momentum of the system. Taking our system to be m_1 alone, the impulse-momentum equation gives

$$\mathbf{I}_1 = m_1\mathbf{v}_1 - m_1\mathbf{u}_1.$$

If a unit vector $\mathbf{n}$ is chosen perpendicular to the line of impact then

$$\mathbf{n}.\mathbf{I} = 0 \Rightarrow (m_1\mathbf{v}_1).\mathbf{n} = (m_1\mathbf{u}_1).\mathbf{n}.$$

Taking m_2 alone as our system, similar deductions can be made and the impulse–momentum equation is represented by Figure 16(b). The interaction principle implies that $I_1 = -I_2$ so that Figure 16(b) and 16(a) can be combined to give Figure 16(c) where the diagonal with an appropriate direction gives either I_1 or I_2. The polygons of Figures 15(b) and 16(c) must be congruent, hence superimposing them we get Figure 17, where **BD** = total momentum, **AC** = I_1, and **CA** = I_2.

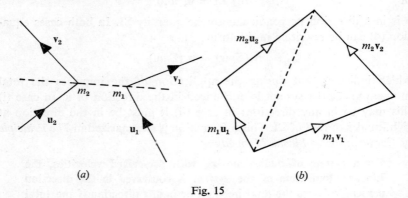

Fig. 15

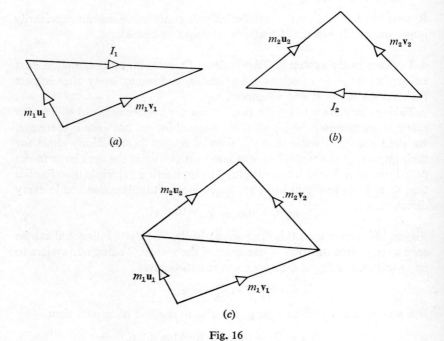

Fig. 16

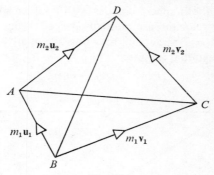

Fig. 17

4.4 Coefficient of restitution. If we examine this situation further we note that the quadrilateral $ABCD$ is defined by the values of the masses and the velocities, in all six quantities m_1, m_2, $\mathbf{u}_1$, $\mathbf{u}_2$, $\mathbf{v}_1$, $\mathbf{v}_2$. Hence in order to be able to draw it, or make the appropriate calculations, five of these values must be known. In general, both $\mathbf{v}_1$ and $\mathbf{v}_2$ cannot be found from the initial conditions. For instance if, from a fixed height, one drops a golf ball, cricket ball, lump of putty, Supaball, etc., onto a fixed surface the initial conditions in each case are the same. The velocities with which they rebound, however, are different and obviously depend on the material concerned. Experiments show that for a particular body striking a fixed surface normally, the speed at which it rebounds is a definite fraction of its speed just before impact. This fraction (called the *coefficient of restitution*, *e*) is a constant for particular surfaces in collision. It is clear on physical grounds that $0 \leqslant e \leqslant 1$ in all cases; for example, putty dropping on glass has a zero coefficient of restitution, while a Supaball bouncing on steel has a coefficient of about 0·95.

For a general impact the same law holds if we replace the word 'speed' by 'component of relative velocity along the line of impact'. In symbols, if $\mathbf{n}$ is a unit vector parallel to the line of impact, then

$$e(\mathbf{u}_1 - \mathbf{u}_2) \cdot \mathbf{n} = (\mathbf{v}_2 - \mathbf{v}_1) \cdot \mathbf{n}. \tag{5}$$

This can be interpreted as: (coefficient of restitution) × (speed of approach) = (speed of separation) *along* the line of impact. This is often called 'Newton's Experimental Law', since it was first formulated by Sir Isaac Newton in the seventeenth century.

Example 10. It is now possible to find the value for *e* between the cushion and the billiard ball in Example 2. The line of impact is perpendicular to the cushion through the point of contact, and u_2 and v_2 are both zero. Substituting in equation (5)

$$e \cdot \cos 30° = 0·58 \cos 59$$

giving $e = 0·3$ to one sig. fig.

Example 11. A smooth sphere collides with another sphere at rest. After the collision their velocities are mutually perpendicular. If the spheres are perfectly elastic ($e = 1$) show that they must be of equal mass.

As there is no external impulse

$$m_1\mathbf{v}_1 + m_2\mathbf{v}_2 = m_1\mathbf{u}_1. \tag{i}$$

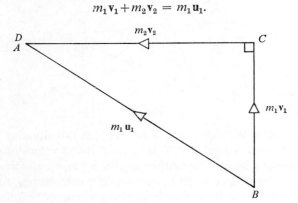

Fig. 18

If $\mathbf{n}$ is a unit vector along the line of impact then equation (5) can be written

$$e\,\mathbf{u}_1.\mathbf{n} = \mathbf{v}_2.\mathbf{n} - \mathbf{v}_1.\mathbf{n}.$$

Now
$$\mathbf{v}_1.\mathbf{n} = 0 \quad\text{and}\quad e = 1$$

so
$$\mathbf{u}_1.\mathbf{n} = \mathbf{v}_2.\mathbf{n} \tag{ii}$$

but from (i) above we have

$$m_1(\mathbf{u}_1.\mathbf{n}) = m_2(\mathbf{v}_2.\mathbf{n}). \tag{iii}$$

Thus from (ii) and (iii)
$$m_1 = m_2.$$

Example 12. Railway trucks of masses 10, 12, 7, 2, and 9 tonnes are travelling with velocities of 7, 5, 5, 4, and 3 km/h respectively along a straight siding. When they hit one another they couple together without rebounding ($e = 0$) and ultimately they are all joined together. Find their final velocity.

Take as our system all the trucks. Since the non-zero impulses all derive from interactions, momentum is conserved in any direction, and in particular in the direction of the track. Therefore

$$10.7 + 12.5 + 7.5 + 2.4 + 9.3 = (10 + 12 + 7 + 2 + 9)v$$

giving
$$v = 5 \text{ km/h}$$

Example 13. A gun of mass M has a fixed elevation θ and recoils horizontally without resistance until a shell of mass m has left the barrel. What is the angle of elevation of the shell when it leaves the barrel?

The full impulse system is given in Figure 19(*a*). For the shell,

$$\mathbf{J} = m(\mathbf{v} - \mathbf{V}),$$

998

where V is the velocity of the gun. This is represented in the triangle ABC in Figure 19(b). The external impulse I is given by

$$I = MV + mv$$

(represented by the triangle ABD in Figure 19(b)).

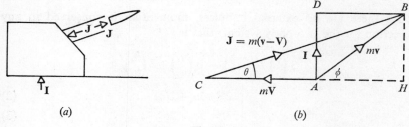

$$\mathbf{J} = m(\mathbf{v} - \mathbf{V})$$

(a)   (b)

Fig. 19

In triangle CHB

$$\mathbf{HA} = MV,$$
$$\mathbf{HC} = (m+M)V,$$
$$BH = (m+M)V \tan \theta,$$

where V is the magnitude of the vector $\mathbf{V}$. Therefore, ϕ, the angle of elevation of the shell, is given by

$$\tan \phi = \frac{BH}{AH} = \frac{M+m}{M} \tan \theta.$$

Example 14. Two small smooth spheres A and B of mass 3 kg and 2 kg collide when their velocities are respectively 5 m/s at $\tan^{-1} \frac{3}{4}$ to $\mathbf{AB}$, and 13 m/s at $\tan^{-1}(-12/5)$ to $\mathbf{AB}$ from the same side of AB. If $e = \frac{2}{3}$ for these spheres, calculate their subsequent velocities.

Figure 20(b) is equivalent to Figure 17. II' is the impulse diagonal and $\mathbf{u}$ and $\mathbf{v}$ are the final velocities of A and B. Take $\mathbf{i}$ and $\mathbf{j}$ as unit vectors parallel and perpendicular to AB (or II') and let

$$\mathbf{u} = \begin{pmatrix} a_1 \\ a_2 \end{pmatrix} \quad \text{and} \quad \mathbf{v} = \begin{pmatrix} b_1 \\ b_2 \end{pmatrix}.$$

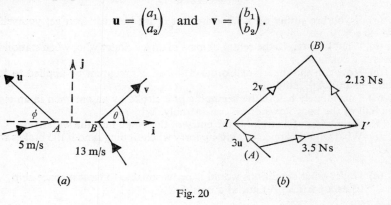

(a)   (b)

Fig. 20

Newton's Experimental Law, equation (5), gives

$$\frac{2}{3}\left[\begin{pmatrix} -5 \\ 12 \end{pmatrix} - \begin{pmatrix} 4 \\ 3 \end{pmatrix}\right]\cdot\begin{pmatrix} 1 \\ 0 \end{pmatrix} = \left[\begin{pmatrix} a_1 \\ a_2 \end{pmatrix} - \begin{pmatrix} b_1 \\ b_2 \end{pmatrix}\right]\cdot\begin{pmatrix} 1 \\ 0 \end{pmatrix},$$

giving
$$6 = b_1 - a_1. \tag{1}$$

As there are no external impulses, momentum is conserved in any direction for the two-body system: that is

$$3\begin{pmatrix} 4 \\ 3 \end{pmatrix} + \begin{pmatrix} -5 \\ 12 \end{pmatrix} = 3\begin{pmatrix} a_1 \\ a_2 \end{pmatrix} + 2\begin{pmatrix} b_1 \\ b_2 \end{pmatrix}$$

$$\Rightarrow \begin{cases} 2 = 3a_1 + 2b_1, & \tag{2} \\ 33 = 3a_2 + 2b_2. & \tag{3} \end{cases}$$

Considering each body in turn, the impulse is along II'. Hence the scalar product of the impulse–momentum equation for each body with $\mathbf{j}$ will give:

For A
$$\begin{pmatrix} 4 \\ 3 \end{pmatrix}\cdot\begin{pmatrix} 0 \\ 1 \end{pmatrix} = \begin{pmatrix} a_1 \\ a_2 \end{pmatrix}\cdot\begin{pmatrix} 0 \\ 1 \end{pmatrix} \Rightarrow a_2 = 3. \tag{4}$$

For B
$$\begin{pmatrix} -5 \\ 12 \end{pmatrix}\cdot\begin{pmatrix} 0 \\ 1 \end{pmatrix} = \begin{pmatrix} b_1 \\ b_2 \end{pmatrix}\cdot\begin{pmatrix} 0 \\ 1 \end{pmatrix} \Rightarrow b_2 = 12. \tag{5}$$

N.B. Equations (3), (4) and (5) are linearly dependent.

From (1) and (2) $a_1 = -2$ and $a_2 = 4$. Hence the final velocities of A and B are

$$\begin{pmatrix} -2 \\ 3 \end{pmatrix} \text{ m/s} \quad \text{and} \quad \begin{pmatrix} 4 \\ 12 \end{pmatrix} \text{ m/s},$$

respectively. In Figure 20(a), $u = 3\cdot6$ m/s and $\phi = 56\cdot3°$; $v = 12\cdot6$ m/s and $\theta = 71\cdot5°$.

Exercise D

1. (a) If you are sitting on a smooth sheet of ice how can you get yourself to the edge?

(b) What happens to the centre of mass of an ice skater who, when stationary, loses her balance?

(c) How can the theory of Conservation of Momentum be applied to long jumping and high jumping?

(d) Immediately before the beginning of a stroke by an oarsman in an eight, the hull of the boat slows down considerably. Why?

(The beginning of a stroke is the entry of the blade into the water.)

(e) What would happen to a tip-up lorry when tipping sand if the brakes were off?

2. (a) Under what conditions would it be reasonable to treat a space-ship
(i) as a particle, (ii) not as a particle?

1000

(b) State the general principle of Conservation of Momentum and say, with explanation, if it can be applied to
      (i) a rocket which explodes when travelling horizontally,
      (ii) a battery-driven car starting from rest on a table, when one considers the system of particles belonging to the car and to the table.
(c) Analyse the situation when a tablecloth is whipped off a table while leaving the crockery behind.

3. An advancing tiger weighing 180 kg and travelling at 2 m/s is hit head on by a bullet weighing 50 g and travelling at 600 m/s. The bullet embeds in the tiger. What is the subsequent speed of the tiger? How many bullets of the same type from an automatic weapon would be needed to halt the tiger if it were springing through the air with a horizontal velocity component of 5 m/s?

4. A pile driver employs a block of mass 800 kg which strikes a pile of mass 100 kg. The velocity of the block immediately before impact is 8 m/s and it does not rebound.
    Find how long the pile and block are moving before they come to rest if the resistance to penetration averages 8×10^4 N.

5. A hammer of mass 6 kg is moving vertically downwards with a speed of 15 m/s and strikes the top of a vertical post of mass 4 kg without rebounding. If the two move for a further 0·3 s before they come to rest, what is the average resistance to motion?

6. Two lumps of putty are travelling at right-angles to each other when they collide and stick together. Their masses are 0·25 kg and 0·35 kg and their speeds are 3 m/s and 4 m/s respectively.
    Draw vector diagrams to illustrate the collision and find the momentum of the combined lump.
    Through what angle is each lump deflected by the impact?
    What is the impulse which each lump of putty experiences?

7. A satellite of mass 200 kg is attached to a nose-cone of mass 12·5 kg. When travelling at a velocity of 9 600 m/s the two are separated by an internal impulse of $1·6 \times 10^5$ s N in a direction at right-angles to the line of flight.
    Find the subsequent speeds of the satellites and nose-cone and the deflection of each from the original line of flight.

8. A bullet of mass 25 g is fired into a fixed block of wood with a velocity of impact of 1000 m/s. If the velocity of departure from the block is 600 m/s in a direction making an angle of 30° with the direction of entry, find the impulse on the block.

9. A ball A of mass 40 g and velocity $\begin{pmatrix} 2 \\ 1 \end{pmatrix}$ m/s collides with a ball B of mass 30 g and velocity $\begin{pmatrix} 1 \\ -2 \end{pmatrix}$ m/s. $\begin{pmatrix} 1 \\ 0 \end{pmatrix}$ is the unit vector along the line of centres.

If the subsequent velocity of B is $\begin{pmatrix} 2 \\ -2 \end{pmatrix}$ m/s, find the subsequent velocity of A.
    Find also the value of 'e' for the two balls.
    (The question should be answered by drawing *and* by calculation.)

10. Two billiard balls A and B, both of mass 120 g, collide: A is moving at 1 m/s and B at 1·5 m/s at 120° to the direction of A's velocity. A is deflected through 90° by the collision and B is then moving perpendicular to it.

Draw vector diagrams and find the speeds of the billiard balls.

What is the impulse between the balls and what is their total momentum?

In which direction is the momentum of either ball unchanged? How is this direction related to the line of centres of A and B at impact?

11. Two spherical satellites A and B, of mass 100 kg and 200 kg respectively, collide in space. A is originally travelling at 9000 m/s in a direction making an angle of $\tan^{-1}\left(\frac{4}{3}\right)$ with the line of centres and B at 8500 m/s at an angle of $\tan^{-1}\left(\frac{15}{8}\right)$. Take $\mathbf{i}$ and $\mathbf{j}$ as unit vectors as shown in Figure 21, and find the final velocities of A and B if A is deflected through an angle of $\tan^{-1}\left(\frac{24}{7}\right)$.

(The question should be answered by drawing and by calculation.)

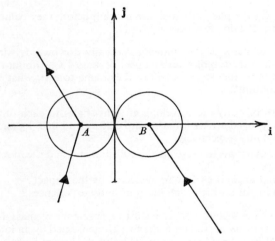

Fig. 21

12. Bullets of mass 45 g are fired from a machine gun of mass 25 kg. The muzzle velocity of each bullet is 600 m/s and the gun fires them at the steady rate of 300 per minute. What is the average force necessary to keep the gun at rest?

13. From a train travelling at 120 km/h a mail bag of mass 40 kg is released into a stationary truck of mass 90 kg.

Find the average horizontal force required to bring the truck to rest in $\frac{1}{2}$ minute.

14. A particle of mass m is enclosed in a straight tube of length a and mass $2m$. The tube has enclosed ends and lies on a smooth table. The coefficient of restitution between the particle and the ends of the tube is $\frac{2}{3}$.

The particle is projected along the tube with velocity v.

Find the distance moved by the tube between the first and second impacts and the time interval between the second and third.

15. Two spheres of masses 30 and 70 g collide when their velocities are $\begin{pmatrix} 8 \\ 4 \end{pmatrix}$ cm/s and $\begin{pmatrix} 5 \\ -15 \end{pmatrix}$ cm/s. $\begin{pmatrix} 1 \\ 0 \end{pmatrix}$ is a unit vector along their line of centres at impact and the coefficient of restitution is $\frac{4}{9}$.

Find the subsequent velocities of the two spheres.

16. A bullet of mass m is fired into a block of wood of mass M, resting on a smooth horizontal table, with a velocity of v. If the opposition to the motion of the bullet through the block is constant and equal to P, find the velocity of the block and the bullet when the latter has come to relative rest in the block. Find the time taken to do so.

17. An aeroplane of mass 2400 kg is towing a glider of mass 600 kg when the tow line inadvertently becomes slack. On becoming taut again the velocities of the aeroplane and glider are $9 \begin{pmatrix} 4 \\ 3 \end{pmatrix}$ m/s and $3 \begin{pmatrix} 5 \\ 12 \end{pmatrix}$ m/s

respectively, where $\begin{pmatrix} 1 \\ 0 \end{pmatrix}$ and $\begin{pmatrix} 0 \\ 1 \end{pmatrix}$

are unit vectors parallel and perpendicular to the tow line. Express the fact that eventually the tow line is unstretched in terms of the subsequent velocities of the aeroplane and glider and hence evaluate the impulse on the glider.

18. A satellite of mass 40 kg has a velocity of

$$\begin{pmatrix} 5 \\ 3 \end{pmatrix} \text{ km/s}$$

when it collides with a second satellite of 30 kg having a velocity at impact of

$$\begin{pmatrix} -2 \\ -4 \end{pmatrix} \text{ km/s.}$$

Referred to the same axes as the velocities, the line of centres of the satellites is in the direction

$$\begin{pmatrix} -2 \\ 1 \end{pmatrix}.$$

If $e = \frac{1}{2}$, calculate the subsequent velocities of the two satellites.

19. Two bodies A and B of equal mass m lie at a distance a apart on a smooth horizontal table. They are connected by a string of length $a\sqrt{3}$. A is given an impulse I in the plane of the table making an angle of $60°$ with **BA**.

Find the velocities of the bodies:

(a) while the string is slack;

(b) after the string becomes taut, assuming that it remains so.

*20. Two equal marbles A and B lie on the diameter AB of a smooth circular groove on a horizontal plane and A is projected round the groove. After time t, A impinges on B. If e is the coefficient of restitution show that a second impact will occur after a further time of $2t/e$. In what way must the impulse–momentum equation be interpreted in these circumstances?

1003

21. A billiard ball hits two adjacent edges of a billiard table in succession. Show that if the coefficient of restitution is e in each case, then the final direction of travel of the billiard ball is parallel to its initial direction.

5. VARIABLE MASS

As we are working within the framework of Newtonian Mechanics, mass is constant, so that this heading is a misnomer. It is, however, a convenient way to describe the motion of a variable subset of the set of mass elements under consideration.

For example, if a raindrop passes through a cloud (compare Exercise E, Question 4), droplets of water condense on the raindrop; if therefore we wish to discuss the motion of the raindrop alone we are essentially considering the motion of a system of particles in which the mass is changing.

Similar circumstances also arise, for instance, in rocket problems; in view of the importance of these, no account would be complete without some consideration of this type of motion. The examples and problems will be restricted to one dimension only, although the theory, in its vector form, does have more general validity.

5.1   Equation of motion. Suppose that at time t a mass m is moving with velocity $\mathbf{v}$ and a mass δm is moving with velocity $\mathbf{u}$. δm coalesces with mass m and at time $(t + \delta t)$ the combined mass is moving with velocity $(\mathbf{v} + \delta \mathbf{v})$. If the resultant external force acting on the system is $\mathbf{F}$ then the impulse–momentum equation gives

$$\delta t . \mathbf{F} \simeq (m + \delta m) . (\mathbf{v} + \delta \mathbf{v}) - m \mathbf{v} - \delta m \mathbf{u};$$

i.e.

$$\delta t . \mathbf{F} \simeq m \delta \mathbf{v} + \delta m \mathbf{v} + \delta m \delta \mathbf{v} - \delta m \mathbf{u};$$

where the approximation is only necessary when $\mathbf{F}$ is variable. Dividing through by δt and proceeding to the limit we get

$$\mathbf{F} = m \frac{d\mathbf{v}}{dt} + \mathbf{v} \frac{dm}{dt} - \mathbf{u} \frac{dm}{dt}. \tag{6}$$

From this we notice that two simplifications are possible. First, if $\mathbf{u} = 0$ (as in the case of a steam locomotive picking up water) the equation (6) reduces to

$$\mathbf{F} = m \frac{d\mathbf{v}}{dt} + \mathbf{v} \frac{dm}{dt},$$

i.e.

$$\mathbf{F} = \frac{d}{dt} (m\mathbf{v}),$$

which is a form in which Newton's Second Law is sometimes couched. Secondly, if $\mathbf{v} = \mathbf{u}$ then equation (6) reduces to

$$\mathbf{F} = m\frac{d\mathbf{v}}{dt}.$$

From these remarks it will be realized that the impulse–momentum equation is used to deduce the Equation of Motion of the system. The result appears as a first-order differential equation.

Example 15. 5 seconds after blast-off the first stage of a two-stage rocket drops away. The second stage is travelling with a vertical velocity of V when the fuel ignites. Matter is ejected from the rocket at a uniform rate with a constant relative velocity of $\mathbf{u}$ in a direction opposite to the direction of travel until the rocket has halved its mass, when the fuel is completely exhausted.

If M is the mass of the rocket just before the second stage ignites and the fuel takes T seconds to burn, show that the velocity at time $(t+5)$ seconds is given by

$$v = V - gt + u.\log (M/m),$$

where

$$m = M\left(1 - \frac{t}{2T}\right).$$

Hence find the velocity of the rocket at burn-out.

Although we could quote equation (6) to establish the equation of motion it is instructive to deduce this from first principles.

If m is the mass of the rocket at time $(t+5)$ s then Figures 22(a) and 22(b) show the system at time $(t+5)$ and $(t+\delta t+5)$ respectively.

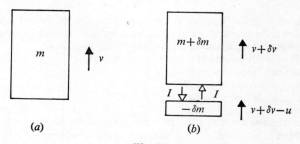

(a)   (b)

Fig. 22

Notice that the ejected matter is given the mass $(-\delta m)$. This can be deduced in the following way. Since $dm/dt = -k$ (say), implying that the mass of the rocket is decreasing, it follows that

$$\delta m \simeq -k\,\delta t \quad \text{and since} \quad \delta t > 0, \quad \delta m < 0.$$

The only external force acting is mg (variable) downwards, and the impulse–momentum equation can be written

$$-mg\,\delta t \simeq (m+\delta m).(\mathbf{v}+\delta\mathbf{v})+(-\delta m).(\mathbf{v}+\delta\mathbf{v}-\mathbf{u})-m\mathbf{v}.$$

This equation reduces to
$$-mg\,\delta t = m\delta\mathbf{v}+\delta m\mathbf{u}.$$

Dividing each side by δt and taking the limit as $\delta t \to 0$, we obtain

$$-mg = m\frac{d\mathbf{v}}{dt}+\frac{dm}{dt}\mathbf{u}. \qquad (1)$$

This could also have been obtained from equation (6) above by putting $\mathbf{F} = -mg$ and replacing $\mathbf{u}$ by $\mathbf{v}-\mathbf{u}$, as indicated by the question.
Now
$$\frac{dm}{dt} = -k \;\Rightarrow\; m = M-kt,$$

since $m = M$ when $t = 0$. Since also $m = \frac{1}{2}M$ when $t = T$, we have $\frac{1}{2}M = kT$, and
$$m = M(1-t/2T).$$

Dividing equation (1) by m and integrating with respect to time from 0 to t, we obtain
$$-gt = v-V+(\log m-\log M)u;$$

since $v = V$ and $m = M$ at $t = 0$; that is,
$$v = V-gt+u\log(M/m).$$

At burn-out, when $t = T$, $M/m = 2$, and we have for the final velocity
$$v = V-gT+u\log 2.$$

Exercise E

1. The case of a rocket is of mass 1·4 kg and the fuel of mass 3·6 kg. The fuel burns out at a constant rate and is completely exhausted after 2 seconds. During this time the rocket experiences a constant thrust of 200 N.

If the rocket is fired vertically what is the velocity:
(a) one second from blast-off;
(b) two seconds from blast-off;
(c) three seconds from blast-off?

2. A rocket of mass km is moving in outer space with velocity u when its motor is started. Matter is ejected with a constant relative velocity of v in a direction opposite to that of the initial motion of the rocket until the mass of the rocket is m. Find the velocity of the rocket when its mass is lm, where $k > l > 1$, if there is no external force acting on the system.

3. A rocket is fixed to a sledge which runs on a smooth horizontal track. The combined mass is M kg and the propellant is ejected at a constant rate of m kg/s, with velocity u m/s relative to the rocket in a direction parallel to the track.

Find the velocity of the rocket and sledge after time t seconds.

4. A raindrop of mass m enters a stationary cloud with velocity u vertically downwards. Water condenses on the raindrop so that its mass increases at a constant rate km. Find the mass M and the velocity v of the raindrop t seconds after entering the cloud.

If the raindrop takes time T to pass through the cloud, find its velocity when (a) $t = T$, (b) $t = 2T$, assuming that the mass remains constant once the cloud has been left.

5. A rocket case of mass M_0, initially containing a mass m_0 of fuel, is mounted on a light frictionless sled and has its jet directed horizontally. It converts fuel into gas at a constant mass-rate, k, and expels it backwards at a constant horizontal velocity u_0 relative to itself. Air resistance is negligible. If the velocities of the rocket are v_1 and v_2 (where $v_2 > v_1$) at the beginning and end respectively of a time interval of length T, find inequalities

    (a) for the final backward momentum of the gas expelled during the interval;

    (b) for the change of backward momentum of the material; and hence

    (c) for the change of forward momentum of the rocket case and remaining fuel.

If the interval begins at a time t after the rocket starts to burn fuel show that

$$(u_0 - (v_2 - v_1))k < (M_0 + m_0 - kt)\frac{v_2 - v_1}{T} < u_0 k.$$

What can be deduced by letting T tend to zero? What are the accelerations of the rocket (i) initially, (ii) at 'burn-out' (i.e. when all the fuel is burnt out)?

6. Graphically or otherwise determine the velocity at burn-out of the rocket in Question 5 if $M_0 = m_0 = 1$ kg, $k = 0.5$ kg/s, $u_0 = 25$ m/s.

Modify your graph to find the velocity at burn-out if the rocket is fired vertically.

34

COMPLEX NUMBERS

1. THE COMPLEX NUMBER FIELD

1.1 You will remember that the concluding section of the chapter on the quadratic function introduced some new numbers called complex numbers. We shall look again at the reasons for inventing complex numbers and then examine our invention.

Consider the quadratic equation

$$x^2 - 2x + 5 = 0.$$

Completing the square we have

$$(x-1)^2 = {}^-4.$$

If we restrict ourselves to the field of real numbers, represented by the set of ordered points on a line, then there is no solution to this equation. That is to say, there is no real number whose square is a negative real number. How do we deal with this limitation? Clearly there is nothing to be gained by looking at the real number field, but we have, on previous occasions, invented new number systems to overcome similar difficulties. For example, negative numbers were invented to solve equations such as $x+5 = 3$; indeed, any equation of the form $x+a = b$, where $a > b > 0$. Let us see how this might work out in our case.

Since

$$^-4 = 4 \times ({}^-1)$$

it would seem reasonable that

$$\sqrt{{}^-4} = \sqrt{(4 \times {}^-1)}$$
$$= \sqrt{4} \times \sqrt{{}^-1}$$
$$= 2\sqrt{{}^-1}.$$

Every negative real number can be treated in a comparable way, so it would appear sufficient to invent a number for $\sqrt{{}^-1}$. This is what we do, and we write

$$j = \sqrt{{}^-1},$$

where j has the property that $j^2 = {}^-1$.

The quadratic equation could now be solved intuitively as follows:

$$x-1 = \pm\sqrt{{}^-4}$$
$$\Rightarrow x-1 = \pm 2j$$
$$\Rightarrow \quad x = 1+2j \quad \text{or} \quad 1-2j,$$

and the solution set could be written as

$$\{1+2j, \ 1-2j\}.$$

This suggests how we should proceed. We must invent a set of numbers, called the *complex number field*, as follows:

$$C = \{z: z = a+bj; \quad a, b \in R\},$$

and call the elements of C *complex numbers*.

Notice that we have used the single letter z to denote the complex number $a+bj$. This is not merely a convenient abbreviation, but emphasizes the need to regard the expression $a+bj$ as a single entity—a complex number.

For the moment we will assume that it is legitimate to regard $2j$ as a number and then to 'add' numbers like 1 and $2j$. A fuller enquiry into these points will be postponed until the end of the chapter.

1.2 Addition and multiplication. Having invented a new number system, what laws do we want these binary operations on the numbers to obey? After all, the system is our invention and we can endow it with whatever properties suit our needs.

You will recollect that if s and t are the roots of

$$ax^2+bx+c = 0,$$

then
$$s+t = -\frac{b}{a} \quad \text{and} \quad st = \frac{c}{a}.$$

This is to imply that

(a) $(1+2j)+(1-2j)$ has to equal 2; and that

(b) $(1+2j)\times(1-2j)$ has to equal 5

if our complex number system is to fit in with the existing theory of the quadratic function.

If we apply the ordinary rules of arithmetic as though they also apply to j then (a) simplifies as follows:

$$\begin{aligned} (1+2j)+(1-2j) &= (1+1)+(2j-2j) \\ &= 2+(2-2)j \\ &= 2+0j \end{aligned}$$

which we write simply as 2.

This is consistent with our needs and suggests that this is a satisfactory way of handling complex numbers.

Generalizing we have:

(i) That the *addition* of two complex numbers $a+bj$, $c+dj$ may be defined as
$$(a+bj)+(c+dj) = (a+c)+(b+d)j.$$

(ii) That the complex number $a+0j$ may be abbreviated to a, and will behave just like the real number a.

Example 1.
$$(3-4j)+(2+3j) = (3+2)+(-4+3)j$$
$$= 5-j.$$

Example 2.
$$(4-3j)+(-4+3j) = (4-4)+(-3+3)j$$
$$= 0+0j,$$

which we write simply as 0.

If we operate in the obvious way with (*b*) we obtain

$$(1-2j)\times(1+2j) = 1\times(1+2j)-2j\times(1+2j)$$
$$= 1+2j-2j-4j^2$$
$$= 1+(2-2)j-4\times(-1)$$
$$= 5+0j$$

which we write simply as 5. Thus this method of proceeding seems to lead to consistent results and suggests

(iii) That the *multiplication* of two complex numbers should be defined as

$$(a+bj)\times(c+dj) = a(c+dj)+bj(c+dj)$$
$$= ac+adj+bcj+bdj^2$$
$$= (ac-bd)+(ad+bc)j.$$

Example 3.
$$(2+j).(3-2j) = 6-4j+3j-2j^2$$
$$= 8-j.$$

Example 4.
$$(4+3j)(4-3j) = 16-12j+12j-9j^?$$
$$= 25+0j,$$

which we write simply as 25.

However, we wish to do more than add and multiply complex numbers. If they are to obey the field laws (Chapter 1, Section 8.3) as rational and real numbers do, then we must be able to do subtraction and division as well.

1.3 Equality of complex numbers. Before we consider either subtraction or division we must state the circumstances under which two complex numbers are equal. So far in using the sign ' = ' to relate two complex numbers we have always assumed that

$$a+bj = c+dj$$

is equivalent to the two equations between real numbers

$$a = c \quad \text{and} \quad b = d.$$

In fact we now define the equality of two complex numbers in this way.

1.4 Subtraction. If complex numbers are to obey the field laws then we can use these laws to deduce a definition for

$$(a+bj)-(c+dj).$$

1010

Regarding subtraction as the addition of the additive inverse, we require first the neutral element for addition. This is obviously $0+0j$ since

$$(a+bj)+(0+0j) = (a+bj) \quad \text{for all } a, b.$$

Generalizing Example 2 we have

$$(c+dj)+(-c-dj) = 0+0j$$

giving $(-c-dj)$ as the additive inverse of $(c+dj)$. Consequently the subtraction of $(c+dj)$ from $(a+bj)$ must be defined as

$$(a+bj)-(c+dj) = (a+bj)+(-c-dj)$$
$$= (a-c)+(b-d)j$$

as might be expected.

1.5   Division. We can follow a similar procedure to deduce a definition for

$$\frac{a+bj}{c+dj}.$$

Regarding division as multiplication by the multiplicative inverse, we require first the neutral element for multiplication. As might be anticipated this neutral element is $1+0j$ since

$$(a+bj).(1+0j) = (a+bj) \quad \text{for all } a, b.$$

A careful look at Example 4 will suggest a way of obtaining the multiplicative inverse of $4+3j$. Since

$$(4+3j)(4-3j) = 25+0j,$$

then

$$(4+3j)(\tfrac{4}{25}-\tfrac{3}{25}j) = 1+0j.$$

Generalizing from this example, we have

$$(c+dj)(c-dj) = (c^2+d^2)+0j$$

$$\Rightarrow (c+dj)\left(\frac{c}{c^2+d^2} - \frac{d}{c^2+d^2}j\right) = 1+0j$$

giving

$$\left(\frac{c}{c^2+d^2} - \frac{d}{c^2+d^2}j\right)$$

as the multiplicative inverse of $(c+dj)$. Consequently the division of $(a+bj)$ by $(c+dj)$ must be defined as

$$\frac{(a+bj)}{(c+dj)} = (a+bj)\left(\frac{c}{c^2+d^2} - \frac{d}{c^2+d^2}j\right)$$

$$= \left(\frac{ac+bd}{c^2+d^2}\right) + \left(\frac{bc-ad}{c^2+d^2}\right)j.$$

Example 5.
$$\frac{5+j}{4+3j} = (5+j)\left(\frac{4}{25} - \frac{3}{25}j\right)$$

$$= \frac{23}{25} - \frac{11}{25}j.$$

However, a second look at Example 4 will suggest an alternative method of obtaining the same result.

$$\frac{5+j}{4+3j} = \left(\frac{5+j}{4+3j}\right) \cdot \left(\frac{4-3j}{4-3j}\right)$$

$$= \frac{(5+j)(4-3j)}{(4+3j)(4-3j)}$$

$$= \frac{23-11j}{25+0j}$$

$$= \frac{23}{25} - \frac{11}{25}j \quad \text{as before.}$$

Exercise A

1. Find the solution sets for the following quadratic equations:
  (i) in the rational field;
  (ii) in the real field;
  (iii) in the complex field.

(a) $x^2 - x - 6 = 0$; (b) $x^2 - 2x - 1 = 0$;
(c) $x^2 - 2x + 2 = 0$; (d) $3x^2 - 7x + 2 = 0$;
(e) $x^2 - 4x + 5 = 0$; (f) $x^2 - 4x + 1 = 0$;
(g) $x^2 - 6x + 10 = 0$; (h) $x^2 - 4x + 8 = 0$;
(i) $2x^2 - 2x + 1 = 0$; (j) $25x^2 - 10x + 2 = 0$.

Under what circumstances does a quadratic equation have solutions in all three fields?

2. Factorize the following expressions:

(a) $z^2 + 1$; (b) $z^2 + 9$; (c) $z^2 + 4$;
(d) $z^2 + 2z + 5$; (e) $z^2 - 6z + 10$; (f) $z^2 + 4z + 20$.

3. Find the sum of each of the following pairs of complex numbers:

(a) $2 + j, 3 - j$; (b) $-2 - 2j, 3 + 4j$;
(c) $4 - j, 1 + 3j$; (d) $2 - 4j, 4 + 2j$;
(e) $-4 + 5j, 4 - 5j$; (f) $2 + 0j, 0 + 5j$;
(g) $7 - 4j, 4 + 7j$; (h) $4 - 2j, 4 + 2j$;
(i) $3 - 2j, -3 - 2j$; (j) $-4 - j, -1 + 5j$.

4. Find $z - w$ where z, w are the complex numbers respectively of Question 3.

5. Find $z \cdot w$ where z, w are the complex numbers respectively of Question 3.

1012

6. Find the sum and product of each of the following pairs of complex numbers:

(a) $1+2j$, $1-2j$; (b) $3-4j$, $3+4j$;

(c) $2-j$, $2+j$; (d) $8+9j$, $8-9j$;

(e) $2+3j$, $2-3j$; (f) $5+6j$, $5-6j$.

Have you any comment to make?

Write down the quadratic equations of which these complex numbers are the roots. Is there anything special about the coefficients? What is the quadratic equation having $1+2j$ and $2-j$ as roots? What do you notice?

7. Find the multiplicative inverses of the following:

(a) $1+j$; (b) $2+j$; (c) $1-2j$; (d) $2-2j$;

(e) $j-1$; (f) $3-j$; (g) $4+3j$; (h) $3-4j$.

8. Find $z \div w$ where z, w are respectively the following pairs of complex numbers:

(a) $1-j$, $1+j$; (b) $1+j$, $2+j$;

(c) $2+j$, $1-2j$; (d) $1+2j$, $2-2j$;

(e) $1+j$, $j-1$; (f) $j-1$, $3-j$;

(g) $3+4j$, $4+3j$; (h) $3+4j$, $3-4j$;

(i) $1-2j$, $5+j$; (j) $3-2j$, $2+3j$;

(k) $a+bj$, $c+dj$.

9. Find the product of each of the following pairs of complex numbers:

(a) $a+bj$, $a+bj$; (b) $a+bj$, $a-bj$;

(c) $a+bj$, $b+aj$; (d) $a+bj$, $b-aj$;

(e) $a+bj$, j; (f) $a+bj$, 1.

In Questions 10–15 you will find it helpful to use $u = a+bj$, $v = c+dj$, $w = e+fj$, $z = g+hj$, etc., in your proofs.

10. Is C closed under: (a) addition, (b) multiplication?

11. Is it true that $z.w = w.z$?

Is it true that $(u.v).w = u.(v.w)$?

Consequently, is the multiplication of complex numbers:

(a) commutative; (b) associative?

12. Repeat Question 11, suitably modified, for:

(a) addition; (b) subtraction; (c) division

of complex numbers.

13. What is the neutral element for:

(a) addition; (b) multiplication

of complex numbers?

14. What is the inverse element of $a+bj$ under:

(a) addition;

(b) multiplication?

1013

15. Is it true that $z.(w+u) = z.w+z.u$?
Is it true that $z+(w.u) = (z+w).(z+u)$?
Consequently, is
(a) multiplication distributive over addition;
(b) addition distributive over multiplication,
for complex numbers?

16. Which of the answers to Questions 10–15 indicate that C satisfies the laws for a field?

17. Are $a+bj, bj+a, a+jb, jb+a$ equivalent forms of the same complex number?

18. Evaluate $P(z) = z^2-jz+(1-3j)$ when:
(a) $z = 1+2j$;   (b) $z = 1+j$;   (c) $z = 3-2j$.
Solve $P(z) = 0$ in the complex field.

19. Solve the following quadratic equations in the complex field:
(a) $z^2-2jz-2 = 0$;   (b) $z^2-4jz-8 = 0$.

20. Show that the subset $\{a+0j: a \in R\}$ of C is isomorphic with the set of real numbers under:
(a) addition;   (b) multiplication.

2. ISOMORPHISMS

2.1 Having invented a new number field it is timely to investigate its structure. This investigation will reveal a considerable variety of isomorphic structures and we begin with the development of a geometrical interpretation of the addition of complex numbers. You will remember that real numbers may be represented by displacements along the number line or by points on the number line. Thus $^+2$ may be represented by a displacement of 2 units from left to right along the line, or by the point 2 on the line. Such a displacement may be represented by directed line segments as in Figure 1.

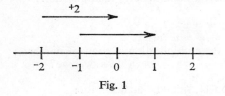

Fig. 1

The question now arises whether there are analogous models for the complex number field.

2.2 An isomorphism with vectors. The fact that the complex number $z = p+qj$ is composed of two parts suggests that we might consider directed line segments having two components. Now the set of directed line segments in a plane having the same two components is called a vector (see Chapter 9, Section 1.2).

1014

In fact we can easily show formally that complex numbers under addition are isomorphic with two-dimensional vectors under addition.

First, it is plain that there is a one-one correspondence between $p+qj$ and the vector $\begin{pmatrix} p \\ q \end{pmatrix}$.

Secondly, since
$$(a+bj)+(c+dj) = (a+c)+(b+d)j$$
and
$$\begin{pmatrix} a \\ b \end{pmatrix}+\begin{pmatrix} c \\ d \end{pmatrix} = \begin{pmatrix} a+c \\ b+d \end{pmatrix}$$

for all a, b, c, d, it follows that the sets

$$\{p+qj, +\} \quad \text{and} \quad \left\{\begin{pmatrix} p \\ q \end{pmatrix}, +\right\} \quad \text{are isomorphic.}$$

2.3 The complex number plane.
Since, for all p, q, the vector $\begin{pmatrix} p \\ q \end{pmatrix}$ is the position vector of the point (p, q) it follows directly that, for all p, q, the complex number $z = p+qj$ can also be represented by the point (p, q).

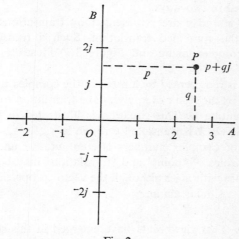

Fig. 2

Complex numbers have been invented to satisfy the need for a number j with the property $j^2 = {}^-1$. If we multiply real numbers by $^-1$ we can interpret this as an operation **H** on the number line, where **H** is a half-turn rotation about 0. If we multiply the real numbers by j and then by j again, we shall have multiplied them by $^-1$. We therefore look for an operation **Q** on the number line such that $\mathbf{Q}^2 = \mathbf{H}$; that is, an operation which, when repeated, is equivalent to a half-turn about 0. The obvious choice for **Q** is a quarter-turn about 0, which suggests that we take axes in the plane such that one axis represents the subset $\{a+0j: a \in R\}$ with the other axis representing the subset $\{0+aj: a \in R\}$ at right-angles to it. Thus $z = p+qj$ can be represented by the point P with coordinates (p, q) referred to these axes. This Cartesian representation of the complex number field is called the *complex number plane*, or the *complex plane* for short. The axes OA and OB in Figure 2 are customarily referred to as the *real* and *imaginary* axes.

Example 6. Represent on the complex plane the complex numbers $w = 2+3j$ and $z = 5+j$ together with $w+z$ and $w-z$. Illustrate the isomorphism with vectors.

In Figures 3(a) and 3(b) $A(2, 3)$ and $B(5, 1)$ represent w and z respectively. In Figure 3(a), $S(7, 4)$ represents $w+z$ and in Figure 3(b), $D(-3, 2)$ represents $w-z$.

The isomorphism between complex numbers and vectors under addition is illustrated in Figures 3(c) and 3(d). It is clear that the triangles PQR and LMN are directly congruent and that they are also directly congruent to triangle OAS in Figure 3(a). Now the vector properties of the sum $w+z$ may be interpreted in two ways.

First, if both w and z are represented by translations then $w+z$ is represented by the combined translation. Such a translation may be applied to the complex plane and Figure 3(e) illustrates this with the triangle OUV.

Secondly, if w is represented by a point in the complex plane then $w+z$ may be regarded as the result of applying the translation representing z to the point representing w. This situation is illustrated in Figure 3(f) in which the triangle OAX is translated through z.

Since the set of complex numbers is commutative under addition it follows that the roles of 'point' and 'translation' may be interchanged. This is not the case with $w-z$ although the vector properties of $w-z$ may be interpreted in a similar manner.

2.4 Summary. Two viewpoints have emerged in this section, namely that the complex number $p+qj$ can be represented by:

(a) the vector $\begin{pmatrix} p \\ q \end{pmatrix}$,

(b) the point (p, q) whose position vector is $\begin{pmatrix} p \\ q \end{pmatrix}$.

Exercise B

1. Represent on the complex plane the complex numbers and their sum from Exercise A, Questions 3 and 6. Does it matter which number is taken first? Why? Illustrate the isomorphism with vectors in the manner of Example 5.

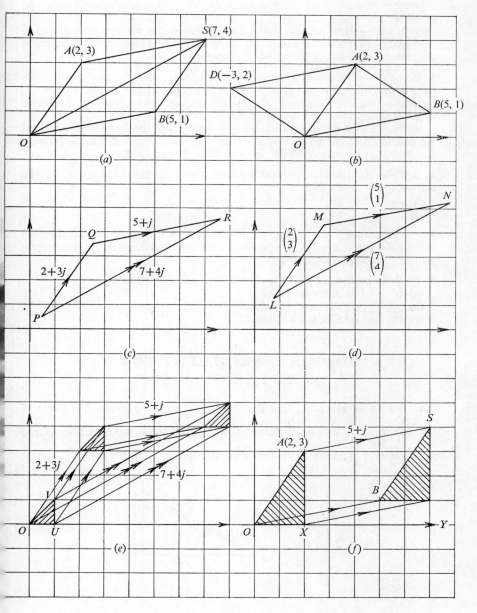

Fig. 3

2. Represent on the complex plane the complex numbers w and z and the differences $z-w$ and $w-z$, where w and z are the complex numbers of Exercise A, Question 3.

What geometrical relationship is there between the position vectors representing the numbers $z-w$ and $w-z$? Illustrate the isomorphism with vectors in the manner of Example 5, applied to subtraction.

3. Using the same scale on the real and imaginary axes plot the points representing the complex numbers and their products of Exercise A, Question 5.

Measure the lengths of each of the vectors representing z, w and $z.w$ in terms of the scale used for the axes. What do you find?

Measure the angle between the positive direction of the real axis and each of the position vectors representing z, w and $z.w$. If the counterclockwise rotation is regarded as positive from the real axis what do you find?

4. Rewrite the complex number $r\cos\theta + jr\sin\theta$ in the form $a+bj$ for the following values of r and θ:

(a) $r = 1$, $\theta = \frac{1}{4}\pi$;   (b) $r = 2$, $\theta = \frac{1}{3}\pi$;
(c) $r = 2$, $\theta = \frac{2}{3}\pi$;   (d) $r = 5$, $\theta = \tan^{-1}(\frac{3}{4})$.

Repeat Question 3 above on the pairs of complex numbers obtained from (a) and (b), (c) and (d). What do you find? How do r and θ define the point representing the complex number?

5. Find the product of the following pairs of complex numbers:

(a) $\cos a + j \sin a$, $\cos a + j \sin a$;
(b) $\cos a + j \sin a$, $\cos b + j \sin b$;
(c) $\cos 2a + j \sin 2a$, $\cos a + j \sin a$.

3. MODULUS–ARGUMENT FORM OF COMPLEX NUMBERS

3.1 You will remember that the vector $\begin{pmatrix} p \\ q \end{pmatrix}$ can be expressed in terms of its magnitude r, and its direction θ, measured from the direction of the base vector $\begin{pmatrix} 1 \\ 0 \end{pmatrix}$. This gives rise to an alternative form for $p+qj$.

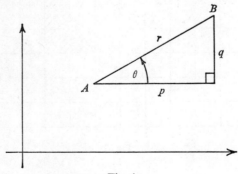

Fig. 4

Thus

$$\binom{p}{q} = \binom{r \cos \theta}{r \sin \theta}$$

and the corresponding form of the complex number

$$z = p + qj$$

becomes

$$z = r(\cos \theta + j \sin \theta).$$

It follows that r and θ are the polar coordinates of the point representing z in the complex plane.

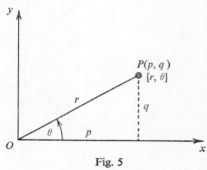

Fig. 5

The quantity r, which is always non-negative, is called the *modulus* of z, written $|z|$, and we write

$$r = |z|.$$

Consequently $z \to |z|$ maps the complex numbers onto the positive reals.

The angle θ, which OP makes with the positive real axis, is called the *argument* of z (or sometimes the amplitude of z) written $\arg(z)$, and we write

$$\theta = \arg(z).$$

Consequently $z \to \arg(z)$ maps the complex numbers into the reals. Now since the circular measure of the angle xOP can be equal to $\theta + 2k\pi$ for any integer k, we must restrict the range of the mapping. This is done by regarding θ as a residue class modulo 2π with its representative number satisfying $-\pi < \theta \leqslant \pi$. This value of θ is called the *principal value* of the argument, and we decree that $-\pi < \arg(z) \leqslant \pi$.

This form of a complex number will be referred to as the modulus–argument form and will be written as $[r, \theta]$. That is

$$z = [r, \theta].$$

3.2 Loci. At this point it is worth interrupting our investigation into the structure of the complex number field to observe the ease with which certain sets of points in the complex plane can be expressed in terms of the modulus–argument form. The following examples will illustrate the general approach.

1019

Example 7. Illustrate in the complex plane the set P where

$$P = \{z: |z| = 2\}.$$

P is the set of points such that the complex numbers represented by these points each have modulus 2. P is thus a circle, centre $(0, 0)$ and radius 2 units. Figure 6 illustrates the locus.

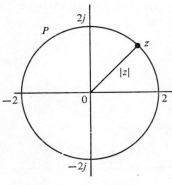

Fig. 6

Example 8. Illustrate in the complex plane the set Q where

$$Q = \{z: |z| = |z+2|\}.$$

In Figure 7(a) A and B represent the complex numbers z and $(z+2)$ respectively. Consequently Q is the set of points, any member A of which has the property that $OA = OB$. (We shall abbreviate this to 'the set of points A for which $OA = OB$'.)

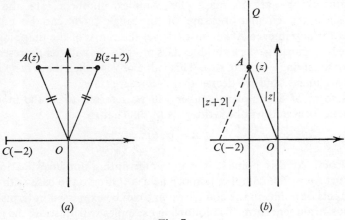

(a)   (b)

Fig. 7

It is easier to visualize this locus if we observe that $|z+2|$ is not only the length of OB, but also that of CA, where C is the point representing -2. The required locus is now the set of points A such that $OA = CA$.

Thus Q is the mediator of OC, and Figure 7(b) illustrates this locus.

In general, just as $\mathbf{AP} = \mathbf{OP} - \mathbf{OA}$, so $z-a$ can be represented by the vector $\mathbf{AP}$, where A represents a, and P represents z. $|z-a| = AP$.

Example 9. Illustrate in the complex plane the set R where

$$R = \{z : |z+2j| = |z-2|\}.$$

In Figure 8(a) A, B and C represent the complex numbers z, $(z+2j)$ and $(z-2)$ respectively. Thus R is the set of points A, such that $OC = OB$.

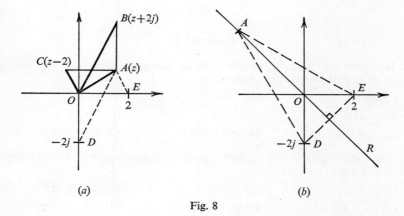

Fig. 8

Again, we may visualize this locus more easily if we regard $z+2j$ as representing the displacement $\mathbf{DA}$, where D represents $-2j$, and $z-2$ as representing the displacement $\mathbf{EA}$, where E represents 2. The required locus is now the set of points A, such that $DA = EA$.

Thus R is the mediator of DE and Figure 8(b) illustrates this locus.

Example 10. Illustrate in the complex plane the set S where

$$S = \{z : \arg (z-2) = \tfrac{3}{4}\pi\}.$$

In Figure 9(a) A and B represent the complex numbers z and $(z-2)$ respectively. Since $\arg (z-2) = \theta$ it follows that S is the set of points A, such that $\theta = \tfrac{3}{4}\pi$. Consequently B must lie on the *half-line*, having one end at O and making an angle of $\tfrac{3}{4}\pi$ with the positive real axis. Thus S is a parallel half-line having one end at $(2, 0)$ and Figure 9(b) illustrates this locus.

1021

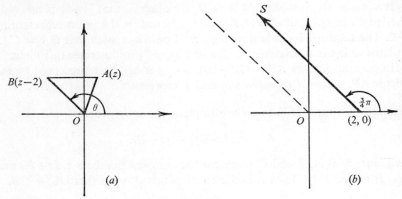

Fig. 9

Exercise C

1. Represent the following numbers in the complex plane and then rewrite them in modulus–argument form:

(a) $3+4j$; (b) $-1+j$; (c) $2-j$;

(d) $-\sqrt{(3)}-j$; (e) $2+j$; (f) $1-2j$;

(g) $-4-3j$; (h) $-5+12j$; (i) $-2-3j$.

2. The following complex numbers are in modulus–argument form. Rewrite them in Cartesian form:

(a) $[3, 0]$; (b) $[2, \frac{1}{3}\pi]$; (c) $[4, -\frac{2}{3}\pi]$;

(d) $[2, -\frac{1}{2}\pi]$; (e) $[1, \pi]$; (f) $[\sqrt{2}, -\frac{3}{4}\pi]$;

(g) $[2, \frac{2}{3}\pi]$; (h) $[5, -\frac{7}{10}\pi]$; (i) $[4, \frac{1}{2}\pi]$.

3. Illustrate in the complex plane the following loci:

(a) $\{z: |z| \geqslant 4\}$; (b) $\{z: |z-2| = 2\}$;

(c) $\{z: |z-j| = 2\}$; (d) $\{z: |z+4| \leqslant 1\}$;

(e) $\{z: |z+3j| > 3\}$; (f) $\{z: |z+1+j| = \sqrt{2}\}$;

(g) $\{z: |z-3-4j| = 4\}$; (h) $\{z: |z-2+j| > 1\}$.

4. Illustrate in the complex plane the following loci:

(a) $\{z: |z-1| = |z+2|\}$; (b) $\{z: |z+j| = |z+1|\}$;

(c) $\{z: |z-2j| \geqslant |z-3|\}$; (d) $\{z: |z-2| < |z-j|\}$.

5. Illustrate in the complex plane the following loci:

(a) $\{z: \arg(z+3) = \frac{1}{2}\pi\}$; (b) $\{z: \arg(z-j) = -\frac{1}{4}\pi\}$;

(c) $\{z: \arg(z-4) = -\frac{3}{4}\pi\}$; (d) $\{z: \frac{1}{2}\pi < \arg(z-2) \leqslant \frac{2}{3}\pi\}$;

(e) $\{z: \arg(z+1+j) = \frac{2}{3}\pi\}$; (f) $\{z: 0 \leqslant \arg(z-1-j) \leqslant \frac{1}{2}\pi\}$.

6. Sketch the following loci giving as many details as you can:

(a) $\{z: |z+1|+|z-1| = 3\}$;

(b) $\{z: |z+1|-|z-1| = 1\} \cup \{z: |z+1|-|z-1| = -1\}$;

(c) $\{z: \arg(z-1)-\arg(z+1) = \tfrac{1}{2}\pi\} \cup \{z: \arg(z-1)-\arg(z+1) = -\tfrac{1}{2}\pi\}$.

How would you alter the definition of the loci of parts (a) and (c) so that the regions enclosed by the loci become the solution sets?

7. Show that $|z|+|w| \geqslant |z+w|$ where z and w are complex numbers. Can this inequality be generalized? If so, give the generalization. Use a representation in the complex plane to substantiate your arguments and state the geometrical fact that you use.

4. AN ISOMORPHISM WITH 2×2 MATRICES

4.1 We will now return to the geometrical interpretation of the multiplication of complex numbers.

From your experience with Exercise B, Question 3, you will realize that the modulus–argument form of complex numbers lends itself to multiplication. In fact you will have guessed that if

$$z = [r, \theta]$$

and

$$w = [s, \phi],$$

then

$$z.w = [rs, \theta+\phi]$$

with the implied refinement that $\theta+\phi$ is reduced mod 2π.

From Figure 10 we can see that the effect of multiplying w by z is to rotate the vector representing w through θ and to enlarge the result by a scale factor of r.

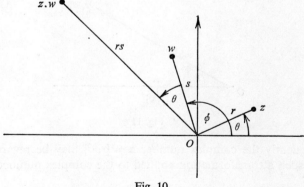

Fig. 10

You will remember from Chapter 8, Section 1.1, that the matrix

$$\mathbf{R}_\theta = \begin{pmatrix} \cos\theta & -\sin\theta \\ \sin\theta & \cos\theta \end{pmatrix}$$

effects a rotation about the origin through an angle θ.

Now $\mathbf{R}_\theta . \mathbf{R}_\phi = \mathbf{R}_{\overline{\theta+\phi}}$ implies

$$\begin{pmatrix} \cos\theta & -\sin\theta \\ \sin\theta & \cos\theta \end{pmatrix} \begin{pmatrix} \cos\phi & -\sin\phi \\ \sin\phi & \cos\phi \end{pmatrix} = \begin{pmatrix} \cos\overline{\theta+\phi} & -\sin\overline{\theta+\phi} \\ \sin\overline{\theta+\phi} & \cos\overline{\theta+\phi} \end{pmatrix}$$

and puts us in a position to establish the isomorphism between

$$[r,\theta] \quad \text{and} \quad r\begin{pmatrix} \cos\theta & -\sin\theta \\ \sin\theta & \cos\theta \end{pmatrix}.$$

There is clearly a one-one correspondence between the two expressions; and further, since $\qquad [r,\theta].[s,\phi] = [rs, \theta+\phi]$
and

$$r\begin{pmatrix} \cos\theta & -\sin\theta \\ \sin\theta & \cos\theta \end{pmatrix} s\begin{pmatrix} \cos\phi & -\sin\phi \\ \sin\phi & \cos\phi \end{pmatrix} = rs\begin{pmatrix} \cos\overline{\theta+\phi} & -\sin\overline{\theta+\phi} \\ \sin\overline{\theta+\phi} & \cos\overline{\theta+\phi} \end{pmatrix}$$

for all r, s, θ and ϕ it follows that, for all r, s, θ and ϕ,

$$\{[r,\theta],\times\} \quad \text{and} \quad \left\{ r\begin{pmatrix} \cos\theta & -\sin\theta \\ \sin\theta & \cos\theta \end{pmatrix}, \times \right\}$$

are isomorphic.

4.2 Spiral similarity. Consider

$$r\begin{pmatrix} \cos\theta & -\sin\theta \\ \sin\theta & \cos\theta \end{pmatrix} \begin{pmatrix} 1 \\ 0 \end{pmatrix} = \begin{pmatrix} r\cos\theta \\ r\sin\theta \end{pmatrix}.$$

From Figure 11 this can be interpreted as a rotation through θ followed by an enlargement by scale factor r of the unit vector $\begin{pmatrix} 1 \\ 0 \end{pmatrix}$. Such a transformation is called a *spiral similarity* with the origin as centre.

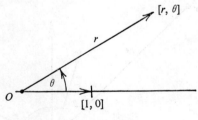

Fig. 11

Consequently the complex number $z = [r,\theta]$ may be regarded as the result of such a transformation applied to the complex number $[1, 0]$.

4.3 Now consider

$$r\begin{pmatrix} \cos\theta & -\sin\theta \\ \sin\theta & \cos\theta \end{pmatrix} \begin{pmatrix} s\cos\phi \\ s\sin\phi \end{pmatrix} = \begin{pmatrix} rs(\cos\theta\cos\phi & -\sin\theta\sin\phi) \\ rs(\sin\theta\cos\phi & +\cos\theta\sin\phi) \end{pmatrix}$$

$$= \begin{pmatrix} rs\cos\overline{\theta+\phi} \\ rs\sin\overline{\theta+\phi} \end{pmatrix}.$$

This is the spiral similarity of Section 4.2, but this time it is applied to the vector representing the complex number $w = [s, \phi]$. Figure 12 shows the effect of the transformation applied to the triangle OAS: that is, the transformation which maps $(1, 0)$ onto (r, θ), as in Section 4.2, also maps (s, ϕ) onto $(rs, \theta + \phi)$.

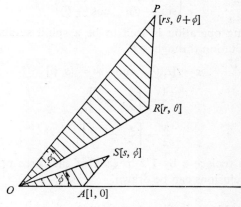

Fig. 12

Consequently the product $z.w$ may be regarded as the result of z operating on w in a similar way. Remembering that multiplication is commutative we deduce that the roles of z and w may be interchanged.

4.4 Lastly, consider

$$r \begin{pmatrix} \cos \theta & -\sin \theta \\ \sin \theta & \cos \theta \end{pmatrix} s \begin{pmatrix} \cos \phi & -\sin \phi \\ \sin \phi & \cos \phi \end{pmatrix} = rs \begin{pmatrix} \cos \overline{\theta + \phi} & -\sin \overline{\theta + \phi} \\ \sin \overline{\theta + \phi} & \cos \overline{\theta + \phi} \end{pmatrix}.$$

This is to say that if two spiral similarities are performed one after the other then the equivalent single transformation is also a spiral similarity.

Consequently if we regard both z and w as spiral similarities, then $z.w$ can be regarded as the single spiral similarity resulting from their combination.

4.5 Division in modulus–argument form. We have previously defined division as multiplication by the multiplicative inverse. Consequently if we wish to divide by $z = [r, \theta]$ then the equivalent matrix operation is to multiply by the inverse of

$$r \begin{pmatrix} \cos \theta & -\sin \theta \\ \sin \theta & \cos \theta \end{pmatrix}, \quad \text{that is, of} \quad \begin{pmatrix} r \cos \theta & -r \sin \theta \\ r \sin \theta & r \cos \theta \end{pmatrix}.$$

Since
$$\begin{vmatrix} r \cos \theta & -r \sin \theta \\ r \sin \theta & r \cos \theta \end{vmatrix} = r^2,$$

this inverse is
$$\frac{1}{r^2} \cdot r \begin{pmatrix} \cos\theta & +\sin\theta \\ -\sin\theta & \cos\theta \end{pmatrix} = \frac{1}{r} \begin{pmatrix} \cos\theta & \sin\theta \\ -\sin\theta & \cos\theta \end{pmatrix}.$$

If we rewrite this in the form
$$\frac{1}{r} \begin{pmatrix} \cos(-\theta) & -\sin(-\theta) \\ \sin(-\theta) & \cos(-\theta) \end{pmatrix}$$

the corresponding operation is seen to be a spiral similarity with scale factor $1/r$ and rotation through $-\theta$.

Consequently if
$$z = [r, \theta] \quad \text{and} \quad w = [s, \phi]$$

then
$$\frac{1}{z} = \left[\frac{1}{r}, -\theta\right]$$

and
$$\frac{w}{z} = \left[\frac{s}{r}, \phi-\theta\right].$$

Further if we replace z by $1/z$ in each of the three previous sections comparable conclusions can be drawn.

4.6 Summary. If $z = [r, \theta]$ and $w = [s, \phi]$ then:

(a) $\dfrac{1}{z} = \left[\dfrac{1}{r}, -\theta\right]$;

(b) $z.w = [rs, (\phi+\theta) \bmod 2\pi]$;

(c) $w/z = [s/r, (\phi-\theta) \bmod 2\pi]$;

(d) z may be regarded as the result of the spiral similarity representing z applied to the vector representing the complex number $[1, 0]$;

(e) $z.w$ may be regarded as the result of applying the spiral similarity representing z to the vector representing w, or vice versa;

(f) $z.w$ may be regarded as representing the single spiral similarity equivalent to the combination of the spiral similarities representing z and w.

Example 11. Express the complex numbers $z = -1 + \sqrt{3}j$ and $w = 2+2j$ in modulus–argument form. Hence calculate $w.z$ and w/z, leaving the answer in modulus–argument form.

Figure 13(a) illustrates w and z on the complex plane.
$$z = -1 + \sqrt{3}j = r\cos\theta + jr\sin\theta$$
$$\Rightarrow \begin{cases} r\cos\theta = -1 \\ r\sin\theta = \sqrt{3}. \end{cases}$$

Squaring and adding gives $r^2 = 4$, implying $r = 2$ since $r \geqslant 0$.

Now $\qquad\qquad \cos\theta = -\tfrac{1}{2} \Rightarrow \theta = \tfrac{2}{3}\pi \text{ or } -\tfrac{2}{3}\pi.$

However $\qquad\quad \sin\theta = \sqrt{\tfrac{3}{2}} \Rightarrow \theta = \tfrac{2}{3}\pi \text{ or } \tfrac{1}{3}\pi.$

1026

The consistent value for θ, namely $\frac{2}{3}\pi$, is also the answer indicated by the figure and demonstrates the usefulness of drawing a representative sketch of the complex plane. Thus $z = [2, \frac{2}{3}\pi].$

A similar procedure leads to $w = [2\sqrt{2}, \frac{1}{4}\pi]$. Consequently

$$zw = [2 \times 2\sqrt{2}, (\tfrac{2}{3}\pi + \tfrac{1}{4}\pi) \bmod 2\pi],$$

or

$$zw = \left[4\sqrt{2}, \frac{11\pi}{12}\right],$$

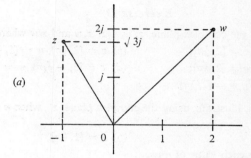

(a)

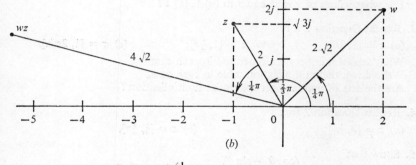

(b)

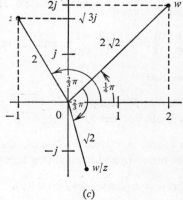

(c)

Fig. 13

and
$$\frac{w}{z} = \left[\frac{2\sqrt{2}}{2}, (\tfrac{1}{4}\pi - \tfrac{2}{3}\pi) \bmod 2\pi\right],$$

or
$$\frac{w}{z} = \left[\sqrt{2}, -\frac{5\pi}{12}\right].$$

Figures 13(b) and (c) illustrate w and z with wz and w/z respectively.

Exercise D

1. Illustrate, using the complex plane, z, w, $1/z$, $z.w$ and z/w where:

(a) $z = [3, \tfrac{1}{6}\pi]$, $w = [2, \tfrac{1}{3}\pi]$;   (b) $z = [2, \tfrac{2}{3}\pi]$, $w = [1, \tfrac{1}{2}\pi]$;

(c) $z = [4, \tfrac{2}{3}\pi]$, $w = [2, \tfrac{5}{9}\pi]$;   (d) $z = [3, -\tfrac{5}{12}\pi]$, $w = [1, \tfrac{5}{12}\pi]$;

(e) $z = [2, -\tfrac{5}{6}\pi]$, $w = [2, \tfrac{1}{6}\pi]$.

2. If $z^2 = z.z$, etc., illustrate, using the complex plane, z^n, when $n = 1, 2, 3, \ldots$, for

(a) $z = [1, \tfrac{1}{4}\pi]$;   (b) $z = [1, \tfrac{4}{9}\pi]$.

Evaluate $|z^n|$ for each value of n used.
For what values of n is z^n equal to (a) 1, (b) z?

3. Repeat Question 2 for:

(a) $z = [1, \tfrac{2}{3}\pi]$;   (b) $z = [1, \tfrac{1}{2}\pi]$;   (c) $z = [1, 2\pi/n]$.

What sets of numbers are generated in each case?
Write down the multiplication table in each case.
Are the sets of numbers groups under multiplication?

4. Repeat Question 2 for:

(a) $z = [2, \tfrac{1}{3}\pi]$;   (b) $z = [\tfrac{1}{3}, \tfrac{3}{4}\pi]$.

5. Show that
$$\begin{pmatrix} \cos\theta & -\sin\theta \\ \sin\theta & \cos\theta \end{pmatrix} = \cos\theta.\mathbf{I} + \sin\theta.\mathbf{J},$$

where
$$\mathbf{I} = \begin{pmatrix} 1 & 0 \\ 0 & 1 \end{pmatrix}, \quad \mathbf{J} = \begin{pmatrix} 0 & -1 \\ 1 & 0 \end{pmatrix} \quad \text{and} \quad \mathbf{J}^2 = -\mathbf{I}.$$

Use this form to prove that
$$\begin{pmatrix} \cos\theta & -\sin\theta \\ \sin\theta & \cos\theta \end{pmatrix}\begin{pmatrix} \cos\phi & -\sin\phi \\ \sin\phi & \cos\phi \end{pmatrix} = \begin{pmatrix} \cos\overline{\theta+\phi} & -\sin\overline{\theta+\phi} \\ \sin\overline{\theta+\phi} & \cos\overline{\theta+\phi} \end{pmatrix}.$$

6. If $z = r(\cos\theta + j\sin\theta)$ and $w = s(\cos\phi + j\sin\phi)$, use the definition of the product of two complex numbers and the addition formulae for $\cos\overline{\theta+\phi}$ and $\sin\overline{\theta+\phi}$ to prove that
$$z.w = rs(\cos\overline{\theta+\phi} + j\sin\overline{\theta+\phi}).$$

5. FURTHER ISOMORPHISMS

5.1 So far we have considered the transformation matrix in the form

$$r \begin{pmatrix} \cos\theta & -\sin\theta \\ \sin\theta & \cos\theta \end{pmatrix}.$$

This is a form suggested in the first place by the geometrical effect of multiplying w by z (see Section 4).

However, if we return to the Cartesian form of a complex number a corresponding form for the transformation matrix should follow.

If $z = p+qj$ then (p,q), the point representing z in the complex plane, is the image of a spiral similarity applied to $(1,0)$ (see Section 4.6). It follows directly that this spiral similarity maps

$$\begin{pmatrix} 1 \\ 0 \end{pmatrix} \to \begin{pmatrix} p \\ q \end{pmatrix} \quad \text{and} \quad \begin{pmatrix} 0 \\ 1 \end{pmatrix} \to \begin{pmatrix} -q \\ p \end{pmatrix}$$

and that the matrix of the transformation is

$$\begin{pmatrix} p & -q \\ q & p \end{pmatrix}.$$

Rewriting the conclusion of Section 4.1 in this form it follows directly that

$$\{p+qj, \times\} \quad \text{and} \quad \left\{ \begin{pmatrix} p & -q \\ q & p \end{pmatrix}, \times \right\} \quad \text{are isomorphic.}$$

Since z is now in a form more appropriate for addition than multiplication you may well be thinking that there may be a corresponding isomorphism. Consider

$$p+qj \quad \text{and} \quad \begin{pmatrix} p & -q \\ q & p \end{pmatrix}$$

in the light of this conjecture.

There is clearly a one-one correspondence between the expressions for all p, q. Further, since

$$(a+bj)+(c+dj) = (a+c)+(b+d)j$$

and

$$\begin{pmatrix} a & -b \\ b & a \end{pmatrix} + \begin{pmatrix} c & -d \\ d & c \end{pmatrix} = \begin{pmatrix} (a+c) & -(b+d) \\ (b+d) & (a+c) \end{pmatrix}$$

for all a, b, c, d, it follows that, for all p, q

$$\{p+qj, +\} \quad \text{and} \quad \left\{ \begin{pmatrix} p & -q \\ q & p \end{pmatrix}, + \right\} \quad \text{are isomorphic.}$$

Thus we have a form which is isomorphic for both operations.

5.2 All the geometrical properties displayed in Sections 4.2 and 4.3 remain applicable and we will show one more as a consequence of

$$\begin{pmatrix} a & -b \\ b & a \end{pmatrix} = a \begin{pmatrix} 1 & 0 \\ 0 & 1 \end{pmatrix} + b \begin{pmatrix} 0 & -1 \\ 1 & 0 \end{pmatrix} = a\mathbf{I} + b\mathbf{J},$$

where $J^2 = -I$; J being the matrix representing a transformation of a quarter-turn.

Consider $(a+bj)$. The matrix equivalent of this may be regarded as operating on the vector $\binom{1}{0}$, giving

$$\begin{pmatrix} a & -b \\ b & a \end{pmatrix} \begin{pmatrix} 1 \\ 0 \end{pmatrix} = aI \begin{pmatrix} 1 \\ 0 \end{pmatrix} + bJ \begin{pmatrix} 1 \\ 0 \end{pmatrix}.$$

aI is an enlargement centre O with scale factor a, and bJ is an enlargement centre O with scale factor b combined with a rotation through a quarter-turn.

$aI + bJ$ is thus represented by the diagonal OC of the rectangle $OACB$ in Figure 14.

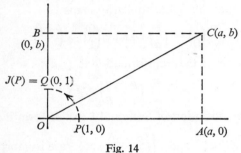

Fig. 14

Now consider $(a+bj)(c+dj)$. If we interpret this as the matrix equivalent of $a+bj$ operating on the vector equivalent of $c+dj$ we have

$$\begin{pmatrix} a & -b \\ b & a \end{pmatrix} \begin{pmatrix} c \\ d \end{pmatrix} = aI \begin{pmatrix} c \\ d \end{pmatrix} + bJ \begin{pmatrix} c \\ d \end{pmatrix}.$$

aI and bJ are the enlargements as before, but this time they are operating on the vector $\binom{c}{d}$. This situation is illustrated in Figure 15 and

$$aI \begin{pmatrix} c \\ d \end{pmatrix} + bJ \begin{pmatrix} c \\ d \end{pmatrix}$$

is seen to be represented by the diagonal OC of the rectangle $OACB$.

5.3   This isomorphism also leads to the verification that if

$$z = p + qj,$$

then

$$\frac{1}{z} = \frac{p}{p^2 + q^2} - \frac{q}{p^2 + q^2} j.$$

As in Section 1.5 the reciprocal of z may be regarded as its multiplicative inverse. Consequently we require the inverse of

$$\begin{pmatrix} p & -q \\ q & p \end{pmatrix}.$$

1030

Since

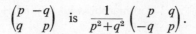

$$\begin{vmatrix} p & -q \\ q & p \end{vmatrix} = p^2 + q^2$$

it follows that the inverse of

$$\begin{pmatrix} p & -q \\ q & p \end{pmatrix} \quad \text{is} \quad \frac{1}{p^2 + q^2} \begin{pmatrix} p & q \\ -q & p \end{pmatrix}.$$

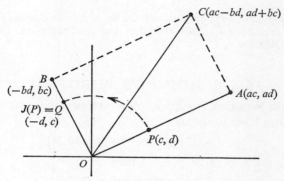

Fig. 15

Rewriting this in the form

$$\begin{pmatrix} \dfrac{p}{p^2 + q^2} & -\dfrac{-q}{p^2 + q^2} \\ \dfrac{-q}{p^2 + q^2} & \dfrac{p}{p^2 + q^2} \end{pmatrix}$$

we deduce that

$$\frac{1}{z} = \frac{p}{p^2 + q^2} - \frac{q}{p^2 + q^2} j$$

as expected.

Exercise E

1. Illustrate the geometrical interpretation of Section 5.2 for:

(a) $2 - 3j$;   (b) $-3 + j$;   (c) $(2 - 3j)(-3 + j)$;

(d) $(-3 + j)(2 - 3j)$;   (e) $(3 + 4j)(5 - 12j)$.

2. Under what circumstances is the rectangle $OACB$, of Figure 14, a square?

3. Modify the geometrical picture of multiplication given in Section 5.2 to give a corresponding geometrical picture of division.
Use the following examples to illustrate your answer:

(a) $\dfrac{3 - 4j}{1 + j}$;   (b) $\dfrac{1 + j}{3 - 4j}$;   (c) $\dfrac{1 - 2j}{2 - 3j}$.

4. What is the area scale factor of the transformation represented by

$$\begin{pmatrix} p & -q \\ q & p \end{pmatrix}?$$

What are the corresponding functions of z in the forms $z = p+qj$, and $z = [r, \theta]$?

5. Show that $\{a+bj, +, \times\}$ is isomorphic with $\{a\mathbf{I}+b\mathbf{J}, +, \times\}$ where

$$\mathbf{I} = \begin{pmatrix} 1 & 0 \\ 0 & 1 \end{pmatrix} \quad \text{and} \quad \mathbf{J} = \begin{pmatrix} 0 & -1 \\ 1 & 0 \end{pmatrix}.$$

6. Show that $\{p+qj\}$ is isomorphic with the set of residue classes $\{p+qx\}$ of real polynomials modulo x^2+1 under addition and multiplication. Cf. Chapter 3, Exercise H, Question 7.

6. DE MOIVRE'S THEOREM

6.1 We have seen that multiplication of complex numbers in modulus–argument form leads to the rule

$$[r, \theta] \times [s, \phi] = [rs, (\theta+\phi) \bmod 2\pi].$$

In particular if $\theta = \phi$ and $r = s = 1$ then

$$[1, \theta]^2 = [1, \theta] \times [1, \theta] = [1, 2\theta].$$

Similarly

$$[1, \theta]^3 = [1, 3\theta]$$

and in general

$$[1, \theta]^n = [1, n\theta],$$

in which we must not forget that $\arg(z^n) = n\theta \bmod 2\pi$.

Expressing this in the algebraic form for complex numbers we have

$$(\cos \theta + j \sin \theta)^n = \cos n\theta + j \sin n\theta.$$

This is de Moivre's theorem for a positive integral index n and is worth illustrating in the complex plane.

If

$$z = \left[1, \frac{2\pi}{5}\right] \quad \text{then} \quad z^n = \left[1, \frac{2n\pi}{5}\right].$$

The complex numbers z^n for $n = 1, 2, \dots, 10$ are illustrated in Figure 16. Notice two features.

(a) $z^n = [1, 0]$ for $n = 0 \bmod 5$.

(b) The points z^n coincide with their predecessors for $n > 5$.

In contrast consider

$$w = [1 \cdot 1, \tfrac{2}{5}\pi].$$

Now $w^n = [1 \cdot 1^n, \tfrac{2}{5}n\pi]$ and those points for which $n = 1, 2, 3, \dots, 10$ are illustrated in Figure 17.

The two corresponding features indicate that:

(a) $\arg(z^n) = 0$ for $n = 0 \bmod 5$.

(b) The points z^n, whilst having the arguments of their predecessors, have different moduli and do not coincide at all.

1032

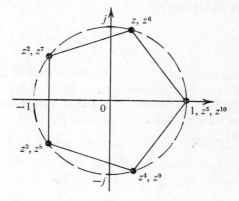

Fig. 16

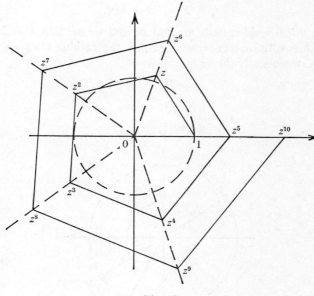

Fig. 17

6.2   *n*th roots. Let us approach the use of de Moivre's theorem from another point of view. If we know z^n and n, then in order to find z, the *n*th root of z^n, the process should, in some respects, be reversed. This can best be illustrated through two examples.

Example 12. Find the square roots of $z = [1, -\tfrac{1}{3}\pi]$ and illustrate z and its square roots in the complex plane.

If $w = [r, \theta]$ is the square root of z then

$$w^2 = z$$

$$\Rightarrow [r^2, 2\theta] = [1, -\tfrac{1}{3}\pi].$$

Before continuing, remember that arg (w^2) will always be given modulo 2π. Now, all members of the residue class $-\tfrac{1}{3}\pi$ modulo 2π are given by $-\tfrac{1}{3}\pi + 2k\pi$ where k is any positive or negative integer, and all the corresponding complex numbers are alternatives to $[1, -\tfrac{1}{3}\pi]$.

It follows that $[r^2, 2\theta] = [1, 2k\pi - \tfrac{1}{3}\pi]$ $(k = 0, \pm 1 \ldots)$

$$\Rightarrow \begin{cases} r^2 = 1, \text{ so that } r = 1 \ (r \geqslant 0) \\ 2\theta = 2k\pi - \tfrac{1}{3}\pi, \text{ so that } \theta = k\pi - \tfrac{1}{6}\pi \ (k = 0, \pm 1 \ldots). \end{cases}$$

Now
$$k = 0 \Rightarrow \theta = -\tfrac{1}{6}\pi,$$
$$k = 1 \Rightarrow \theta = \tfrac{5}{6}\pi,$$
$$k = 2 \Rightarrow \theta = \tfrac{11}{6}\pi.$$

But again θ is a residue class modulo 2π and we see that $k = 2$ and any further value will give a member of either the residue class $-\tfrac{1}{6}\pi$ or the class $\tfrac{5}{6}\pi$. Consequently the square roots of

$$z = [1, -\tfrac{1}{3}\pi]$$

are
$$w_1 = [1, -\tfrac{1}{6}\pi]$$

and
$$w_2 = [1, \tfrac{5}{6}\pi].$$

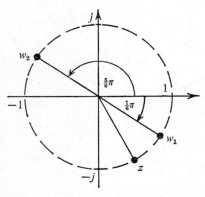

Fig. 18

Figure 18 illustrates w_1, w_2 and z, and incidentally shows that $w_1 = -w_2$ as with real square roots. However, this does not imply that either root is positive or negative in the sense applied to real numbers. The concept of a positive or negative (real) number is associated with the existence of a zero number *and* a linear representation of the number field. Complex numbers, being represented by points of a plane, can obviously not be ordered in this way.

Example 13. Find the cube roots of -8 and hence factorize the expression z^3+8.

We are seeking z where $z^3 = -8$. Consequently the complex number -8 must be written in its modulus–argument form. Now

$$-8 = [8, \pi].$$

If $z = [r, \theta]$ then
$$z^3 = -8$$
$$\Rightarrow [r^3, 3\theta] = [8, \pi].$$

Recollecting that $\arg(-8) = \pi$ modulo 2π we have

$$[r^3, 3\theta] = [8, (2k+1)\pi] \quad (k = 0, \pm 1 ...)$$

$$\Rightarrow \begin{cases} r^3 = 8, \text{ so that } r = 2 \quad \text{since} \quad r \geqslant 0 \\ 3\theta = (2k+1)\pi, \text{ so that } \theta = \left(\dfrac{2k+1}{3}\right)\pi \quad (k = 0, \pm 1 ...). \end{cases}$$

Now
$$k = 0 \Rightarrow \theta = \tfrac{1}{3}\pi,$$
$$k = 1 \Rightarrow \theta = \pi,$$
$$k = 2 \Rightarrow \theta = \tfrac{5}{3}\pi \bmod 2\pi = -\tfrac{1}{3}\pi,$$

and further values of k will give a member of these three residue classes for θ. Consequently the cube roots of -8 are:

$$z_1 = [2, \tfrac{1}{3}\pi] = 1 + j\sqrt{3},$$
$$z_2 = [2, \pi] = -2 + j0$$

and
$$z_3 = [2, -\tfrac{1}{3}\pi] = 1 - j\sqrt{3}.$$

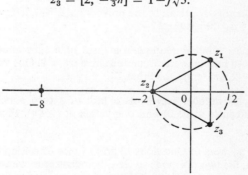

Fig. 19

Figure 19 illustrates $[-8, \pi]$ and its three cube roots. Lastly, since we have effectively solved the equation $z^3+8 = 0$ we can factorize the polynomial z^3+8 as

$$z^3+8 = (z+2)(z-1-j\sqrt{3})(z-1+j\sqrt{3}).$$

Exercise F

1. If $z^2 = -1$, what are the complex numbers z? Factorize $z^2 + 1$.

2. If $z^3 = -1$, find the three possible complex numbers z.
Plot their corresponding points on the complex plane. Factorize $z^3 + 1$.

3. Find the values of z which satisfy $z^2 = j$ and plot their corresponding points on the complex plane.

4. Find the value of z which satisfy $z^4 + 1 = 0$. Plot their corresponding points on the complex plane and factorize $z^4 + 1$ into its four factors.

5. Find the values of z which satisfy $z^5 + j = 0$. Plot their corresponding points on the complex plane and factorize $z^5 + j$.

6. Can you say how many of the roots of $z^n + 1 = 0$ are real if (*a*) n is even, (*b*) n is odd?
Repeat for $z^n - 1 = 0$.

7. If $z^n = [1, \theta]$ give the general form for z in terms of θ, n and k where k is any integer between 0 and $n-1$.

8. If $z^4 = 4$ find the possible values of z and factorize $z^4 - 4$.

9. If $z^5 = 32$ find the possible values of z and factorize $z^5 - 32$.

10. If $z^5 = 1 + j$ find the possible values of z and factorize $z^5 - 1 - j$ into its five factors.

11. If $z^n = [r, \theta]$ give the general form for z in terms of r, n, θ and k where k is any integer satisfying $0 \leqslant k \leqslant n-1$.

12. How many factors are there in the polynomial $z^{10} + a$? How many roots of the equation $z^{10} + a = 0$ are there?

13. Which complex number represents a third of a turn about O? An equilateral triangle is to have its vertices on the circle $|z| = 2$. One vertex is the point representing $z = [2, \frac{1}{6}\pi]$. Find the other two vertices.

14. Which complex number represents a fifth of a turn about O? A regular pentagon has its centre at $(0, 0)$ and one vertex at $(3, \frac{3}{4}\pi)$. Find the remaining four vertices.

15. Convert the answers to Questions 13 and 14 into Cartesian form. Translate, without rotation, the two polygons so that their centres move to the point $(3, 4)$. Give the new coordinates of the vertices of the two polygons and write the complex numbers represented by these points in Cartesian form.

16. Write down the complex number representing a rotation of $\frac{1}{8}\pi$ about the origin. A regular octagon has its centre at $(1, 1)$ and a vertex at $(2, 2)$. Find the remaining vertices.

1036

7. CONJUGATE COMPLEX NUMBERS

Look again at the form of the complex roots of the quadratic equation of Section 1.1, and the form of the complex numbers of Question 6 of Exercise A. Each pair of numbers is of the form $a+jb$, $a-jb$. Pairs of complex numbers of this form are called conjugate complex numbers.

Generally if $z = a+jb$ then its conjugate is written

$$\bar{z} = a-jb.$$

Further, a is called the real part of z, written re z, and b is called the imaginary part of z, written im z. These terms correspond with the real and imaginary axes introduced in Section 2.3 and are a relic of the days when some numbers were considered more real than others.

We have

$$\left.\begin{array}{l} \text{re } z = a \\ \text{im } z = b \end{array}\right\} \Leftrightarrow z = a+jb.$$

Exercise G

1. Write down the conjugates of:

(a) $5+2j$;   (b) $2+j$;   (c) $3-4j$;

(d) $-7j$;   (e) -3;   (f) $-3-2j$.

2. Illustrate on the same complex plane, with $z = 3+4j$:

$$z, \quad \bar{z}, \quad z+\bar{z}, \quad z.\bar{z}, \quad \frac{1}{z}, \quad \frac{1}{\bar{z}}, \quad \frac{\bar{z}}{z}, \quad \frac{z}{\bar{z}}.$$

3. If z and $\bar{z}$ are represented on the complex plane, what can you say about:

(a) their relation to the real axis?;

(b) arg (z) and arg $(\bar{z})$?

4. If $z = a+jb$ and $w = c+jd$:

(a) what can you say about (i) $z+\bar{z}$, (ii) $z.\bar{z}$?

(b) prove:

    (i) $|z| = |\bar{z}|$;

    (ii) $z.\bar{z} = |z|^2 = |\bar{z}|^2$;

    (iii) $\bar{w}+\bar{z} = \overline{w+z}$;

    (iv) $\bar{z}.\bar{w} = \overline{z.w}$;

(c) explain, without detailed working, why

$$z\bar{w} + w\bar{z}$$

is real.

5. Use matrix algebra and the isomorphism between

$$\{p+qj, +, \times\} \quad \text{and} \quad \left\{\begin{pmatrix} p & -q \\ q & p \end{pmatrix}, +, \times\right\}$$

to answer Questions 4(a) and (b).

6. Use de Moivre's theorem to prove $(\bar{z})^n = \overline{(z^n)}$.

7. Look again at the form of the complex roots of the polynomials of Questions 1, 2, 4, 8 and 9 from Exercise F. Do the complex roots occur in conjugate pairs? Now look again at the complex roots of the polynomials of Questions 3, 5 and 10 of Exercise F and Questions 18 and 19 of Exercise A. Do these roots occur in conjugate pairs?

Under what circumstances does it seem that the roots of a polynomial occur in conjugate pairs?

8. If $P(z)$ is a polynomial in z with real coefficients—called a real polynomial—prove:

(a) $P(\bar{z}) = \overline{P(z)}$;

(b) if $P(z_1) = 0$, then $P(\bar{z}_1) = 0$; i.e. if z_1 is a root of $P(z) = 0$, then $\bar{z}_1$ is also a root of $P(z) = 0$.

8. COMPLEX FUNCTIONS

You are familiar with functions which map R onto (or into) R. Examples of these are $x \to 2x+1$ and $x \to x^2$. Can we attach a similar interpretation to $z \to z+p$, for example? Such a function maps C onto C and in view of the fact that we are mapping a plane onto a plane it is usually convenient to superimpose the two planes, giving them a common origin and common axes.

If $f(z) = z+p$ then the mapping is $z \to f(z)$. We already have a geometrical interpretation of $z+p$ from Section 2.3, Example 5, namely, that any point z is translated through p. Consequently C is translated through p by f.

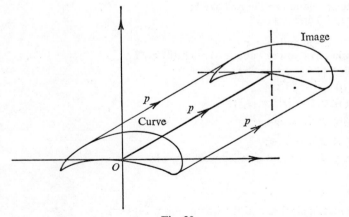

Fig. 20

Figure 20 illustrates this mapping with a curve and its image under f.

Example 14. Investigate the mapping $z \to pz$.

This time we make use of the geometrical interpretation developed in Section 4.3. This implies that multiplication by p enlarges, centre $(0, 0)$, by scale factor $|p|$ and rotates about $(0, 0)$ through arg (p).

Figure 21 illustrates this mapping for $p = [r, \alpha]$ where $r > 1$.

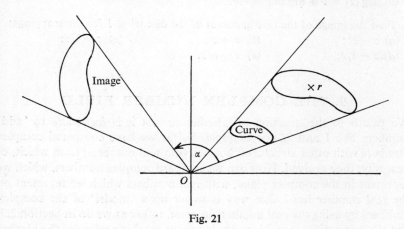

Fig. 21

Exercise H

1. Discuss the image of the circle $|z| = 1$ under the mappings

   (a) $z \to z+2+3j$;   (b) $z \to (1+\sqrt{3}j)z$.

2. Illustrate Example 14 for:

   (a) $p = [4, 0]$;   (b) $p = [2, \frac{1}{4}\pi]$;   (c) $p = [3, \frac{2}{3}\pi]$.

Use, as the object to be mapped, the rectangle $A(1, 1)$; $B(1, 2)$; $C(3, 2)$; $D(3, 1)$.

3. Find the image of the rectangle $A(2, 1)$; $B(-2, 1)$; $C(-2, -1)$; $D(2, -1)$ under the mappings:

   (a) $z \to z+3+4j$;

   (b) $z \to bz$ where

       (i) $b = \frac{1}{2}+0j$;   (ii) $b = 0-3j$;   (iii) $b = 4-3j$.

4. Find the lines whose images are $x = 0$, $y = 0$ under the mapping $z \to z^2$.

5. Find the lines whose image is $x-y = 0$ under the mapping $z \to z^2$. [You should obtain two perpendicular lines intersecting at $(0, 0)$.]

6. Repeat Question 5 for the line $x+y = 0$.

7. What mappings are represented by:

   (a) $z \to \bar{z}$;   (b) $z \to \bar{z}+a$?

8. For the mapping $z \to 4/z$ plot the points representing z and its image for
$$z = 1+j; \quad 2+2j; \quad -1+j; \quad \text{and} \quad -2+2j.$$
If $w = 4/z$ show that $|z| = 2 \Rightarrow |w| = 2$.
What can you say about the mapping from the facts that:
(a) $|z| > 2 \Rightarrow |w| < 2$;
(b) $\arg(z) = \theta \Rightarrow \arg(w) = -\theta$.

9. Find the image of the first quadrant of the disc $|z| \leqslant 1$ for the mappings:

(a) $z \to z^{\frac{1}{2}}$;   (b) $z \to z^2$;   (c) $z \to 1/z$;

(d) $z \to 1/\bar{z}$;   (e) $z \to \text{re } z$.

9. THE COMPLEX NUMBER FIELD

We return to the question of whether or not it is *legitimate* to 'add' numbers like 1 and $2j$, for example. So far we have compared complex numbers with other structures, but not with real numbers, from which, of necessity, they evolved. How can we compare complex numbers, which we represent in the complex plane, with real numbers which we represent on the real number line? One way is to set up a 'model' of the complex numbers by using the real numbers in pairs, rather as we do in Section 2.3. But there is a difference. Now, we lay down working rules for the algebra of the ordered pairs of real numbers, (a, b), which we are going to call complex numbers.

That is $\qquad C = \{(a, b): a, b \in R\}.$

The rules are:

(i) Equality of complex numbers

$$(a, b) = (c, d) \quad \Leftrightarrow \quad a = c, b = d.$$

(ii) Addition of complex numbers is defined by

$$(a, b)+(c, d) = (a+c, b+d).$$

(iii) Multiplication of complex numbers is defined by

$$(a, b)\times(c, d) = (ac-bd, ad+bc).$$

It follows from these definitions that $\{R, \times, +\}$ is isomorphic with $\{(a, 0), \times, +\}$.

Now $(0, 1)\times(0, 1) = (-1, 0)$; so that if $(0, 1)$ is denoted by j then j^2 corresponds to the real number -1. Further

$$(a, b) = (a, 0)+(0, b)$$
$$= (a, 0)+(b, 0)\times(0, 1)$$
$$= (a, 0)+(b, 0)\times j;$$

so that (a, b) corresponds to $a+bj$ where a and b are reals, and this is our justification for the use of the plus sign.

1040

All the properties of complex numbers follow from the three definitions above. If you are interested you might like to work Exercise A again from these definitions.

Miscellaneous Exercise

1. Solve the following equations in the complex field:
    (a) $z^4 + 4 = 0$;   (b) $z^3 - (1+j) = 0$;
    (c) $z^5 - (3-4j) = 0$;   (d) $2z^8 + (\sqrt{3}-j) = 0$.

2. Illustrate in the complex plane the following sets of points:
    (a) $|z| = 3$;   (b) $|z| < 5$;
    (c) $\arg(z) = \frac{1}{6}\pi$;   (d) $|z - 2j| = 2$;
    (e) $\arg(z - j) = 0$;   (f) $|z - 1| \leqslant |z + 1|$;
    (g) $\arg(z + j) - \arg(z - j) = \frac{1}{2}\pi$.
    This does not give all you might think.
    What is needed to complete the circle $|z| = 1$?

3. Find a polynomial having real coefficients with $3 + 4j$ as a root.

4. Illustrate the set of points on the complex plane representing z when
$$z = j + t(1 + 2j),$$
where t can be any real number.

5. If z has no reciprocal, that is if $1/z$ is not defined, what can you say about z?

6. If $z = a + jb$ and $w = c + jd$, show that:
    (a) $z\bar{w} + w\bar{z}$ is of the form $p + 0j$;
    (b) $z\bar{w} + w\bar{z} \leqslant 2|z \cdot \bar{w}|$;
    (c) $|z\bar{w}| = |\bar{z}w| = |z| \cdot |w|$.
    Hence by expanding $(z + w)(\bar{z} + \bar{w})$ show that $|z + w| \leqslant |z| + |w|$.
    N.B. This is an algebraic proof of the geometrical fact used in Question 7 of Exercise C.

7. Prove that the mapping $z \to z/(z-1)$ maps the line $x = \frac{1}{2}$ onto the circle $|z| = 1$.

    Method. If $w = \dfrac{z}{z-1}$ then $z = \dfrac{w}{w+1}$.

    The line $x = \frac{1}{2}$ may be written $\arg(z - \frac{1}{2}) = \pm\frac{1}{2}\pi$. Hence find $(z - \frac{1}{2})$ as a function of w and use Question 6(c) of Exercise C.
    What happens to the line $x = k$ (constant) under this mapping?

8. If u, v, w are three unequal complex numbers, under what circumstances will the points representing them in the complex plane be collinear?
    Prove that the points are collinear if and only if real numbers λ, μ, ν can be found so that
$$\lambda u + \mu v + \nu w = 0 \quad \text{and} \quad \lambda + \mu + \nu = 0$$
where λ, μ, ν are not all zero.

9. Describe a geometrical construction to give the image of a point under the mapping $z \to z + (1/z)$.

If this transformation is applied to any circle passing through $z = -1$, enclosing $z = 1$ and having its centre off the real axis the result is an aerofoil. This is known as Joukowski's Aerofoil and can be adjusted to approximate to the cross-section of an aeroplane's wing. This enables problems, such as the air flow round a wing, to be related to problems associated with a cylinder: an easier representation.

Find the image of the circle $|z - (1 + \frac{3}{2}j)| = \frac{5}{2}$ under this mapping.

10. Prove that $\{a + b\omega : a, b \in R$ and $\omega^3 = 1\}$ is isomorphic under addition and multiplication with $\{a + bx : +, \times, \text{modulo } x^2 + x + 1\}$.

35

POLYNOMIAL EQUATIONS

In the last chapter we saw that the equation $z^n = a$ has n roots. We shall now see that the same result can be extended to all equations $P(z) = 0$, where P is a polynomial over the complex field, and that it tells us something about the solution of polynomial equations over the real field. We solve a number of such equations approximately, and illustrate the solutions by using the graphs of some real polynomial functions.

1. POLYNOMIALS OVER THE COMPLEX FIELD

The general polynomial of degree n may be written

$$P = a_0 + a_1 z + a_2 z^2 + \ldots + a_n z^n,$$

where a_n is not equal to zero. Although our main intention is to solve polynomial equations whose coefficients a_i are drawn from the real field, we shall sometimes find it useful to work more generally with polynomials over the complex field. All the results of Chapter 3 still hold, because they depend only on the laws which govern operations upon the members of a field, and the complex number system obeys those laws.

Thus we can add, subtract and multiply polynomials. We can express a given polynomial P as $A \cdot Q + B$, where A is any given polynomial, B (the remainder) a polynomial of lower degree than A, and Q (the quotient) another polynomial to be found. If the remainder B is the zero polynomial, and therefore $P = A \cdot Q$, we say that A is a factor of P, and that P is *reducible*. There is essentially only one way (apart from numerical multiples and rearrangements) in which P can be expressed as a product of irreducible polynomials, though this statement remains to be proved.

Besides the polynomial form, we are interested in the polynomial function

$$P: z \to P(z)$$

and in the polynomial equation

$$P(z) = 0.$$

We also know the *factor theorem*,

$$P(b/a) = 0 \quad \Leftrightarrow \quad (az - b) \quad \text{is a factor of } P.$$

The z of the polynomial form is indeterminate—that is to say, it acts merely as a place-holder, like the t in the generator

$$G(t) = \sum_{i=0}^{i=n} p_i t^i.$$

But we shall usually suppose that the domain of the polynomial function is the field from which the coefficients are drawn; its codomain will then be the same field again.

Exercise A

1. Which of the following are polynomials, and what is the degree of those that are? Name the simplest field from which the coefficients may be drawn.

(a) $z^3 - 3z + 2$; (b) $z^2 - 2jz - 2$; (c) $3 . \sqrt[3]{2}^2 - 4 . \sqrt[3]{2} + 1$;

(d) πz^2; (e) $4z^2 + 1/z$; (f) $\sum_{i=0}^{i=n} z^i/i!$;

(g) $e^{j\pi} z + 1$; (h) $\begin{pmatrix} 1 & 0 \\ 0 & 1 \end{pmatrix} \mathbf{Z}^2 - \begin{pmatrix} 3 & -2 \\ 2 & 3 \end{pmatrix} \mathbf{Z} + \begin{pmatrix} 2 & -3 \\ 3 & 2 \end{pmatrix}$;

(i) $(1 - z^3)/(1 - z)$; (j) $3z^2 + 2z + 1$; (k) $\sum_{i=0}^{i=\infty} (\tfrac{1}{2} z)^i$.

2. What is the coefficient of z^i in the polynomials:

(a) $(1 + 2z)^4$; (b) $(1 - z)(1 + z + z^2 + z^3)$;

(c) $(b + az)^n$; (d) $(z - \alpha)(z - \beta)(z - \gamma)$;

(e) $\left(\sum_{i=0}^{i=2} a_i z^i \right) . \left(\sum_{i=0}^{i=1} b_i z^i \right)$; (f) $(1 + z) \sum_{i=0}^{i=n} \binom{n}{i} z^i$?

3. Find a simpler form for the polynomial function

$$\mathbf{x} \rightarrow \mathbf{x}^4 + 2\mathbf{x}^3 + 2\mathbf{x}^2 + \mathbf{x}$$

whose coefficients are drawn from the integers modulo 3, by considering the images of **0, 1, 2** under the function. Show also that

$$\mathbf{x}^4 + 2\mathbf{x}^3 + 2\mathbf{x}^2 + \mathbf{x} = \mathbf{x}(\mathbf{x} + 1)(\mathbf{x} + 2)^2.$$

Can the polynomial be factorized in any other way? Can the function be expressed as a product of linear functions in any other way?

*4. Show that the set of all polynomials over C forms an integral domain (see *S.M.P. Advanced Tables*, p. 3). Is this true (a) of polynomials over C of degree less than n, (b) of polynomials over the integers modulo 5? Is it true of the set of images under the corresponding polynomial functions of all points in the domain?

2. POLYNOMIALS OF DEGREE n OVER C

We now lead towards the following very powerful result:

Every polynomial P over C, of degree n, has just n zeros.

It can also be expressed in another form:

Every polynomial equation $P(z) = 0$ over C, of degree n, has just n roots.

Examples like z^2-10 and z^2+10 show that this rule is true neither of the rationals Q, nor of the reals R. For z^2-10 is irreducible over Q, and therefore has no zeros; over R, however, it can be expressed as

$$(z-\sqrt{10})(z+\sqrt{10}).$$

On the other hand, z^2+10 is irreducible over R; while over C it can be expressed as $(z-j\sqrt{10})(z+j\sqrt{10})$.

Indeed, as we have seen, it was the desire to be able to handle more and more general polynomial equations that led mathematicians to extend the number system in the first place. Starting from the counting numbers, they introduced wider classes of numbers—integers, rationals, reals, and finally the complex numbers. The theorem tells us that it is unnecessary to invent any further system of numbers to solve polynomial equations; for all the zeros of all the polynomials over C are included in C.

2.1 Multiple roots. The main difficulty with this theorem is that the n roots are sometimes not all distinct. This can be seen from the equation

$$z^3-3jz^2-3z+j = 0,$$

for example, where the unique factorization

$$(z-j).(z-j).(z-j)$$

suggests that the root j should be counted three times over. Compare Example 2 with Example 1.

Example 1. Consider the zeros of $z^2-2jz-2$.

$$z^2-2jz-2 = (z-j-1).(z-j+1),$$

so that $(j-1)$ and $(j+1)$ are the zeros of the polynomial. There can be no other zeros; for if a is distinct from these two zeros,

$$(a-j-1).(a-j+1) \neq 0.$$

The second degree polynomial, then, has two linear factors, and the corresponding equation has two roots.

Example 2. Consider the zeros of $z^2-2jz-1$.

$$z^2-2jz-1 = (z-j).(z-j),$$

so that j is the only zero of the polynomial. As the factor $(z-j)$ appears twice in the expression for P, it would seem reasonable to count the zero j twice. We may say, similarly, that the equation

$$(z-j)^3 = 0$$

has a three-fold root j.

We therefore frame this definition:

> *Definition*: If $P(z)$ can be written as $(z-a)^m.Q(z)$, where a is not a zero of Q, we say that a is an *m-fold zero*, or a *zero of multiplicity m*, of P; and that it is an *m-fold root* of $P(z) = 0$.

Example 3. List the roots of the equation $(z-2)^3.(z+1)^2.(z-3j) = 0$.

The equation has a three-fold root at 2, a double root at -1, and a simple root at $3j$. If therefore we count m-fold roots m times, the total number of roots, six, corresponds exactly to the degree of the equation.

Example 4. List the zeros of the polynomial z^3-3z+2.

We see at once, by the factor theorem, that 1 is a zero of this polynomial. We therefore write it in the form

$$(z-1).(z^2+z-2).$$

Again it appears that 1 is a zero of the quadratic. We finally display the polynomial in the form

$$(z-1)^2.(z+2).$$

Thus there is a single zero at -2, and a double zero at 1.

2.2 Remainder theorem and factor theorem. The division process of Chapter 3 shows that it is always possible to express a polynomial P in the form

$$P(z) = (az-b).Q(z)+r.$$

By the definition of equal forms, the coefficient of each power of z must be the same on either side of the equation, just as when two geometrical vectors are equal each pair of components must be equal. The images under the corresponding functions are therefore equal for all values of z, and in particular when $z = b/a$ we may deduce the *remainder theorem*

$$P(b/a) = r,$$

and the *factor theorem*

$$P(b/a) = 0 \iff P(z) = (az-b).Q(z),$$

where P is a polynomial of degree n, and Q some polynomial of degree $n-1$.

Example 5. What is the remainder when $2z^2-4z+7$ is divided by $z-3j$?

By the remainder theorem, the answer is

$$P(3j) = -2.9-4.3j+7 = -11-12j.$$

Example 6. Is $2z+5$ a factor of $6z^3-5z^2-36z+35$?

$$P(-\tfrac{5}{2}) = -6.(\tfrac{125}{8})-5.(\tfrac{25}{4})+36.(\tfrac{5}{2})+35 = 0,$$

so, by the factor theorem, $2z+5$ is a factor of the polynomial.

The factor theorem tells us, then, that if b/a is a zero of P, $az-b$ is a factor of P. We therefore have a very close connection between factors, roots and zeros, and indeed it is clear that in any particular domain the existence of roots and zeros is intimately bound up with the reducibility of the polynomial to a product of linear factors.

Exercise B

1. Find the remainder when:
(a) $z^3 - z$ is divided by $z - 2$;
(b) $2z^2 - 4z + 7$ is divided by $3z + 5$;
(c) $z^2 - 5z + 1$ is divided by $z - j$;
(d) $az^2 + bz + c$ is divided by $mz - n$.

2. Which, if any, of (i), (ii), (iii) are factors of the polynomial?
(a) $z^3 + z - 6$: (i) $z + 1$, (ii) $z - 2$, (iii) $z + 3$;
(b) $2z^2 - 7z + 5$: (i) $z + 1$, (ii) $z - 1$, (iii) $2z - 5$;
(c) $z^2 - 2zw - 8w^2$: (i) $z - 2w$, (ii) $z + 4w$, (iii) $z + 2w$; this is a polynomial in two indeterminates z, w over C;
(d) $z^2 + 36$: (i) $z - \sqrt{6}$, (ii) $z - 6j$, (iii) $z + 6j$.

3. (a) What is the value of a if $z - 2$ is a factor of $3z^7 - az^2 + 4$?
(b) What are the values of b, $c \in Q$ if $bz^7 - cz^2 + 4$ has a factor $z - \sqrt{2}$?

4. A polynomial over Q has $z - \sqrt{2}$ as a factor. Prove that $z + \sqrt{2}$ is another factor. Is the same thing true of polynomials over R?

5. Criticize the following argument:
If $h(z) = 1 - \sin z$, $h(\tfrac{1}{2}\pi) = 0$; so $z - \tfrac{1}{2}\pi$ is a factor of $1 - \sin z$.

6. Criticize the following argument:
$P(z) = z^3 - z$ over the integers modulo 3. Since $P(0) = P(\pm 1) = P(\pm 2) = 0$, $z.(z+1).(z-1).(z+2).(z-2)$ are the factors of $z^3 - z$.

7. Show that if $\Sigma\alpha\beta$ means 'the sum of the products of pairs of distinct elements of the set $\{\alpha, \beta, \gamma\}$', and so on,
$$(z-\alpha).(z-\beta).(z-\gamma) = z^3 - \Sigma\alpha.z^2 + \Sigma\alpha\beta.z - \alpha\beta\gamma,$$
and state a similar result for an equation with four roots.
(The coefficients of the cubic are called *symmetric functions* of the roots, because the interchange of any two of α, β and γ leaves their values unaltered.)

8. Use the result of Question 7 to write down polynomials whose zeros are:
(a) $3, \sqrt{2}, -\sqrt{2}$;   (b) $-2, 2+j, 2-j$;   (c) $\pm 1, 1 \pm \sqrt{3}$;
(d) $1, a \pm bj$;   (e) $0, \pm 1$;   (f) $5 - 2j, 4 + 3j$.

9. By using the factor theorem with suitable rational numbers, solve:
(a) $z^3 - 6z^2 + 11z - 6 = 0$;   (b) $z^3 - z^2 - z - 2 = 0$;
(c) $z^3 + z^2 - 2z - 8 = 0$;   (d) $3z^3 - 4z^2 - 13z - 6 = 0$.

10. Solve:
(a) $z^4 + 2z^3 + z^2 - 4 = 0$;   (b) $2z^4 + z^3 - z - 2 = 0$;
(c) $z^4 + 4z^3 + 8z^2 + 11z + 6 = 0$;   (d) $z^3 + 1 = 0$.

11. Investigate the factors (i) over Q, (ii) over R, (iii) over C of:
(a) $z^3 + 1$;   (b) $z^4 - 1$;   (c) $z^4 + 1$.

12. Find the factors of $z^2 + 2$ over the integers modulo 3, and of all other reducible quadratics over this field.

3. THE FUNDAMENTAL THEOREM
OF ALGEBRA

In Exercise B, there has been no difficulty in finding at least one root of each of the equations with which we have been confronted. When we have found such a root, we can reduce the problem to a simpler one; and again there has been no difficulty in finding a root of the reduced equation. We can reduce the original equation, root by root, to a quadratic and eventually to a simple equation.

This process is in fact always possible. It enables us to state the theorem suggested above in a form which is much neater, and looks much more innocuous. It may be written:

Every polynomial equation over C has a root,

or, more shortly still,

Every polynomial over C has a zero.

This is called the *fundamental theorem of algebra*. We can use the division process and the theorem of unique factorization to extend it inductively to the result stated in Section 2. For as soon as we have identified a root of $P(z) = 0$, an equation of degree n, we can reduce the problem to the solution of $Q(z) = 0$, an equation of degree $n-1$. We can thus in principle reduce any polynomial equation to a linear one, provided that we can find some means of actually locating the roots. The full proof is too difficult for this course; but it is of interest to see the lines on which it is developed.

In Section 3.1 we sketch a proof of the theorem; for a fuller discussion see, for example, Hardy, *Pure Mathematics* (ninth edition, Cambridge, 1944), or Courant and Robbins, *What is Mathematics?* (Oxford, 1941).

*3.1 Sketch proof of the fundamental theorem of algebra.We shall illustrate the theorem by considering the polynomials $z^3 + 10j$ and $z^3 + z + 1$. The ideas that emerge are in fact the essential ideas of the general proof.

Unfortunately the graphical representation of a function of a complex variable is by no means as simple as the graph of a function of a real variable. Members of domain and codomain are each represented by the points of a plane, instead of the points of a line; we therefore represent the domain by one plane, which we usually call the z-plane, and the codomain by another, which we usually call the w-plane, as in Figures 1 and 2. Each point will have an image, $w = P(z)$; if z is a zero of P, what will w be?

Each point of the z-plane has an image in the w-plane, and the question is whether any point has an image at O, for it would then be a zero of P. We shall consider the points of the z-plane systematically, by plotting the images of the points of the circles $|z| = r$ as r increases from zero. Figure 1 shows these circles for $r = 0, 1, 2, 3$, and Figure 2 shows their images $w = z^3 + 10j$ for these values of r.

1048

Study the lettered points in Figure 1, and their lettered images in Figure 2, carefully. The circle in Figure 2 must be described three times while the circle in Figure 1 is described once; for if the argument of z is θ, then the argument of $(w - 10j)$ will of course be 3θ.

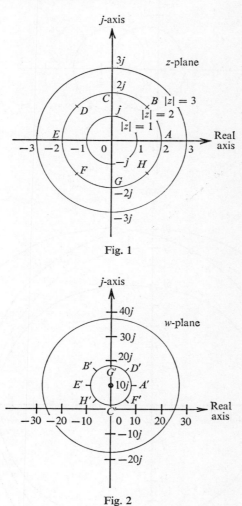

Fig. 1

Fig. 2

Figure 3, similarly, shows the images of $|z| = 1$ and $|z| = 2$ under the function $z \to z^3 + z + 1$; the circles of Figure 2 were by no means typical, and this more complicated graph shows what we must expect. What is the image of $|z| = 0$ under this mapping? The reader would be well advised to trace on Figure 3 how the image point moves as z describes the circles

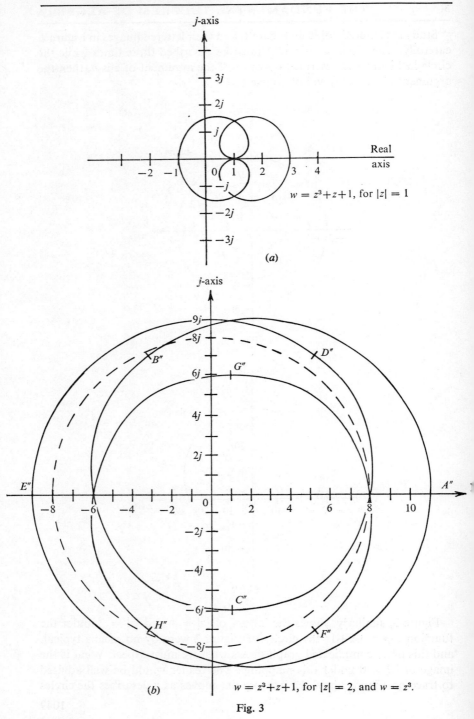

j-axis

$3j$
$2j$
j

Real axis

-2 -1 0 1 2 3 4

$-j$

$w = z^3 + z + 1$, for $|z| = 1$

$-2j$

$-3j$

(a)

j-axis

$9j$
$8j$
B'' G'' D''
$6j$
$4j$
$2j$

E'' A''

-8 -6 -4 -2 0 2 4 6 8 10

$-2j$
$-4j$
C''
$-6j$
H'' F''
$-8j$

(b) $w = z^3 + z + 1$, for $|z| = 2$, and $w = z^3$.

Fig. 3

$|z| = 1$ and $|z| = 2$. In the latter case, notice how the points of the main curve in Figure 3(b) are related to points z^3 of the pecked circle. Start at $\theta = 0$ in each case, and work round the circle anticlockwise.

Example 7. Consider the existence of zeros of $z^3 + 10j$.

When $r = 0, 1, 2, 3$, the image curve passes completely round the origin 0, 0, 0, 3 times. Obviously this number depends upon r; we may call it the *order* of O with respect to P, and denote it, say, by $\phi(r)$. The point that has to be left a little vague at the moment, though it is intuitively 'obvious', is that if the image curve does not pass through the origin, ϕ is a *continuous* function—that is to say, a small change in r will only produce a small change in $\phi(r)$. In fact, $\phi(r)$ can only take integral values; therefore, since it starts at zero for $r = 0$, it must remain at zero if none of the image curves ever passes through O.

But in this case, clearly, the image curve passes through O when $r = \sqrt[3]{10}$, and there is a jump there in the value of $\phi(r)$ (of what size?). It is instructive to imagine the image curve being displayed on a television screen, and being expanded continuously as r varies from, say, 0 to 4. The picture would be of an expanding circle, in each case described three times, and $\phi(r)$ would increase from 0 to 3—the degree of P.

Since $\phi(r)$ changes, there must be at least one zero of $z^3 + 10j$.

Example 8. Consider the existence of zeros of $z^3 + z + 1$.

Here again $r = 0 \Rightarrow \phi(r) = 0$, and this will be true for any polynomial P, provided $P(0) \neq 0$. We see from Figure 3(a) that $\phi(1) = 1$, and from Figure 3(b) that $\phi(2) = 3$. Again, it is instructive to try to imagine a television presentation of the image curve as r increases from 0 to 2; because $\phi(r)$ changes, this rather more complicated curve must pass through the origin at some stage of the process.

In both cases, $\phi(r)$ has taken a value which is also the degree of the equation, for sufficiently large r. This is also generally true, and we can prove it without actually drawing any graphs at all. For as r increases, the term z^3 becomes more and more important, just as x^3 does in the corresponding function over R. In fact, if in this case we consider the values of z^3 and of $z + 1$ separately, for each point of the circle $|z| = r$, we see that z^3 has modulus r^3, while $z + 1$ cannot have a modulus greater than $r + 1$. Figure 3(b) illustrates this well.

When r is large enough, the images $w = P(z)$ and $w = z^3$, for each value of z, will be relatively close to each other. There is certainly no danger that the line segment joining them can pass through O; indeed, $P(z)$ must lie outside the circle $|w| = r^3 - (r + 1)$. Confirm this by plotting a few points $w = z^3$ and $w = P(z)$ in Figure 3(b), where $|z| = 2$.

If we define the polynomial $P_k(z)$ as $z^3 + k(z + 1)$, so that $P_0(z) = z^3$ and $P_1(z) = P(z)$, we can see that as k decreases from 1 to 0 the curve will be *continuously deformed* from the original image curve into a circle described three times. (In fact, in this deformation, each point moves on a line segment.) Again, it is quite easy to imagine this process on a television screen; it is interesting to draw the line segments along which, say, the lettered points move in Figure 3(*b*). This should bring out both the idea of a continuous deformation and of the relative closeness of the curve to the dotted circle.

We are now ready for a sketch of the general proof. We take the hypothesis that the equation has *no* root, and that therefore none of the image curves passes through O. Since ϕ is a continuous function, but can only take integral values, $\phi(r) = \phi(0) = 0$ for all values of r. But we know that the set of points $\{w: w = P(z)$, where $|z| = r\}$ can be deformed into the set of points $\{w: w = z^n$, where $|z| = r\}$ without passing through the origin, if r is large enough. The order of O with respect to P is therefore the same as its order with respect to z^n; and since the latter has an image curve which is simply a circle described n times, $\phi(r) = n$ for large r. This contradicts the previous conclusion that $\phi(r) = 0$ for all r, and shows that the hypothesis was false. The equation therefore has a root.

3.2 Consequences of the fundamental theorem. Apart from the result already stated, that $P(z) = 0$ has in fact not just one root, but n roots (*m*-fold roots being counted m times), there is another conclusion that may be drawn. That is, that the complex number system is in an important sense final. When we were considering the solutions of quadratic equations over the real field, we had to extend the real number system into the complex number system, to ensure that we could say that every quadratic equation had just two roots. It might reasonably have been supposed that this was only the first of a number of such extensions which might become necessary as the generality of the equations to be considered increased. Indeed, it would not have been surprising if $\sqrt{j}$, for example, had not been a member of the complex field. To complete the system, then, we should have wanted to adjoin to it all numbers of this type as well. However, although we have progressed from degree 2 to degree n, and from the real field to the complex field, with all the possibilities of extra complication that these changes involve, it has turned out that to solve all polynomials of every degree over the complex field we need no more than the complex numbers. No further extension is necessary; there are no loose ends to tie up, and our search for numbers to solve polynomial equations does indeed end here.

Exercise C

1. Draw the circle $|z| = 2$, and pencil in the radii at intervals of $10°$, on graph paper. Draw axes for the w-plane on tracing paper, and draw the image curve $w = z^3$. Mark the points corresponding to the ends of the radii in the z-plane.

Now draw the image curve $w = z^3 + 1$ of $|z| = 2$, again marking the points corresponding to the ends of the radii in the z-plane.

By placing the tracing paper over the circle in the z-plane, plot the points of the w-plane which are the images of the marked points of $|z| = 2$ under the function $z \to z^3 + z + 1$, and sketch the image curve.

In Questions 2–7, plot the images in the w-plane of the circles $|z| = 0, 1, 2$ under the given functions; in each case, use the values of $\phi(0)$, $\phi(1)$, $\phi(2)$ to estimate very roughly where the zeros lie.

2. $z \to z^2 + 1$.

3. $z \to z^3 + 3 + 4j$.

4. $z \to (z-1)^2$.

5. $z \to (z-j)^3$.

6. $z \to z^3 - 3z + 1$.

7. $z \to z^4 + z^2 + 1$.

4. POLYNOMIALS OVER THE REAL FIELD

The case of polynomials over the real field is a good deal less simple than the case of polynomials over the complex field, as even our experience of quadratic equations suggests. Of course, when the coefficients are real, there will still be n complex roots, since $R \subset C$; we shall therefore continue to work in the complex field, but with special reference to the number and position of the real roots of a real polynomial equation.

4.1   Conjugate complex pairs. If one of the roots of a real quadratic equation is $a + bj$, where $b \neq 0$, we already know that the other is $a - bj$. We can see that this is true by thinking of the method of solution; for we finally reduce the equation to the form

$$(x - a)^2 = c.$$

If c is negative, and therefore equal, say, to $-b^2$, it follows at once that the solutions are $a \pm bj$. It is also useful to confirm that the sum and product of these roots are both real—compare Exercise B, Question 7.

But there is a better reason for the fact than this. For if we replace j everywhere by $-j$, and so replace every complex number z by its conjugate $\bar{z}$, we find that a polynomial P with *real* coefficients is unchanged. But since

$$\bar{z}_1 + \bar{z}_2 = \overline{(z_1 + z_2)}$$

and

$$\bar{z}_1 . \bar{z}_2 = \overline{(z_1 z_2)}$$

it follows that

$$P(\bar{z}) = \overline{P(z)}$$

and therefore that

$$P(z) = 0 \;\Leftrightarrow\; P(\bar{z}) = 0.$$

We can express the reason shortly by saying that $a + bj \leftrightarrow a - bj$ is an isomorphism of C with itself (as addition and multiplication are preserved). The isomorphism can be represented, say in Figures 1 and 2, by a reflection in the real axis. Under the isomorphism, the coefficients of P and the number 0 (since they are all real numbers) are unchanged; therefore

$$P(z) = 0 \Leftrightarrow \overline{P(z)} = 0 \Leftrightarrow P(\bar{z}) = 0.$$

Roots of the equation which are not real numbers therefore occur in complex conjugate pairs; and what was true for the quadratic turns out to be true for all polynomials with real coefficients.

4.2 Irreducible polynomials over the real field. If $a - bj$ and $a + bj$, then, are (distinct) roots of a polynomial equation with real coefficients, $(z - a + bj)$ and $(z - a - bj)$ are factors of the polynomial over the complex field. Their product, however, is the quadratic polynomial

$$(z^2 - 2az + a^2 + b^2),$$

which has real coefficients and is irreducible over the real field.

Since the previous section shows that complex roots of such equations always occur in conjugate pairs, it follows that all the factors of the polynomial can be combined together into real linear or quadratic factors. We sum up by saying

> Every polynomial with real coefficients can be expressed as a product of real linear or quadratic factors;

or

> The only irreducible polynomials over the real field are linear or quadratic.

4.3 Roots of real polynomial equations. This proves an important result about real polynomial equations. The number of real roots must have the same *parity* as the degree of the polynomial. Thus, an equation of even degree has an even number of real roots, and an equation of odd degree an odd number—and therefore at least one.

If we look at the graphs of some typical polynomials, as in Figure 4, we can see the truth of this at once. For if P is of odd degree large positive and large negative values of x make $P(x)$ take opposite signs, and the graph must cross the axis an odd number of times (since it is essentially continuous). Similarly, if P is of even degree, the graph must cross the axis an even number of times.

Figures 4(a) and (b) show typical graphs of cubics, and 4(c) and 4(d) of quartics. Notice that no amount of translation, reflection in the axes, or stretching can alter the parity of the number of roots, provided that multiple roots are suitably allowed for.

For this purpose, of course, an m-fold root must be counted m times; Figure 5(a) shows a typical case of a two-fold root, and 5(b) of a three-fold root.

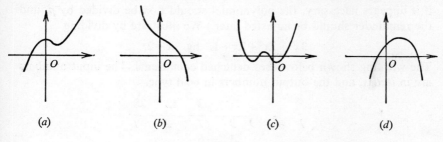

(a)   *(b)*   *(c)*   *(d)*

Fig. 4

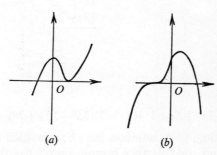

(a)   *(b)*

Fig. 5

Exercise D

Reduce the given polynomials to their simplest real factors, and sketch the graphs of the corresponding functions. (Note the positions of maxima and minima.)

1. $x^3 - 3x$.

2. $x^3 + x$.

3. $x^3 + 1$.

4. $x^3 - x^2$.

5. $x^3 - 3x^2 + 3x - 1$.

6. $x^4 - 3x^2 + 2$.

7. $x^4 + 3x^3 - x^2 - 3x$.

8. $x^4 + x^2 - 2$.

9. $x^4 + 16$.

10. $x^4 + x^3$.

11. $x^4 - 2x^2 + 1$.

12. $x^5 - x$.

13. $x^4 - 5x^3 + 9x^2 - 7x + 2$.

14. $x^5 - 4x^3$.

5. SYNTHETIC DIVISION

(The reader is advised to work Questions 11–13 on p. 80 of *Advanced Mathematics, Book* 1, before reading this section.)

5.1 It is convenient at this stage to revise the methods of division used on p. 65 and programmed on p. 863 for dividing by a linear factor $(x - a)$. (It is usually preferable not to divide by a factor $(px - q)$, unless $p = 1$;

if it appears necessary, the polynomial should first be divided by p, and the remainder should be adjusted later.) We illustrate by dividing

$$3x^3 + 7x^2 + 2x + 1 \quad \text{by} \quad x - 2.$$

The working shown below uses detached coefficients. The input numbers are in *italics*, and the output numbers in **bold** type.

$$
\begin{array}{r}
\mathbf{3} \quad \mathbf{13} \quad \mathbf{28} \\
\textit{1} \quad -\textit{2} \;)\; \textit{3} \quad \textit{7} \quad \textit{2} \quad \textit{1} \\
\mathbf{3} \quad -6 \\
\hline
13 \quad 2 \\
\mathbf{13} \quad -26 \\
\hline
28 \quad 1 \\
\mathbf{28} \quad -56 \\
\hline
57
\end{array}
$$

This shows that

$$3x^3 + 7x^2 + 2x + 1 = (x-2)(3x^2 - 13x + 28) + 57.$$

But in this working, some numbers have been written three times. If we omit all duplications, we can write it more simply like this:

$$
\begin{array}{r}
\textit{1} \quad -\textit{2} \;)\; \textit{3} \quad \textit{7} \quad \textit{2} \quad \textit{1} \\
-6 \\
\hline
13 \\
-26 \\
\hline
28 \\
-56 \\
\hline
57
\end{array}
$$

or more compactly still:

$$
\begin{array}{r}
\textit{1} \quad -\textit{2} \;)\; \textit{3} \quad \textit{7} \quad \textit{2} \quad \textit{1} \\
-6 \quad -26 \quad -56 \\
\hline
\mathbf{3} \quad \mathbf{13} \quad \mathbf{28} \quad \mathbf{57}
\end{array}
$$

If we examine the process, we can see that it works like this:

take *3*	**3**
multiply by -2	-6
subtract from 7	**13**
multiply by -2	-26
subtract from 2	**28**
multiply by -2	-56
subtract from *1*	**57**

This is very like the flow diagram of p. 67, formalized on p. 70, applied to the task of evaluating $P(2)$. Indeed, if instead of writing

$$\text{multiply by } -2$$
$$\text{subtract from } \ldots$$

we write

$$\text{multiply by } 2$$
$$\text{add to } \ldots$$

we can see that it is exactly the same process, and leads to the same working. We therefore finally prefer to write

$$
\begin{array}{c|cccc}
(x-2): & 3 & 7 & 2 & 1 \\
       &   & 6 & 26 & 56 \\
\hline
       & 3 & 13 & 28 & 57 \\
\end{array}
$$

The reader should now work Exercise E, Question 1 (a)–(d).

5.2   Repeated division by $x-a$. If we repeat the process as often as we can, we have the following working:

$$
\begin{array}{c|cccc}
(x-2): & 3 & 7 & 2 & 1 \\
       &   & 6 & 26 & 56 \\
\hline
       & 3 & 13 & 28 & 57 \\
       &   & 6 & 38 &   \\
\hline
       & 3 & 19 & 66 &   \\
       &   & 6 &   &   \\
\hline
       & 3 & 25 &   &   \\
\end{array}
$$

This tells us that

$$3x^3 + 7x^2 + 2x + 1 = 3(x-2)^3 + 25(x-2)^2 + 66(x-2) + 57.$$

If we write $T(x) = 3x^3 + 25x^2 + 66x + 57$, we can see at once that the graph of $y = P(x)$ is simply the graph of $y = T(x)$, translated through $\binom{2}{0}$. Clearly, if we consider the graph of $y = T(x)$, the numbers 57 and 66 have a special significance; they are $T(0)$ and $T'(0)$, the intercept on the y-axis and the gradient at $x = 0$, on the curve. It follows that $P(2) = 57$ (as we knew previously); but it also follows that $P'(2) = T'(0) = 66$, and if $Q(x)$ is the first quotient, $Q(2) = P'(2)$ is the gradient of the original curve at $x = 2$.

Example 9. Divide $x^4 - 4x^3 + 3x^2 + 4x - 4$ repeatedly by $x - 2$, and comment on the result.

$$
\begin{array}{r|rrrrr}
(x-2): & 1 & -4 & 3 & 4 & -4 \\
       &   & 2 & -4 & -2 & 4 \\
\hline
       & 1 & -2 & -1 & 2 & \ \ 0 \\
       &   & 2 & 0 & -2 & \\
\hline
       & 1 & 0 & -1 & \ \ 0 & \\
       &   & 2 & 4 & & \\
\hline
       & 1 & 2 & \ \ 3 & & \\
       &   & 2 & & & \\
\hline
       & 1 & \ \ 4 & & &
\end{array}
$$

This shows that
$$P(x) = (x-2)^4 + 4(x-2)^3 + 3(x-2)^2.$$

Thus, (a) 2 is a double zero of P,

(b) $P(2) = P'(2) = 0.$

Here we can see that if a is a repeated zero of P, then of course $Q(a) = 0$; it therefore follows that $P'(a) = 0$ also.

5.3 Two general results. The results of Section 5.2 are generally true, and can be formulated as follows:

(a) If Q is the quotient when P is divided by $x-a$, $Q(a) = P'(a)$. For

$$P(x) = (x-a) \cdot Q(x) + r \ \Rightarrow \ P'(x) = (x-a) \cdot Q'(x) + Q(x)$$

(using the product rule)

$$\Rightarrow P'(a) = Q(a).$$

In particular, this is true when a is a zero of P, but the general result confirms the remark in Section 5.2.

(b) If a is a repeated zero of P, then $P'(a) = 0$.
For $x-a$ divides Q, so that $Q(a) = 0$; and then, by result (a), $P'(a) = 0$. It is also easy to prove by induction that if a is an m-fold zero of P, then

$$P^{(i)}(a) = 0 \quad \text{for} \quad i = 1, 2, \ldots, m-1.$$

5.4   Unique factorization. We know that (working with polynomials throughout)
$$P(a) = 0 \;\Rightarrow\; P(z) = (z-a).Q(z), \quad \text{for some } Q;$$

if $z-b$ is a factor of P distinct from $z-a$, does it follow that

$$P(z) = (z-a).(z-b).R(z), \quad \text{for some } R?$$

This corresponds closely to the prime factorization of integers. The need for the theorem is indicated by the fact that if we take factors of integers which are not prime, the result is false; for although 4 and 6 are distinct factors of 12, there is no integer k such that $4.6.k = 12$.

The factor theorem does show easily that the result is correct.

Proof.
$$P(z) = (z-a).Q(z), \quad \text{by hypothesis,}$$

and
$$P(b) = 0, \quad \text{since } z-b \text{ is a factor of } P,$$

$$\Rightarrow (b-a).Q(b) = 0$$

$$\Rightarrow Q(b) = 0, \quad \text{since } b \neq a,$$

$$\Rightarrow Q(z) = (z-b).R(z), \quad \text{for some polynomial } R,$$

$$\Rightarrow P(z) = (z-a).(z-b).R(z).$$

This can be extended immediately to any number of factors; thus,

$$P(a_1) = P(a_2) = \ldots = P(a_n) = 0$$

$$\Rightarrow P(z) = (z-a_1).(z-a_2)\ldots\ldots(z-a_n).Q(z),$$

and, if P is of degree n, with n distinct zeros, Q must be a mere constant. Thus, apart from constant multiples, the factorization of P is unique.

Exercise E

1. Use the method of synthetic division to obtain the quotient and remainder when the first named polynomial is divided by the second:

(a) $2z^2 - 4z + 7$, $z+3$;   (b) $2z^2 - 4z + 7$, $z-3$;

(c) $2z^3 - 4z + 7$, $z-3$;   (d) $z^3 - z$, $z-2$;

(e) $z^2 + \sqrt{2}z - 4$, $z + \sqrt{2}$;   (f) $az^2 + bz + c$, $mz + n$;

(g) $4z^3 - 3z - 2$, $z - j$;   (h) $z^5 - 1$, $z - 1$;

(i) $2z^3 - 4z + 7$, $3z + 5$;   (j) $ax^4 + bx^3 + cx^2 + dx + e$, $x - k$;

(k) $z^4 - 7z + 5$, $z - 3 + 2j$;   (l) $z^4 + 4$, $z - 1 - j$.

2. Divide $x^4 - 6x^3 + 11x^2 - 6x$ repeatedly by $x-1$. Explain your result in terms of the graph of $y = P(x)$. What are $P(1)$, $P'(1)$, $P''(1)$, $P'''(1)$?

21-2

3. Find $P(a)$ and $P'(a)$ in each of the following cases:

(a) $x^3 - 3x + 1$; $a = 2$;
(b) $x^3 - 7x + 7$; $a = -3$;
(c) $x^3 - 6x^2 + 12x - 8$; $a = 2$;
(d) $2x^3 + 2x^2 + 8x + 7$; $a = -1$;
(e) $x^3 - 3x^2 - 3x + 1$; $a = 3$;
(f) $x^3 + 5x^2 + 8x + 4$; $a = -2$.

*4. Write a flow diagram to compute the first n successive derivatives of

$$P(x) = \sum_{i=0}^{i=n} a_i x^i \quad \text{at} \quad x = p.$$

*5. (Lagrange's Interpolation Formula.) It is required to find a cubic polynomial function under which the images of a_0, a_1, a_2, a_3 are b_0, b_1, b_2, b_3. Carry out the following procedure for $a_i = i$ and chosen numerical values of b_i, and show that it will always work.
Define

$$P(x) = (x - a_1).(x - a_2).(x - a_3).(x - a_0).$$

Define $Q_i(x)$ as the quotient when P is divided by $x - a_i$. Then the required function is

$$\sum_{i=0}^{i=3} (b_i . Q_i(x)/Q_i(a_i)).$$

*6. Consider the form $(x + 2)^2$ over the integers modulo 4, and explain where the proof of Section 5.4 breaks down if the set of numbers over which the form is defined is not an integral domain.

*7. For each value of x, in the system of integers modulo 3, $x.(x + 1).(x + 2) = 0$, and yet the system is an integral domain. Explain the apparent contradiction of the unique factorization theorem. (Distinguish between a form and a function.)

6. SOLUTION OF POLYNOMIAL EQUATIONS

If it is not possible to find a rational root of a polynomial equation by inspection, we must fall back on an approximation such as the Newton–Raphson method, which applies to any equation of the form $f(x) = 0$. It depends upon the fact that if a is an approximation to a root of $f(x) = 0$, then

$$a - \frac{f(a)}{f'(a)}$$

is in general a better approximation to that root.

In the method developed in Section 5, we calculated not only $P(a)$, but also $P'(a) (= Q(a))$, by synthetic division. Example 10 shows how the work may be laid out.

The most frequent error is to treat $P(a)$ as if it were another coefficient, taking the work one step too far. Beware of this.

1060

Example 10. Find the real root of the equation $3x^3+7x^2+2x+1 = 0$.
We start by calculating $P(-2)$ and $P'(-2)$. The working is:

$a = -2$:	3	7	2	1	
		-6	-2	0	
	3	1	0	$\boxed{+1}$	Correction:
		-6	10		$-1/10 = -0.1$
	3	-5	$\boxed{10}$		

$a = -2.1$:	3	7	2	1	
		-6.3	-1.47	-1.113	
	3	0.7	0.53	$\boxed{-0.113}$	Correction:
		-6.3	11.76		$+0.113/12.29$
	3	-5.6	$\boxed{+12.29}$		$\simeq +0.0091$

$a = -2.0909$:	3	7	2	1	
		-6.2727	-1.5207	-1.0022	
	3	0.7273	0.4793	$\boxed{-0.0022}$	Correction:
		-6.2727	11.6101		$+0.0022/12.0883$
	3	-5.5532	$\boxed{12.0883}$		$\simeq +0.0002$

$a = -2.0907$:	3	7	2	1	
		-6.2721	-1.5218	-0.9998	Answer:
	3	0.7279	0.4782	$\boxed{+0.0002}$	-2.0907

The working speaks for itself. In each case we calculate $P(a)$ and $P'(a)$, except that in the last case it is unnecessary to perform the second division.

The numbers 3, 0.7279, 0.4782 have a special significance in the problem as a whole. For they are the coefficients of the quadratic which is left when the factor $(x+2.0907)$ is removed from the original equation, and would form the starting point of the calculations which lead to the next root. In this case, however, '$b^2 < 4ac$', and the only real root is -2.0907, to five significant figures.

6.1 Comments on the method of solution. This elegant process not only applies the Newton–Raphson method quickly and efficiently, but it also provides an iterative method very suitable for computer programming, and indeed displays the coefficients of the reduced equation to be solved when the first root has been located.

The remaining problem is to find a suitable first approximation. For a computer program, it is usually sufficient to start with $a = 0$, and it is interesting to start there occasionally with hand calculations, to see how long it takes to converge. Difficulties will sometimes arise because $P'(a)$ is too small, or for one or two other possible reasons; but it is not difficult to avoid these problems when the calculations are done by hand.

If a more accurate starting point is required, it will usually be enough to evaluate $P(x)$ for a few small integers, positive and negative, and to find a and b such that $P(a)$ and $P(b)$ have opposite signs. A linear interpolation will often give us a good idea of the first decimal place; thus, in Example 10 we should find that $P(-2) = +1$, $P(-3) = -11$, which suggests starting at $-2{\cdot}1$.

If even this is not enough, it will be necessary to consider the zeros of P'. A polynomial of odd degree will have at least one real root; and a polynomial of even degree, therefore, at least one maximum or minimum. The values of $P(x)$ at maxima and minima will indicate possible positions of roots by their changes of sign.

6.2 Checks for the solutions. To check the solutions we study the *symmetric functions* of the roots (see Exercise B, Question 7 for the notation). It will be recalled that if α, β are the roots of the quadratic

$$ax^2+bx+c = 0,$$

the polynomials
$$ax^2+bx+c \quad \text{and} \quad a(x-\alpha).(x-\beta)$$

are identical, so that
$$\alpha+\beta = -b/a \quad \text{and} \quad \alpha\beta = c/a.$$

Similarly, for polynomials of a higher degree, the sum of the roots will still be equal to $-b/a$, and the product to $\pm k/a$, where k is the constant term. Thus, if α, β, γ, δ, ϵ are the roots of the fifth degree polynomial

$$ax^5+bx^4+cx^3+dx^2+ex+f,$$

then
$$a.(x-\alpha).(x-\beta).(x-\gamma).(x-\delta).(x-\epsilon)$$

is the identical polynomial, and

$$\Sigma\alpha = -b/a, \qquad \Sigma\alpha\beta = +c/a,$$

$$\Sigma\alpha\beta\gamma = -d/a, \qquad \Sigma\alpha\beta\gamma\delta = +e/a,$$

$$\alpha\beta\gamma\delta\epsilon = -f/a.$$

One or more of these equations may be used as a check on the accuracy of the solutions of the original equation; indeed, it is often useful to use the product of the roots to calculate the last root to be found and their sum to check the solutions.

Exercise F

(The use of a desk calculator is a great help in this exercise. It is often wiser to solve $P(-x) = 0$, rather than $P(x) = 0$, if negative roots are required; and it is always wise to check any transfer of numbers from one register to another, or to or from a paper store. Checks based on Section 6.2 should be used as a matter of routine.)

1. Use the method of Section 6 to solve the equation $x^2 - 2 = 0$, to five significant figures.

2. Solve the equation $x^2 - 3x + 1 \cdot 75 = 0$ by this method, and check that the sum of the roots is 3 and their product $1 \cdot 75$.

3. Find consecutive integers between which any roots of the following equations must lie:

(a) $x^2 - 5 \cdot 92x + 7 \cdot 51 = 0$;   (b) $1 \cdot 1x^3 - 2 \cdot 3x - 4 \cdot 9 = 0$;
(c) $x^3 + 2x^2 + x + 3 = 0$;   (d) $x^3 - 4x^2 - x + 5 = 0$;
(e) $x^4 - 5x^2 + 4 \cdot 25 = 0$;   (f) $4x^3 + x^2 + 12x - 4 = 0$.

4. Take the line through $(a, P(a))$ and $(b, P(b))$ as an approximation to the polynomial function, and use it to find a first approximation to the root of $P(x) = 0$ which lies between a and b:

(a) $x^3 - 7x + 7 = 0$, $a = -4$, $b = -3$;
(b) $x^3 - 3x + 1 = 0$, $a = 1 \cdot 5$, $b = 2$;
(c) $3x^3 + 2x^2 + 8x + 7 = 0$, $a = 0$, $b = -1$.

5. Multiply out the product of five factors in Section 6.2, and confirm the values given for the symmetric functions.

Verify that when $\alpha = \cos 2\pi/5 + j \sin 2\pi/5$, the roots of $x^5 = 1$ are 1, α, α^2, α^3, α^4, and that the symmetric functions have the correct values.

*6. Identify the group of substitutions under which the symmetric functions on five roots remain invariant.

7. Express $(\alpha - \beta)^2$ in terms of $\alpha + \beta$ and $\alpha\beta$ and hence solve (to three significant figures, for irrational roots):

(a) $2x^2 + 6x + 5 = 0$;   (b) $3x^2 - 7x + 4 = 0$;
(c) $x^2 - 5x - 14 = 0$;   (d) $4x^2 - 12x + 7 = 0$.

8. Find to four significant figures the roots of $x^2 - 3x - 0 \cdot 002 = 0$.

Questions 9 and 10 should be treated as group projects.

9. Obtain the root between 0 and 1 and the root between 3 and 4 of the equation

$$x^3 - 3x^2 - 3x + 1 = 0,$$

correct to five significant figures, and check by solving the quadratic formed when the factor $(x + 1)$ is removed.

1063

10. Find, correct to four significant figures, the real roots of the following equations, and check your solutions:

(a) $x^3 - 3x + 1 = 0$;   (b) $x^3 - 7x + 7 = 0$;

(c) $2x^3 + 2x^2 + 8x + 7 = 0$;   (d) $x^3 - 4x - 1 = 0$;

(e) $x^3 + 2x^2 + 1 = 0$;   (f) $x^4 - 3x^2 - 4x - 3 = 0$.

11. Write a flow diagram to compute all the real roots of a cubic equation, to a prescribed standard of accuracy.

12. Examine the effect on the symmetric functions of (a) increasing the roots of an equation by $-k$, (b) multiplying the roots of an equation by 10, and solve Question 10(a) by repeatedly applying this process.

13. Show how squaring the roots of an equation can be effected by combining the symmetric functions together suitably, and find the largest root of Question 10(a) by applying the process repeatedly.

*14. How could you adapt the process of Question 12 to take advantage of the binary scale in which many computers work? Find $\sqrt{2}$ to within 0·001 by this method, but add (or subtract) to avoid multiplying.

SUMMARY

Any polynomial P can be expressed in the form $P(z) = (z-a) \cdot Q(z) + r$ where Q is a polynomial of lower degree, for any a.

If $P = A \cdot Q$, A and Q are factors of P, and P is reducible.

$P(b/a) = 0 \Leftrightarrow (az - b)$ is a factor of P.

A polynomial of degree n over C has just n zeros, counting m-fold zeros m times (the fundamental theorem of algebra).

In polynomial equations with real coefficients, complex roots occur in conjugate pairs, so that the only real polynomials irreducible over the reals are linear and quadratic.

If $P(z) = (z-a) \cdot Q(z)$, $P'(a) = Q(a)$; in particular, if a is a repeated zero of P, it is also a zero of P'.

The Newton–Raphson method may be applied to solve $P(z) = 0$ by using synthetic division by $(x-a)$ to find the correction $-P(a)/P'(a)$.

Solutions may be checked thus: if α, β, γ are roots of

$$az^3 + bz^2 + cz + d = 0$$

then $\qquad \Sigma \alpha = -b/a; \quad \Sigma \alpha\beta = +c/a; \quad \alpha\beta\gamma = -d/a;$

and similarly for equations of higher degree.

1064

REVISION EXERCISES

32. RELATIVE MOTION

1. At 06.00 a ship is 8 n.m south of a lighthouse L. Her speed is 10 knots in still water, but there is a current flowing at 3 knots in the direction N 30° E. The ship wishes to pass 10 n.m due east of L. Find the course to be set, and the time when L is closest.

2. A ship A with speed 10 knots sights a ship B 10 miles to the south, sailing on a course of 100°. B's speed is 15 knots; how close can A approach B, and how long will it take her to the point of closest range?

3. A rod AB, 10 cm long, is constrained to move so that its ends slide in two perpendicular grooves. Suppose that A moves on the x-axis, and B on the y-axis. The rod rotates with constant angular velocity relative to these axes, making 1 revolution in 5 seconds.

  (*a*) Find the velocities of A and B when A is 6 cm from the origin.

  (*b*) Describe the motion of the centre of the rod.

  (*c*) Where is the instantaneous centre in a general position?

  (*d*) If the origin and the rod's centre are fixed, but the grooves are cut in a circular plate which is free to turn about the origin, can the rod be used to drive the plate, and if so, what will the gear ratio be?

4. Suppose the earth were a sphere of radius 6.4×10^6 m. Then it would attract bodies near its surface to its centre with an absolute acceleration of 9.8 m/s². What would be the acceleration (relative to the earth) of a freely falling body in latitude 50°? (This is of course the *observed* value of g.)

  If the earth were covered with calm water, its surface would be at right-angles to this relative acceleration. Sketch the form it would take. (In fact the earth itself approximates to this form.)

5. Two gear-wheels A and B of radii 3 cm and 5 cm are mounted on the same axle; the outer one has internal teeth. A triangular frame C carries three pinions, each 2 cm in diameter, meshing with the gear-wheels (see Figure 1, p. 1066).

  (*a*) If A is fixed, and C rotates at 30 rev/min, what will be the angular velocity of B?

  (*b*) If C is fixed, and B rotates at 30 rev/min, what will be the angular velocity of A?

  (*c*) Write down two equations connecting

  (i) ω_A, ω_B, and ω_C;

  (ii) ω_A, ω_B, and ω, where ω_A, ω_B, ω_C and ω are the angular velocities of A, B, C and of the pinions relative to the frame C. Find the angular velocity of the pinions relative to the fixed gear A in case (*a*).

6. The velocity of a car of a fairground 'octopus' at the highest point of its path is 5 m/s horizontally. At this moment it is

  (*a*) travelling in a horizontal circular path of radius 4 m;

  (*b*) describing a vertical sine curve whose radius of curvature at this point is 2.5 m vertically downwards;

  (*c*) being retarded in the direction of motion at 0.7 m/s².

What is the acceleration of the car?

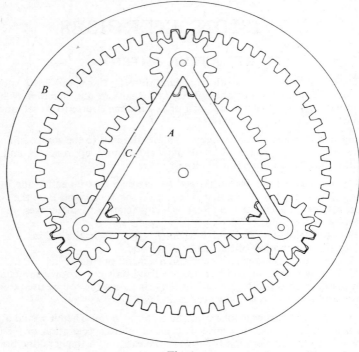

Fig. 1

33. MOMENTUM

1. A ball is thrown vertically downwards so as to strike a horizontal floor with velocity $10\sqrt{6}$ m/s. It rebounds and strikes a horizontal ceiling 5 m above the floor. Find the speed with which it again hits the floor, given that the coefficient of restitution for each impact is 0·7. Will it hit the ceiling again?

2. A shell moving horizontally at 300 m/s explodes into two parts, one of which is three times as massive as the other. They are then observed to move in the same vertical plane as before, the more massive part at 25° below the horizontal, and the lighter part at 25° above the horizontal. Find their speeds, and the direction of the explosive impulse.

3. A rocket ejects matter at a speed of 500 m/s, discharging 500 g in 4 seconds. Find the thrust produced.

   The mass of the rocket is 5 kg, and the fuel takes up 20 % of this. Show that the rocket begins to rise immediately on ignition, and find its velocity at burn-out if it rises vertically.

4. A jet of water 1 cm in diameter and moving at 10 m/s impinges tangentially on the buckets of a Pelton wheel and has its relative velocity reversed. If the buckets are 60 cm from the axle of the wheel, find the thrust of the jet:

   (*a*) when the wheel is at rest;
   (*b*) when it is rotating at 1·25 rad/s.

5. A line of pennies rests on a smooth table, each penny touching its neighbours. A single penny, moving along the direction of the line at 10 cm/s, strikes an end penny. Explain what is observed to happen.

If the experiment is conducted with two striking pennies, two pennies usually are seen to detach themselves from the line. Can you give an explanation of this?

If there are 10 pennies originally in the line, and the last penny moves off at 5 cm/s,

   (*a*) explain what has happened to the conservation of momentum;

   (*b*) give an estimate of the coefficient of restitution.

6. A machine gun of mass M contains shot of total mass M'. The shot is fired with muzzle velocity u (relative to the gun) which can be taken to be horizontal. The gun rests on rough ground with coefficient of friction μ. Show that the velocity of recoil when all the shot is fired is approximately $u(r - r^2/2) - \mu g t$, where r is the ratio M'/M, and t is the time it takes to fire the shot.

34. COMPLEX NUMBERS

1. If I, J, K are the complex matrices

$$\begin{pmatrix} 0 & 1 \\ -1 & 0 \end{pmatrix}, \quad \begin{pmatrix} 0 & j \\ j & 0 \end{pmatrix}, \quad \begin{pmatrix} j & 0 \\ 0 & -j \end{pmatrix}$$

respectively, prove that

$$\mathbf{I}^2 = \mathbf{J}^2 = \mathbf{K}^2 = -1; \quad \mathbf{IJ} = -\mathbf{JI} = \mathbf{K},$$
$$\mathbf{JK} = -\mathbf{KJ} = \mathbf{I}, \quad \mathbf{KI} = -\mathbf{IK} = \mathbf{J}.$$

A group of matrices is to be generated by I and J. What is the order of this group? List its elements.

2. Given that $2 + j$ is a root of a quadratic equation with real coefficients, what must the other root be? What is the square of the difference of the roots? Find the quadratic equation whose roots have a sum of 6 and a squared difference equal to -5.

3. Show that the two numbers $(-1 + j\sqrt{3})/2$ and $(-1 - j\sqrt{3})/2$ are such that each is the square of the other. Are there any other complex numbers with this property?

Find all the roots of $z^6 = 1$ in this form.

4. Find integers a, b such that $(a + jb)^2 = 9 + 40j$. By using $|z^2| = |z|^2$, show that

$$(a^2 + b^2)^2 = (a^2 - b^2)^2 + (2ab)^2.$$

Obtain a similar algebraic identity by expressing the modulus of the product $(a + jb)(c + jd)$ in two ways.

Express 65×41 as the sum of two squares of integers in as many ways as possible.

5. Sketch the locus of the point represented in the complex number plane by z, given that $|z + 4| = 2|z + 1|$.

Show algebraically that this is the same as the locus given by $|z| = 2$.

6. Find the image under the mapping $z \rightarrow 6/z$ of the circles

   (*a*) $|z - 2| = 3$;   (*b*) $|z - 2| = 2$;   (*c*) $|z - j| = 5$.

35. POLYNOMIAL EQUATIONS

1. Find cubic equations whose roots are

$$(a)\ 2, 3-j, 3+j; \qquad (b)\ -3, 1-j, -1+j.$$

In what sense are your solutions unique?

2. Express the following polynomials as the product of irreducible polynomials: (i) over the integers, (ii) over the real numbers, (iii) over the complex numbers:

(a) $x^3 + 2x^2 + 2x + 4$; (b) $2x^3 - x^2 + 9$;

(c) $x^4 + 2x^2 - 8$; (d) $8 + x^3$.

3. Show that a general polynomial of the second degree can be written in the form

$$A(x-b)(x-c) + B(x-c)(x-a) + C(x-a)(x-b),$$

where a, b, c are any given unequal real numbers.

Use this to find the quadratic polynomial Q for which

$$Q(1) = -4, \qquad Q(-1) = -8, \quad \text{and} \quad Q(3) = 16.$$

Extend the method to find a cubic polynomial P for which

$$P(-2) = -4, \quad P(-1) = 6, \quad P(1) = 18, \quad \text{and} \quad P(2) = 3.$$

4. (a) Prove that if $a+bj$ is a zero of a polynomial with real coefficients, then $a-bj$ is also a zero.

(b) Express $P(x) = 6x^4 - 13x^3 + 60x^2 - 6x - 20$ as the product of irreducible polynomials over the complex numbers, given that $P(1+3j) = 0$.

(c) What can you say about the zeros of a polynomial with real coefficients of degree $2n+1$?

5. Find, correct to three significant figures, the zeros of the quartic polynomial

$$P(x) = x^4 + 5x^3 + 4x^2 - 3x - 3.$$

Sketch the graph of $y = P(x)$.

6. Show that if $a^2 + a + 2 = 0$, then the equation whose roots are the squares of the roots of

$$x^3 + (a+1)x^2 + ax - 1 = 0$$

is the same equation. What must then the roots of this equation be?

APPENDICES TO BOOK 3:
PROGRAMMING LANGUAGES

APPENDIX 1. ALGOL

Algol is an internationally standardized language, with many advantages for school use. It is, however, usually written to be punched on paper tape, which makes access to a perforator and to some sort of print-out mechanism necessary. This equipment is expensive, and, besides, a single error will usually make it necessary to copy a whole program again—a lengthy and frustrating process, which can be avoided by the use of punched cards.

There are also minor variations from compiler to compiler, some of them depending upon the number of holes in the paper tape available; but the system described here can easily be adjusted by reference to the description of the compiler used in any particular computer.

1. *Programming symbols*

The symbols we shall use are:

(*a*) The letters of the alphabet (in *italic*);

(*b*) the digits from 0 to 9 inclusive; the decimal point · , and a special symbol $_{10}$, used so that, for example, $_{10}3$, $_{10}+3$, $_{10}-3$ mean 1000, 1000, and 0·001 respectively;

(*c*) the operations +, −, * (multiplication), / (division), and ↑ (raising to a power, so that, for example, $x \uparrow 2$ means x^2);

(*d*) the relations =, ≠, >, ⩾, <, ⩽;

(*e*) the punctuation marks , : ; ( ) [ ] ' ';

(*f*) the space (referred to as *Sp*) and *Newline* (which for some compilers must be written *Cr Lf*—for Carriage Return, Line Feed—especially when 5-hole tape is used).

The compiler uses *Sp* and *Newline* only to separate one word from another, and of course to determine the output layout; and although the general layout of the program is ignored, it is a great help to the human reader and writer of programs to use a clear layout. For this reason, basic words are printed in **bold** type (they are underlined in typewritten or manuscript programs), and a sensible convention of lines and spaces has been tacitly adopted.

Unfortunately, only 5-hole tape perforators will be available to most schools, and because only 32 tape symbols are possible there is usually also a *Letter shift* and a *Figure shift*, so that, for example, the same symbol may be used for *a* or for 1, according to which shift last occurred. Similarly, blank tape is sometimes needed for special purposes, and programs conventionally begin with *Newline* and end with *Newline* repeated three times. This does not affect the writing of programs, however, but only their preparation for the computer.

Compilers also have a wide variety of input and output conventions; here, we write '*a* := *read*'; and '*print(x)*', and '*printtext('error')*', though some modification would be needed for any actual compiler.

2. *Statements*

All Algol instructions are called *statements*, and they are separated from each other by the symbol ; instead of by the 'boxes' of the main text, which cannot be presented easily to the compiler. Thus, part of a program might read:

> **begin** $a := read$; $b := read$; $c := read$;
>
> $p := sqrt(b \uparrow 2 - 4*a*c)/a/2$;
>
> $x := b/a/2 + p$; $y := b/a/2 - p$;
>
> $print(x)$; $print(y)$;
>
> **end**;

Notice that highly complicated sequences of instructions can be compressed into single statements, which the compiler will be able to analyse systematically. For **begin** and **end**, see Section 3; for *sqrt(E)*, see Section 8.

The other symbols are interpreted according to the following rules:

(*a*) $\uparrow$ binds more tightly than any other operation;

(*b*) * and / bind more tightly than + and −, and are interpreted successively from left to right (so that $b/a/2$ means $(b/a)/2$, and so forth);

(*c*) + and − are the weakest bonds, and again are interpreted from left to right, according to the normal arithmetic convention.

3. *Basic words*

One of the most ingenious features of Algol is the large number of *basic words*. The compiler will regard each basic word as a single symbol, which enormously increases the number of abbreviations available.

(Some compilers have to go still further, and introduce basic words such as **gr** and **lesseq** (instead of > and ⩽), because their keyboards are too limited, and some use **read** and **print** as basic words; but this is a matter of local convention.)

begin and **end** are of particular importance. They are used as brackets, to bind together a sequence of statements into one *compound statement*. When this type of statement contains declarations as well (see Section 4), it is called a *block*; and it is another of the distinctive features of Algol that a program may be written in several separate blocks, by different people and with independently chosen names for the variables (*identifiers*), and fitted together with a minimum of fuss.

Other basic words are introduced as they are needed.

4. Declarations and blocks

It is necessary to warn the compiler how many stores of different types to reserve for each different purpose, and so every block must be headed by *declarations* of all the identifiers that are going to be used within it. The main distinction is between **real** and **integer**. Stores of the latter type hold only whole numbers, and hold them exactly; stores of the former type can hold any numbers (of a reasonable size), with a limited number of significant figures and the possibility of small errors affecting the last few binary places. It is best to use **integer** stores for counting, wherever possible, and to avoid them for all other purposes. Thus, even if the quadratic equations to be solved by the program above had integral coefficients, it would be better to write:

$$\textbf{begin real }\ a, b, c, x, y, p;$$
$$a := read; b := read; c := read;$$
$$p := sqrt(b \uparrow 2 - 4*a*c)/a/2;$$
$$x := b/a/2 + p; y := b/a/2 - p;$$
$$print(x); print(y);$$
$$\textbf{end};$$

Every program must itself be a block, but blocks may occur within blocks, to any depth; identifiers declared in any block retain their meaning throughout the block, unless they are re-declared in an inner block; but the beginner is advised not to re-declare, just as he would be wiser to use different identifiers in different blocks; for it would confuse him (though not the compiler) to use the same letter to identify one store when it is used in one block, and another when it is used in another block.

Two further declarations are, for example:

$$\textbf{integer array }\ a\,[1:4];$$

$$\textbf{real array }\ tensor\,[0:3,\ 0:3,\ 0:3];\dagger$$

The former reserves four integer stores, and the latter 64 real stores, referred to by the names $tensor\,[p, q, r]$, where p, q, r may be any integers between 0 and 3. One-dimensional arrays (vectors) and two-dimensional arrays (matrices) are, however, the most useful, and, provided that m and n have been assigned integer values (and declared as integer identifiers) in an outer block, may even be declared as

$$\textbf{real array }\ coeff\,[1:m,\ 1:n];$$

It is customary in Algol to give variables names (identifiers) which remind us of their nature, and almost any sequence of letters and numbers (beginning with a letter) may be used. Most compilers, however, ignore

† **real array** is preferred to the alternative **array**.

symbols after the sixth, and it is generally wise not to use basic words also as identifiers. Thus, we may use *count*, *sum*, *sumsq*, *term*, *x1*, *d2x*, *int*, and so forth, quite freely.

5. *Conditional statements*

The basic words **if, then, else** are used to give alternative courses of action. An instruction such as

$$\textbf{if} \quad p < 0 \quad \textbf{then} \quad p := -p;$$

will change the sign of p if p is negative, but will otherwise be ignored; and provision in the program above may be made for $(b^2 - 4ac)$ to be negative as follows:

> **begin real** a, b, c, *root1*, *root2*, p;
>
> $a := read; b := read; c := read;$
>
> **if** $b \uparrow 2 < 4*a*c$ **then** *printtext*('*error*') **else**
>
> **begin** $p := sqrt(b \uparrow 2 - 4*a*c)/a/2;$
>
> $root1 := b/a/2 + p; root2 := b/a/2 - p;$
>
> *print*(*root1*); *print*(*root2*);
>
> **end**;
>
> **end**;

Notice that **then** and **else** must be followed by *single* statements, which is why the second **begin** and **end** are necessary in this program (can you see what would happen if they were omitted?); and that **else** must never be preceded by a semi-colon.

Notice that a further condition would be needed to guard against the possibility that $a = 0$.

6. *Labels and jump instructions*

The basic word **goto** may also be used for jumps to statements marked by *labels*, as in this version of the Newton–Raphson process for extracting a square root:

> **begin real** x, y, z, *root*;
>
> $x := read; y := 1;$
>
> *repeat*: $z := y/2 - x/(2*y);$
>
> $root := y - z;$
>
> **if** $abs(z) < {}_{10}-8$ **then goto** *output*;
>
> $y := root;$
>
> **goto** *repeat*;
>
> *output*: *print*(*root*);
>
> **end**;

Notice that the labels (which may look like any other identifiers) are distinguished by the colon (:); and that some compilers will expect a declaration of labels used within the block, such as:

$$\textbf{switch } s := \textit{repeat, output};$$

7. Loops and **for** statements

By far the commonest form of jump instruction, however, is the **for** statement, which is available in three main forms:

$$\textbf{for } k := 1, 2, 5 \textbf{ do } \dots$$
$$\textbf{for } k := 1 \textbf{ step } 1 \textbf{ until } 20 \textbf{ do } \dots$$
$$\textbf{for } k := 1, 2*k \textbf{ while } k < 100 \textbf{ do } \dots$$

In these loops, k takes three, twenty, and seven values respectively; the loop is cycled that number of times, and at the end of the process k becomes undefined.

Useful variations are:

$$\textbf{for } k := m \textbf{ step } -1 \textbf{ until } n \textbf{ do } \dots$$
$$\textbf{for } k := 0 \textbf{ step } 0 \cdot 1 \textbf{ until } 1 \cdot 05 \textbf{ do } \dots$$

(notice the provision made for avoiding the effects of small rounding errors) and

$$\textbf{for } root := (y + x/y)/2 \textbf{ while } abs(root - y) > {}_{10} - 8 \textbf{ do } y := root;$$

which effectively replaces the whole program of Section 6 from *repeat*: to *output*: inclusive, except that since *root* is now undefined the last instruction must be *print(y)*;

The use of this device is well illustrated by a program to find the mean and standard deviation of a population of size n. The number n is placed first on the data tape, followed by the population members, in any order:

```
begin real x, sum, sumsq; integer m, n;
    n := read; sum := sumsq := 0;
    for m := 1 step 1 until n do
    begin x := read;
        sum := sum + x;
        sumsq := sumsq + x*x;
    end;
    print(sum/n); print(sqrt(sumsq/n - (sum/n) ↑ 2));
end;
```

Here the inner compound statement is executed n times in all, and, although here the value of m is not used for any other purpose, it is in fact available at all times during the **do** loop. Thus, to print out the binomial probabilities:

```
begin real a, b, pr; integer n, i;
    n := read; a := read;
    b := 1 − a; pr := b ↑ n;
    for i := 0 step 1 until n do
    begin print(i); print(pr);
        pr := pr*a*(n−i)/(b*(i+1));
    end;
end;
```

What would happen here if the inner **begin** and **end** were omitted?

8. *Functions and procedures*

An Algol compiler provides nine functions automatically:

sqrt(E);	
exp(E)	*(the exponential function)*;
ln(E)	*(the natural logarithm)*;
sin(E)	*(where E is measured in radians)*;
cos(E)	*(where E is measured in radians)*;
arctan(E)	*(which is given in radians)*;
sign(E)	$(+1, 0,$ *or* $−1,$ *according to the sign of E)*;
abs(E)	*(that is, E*sign(E))*;
entier(E)	*(the largest integer not greater than E)*.

All these functions may be used as *sqrt* was in Section 7, with any arithmetic expression. *exp* and *ln* are considered later in the course.

But it is possible to invent functions and routines of your own, and to refer to them simply by the name you give them, provided only that you declare them at the head of the block in which they are needed (or of an outer block). Indeed, they may be regarded as perfectly normal declarations whose names are **real procedure, integer procedure,** and **procedure,** for which the procedure body gives the definition; their uses are illustrated below.

First, here is a rather inefficient program which evaluates $\binom{n}{r}$ and stores it in *coeff*[n, r], by using the function *fac(n)* to produce *n*!:

```
begin real procedure fac(n); integer n;
            begin integer i; real faci;
                    if n = 0 then fac := 1 else
                    begin faci := 1;
                            for i := 1 step 1 until n do
                                faci := faci*i; fac := faci;
                    end;
            end;
            integer n, r; integer array coeff[1:20, 1:20];
            n := read; r := read;
            coeff[n, r] := fac(n)/(fac(r)*fac(n−r));
    end;
```

Notice that the function (declared by **real procedure** rather than **integer procedure** to avoid overflowing) produces a single number as its output, and that its parameters (in this case, simply n) are unchanged by it. Notice also that the parameters have their type declared before the procedure body.

Routines, however, declared without a type, normally change the values of some of the parameters; so, as our second example, we give a method for multiplying two vectors of dimension n, which have to be read from tape; the result will be analogous to $a_1 b_1 + a_2 b_2 + a_3 b_3$.

```
begin integer m, n; m := read; n := read;
    begin procedure vectin(p, q); real array p; integer q;
        comment p is the name of the vector and q is its dimension;
            begin integer r;
                    for r := 1 step 1 until q do p[r] := read;
            end;
        real procedure prod(x, y, z); real array x, y; integer z;
        comment x and y are the names of the vectors and z of their
                common dimension;
            begin integer r; real sum; sum := 0;
                    for r := 1 step 1 until z do sum := sum+x[r]*y[r];
                    prod := sum;
            end;
        real array a[1:m], b[1:n];
        vectin(a, m); vectin(b, n);
        if m = n then print(prod(a, b, m)) else printtext('different
                dimensions');
    end;
end;
```

Notice how anything from **comment** to the next semi-colon will be ignored by the compiler, and why it is necessary to have an outer block simply to declare the values of *m* and *n*. Notice also the distinction between the declaration of procedure parameters and of variables used in the procedure body; in particular, that the arrays are declared simply as *x*, *y* rather than as $x[1:m]$, $y[1:n]$, and so forth.

9. *Adaptation to particular compilers*

There is little point in giving details of any particular compiler or keyboard; but points which should be watched are these:

(*a*) What symbols are not available on the keyboard, and how are they to be represented?

(*b*) What format is necessary for a 'read' instruction?

(*c*) How is the format for a 'print' instruction determined?

(*d*) What is expected in the way of a title, and at the end of a program?

APPENDIX 2. FORTRAN

Fortran is an internationally standardized language which, despite some difficulty over input and output, has many advantages for school use. It is usually punched on cards, so that if there is an error in a program only a single card needs to be replaced to correct it; since card punches may be hand operated, they are relatively cheap, though print-outs of programs—best done on the computer while compiling—are more expensive.

There are two main varieties of Fortran—Fortran II, or Basic Fortran, which is described here; and Fortran IV, or Standard Fortran, which has rather more facilities available. There are a very few small differences between compilers.

1. *Programming symbols*

The symbols used are:

(*a*) The letters of the alphabet, in small capitals. In manuscript, ϴ is always written for the letter o and Ƶ for the letter z, to avoid confusion with the figures 0 and 2, and Ɪ is always written with serifs, to avoid confusion with 1.

(*b*) The digits from 0 to 9 inclusive; the decimal point . (written or printed on the line), and a special symbol E, which gives powers of ten, so that (for example) 2.0E3 or 2.0E+3 means 2000, while −0.5E−2 means −0.005.

(*c*) The operations +, −, * (multiplication), / (division), and ** (raising to a power, so that x**2 means x²).

(*d*) The assignment symbol, = (not :=, as in the main text).

(*e*) The punctuation marks ( ) , only. Spaces are always neglected, except in the input and output of text.

1076

A new line on a written or typed program indicates the beginning of a new statement of the program, and also the beginning of a new card. It is not legitimate to write two statements on one card.

2. REAL *and* INTEGER *modes*

Fortran distinguishes very sharply between REAL and INTEGER modes, and this is one of its greatest disadvantages for school use. INTEGER arithmetic gives integral division, truncating the answer, so that, for example, 22/7 means 3; and although compilers can handle some 'mixed mode' expressions, it is better to avoid them completely.

INTEGER stores hold integers, exactly, and are represented by identifiers (strings of letters and numbers beginning with a letter) whose first letter is I, J, K, L, M, or N; they should be used only for counters.

REAL stores hold any numbers of a reasonable size, using a floating point system, and with small errors possible in the last few binary digits. If integers are to be treated as real numbers, they must be written with a decimal point and (preferably) a zero; thus, $22.0/7.0$ would be handled in REAL arithmetic and not in INTEGER arithmetic. But the contents of INTEGER stores can be fed into REAL stores, and given a floating point; thus, the statements

$$AJ = J,$$
$$B = 2$$

are perfectly legitimate, and indeed indicate an easy way of avoiding the use of INTEGER arithmetic. (This does not apply to input data; if 2 is to be read into a REAL store it should be written 2.0.)

Any store whose name begins with a letter from A to H or from O to Z is regarded as a REAL store; but it is possible to declare

INTEGER A, H

REAL MEAN

for example, at the beginning of a segment.

3. *Arrays*

If an array of numbers is needed, a DIMENSION statement must be made at the head of the segment, to warn the compiler how many stores to reserve. The type is again determined by the initial letter. Thus, a statement like

DIMENSION N(4), X(3, 3), ITEM (2, 2, 2)

reserves four INTEGER stores for the vector N, nine REAL stores for the matrix X, and eight INTEGER stores for the array ITEM. It is a minor disadvantage that elements can only be referred to by positive integral suffices, so that it is not possible to start an array of coefficients with A(0) (representing the familiar a_0).

If it is not certain how many elements there are to be in an array, there is of course no harm in reserving too many stores.

4. *Statements*

All Fortran instructions are called *statements*. Thus, these five statements might form part of a program for solving quadratic equations:

> READ A, B, C
>
> P = SQRT(B**2−4.0*A*C)/(A*2.0)
>
> X = B/(A*2.0)+P
>
> Y = X−2.0*P
>
> PRINT X, Y

Notice that highly complicated sets of instructions can be compressed into single statements. The operations obey these rules:

(*a*) Two operations may not occur together: thus, we may not write A = B/−2.0, but must write A = −B/2.0 or A = B/(−2.0).

(*b*) ** binds most tightly of all.

(*c*) * and / bind next most tightly, interpreted as they occur from left to right; thus B/A/2.0 would mean (B/A)/2.0, and so on.

(*d*) + and − bind least tightly, and are interpreted as they occur from left to right, as in ordinary arithmetic.

5. *Segments and the master segment*

At the school level, most programs consist simply of a single segment, which is a MASTER segment. (There must be just one MASTER segment in each program.) The operating system most used demands that this segment should begin with MASTER and a title, and that the last segment should end with FINISH; other segments may define functions and subroutines (see below), but every segment must terminate with END. The last instruction to be carried out will always be STOP, which deletes the program from the stores of the computer; and a function or subroutine segment will end with RETURN. Thus, to make the quadratic program acceptable, we write

> MASTER QUAD
>
> READ A, B, C
>
> P = SQRT(B**2−4.0*A*C)/(A*2.0)
>
> ROOT1 = B/(A*2.0)+P
>
> ROOT2 = ROOT1−2.0*P
>
> PRINT ROOT1, ROOT2
>
> STOP
>
> END
>
> FINISH

6. GOTO *and* IF *statements*

Jumps and alternatives are generally managed by numbering statements. Thus, except that it provides no means of ending the process, the Newton–Raphson process for finding square roots might be written

$$21 \qquad Y = (Y+X/Y)/2.0$$
$$\text{GOTO } 21$$

An IF statement, however, provides three such jumps simultaneously, according as the value of the expression quoted in brackets is negative, zero or positive. Thus, the loop could end

```
21      Y = ROOT
        CORR = Y/2.0 - X/(2.0*Y)
        ROOT = Y - CORR
        IF (ABS(CORR) - 0.000001) 22, 22, 21
22      PRINT ROOT
```

although with some compilers the 22 may be omitted, and 0 substituted for it in the IF statement (0 leading to the next statement).

With this convention, the QUAD program may be protected from the two main dangers, thus:

```
        MASTER QUAD
        READ A, B, C
        IF (A) 0, 40, 0
        IF (B**2 - 4.0*A*C) 40, 0, 0
        P = SQRT(B**2 - 4.0*A*C)/(2.0*A)
        ROOT1 = B/(2.0*A) + P
        ROOT2 = ROOT1 - 2.0*P
        PRINT ROOT1, ROOT2
        GOTO 41
40      PRINT (7H ERROR )
41      CONTINUE
        STOP
        END
        FINISH
```

Notice the dummy statement CONTINUE; it is unnecessary here, in fact, because STOP itself could have been numbered 41.

Six spaces are normally reserved at the left of the paper, and of the cards, of which the first five may be used for such statement numbers.

7. DO *loops*

By far the commonest instruction for loops, however, is the DO statement, which instructs the computer to carry out all the instructions down to the statement whose number is quoted, giving the variable all the named values in turn. J = 1, N means that J takes all successive integral values from 1 to N inclusive; J = 2, 100, 7 that it takes the values 2, 9, 16, etc., up to and including 100.

This elegant program stores up to 200 numbers and finds their mean and standard deviation; the numbers are given on cards or tape, and are preceded by the number, *n*, that we are to expect.

```
              MASTER STATS
              DIMENSION X(200)
              READ N
              AN = N
              SUM = 0.0
              SUMSQ = 0.0
              DO 51 J = 1,N
              READ X(J)
              SUM = SUM+X(J)
    51        SUMSQ = SUMSQ+X(J)**2
              AMEAN = SUM/AN
              VAR = (SUMSQ/AN−AMEAN**2)
              PRINT AMEAN, SQRT(VAR)
              STOP
              END
              FINISH
```

If there is no need to keep the numbers for future reference, the DIMENSION statement may be omitted, and X(J) may be replaced everywhere by X. With some compilers, the mixed-mode expression SUM/N is allowed, and there is no need to introduce AN.

Notice that J is essentially a *positive* integer, and so are all three indices of the DO statement—another annoying restriction.

8. *Functions and sub-routines*

A number of standard functions are provided in Fortran, of which the most important are these: (notice that circular measure is used for all trigonometrical functions)

SIN(E)	ASIN(E) (inverse of SIN)	ABS(E) (E or −E, as E $\geqslant 0$ or < 0)
COS(E)	ACOS(E)	IABS(E) (as ABS, but for integers)

1080

TAN(E)   ATAN(E)   INT(E) (truncating a REAL)

SQRT(E)   NINT(E) (rounding a REAL)

ALOG(E)   EXP(E)

ALOG10(E) ANTILOG(E) (both to base ten)

But it is also possible to define your own functions, valid throughout a segment, as, for example, the following, which must be placed before any executable statements of the segment:

> Y(X) = EXP(−X*X/2.0)*0.39894228
> AREA(P, Q, R, H) = (P+4.0*Q+R)*H/3.0

These two functions may be used to print out a table of ordinates and areas under the Normal curve, using Simpson's Rule:

> MASTER NORMAL
> Y(X) = EXP(−X*X/2.0)*0.39894228
> AREA(P, Q, R, H) = (P+4.0*Q+R)*H/3.0
> TOT = 0.5
> DO 2 J = 1, 400
> AJ = J
> X = AJ*0.01
> TOT = TOT+AREA(Y(X−0.01), Y(X−0.005), Y(X), 0.005)
> 2   PRINT X, Y(X), TOT
> STOP
> END
> FINISH

Functions of this sort, however, are only valid in the segment in which they are named, and may only involve one statement. If they need more than one statement, or are needed in more than one segment, they are defined in a FUNCTION SEGMENT, as, for instance,

> FUNCTION Y(X)
> Y = EXP(−X*X/2.0)*X/2.0
> RETURN
> END

where the RETURN statement returns control to the place where the function Y(X) was first found. We could then write, for example, anywhere in the program

$$Q = Y(R)/Y(R+0.01)$$

1081

Another example of this may be given where it is required to work out $n!$ (factorial n). Notice that although this is essentially an integral function, 11! exceeds the capacity of an integer store, and the working is in REAL mode:

```
FUNCTION FAC(N)
FAC = 1
DO 51 K = 1, N
AK = K
51   FAC = FAC*AK
RETURN
END
```

so that we might write the binomial coefficients (inefficiently) as

```
COEFF(N, I) = FAC(N)/(FAC(I)*FAC(N−I))
```

More complicated procedures still need a SUBROUTINE SEGMENT; thus, if vector multiplication, giving a result such as $a_1 b_1 + a_2 b_2 + a_3 b_3$ is needed more than once, and if the n-dimensional vectors concerned need to be read in, we might write:

```
MASTER VECPRO
DIMENSION A(15), B(15)
READ M
CALL VECTIN(A, M)
CALL VECTIN(B, M)
PRINT PROD(A, B, M)
STOP
END
SUBROUTINE VECTIN(P, I)
C    P IS THE NAME OF THE VECTOR AND I ITS DIMENSION
DIMENSION P(15)
DO 1 K = 1, I
1    READ P(K)
RETURN
END
FUNCTION PROD(P, Q, I)
C    P, Q ARE THE VECTORS AND I THEIR DIMENSION
DIMENSION P(15), Q(15)
PROD = 0.0
DO 2 K = 1, I
```

2   PROD = PROD + P(K)*Q(K)

RETURN

END

FINISH

This shows the construction of a Fortran program clearly. The compiler ignores comments labelled C.

9. *Input and output*

In the previous Sections, the READ and PRINT instructions were over-simplified. In fact, instead of READ A, B, C we should probably have to write

READ (1, 4) A, B, C

where the 1 refers to a statement such as

PERIPHERAL (1, CR0), (11, LP0)

which specifies that 1 always refers to the (first) card-reader, and 11 to the (first) line-printer; a series of programs may often make this convention without actually repeating the PERIPHERAL statement each time.

Similarly, the 4 refers to a FORMAT statement such as

4   FORMAT (3F10.3)

which is explained below. We need to know about three of the possible formats, F, I, and H, which are outlined below, and for each we need the idea of a *field* of characters—a number of consecutive characters on card or line of the input or output medium. 'A field of 10 characters' will always mean the next ten characters available, on the same card or line unless the symbol / occurs.

9.1 *The* F *format*

F10.3, for example, means that the number to be read in or printed out must be in a field of ten characters (including signs, spaces, and decimal point), and that there will be three figures after the decimal point. (If, however, a decimal point is shown in the input data it will supersede this requirement.) A number before the F indicates how often it is repeated. Thus,

4   FORMAT (3F10.3, F10.1/F10.3)

WRITE (11, 4) A, B, C, D, E

with the number 1.23456 held in each of the stores named will produce (a point is put above each character to help to count spaces; each fifth space is marked by a colon)

````
. . . . : . . . . : . . . . : . . . . : . . . . : . . . . : . . . . : . . . . :
      1.235      1.235      1.235      1.2
      1.235
````

as the output, and the input would be expected in the same form.

1083

9.2 *The I format*

This is exactly similar, except that, being designed for integers, no decimal point is needed. Thus, if I, J, K, L contain 2, -3, 4, -5,

$$4 \quad \text{FORMAT (2I6, I4/I6)}$$
$$\text{WRITE (11, 4) I, J, K, L}$$

gives

```
...:....:....:....:....:....:....:....:....:
      2    -3    4
     -5
```

The input is expected in the same form.

9.3 *The H format*

This is for the output of characters, including spaces, and the number before the H indicates how many characters are to be expected. Thus, in the program of Section 6, $\quad 4 \quad$ FORMAT (7H ERROR)

$$\text{WRITE (11, 4)}$$

would produce

```
...:....:...:....:....:....:....:....:....:
    ERROR
```

and the next output would begin at the eighth space.

9.4   These can, of course, be mixed; thus, the instructions for the input and output of a program calculating binomial frequencies might be:

Part of program:

```
4       FORMAT (I2,F10.6)
        READ (1,4) N,P
5       FORMAT (20HBINOMIAL FREQUENCIES/3HN =,I2/ 12H I      PR(I))
6       FORMAT (I2,F10.4)
        WRITE (11,5) N
        WRITE (11,6) I,PR
```
                                        (this statement in a DO loop)

Data tape:

```
4    .166667
```

Result as printed:

```
BINOMIAL FREQUENCIES
N = 4
  I     PR(I)
  0    .4823
  1    .3858
  2    .1157
  3    .0154
  4    .0008
```

INDEX